Promoting Health and Emotional Well-Being in Your Classroom

Sixth Edition

Randy M. Page, PhD | Tana S. Page, MS
Brigham Young University

JONES & BARTLETT LEARNING

World Headquarters
Jones & Bartlett Learning
5 Wall Street
Burlington, MA 01803
978-443-5000
info@jblearning.com
www.jblearning.com

Jones & Bartlett Learning books and products are available through most bookstores and online booksellers. To contact Jones & Bartlett Learning directly, call 800-832-0034, fax 978-443-8000, or visit our website, www.jblearning.com.

> Substantial discounts on bulk quantities of Jones & Bartlett Learning publications are available to corporations, professional associations, and other qualified organizations. For details and specific discount information, contact the special sales department at Jones & Bartlett Learning via the above contact information or send an email to specialsales@jblearning.com.

Copyright © 2015 by Jones & Bartlett Learning, LLC, an Ascend Learning Company

All rights reserved. No part of the material protected by this copyright may be reproduced or utilized in any form, electronic or mechanical, including photocopying, recording, or by any information storage and retrieval system, without written permission from the copyright owner.

The content, statements, views, and opinions herein are the sole expression of the respective authors and not that of Jones & Bartlett Learning, LLC. Reference herein to any specific commercial product, process, or service by trade name, trademark, manufacturer, or otherwise does not constitute or imply its endorsement or recommendation by Jones & Bartlett Learning, LLC and such reference shall not be used for advertising or product endorsement purposes. All trademarks displayed are the trademarks of the parties noted herein. *Promoting Health and Emotional Well-Being in Your Classroom, Sixth Edition* is an independent publication and has not been authorized, sponsored, or otherwise approved by the owners of the trademarks or service marks referenced in this product.

There may be images in this book that feature models; these models do not necessarily endorse, represent, or participate in the activities represented in the images. Any screenshots in this product are for educational and instructive purposes only. Any individuals and scenarios featured in the case studies throughout this product may be real or fictitious, but are used for instructional purposes only.

The authors, editor, and publisher have made every effort to provide accurate information. However, they are not responsible for errors, omissions, or for any outcomes related to the use of the contents of this book and take no responsibility for the use of the products and procedures described. Treatments and side effects described in this book may not be applicable to all people; likewise, some people may require a dose or experience a side effect that is not described herein. Drugs and medical devices are discussed that may have limited availability controlled by the Food and Drug Administration (FDA) for use only in a research study or clinical trial. Research, clinical practice, and government regulations often change the accepted standard in this field. When consideration is being given to use of any drug in the clinical setting, the health care provider or reader is responsible for determining FDA status of the drug, reading the package insert, and reviewing prescribing information for the most up-to-date recommendations on dose, precautions, and contraindications, and determining the appropriate usage for the product. This is especially important in the case of drugs that are new or seldom used.

Production Credits

Executive Publisher: William Brottmiller
Publisher: Cathy L. Esperti
Executive Editor: Rhonda Dearborn
Editorial Assistant: Jillian Porazzo
Associate Production Editor: Sara Fowles
Senior Marketing Manager: Andrea DeFronzo
VP, Manufacturing and Inventory Control: Therese Connell
Composition: Aptara®, Inc.
Cover Design: Kristin E. Parker
Photo Research and Permissions Coordinator: Amy Rathburn
Cover Images: (left to right) © Pressmaster/ShutterStock, Inc.; © Pressmaster/ShutterStock, Inc.; © lightpoet/ShutterStock, Inc.
Printing and Binding: Edwards Brothers Malloy
Cover Printing: Edwards Brothers Malloy

Library of Congress Cataloging-in-Publication Data
Page, Randy M.
Promoting health and emotional well-being in your classroom / Randy M. Page, PhD, Brigham Young University, Provo, Utah, Tana S. Page, MS, Brigham Young University, Provo, Utah.—Sixth edition.
    p. ; cm.
Includes bibliographical references and index.
ISBN 978-1-4496-9026-7 (pbk.)
1. Students—Mental health. 2. Mental health promotion. 3. Self-esteem in children. 4. Self-esteem in adolescence. 5. Classroom environment.
I. Page, Tana S. II. Title.
LB3430.P34 2015
371.4′04—dc23

2013035205

6048

Printed in the United States of America
18 17 16 15 14   10 9 8 7 6 5 4 3 2

BRIEF CONTENTS

Chapter 1   Teaching to Make a Difference   1

Chapter 2   Teaching Today's Students   23

Chapter 3   Life Skills   49

Chapter 4   Stress Management Skills   97

Chapter 5   Media Literacy Skills   133

Chapter 6   Promoting Healthy Eating and Physical Activity   161

Chapter 7   Promoting a Tobacco- and Drug-Free Lifestyle   197

Chapter 8   Promoting Sexual Health   247

Chapter 9   Violence Prevention and Safety   281

Chapter 10   Dealing with Crises and Critical Issues   311

CONTENTS

Preface ix
Acknowledgments xi

CHAPTER 1   Teaching to Make a Difference 1
You Can Make a Difference 2
Modeling: Personal and Professional
  Characteristics of Effective Teachers 5
Interacting with Students 6
  Expectations 7
  Discipline and Procedures 8
  Teeter-Tottering and Hydraulic Lifts 10
  Sensitivity to Diversity 12
Students with Special Needs 13
  Emotional Needs 13
  English Language Needs 14
  Learning Needs 15
Common K–12 Health Problems 17
  Communicable Health Conditions 17
  Chronic Health Conditions 18
Key Terms 21
Knowledge Check! 21
References 22

CHAPTER 2   Teaching Today's Students . . 23
Today's Learners and the Brain 23
Teaching with the Brain in Mind 25
  Relaxed Alertness .26
  "So What?" 26
  Active Learning 27
  RAD Teaching 27
  Other Considerations 28
Teaching Health Literacy in the Twenty-First
  Century 29
  Guide on the Side 29
  Learning Styles 29
Deciding What to Teach 31
  National Hezalth Education Standards: Skills . .31
  CDC's Categories of Risk Behavior 32
  State and District Guidelines 33
  Health Education Curriculum Analysis Tool 34
  Characteristics of Effective Health
    Education Curricula 34

  Coordinated School Health Program 35
  NCATE Preparation Standards 37
Teaching for Behavior Change 38
  Health Belief Model 38
  Social Cognitive Theory 38
  Theory of Planned Behavior 39
  Stages of Change Model 40
Instructional Planning 40
  Assessing Needs .40
  Setting Learning Goals 41
  Instruction Mapping 41
  Unit Planning 41
  Unit Design 42
  Lesson Plan 44
Key Terms 46
Knowledge Check! 47
References 47

CHAPTER 3   Life Skills 49
Teaching Life Skills 50
Self-Awareness and
  Self-Evaluation Skills 52
  Self-Esteem 53
  Self-Worth 53
  Ideal-Self 54
  Pygmalion-Self 56
  Self-Evaluation 57
Communication and Interpersonal Skills 58
  Sending and Interpreting Messages 58
  Assertiveness and Advocacy 60
  Empathy 61
  Relationship Building 62
Goal-Setting and Self-Management Skills 65
  Being Proactive .66
  Anger Management 68
Decision-Making and Problem-Solving Skills 69
  Problem-Solving Steps 69
  Making Decisions 70
  Conflict Management 70
  Resilience 71
  Asset Development 71
Key Terms 95

v

Knowledge Check! 95
References 96

CHAPTER 4   Stress Management Skills . . 97

Understanding the Nature of Stress. 97
Disease and Stress 98
Understanding Your Stress. 99
    Cognitive Distortions 100
    Restructuring Your Thinking. 101
Understanding Your Students' Stress 101
    Day-to-Day Hassles 102
    Economic Stressors. 102
    Immigration 102
    Natural Calamities 102
    Home-Based Stress. 103
    School-Based Stress 105
Stress and Mental Disorders. 108
    Depressive Disorders. 108
    Assisting Young People Who Are
       Depressed. 110
    Anxiety Disorders. 110
Stress Reduction Skills 112
    Time Management 113
    Money Management 113
    Study and Test-Taking Skills. 114
    Rest and Sleep 114
    Giving and Serving. 114
Stress Coping Skills 115
    Think About Thinking 115
    Humor 115
    Journal Writing 116
    Play. 116
    Physical Exertion 117
Relaxation Skills 117
    Diaphragmatic Breathing. 117
    Autogenic Training. 117
    Visualization/Imagery. 118
    Progressive Muscular Relaxation. 118
    Music and Art 118
Key Terms. 131
Knowledge Check! 131
References 132

CHAPTER 5   Media Literacy Skills. 133

Media Use and Concerns 134
    Internet Use Concerns 136
    Recommendations for Media Use 137

Advertising Power 138
    Ad Creep. 139
    Targeting Children 140
    Vulnerability of Children 140
    School-Based Marketing 140
    Internet Marketing. 141
Using Technology in the Classroom. 141
    PowerPoint 142
    Social Media in the Classroom 143
Accessing Valid Information 144
    Evaluating Information on the Internet. . . . 145
Analyzing Media and Technology Influences. . . . 146
    Who Created This? 146
    Why Was It Made? 147
    What Is Sold or Omitted? 147
    Targeted to Whom? 148
    How Is It Constructed? 148
Practicing Media Management 148
    Limit Use 149
    Online Safety Tips 149
    Make Positive Media Choices 150
    Select Creative Alternatives.   150
Key Terms. 159
Knowledge Check! 159
References 159

CHAPTER 6   Promoting Healthy Eating
        and Physical Activity 161

Trends and Influencing Factors 162
    Physical Inactivity. 162
    Too Many Calories 164
    Family and Social Factors 164
    Media Use. 165
    Energy Drinks 166
    Food in Schools. 166
    Media's Influence on Body Image 167
Problems Related to Unhealthy Eating and
    Inactivity. 168
    Unsafe Weight-Loss Methods 169
    Anorexia Nervosa. 170
    Bulimia 171
Diseases Related to Unhealthy Eating and
    Inactivity 171
    Diabetes. 172
    Coronary Heart Disease 173
    Cancer 174

Osteoporosis and Arthritis............174
Dental Decay.....................175
School Health Guidelines to Promote Healthy
 Eating and Physical Activity..........175
 Supportive School Environment........176
 School Personnel Collaboration........176
 Parental Involvement...............176
 Community Involvement.............177
Healthy Eating Curricula...............177
 Dietary Guidelines................177
 MyPlate........................179
 National Standards................180
Physical Activity Curricula.............181
 Physical Activity Guidelines..........182
Activities for Healthy Eating and Physical
 Activity.........................183
Key Terms.........................193
Knowledge Check!....................193
References........................194

**CHAPTER 7   Promoting a Tobacco- and
              Drug-Free Lifestyle......197**
Monitoring Substance Use Trends..........198
Media Promotion of Alcohol and Tobacco
 Use............................200
Substance Abuse Prevention Education......201
 School-Based Programs That Work......202
 Information-Based Strategies..........202
 Normative Education...............203
 Resistance Strategies...............203
 Personal and Social Skills Training and
  Enhancement Approaches..........203
 Peer Approaches..................204
 Drug-Free Activities and Alternatives
  to Drugs.....................204
 Student Assistance Programs..........204
 Parent Approaches.................205
Substance Abuse Prevention Curricula......206
 Developmental Considerations.........206
 High-Risk Students.................210
 Infusion of Substance Abuse Prevention
  Education into the Curriculum.......211
Tobacco...........................211
 Nicotine........................212
 Health Consequences of Smoking......212
 Smoking and Girls.................214

Smokeless Tobacco..................215
Hookahs, Bidis, and Kreteks...........215
Tobacco Use Prevention and Cessation
 Programs in Schools...............216
Alcohol............................217
 Alcoholism......................217
 Addiction in the Family..............219
 Al-Anon and Alateen...............222
Marijuana and Cannabis................223
Other Drugs of Abuse..................224
 Oxycodone......................225
 Inhalants.......................225
 Anabolic Steroids..................226
 Cocaine........................227
 Methamphetamine.................227
 Heroin.........................228
 Club Drugs......................229
 Date-Rape Drugs..................231
 Drug Injection and Disease Transmission....232
Activities for Tobacco, Alcohol, and Drugs.....233
Key Terms.........................245
Knowledge Check!....................245
References........................246

CHAPTER 8   Promoting Sexual Health..247
Sexual Trends......................248
Media and Sexual Content..............249
Culture and Sexual Development..........250
 Puberty Hormones.................250
 The Big Talk.....................251
Sex Education......................251
 Abstinence Education...............253
 HIV Prevention Education............254
 Contraceptives...................255
 Controversial Issues................256
 Peer-Led Prevention Programs.........257
 Teen Parenthood Programs...........257
 Programs for Out-of-School Youths......257
 National Sexuality Education Standards....257
Problems Associated with Youth Sexual
 Activity.........................260
 Emotional Consequences............260
 Unintended Teen Pregnancy..........262
Diseases Associated with Youth Sexual
 Activity.........................264
 HIV Infection....................264

Sexually Transmitted Infections 264
Common STIs Among Teens 266
Key Terms. 279
Knowledge Check! 279
References 280

CHAPTER 9   Violence Prevention and Safety 281
Bullying. 282
Cyberbullying 283
Risk Factors 283
Effects and Warning Signs. 284
Responding to Bullying. 284
Preventing Bullying 285
Violence. 285
Family Factors. 286
Exposure to Media Violence 286
Substance Use and Abuse 287
Immediate Access to Weapons 288
Personal and Peer Characteristics 288
Gang Involvement 288
Violence and Learning Potential. 289
Violence-Free School Environment 290
School Security Measures 290
School Gun Laws 290
A Safe Physical Environment 290
A Safe Social Environment 290
Discipline and Dress Codes 291
Warning Signs of Violence 291
Effective Violence Prevention Programs 292
Violence Prevention Curriculum 292
Child Abuse 293
Recognizing Abuse 294
Handling Disclosure 295
Reporting Abuse 295
Preventing Child Abuse 295
Sexual Violence. 298
Date Rape 298
Intimate-Partner Violence 298
Safety 299
Traffic-Related Injuries 299
Home-Based Injuries 299
Outdoor Injuries 300
Safety and Hazard Assessments 300
Safety Curricula. 300
Key Terms. 309
Knowledge Check! 309
References 310

CHAPTER 10   Dealing with Crises and Critical Issues 311
Crisis Response Plans 311
Preparations for a Crisis 312
Short-Term Responses and Services. 313
Long-Term Responses and Services 314
Youth Suicide 314
Warning Signs of Suicide 315
Prevention and Intervention 317
Self-Injury 320
Helping Children and Adolescents
Deal with Death 321
Culture and Death Practices 321
Age-Related Concepts and Needs 323
Death of a Parent 327
Death of a Sibling 328
Death of a Pet 329
Providing a Supportive Environment for the
Terminally Ill Child 329
Understanding the Dying Child 330
The Teacher's Role 330
The Classmates' Role 331
Responding Appropriately to Death 331
Death of a Student 331
Suicide 332
When Tragedy Comes to School 333
Death Education 336
Key Terms. 345
Knowledge Check! 345
References 345

Index 347

PREFACE

This sixth edition of *Promoting Health and Emotional Well-Being in Your Classroom* makes teaching vital health issues fun and easy! It was written with readers in mind, to motivate and empower them to make a difference in the lives of young people.

How to Use This Book

The chart on the inside cover identifies key elements of health curriculum. It illustrates how this book incorporates these elements and simplifies health instruction. Using the chart, consider the following:

- The traditional ten content areas of health are overwhelming for elementary teachers—the long list can discourage them from even trying to teach health. This amount of content also frustrates secondary teachers who have limited classroom time. The organization and approach in this book will help you overcome that obstacle.
- It is better to organize health instruction around the CDC's six risk behaviors, while still addressing the traditional content areas. These can easily be grouped into just four content areas, indicated by color. Emotional well-being is a core component of all these units. It needs to be included in each and can also be taught as a unit by itself. Color identifies how these units match up with the ten content areas.
- The National Health Education Standards are also essential in health instruction. Their key words are highlighted in blue. They focus on skills rather than on content areas. By blending these blue highlighted skills with the color-coded risk behaviors, you will be able to focus and streamline your health education instruction.
- The column to the far right illustrates how this book brings all of these elements together in a very simple way. Chapter titles are in blue to indicate their focus on national standards and skill instruction. Chapters 3–5 are devoted to skill development and comprise what is typically taught in emotional health units. Chapters 6–10 address the CDC's risk behaviors. As you will note, the skill chapters precede the risk behavior chapters so that the foundation for skills and emotional well-being is established first and can easily be incorporated into the risk chapters that follow. The last chapter helps students understand how to deal with critical issues in the classroom and serves as a culminating chapter.

What Is New and Unique About This Edition

New Design!

The new design with perforated pages makes it easy for students to complete and turn in application assignments and activities. These include worksheets where students process more than 275 interactive assessments and learning activities, many new to or revised in this edition.

Engaging Activities!

Each chapter ends with creative and engaging activities that make health instruction memorable and impacting.

Risk behavior chapters also include activities for advocacy, family and community involvement, and integration into core subjects including math, language arts, and social studies.

New and Expanded Sections

- Students with Special Needs
- Common K-12 Health Problems
- Instructional Planning (including chapter worksheets)
- Building Willpower and Self-control
- Depressive Disorders
- Anxiety Disorders
- Using Technology in the Classroom
- Trends in risk behaviors
- Dietary Guidelines
- Myplate
- Tobacco and Drug Laws
- Hooka
- Puberty
- The *Big Talk*
- Laws and Teen Pregnancy
- Bullying
- Partner Violence
- Culture and Death Practices
- Terminal Illness.
- Key Features.

Favorite key features are included to facilitate student learning and effective health teaching preparation:

- Case studies or stories open each chapter and provide an introduction to chapter material.
- Application exercises help readers personally assess or apply chapter content.
- Internet support boxes identify where students can gain additional information on key issues or help in developing health curricula including unit and lesson plans.
- National Health Education Standards, Health Behavior Outcomes (HBOs) and HECAT Modules are highlighted throughout the book. They help students identify what needs to be taught at various grade levels.
- Chapters end with a multitude of activities for students to use while teaching health.
- Worksheets guide students through effective unit and lesson plan development.
- Knowledge Check exercises help students identify and process chapter concepts.

This book helps you **Flip Your Classroom!** Simply require students to read chapters and complete application exercises before coming to class. Assign them Knowledge Checks or have students be prepared to answer the questions in online quizzes before class, or give a two- or three-question quiz at the beginning of class from the assigned Knowledge Check. Then use your class time for more engaging and interactive discussions, group activities, and so much more! Flipping your classroom helps students learn at a deeper level, facilitates meaningful class discussions, and provides more in-class time for applying the material.

Instructors using this book appreciate the great online resources available to them:

- Examples of syllabi for courses using this book
- Chapter PowerPoint slides that facilitate discussion and make concepts memorable
- Detailed chapter outlines that can serve as lecture notes or for quiz/test development
- Numerous additional activities that can be used while teaching a college level course
- Examples of completed lesson plan and unit planning worksheets
- A test bank created by the authors

Enjoy using this book designed to make teaching health issues easy, fun, and life-changing for both instructors and students!

ACKNOWLEDGMENTS

We are very grateful for all of those who helped bring about this *Sixth Edition* of *Promoting Health and Emotional Well-Being in Your Classroom*. Cathy Esperti, publisher; Jillian Porazzo, editorial assistant; Andrea DeFronzo, senior marketing manager; and Sara Fowles, associate production editor, were great sources of support and guidance. We also are grateful for the young artists who lent us their drawing talents.

The comments and suggestions of students and reviewers, past and present, helped facilitate many changes in this edition:

- Diane Davis, Bowie State University
- Jennifer Dearden, Morehead State University
- David Durbin, Pikeville College
- N. C. Eburne, Brigham Young University at Hawaii
- Brian Geiger, University of Alabama–Birmingham
- Steven Godin, East Stroudsburg University
- Steve Goodwin, University of Delaware
- Marsha Greer, California State University at San Bernardino
- Melissa Hedstrom, Western Oregon University
- Linda L. Hendrixson, East Stroudsburg University
- Tammy James, West Chester University
- Katie Flynn, Union College
- Judith Nuno, University of San Diego
- Jeanette Tedesco, Western Connecticut State University
- Karen Vail-Smith, East Carolina University
- Patti Warner, James Madison University
- David M. White, East Carolina University

We also want to thank all of our incredible children and grandchildren for their love, support and inspiration. You add meaning to everything we do.

Chapter 1
Teaching to Make a Difference

Cipher in the Snow

It started with tragedy on a biting cold February morning. I was driving behind the Milford Corners bus as I did most snowy mornings on my way to school. It veered and stopped short at the hotel, which it had no business doing, and I was annoyed, as I had to come to an unexpected stop. A boy lurched out of the bus, reeled, stumbled, and collapsed on the snowbank at the curb. The bus driver and I reached him at the same moment. His thin, hollow face was white, even against the snow.

"He's dead," the driver whispered.

It didn't register for a minute. I glanced quickly at the scared young faces staring down at us from the school bus. "A doctor! Quick! I'll phone from the hotel. . . ."

"No use. I tell you he's dead." The driver looked down at the boy's still form. "He never even said he felt bad," he muttered, "just tapped me on the shoulder and said, real quiet, 'I'm sorry, I have to get off at the hotel.' That's all. Polite and apologizing like."

At school, the giggling, shuffling morning noise quieted as the news went down the halls. I passed a huddle of girls. "Who was it? Who dropped dead on the way to school?" I heard one of them half-whisper.

"Don't know his name; some kid from Milford Corners," was the reply.

It was like that in the faculty room and the principal's office. "I'd appreciate your going out to tell the parents," the principal told me. "They haven't a phone and, anyway, somebody from school should go there in person. I'll cover your classes."

"Why me?" I asked. "Wouldn't it be better if you did it?"

"I didn't know the boy," the principal admitted levelly. "And in last year's sophomore personalities column I note that you were listed as his favorite teacher."

I drove through the snow and cold down the bad canyon road to the Evans' place and thought about the boy, Cliff Evans. His favorite teacher! I thought. He hasn't spoken two words to me in two years! I could see him in my mind's eye all right, sitting back there in the last seat in my afternoon literature class. He came in the room by himself and left by himself. "Cliff Evans," I muttered to myself, "a boy who never talked." I thought a minute. "A boy who never smiled. I never saw him smile once."

The big ranch kitchen was clean and warm. I blurted out my news somehow. Mrs. Evans reached blindly toward a chair. "He never said anything about bein' ailin'."

His stepfather snorted. "He ain't said nothin' about anything since I moved in here."

Mrs. Evans pushed a pan to the back of the stove and began to untie her apron. "Now hold on," her husband snapped. "I got to have breakfast before I go to town. Nothin' we can do now anyway. If Cliff hadn't been so dumb he'd have told us he didn't feel good."

After school I sat in the office and stared bleakly at the records spread out before me. I was to close the file and write the obituary for the school paper. The almost bare sheets mocked the effort. Cliff Evans, white, never legally adopted by his stepfather, five young half-brothers and sisters. These meager strands of information and the list of D grades were all the records had to offer.

Cliff Evans had silently come in the school door in the mornings and gone out the school door in the evenings, and that was all. He had never belonged to a club. He had never played on a team. He had never held an office. As far as I could tell he had never done one happy, noisy kid thing. He had never been anybody at all.

How do you go about making a boy into a zero? The grade school records showed me. The first- and second-grade teachers' annotations read "sweet, shy child," "timid but eager." Then, the third-grade note had opened the attack. Some teacher had written in a good, firm hand, "Cliff won't talk. Uncooperative. Slow learner." The other academic sheep had followed with "dull," "slow-witted," "low IQ." They became correct. The boy's IQ score in the ninth grade was listed at 83. But his IQ in the third grade had been 106. The score didn't go under 100 until the seventh grade. Even shy, timid, sweet children have resilience. It takes time to break them.

I stomped to the typewriter and wrote a savage report pointing out what education had done to Cliff Evans. I slapped a copy on the principal's desk and another in the sad, dog-eared file. I banged the typewriter and slammed the file and crashed the door shut, but I didn't feel much better. A little boy kept walking after me, a little boy with a peaked, pale face; a skinny body in faded jeans; and big eyes that had looked and searched for a long time and then had become veiled.

I could guess how many times he'd been chosen last to play sides in a game, how many whispered child conversations had excluded him, how many times he hadn't been asked. I could see and hear the faces and voices that said over and over, "You're dumb. You're a nothing, Cliff Evans."

A child is a believing creature. Cliff undoubtedly believed them. Suddenly it seemed clear to me: When finally there was nothing left at all for Cliff Evans, he collapsed on a snowbank and went away. The doctor might list "heart failure" as the cause of death, but that wouldn't change my mind.

We couldn't find 10 students in the school who had known Cliff well enough to attend the funeral as his friends. So, the student body officers and a committee from the junior class went as a group to the church, being politely sad. I attended the services with them, and sat through it with a lump of cold lead in my chest and a big resolve growing through me.

I've never forgotten Cliff Evans nor that resolve. He has been my challenge year after year, class after class. I look up and down the rows carefully each September at the unfamiliar faces. I look for veiled eyes or bodies scrounged into a seat in an alien world. "Look, kids," I say silently. "I may not do anything else for you this year, but not one of you is going to come out of here a nobody. I'll work or fight to the bitter end doing battle with society and the school board, but I won't have one of you coming out of here thinking himself into a zero."

Most of the time—not always, but most of the time—I've succeeded.

Source: Reproduced from J. E. Mizer, Cipher in the snow. NEA J. 1964;50:8–10. Reprinted with permission. A movie of this story also exists and has the same title.

The potential for teachers to have a positive influence upon their students is great, as is the need for such influence. School-age children and adolescents spend more time with their teachers at school than they do with their parents. Although it is unrealistic to expect every teacher to successfully help every "Cliff Evans" feel better about himself, there are countless young people who have been, and are yet to be, touched by a special teacher who makes a big difference in their lives. The purpose of this is chapter is to give you information and insights into how to be such a teacher.

■ YOU CAN MAKE A DIFFERENCE

Education is all about influencing others. **Figure 1-1** depicts our **pyramid of influence** as teachers. It is interesting to note that even though most of our coursework in preparation for entering the teaching profession centers on the tip of the pyramid, it is actually the least influential area. We spend a great deal of energy learning how to write effective objectives and lesson plans, prepare materials,

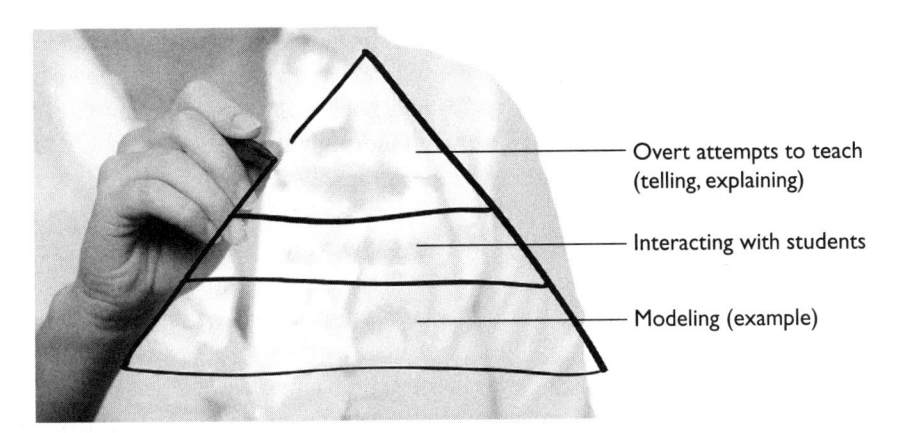

FIGURE 1-1 A teacher's pyramid of influence.
Photo: © Kalim/Shutterstock, Inc.

present information, and evaluate student learning. These are vitally important skills for educators. More vital and perhaps overlooked are the larger two areas of the pyramid. The foundation for influencing others is modeling—that is, being an example of what we are trying to teach. This includes the obvious, such as a teacher reading while having students do silent sustained reading or being a nonsmoker while discussing the harmful effects of tobacco. It also includes less obvious and, unfortunately, sometimes negative acts, such as modeling dislike for things or people. The large midsection of the pyramid of influence deals with interacting with or relating to students. Our ability to influence here is exemplified by the saying "I don't care how much you know until I know how much you care." This chapter looks in depth at the bottom two sections of the pyramid. The *Teaching Today's Students* chapter is devoted to the top section.

Now that we have discussed our pyramid of influence, we need to consider our circle of influence. Have you ever stopped to think about your circle of influence? To better understand this concept, do the following activity. On a sheet of paper, draw a large circle and label it your **circle of concern** (see **Figure 1-2**). Inside the circle write everything you are concerned about—from world peace to what you are going to eat for your next meal. Your circle might contain items such as these: kids living in dysfunctional situations, teen pregnancy, hatred, violence, bigotry, drug abuse, poverty, apathy, conflicts with roommates or family members, car problems, money for next semester, lack of parking on campus, an egotistical professor, a family member's health, obtaining a meaningful position within your career, paying bills, meeting deadlines, lack of time, or finding a soul mate. You will find that you can probably easily fill the entire circle with your specific concerns.

Next, draw a smaller circle within this large circle. Label this as your **circle of influence**. This smaller circle represents what you have control over—what you can influence. Now, think about the items within your circle of concern and ask yourself the following questions: Which of these concerns

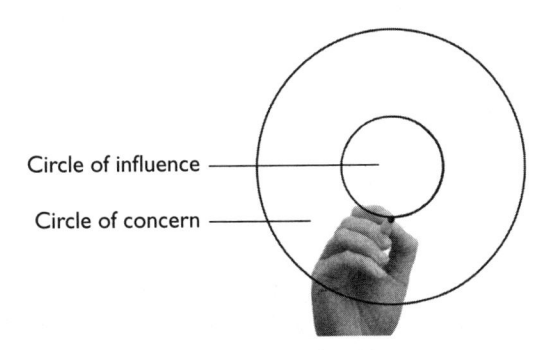

FIGURE 1-2 A teacher's circle of concern and influence.
Photo: © iStock/Thinkstock

You Can Make a Difference

can you personally influence? Which items belong in the circle of influence and which belong in the outer circle of concern? Finally, and most important, ask yourself, "Where do I put most of my efforts, thoughts, and actions? Are they within my circle of influence or within my circle of concern?"

Proactive people (see Chapter 3) focus their thoughts and activities inside their circle of influence. They spend their time and energy on things they can do something about, and as a result their circle of influence naturally grows over time. **Reactive people**, in contrast, spend most of their time in their circle of concern. They focus on the weaknesses of other people, problems in their environment, and circumstances over which they have no control. Their focus creates blaming and accusing attitudes as well as feelings of victimization. Focusing on one's circle of concern causes one's circle of influence to shrink for lack of attention.[1]

Teachers often deeply feel the effects of social problems on a very personal level. Within their own classrooms, they witness the devastating effects of dysfunctional homes, poverty, drugs, violence, teen pregnancy, and other problems affecting our communities and society. Because teachers care about people, they are prone to have very large circles of concern. However, focusing more on one's circle of concern rather than on the inner circle of influence can create feelings of being overwhelmed, disempowered, and "burned out." Novice teachers are especially susceptible to becoming fixated upon their circle of concern as they begin dealing with students and their problems.

Spanish Harlem (New York City) junior high teacher Bill Hall provides an excellent example of how one teacher made a positive difference in the lives of his students by being focused on his circle of influence.[2] It would have been easy for Bill to fall into the trap of being focused on his circle of concern. He taught in a neighborhood where infant mortality rates were high, where the average male life expectancy was even less than in Bangladesh, and where language and a few walls separated the stark contrast of poverty and affluence. Rather than focusing on these conditions, Bill devoted his energy to what he could do—that is, to his circle of influence. Bill organized an after-school chess club to help students better learn English. Many of his students had recently arrived from Central and South America, Pakistan, and Hong Kong and could speak only minimal English. This chess club became known as the Royal Knights of Harlem.

The members of the club not only learned English, but also grew in confidence as they came to see themselves through Bill's eyes. Their schoolwork improved as they became more proficient at chess. In its first year, the club finished third at the state finals in Syracuse, becoming eligible for the junior high school finals in California. Bill raised funds to fly the team to California, where they finished 17th out of 109 teams in the national competition. Then, his team met a girl from the Soviet Union who was the women's world champion. The team reasoned that if this girl could come all the way from Russia, why couldn't they go there? The team traveled to Russia with the help of corporate sponsors, particularly Pepsi-Cola. There, the Royal Knights of Harlem won about half of their matches and uncovered a home-grown advantage in the special event of speed chess. Remember, these were not chess protégés, but rather students who were selected for their need to learn English.

Bill never dreamed that all of this would happen within a few short years of starting the chess club. Neither did he foresee the day that his junior high auditorium would be chosen by a Soviet dance troupe as the site of a New York performance because of his chess club's tour in Russia. But all of this did happen—and it happened because Bill chose to be circle-of-influence focused. As time passed, his circle of influence naturally grew. When the Royal Knights were asked by one interviewer what they were doing before Bill Hall and chess playing had come into their lives, one boy said, "Hanging out in the street and feeling like shit." "Taking lunch money from younger kids and a few drugs now and then," admitted another. "Just laying on my bed, reading comics, and getting yelled at by my father for being lazy," said a third. When asked if there was anything in their schoolbooks that made a difference, one explained to the agreement of all, "Not until Mr. Hall thought we were smart and then we were."[2(p.139)]

They were smart and Bill Hall helped them discover their potential. Others, too, came to realize it. When they were ready to graduate from junior high, the Royal Knights members received numerous offers from high schools to join their "gifted" student programs. One private school from California even provided a full-ride scholarship. At the time of junior high graduation, club members were convinced that they could do anything and had career aspirations of law, accounting, teaching, and computer science.

It is common for educators to wish that we could take our students out of less than ideal circumstances. But this is rarely possible. Bill Hall made a difference by working within his circle of influence—by showing his students that they had the power within themselves to rise above their circumstances. We can all expand our ability to influence, and thereby make a difference, by focusing on what we can do—not on what others should be doing.

■ MODELING: PERSONAL AND PROFESSIONAL CHARACTERISTICS OF EFFECTIVE TEACHERS

The importance of modeling healthy and ethical behaviors cannot be overemphasized. Modeling is a major means by which skills are taught and learned. Observing how others act provides a pattern for youth to follow when in similar circumstances. Next to parents, educators—whose behavior patterns are watched and imitated—are often the most influential adults in a young person's life. Students often learn more from what we do than what we say. The way an educator reacts to frustration or stress can make a lasting impression on a young person. Both displays of positive coping skills and negative responses have modeling effects. Therefore, educators must give serious attention to their emotional health and to their own practices and skills.

Consider which behaviors you model, what you might be teaching students. Do you model healthy behaviors including eating lots of fruits and vegetables, watching your weight, and being physically active? Do you abstain from tobacco and other drug abuse? Do you consistently wear a seat belt? Do you model professional ethical behaviors including acting with integrity, respect, and confidentiality? Do you refrain from gossip and negative discussion of others, including students? Do you interact with students with sensitivity to their needs and diversity? Reviewing the characteristics in **Box 1-1** will help you assess the characteristics you model to your students.

1-1

Characteristics of Effective Teachers

Effective teachers:

- Are caring, warm, and very interested in students' total well-being.
- Are organized, prepared, and clear.
- Have deep preparation in and infectious enthusiasm for the subject and teaching.
- Maintain high standards of conduct and create a sense of belonging.
- Have high academic expectations for their students and are able to inspire and motivate students effectively with their expectations.
- Make coursework relevant, meaningful, and important to students.
- Use a variety of teaching methods and are creative in helping students learn.
- Inject humor.
- Demonstrate a willingness to admit mistakes.
- Demonstrate fairness in grading and respect in their interactions.

INTERACTING WITH STUDENTS

How we interact with students affects the degree of our influence in and out of the classroom. Frank O'Malley, an English professor at Notre Dame for four decades, was a teacher who made a difference in the lives of his students. He taught reading, writing, and *caring*. At the beginning of each semester, O'Malley would memorize each student's name and have everyone submit a brief autobiography so that he could understand each student better. He focused on the fact that as a teacher he was assisting the growth of unique minds and spirits. He read each paper closely and covered it with red-inked comments of both criticism and praise. O'Malley taught his students to

Teachers who make a difference create high academic and behavioral expectations and communicate a feeling of love and belonging.

How a teacher interacts with just one student influences that teacher's relationship with each student in the classroom.

exceed their own expectations under his prodding. He gave them a vision of great literature, but also a vision of how they could excel.[3]

We need more Frank O'Malleys in education today—that is, teachers who know and care for each of their students (not just the standouts), teachers who set high behavior and academic standards for all their students and who take the time and energy to help students achieve that higher expectation. As William Glasser said, "When you study great teachers . . . you will learn much more from their caring and hard work than from their style."[4(p.38)]

While serving as Secretary of Education, William Bennett took the sound advice of his wife to get out of his office and get into the schools. He chose to visit schools weekly that had been identified as exemplary. These schools were located in all sorts of settings, including many from poorly funded inner cities. Bennett visited these schools for the purpose of finding out why they were successful. Two children at Garrison Elementary School in the South Bronx, New York, summed up Bennett's key findings for what makes for a successful school when they told him they went to "America's greatest school" because "(1) there's no messin' around, (2) there's no foolin' around, and (3) everybody loves you."[5(p.75)] Research has consistently shown what these two children knew: that effective teachers and schools interact with students in ways that (1) create high academic expectations, (2) maintain high behavioral expectations, and (3) communicate a feeling of love, belonging, and community.

The importance of **connectedness**—a belief held by students that the adults and peers at their school care about their learning and about them as individuals—cannot be overemphasized. Students who feel connected to their school are more likely to engage in healthy behaviors and succeed academically. In particular, connected students are less likely to use alcohol and other drugs, miss school, have sex at an early age, or be involved in violence or behaviors that increase their risk for injury (such as drinking and driving).[6]

Expectations

Expectations can lead people to form negative or positive self-fulfilling prophecies. **Self-fulfilling prophecies** are expectations about future behavior and performance that emanate from labels and self-image. Children who are labeled "dumb" are likely to live up to that expectation, just as children labeled "bright" are likely to prove that prophecy correct.

A teacher can formulate labels and expectations for new students even before the beginning of an academic year. For example, a label can form in a teacher's mind through subconscious stereotyping or prejudices based on attractiveness, ethnicity, socioeconomic level, or gender. Teachers can also attach labels to students based on discussions with previous teachers, school administrators, students, or parents. The reputations that older siblings establish in school get passed on to younger brothers and sisters. School records of performance and teachers' impressions are also sources of predetermined labels. Cliff Evans, in the story at the beginning of this chapter, is an example of the tragic effect that negative labels and expectations can have.

Rosenthal and Jacobson conducted some of the early work relating teacher expectations to student performance and behavior in school.[7] In their study, students in an elementary school were given the "Test for Intellectual Blooming." In each of the classes, an average of 20% of the children were identified as having test scores that suggested they would show unusual academic gains during the school year. The identified children had actually been picked at random from the total population taking the test. Eight months later, all the children in the school were retested. Those children whom the teachers expected to show greater intellectual growth had significantly higher scores than other children in the school. This outcome resulted, apparently, from the teachers interacting more positively and favorably with the "brighter" children.

Although Rosenthal's original expectancy research has been criticized for shortcomings in design and methodology, none of the criticisms have denied that teacher expectations have a significant influence on student performance, a fact supported by many subsequent studies. Hamachek cites studies that demonstrate that teachers tend to expect, and therefore get, the same performance from younger siblings that they had come to expect from older brothers and sisters.[8] Hamachek also reviews how children whose IQs have been overestimated by teachers demonstrated higher reading achievement. This relationship was especially evident with first-grade teachers who expected the girls to outperform the boys. In contrast, teachers who did not have this expectation found no significant difference between the sexes in aptitude for learning to read.

Physical attractiveness also influences teacher expectations and interactions. Teachers are more likely to interact with and respond more positively to attractive children. Some research studies show that even the academic grades assigned to students are influenced by the attractiveness of the students. An example of this is when athletes receive higher grades than their schoolwork merits.

Physical attractiveness also affects how students interact with one another. Early in life, children learn the high value that society places on beauty. Popular children's stories (e.g., *The Ugly Duckling*, *Sleeping Beauty*, *Rudolph the Red-Nosed Reindeer*, *Dumbo the Elephant*, *Snow White and the Seven Dwarfs*, and *Cinderella*) reinforce this value, showing the errors of this way of thinking. Unattractive children are often mocked and teased by other children. During adolescence—a period of rapid changes in body appearance, form, and size—youth often become fixated on physical appearance. They want to look like the media images of firm, sleek, beautiful bodies displayed everywhere. This is a time when peer perceptions become dominant, when expectations for conformity are intense, and when deviations are not easily tolerated.

Teachers must be careful regarding the nonverbal messages they send to their students concerning their students' competence and lovableness. First, teachers must be honest with themselves about any negative feelings or expectations they have. Although you would never dream of telling a student that he or she is "dumb" or "ugly," these perceptions can be communicated nonverbally without your even knowing it. Communication experts tell us that more than half of what we communicate is conveyed by our body posture and facial expressions and that the tone of voice is by far the most important part of our verbal message.

As a teacher, you should take a hard look at the expectations you have for your students. Strive to remove negative labels that have been established by previous experiences, teachers, or older siblings, and try to replace negative expectations with positive ones. It is critical to realize that many children in our school systems have rarely or never been viewed in a positive light by a significant adult. The likelihood of positive performance in children increases when they feel warmth from others and believe that they are regarded as capable.

Discipline and Procedures

Erroneously, discipline is often thought to be synonymous with punishment. The true purpose of **discipline**, however, is the training of self-control. Having and maintaining classroom policies and procedures (e.g., when and how to speak, leave your seat, line up, turn in homework, do make-up work) helps students learn self-discipline. Effective teachers spend the first weeks of school teaching procedures and having their students practice these procedures. This takes classroom time in the beginning, but it saves a great deal of time, and teacher energy, over the course of the school year.

Self-control is best learned from people who exemplify it. Therefore, the key to positive and effective discipline lies in the character of the teacher. Disciplinary efforts tend to be unfair and ineffective when teachers display angry or harsh behavior. Teachers who have unstructured classrooms and who do not enforce classroom rules nurture unpleasant and unruly environments. Successful teachers demonstrate warm, friendly attitudes toward students. They have an air of self-assurance that demands respect and have well-defined behavioral expectations of their students. Such teachers have classroom environments wherein students are comfortable and ready to learn.

Teacher Behavior

We usually think of discipline in terms of student conduct. Before addressing student behavior, please carefully review these rules for teacher behavior that effective teachers live by.

Teachers' 10 Commandments

1. Know students' names. Call students by name, become familiar with their interests and talents, and show respect for each student.
2. Ask, "So what?" when preparing lessons. Make learning and the subject matter relevant, challenging, and fun to students.
3. Establish and maintain routines and procedures for taking attendance, opening class, and so on. Begin class promptly.
4. Use the three F's for good discipline: be firm, fair, and friendly.
5. Don't expect problems; don't look for them. Expect students to be competent, capable, and eager to learn. It is better to be proved wrong than to have students live up to negative expectations.
6. When problems arise, handle them immediately and consistently before they escalate into larger ones. For example, you can walk toward, stop, and look at or call a misbehaving student by his or her last name. Don't use major "artillery" for minor infractions.
7. Correct students in private whenever possible.
8. Avoid sarcasm, ridicule, and belittling remarks, and help students do likewise.
9. Encourage hydraulic-lift experiences in and out of the classroom.
10. Involve students in the setting of individual academic goals.

Student Behavior

Now let us address behavioral expectations for students. Establishing and maintaining classroom procedures for things such as group work, coming to attention, or computer use helps students know what they are to do and how to do it. Procedures are steps to be followed, not rules that can be broken. When a student doesn't enact a procedure, the teacher can simply say, "What is the procedure for . . . ?" After the student articulates the procedure, the teacher can then say, "Show me."[9] Having procedures facilitates students becoming responsible for their behavior and allows teachers to manage rather than discipline their classroom.

Clearly defining rules for student behavior at the beginning of the academic year is also important. Rules can give students a sense of security and can curtail discipline problems. It has been said that cows in a new pasture will seek out the fences to see how far they can roam. So it is with students. For this reason, it is imperative that teachers clearly define the boundaries. It is inevitable that some students will test the "fences" to see how strong they are (in other words, whether the teacher will, in fact, enforce the established rules). A student contract is often useful in establishing classroom rules. **Box 1-2** contains an example of a student behavior contract that has been used in a junior high setting. Note item 7; the teacher who developed and used this form felt it was the most important item in the list.

Many teachers believe that students are more willing to follow rules that they are part of developing. It is often helpful to involve students in a discussion about classroom rules on the first day of class. Encouraging their input enhances the children's sense of having some control. Rules can be printed on a large sheet of paper and hung in a prominent place in the classroom. The process by which rules are developed is perhaps not as important as making sure that they are clearly defined from the beginning and that they are consistently and fairly enforced.

1-2

Classroom Policies

1. Bring pencil/pen and notebook daily. Sharpening of pencils is to be done before class, never during a lecture or discussion.
2. Be in your seat when the bell rings, or have a late excuse. Take care of drinks and restroom needs during class changes.
3. When you have been absent, it is *your* responsibility to follow established procedures to acquire missed information, turn in assignments, and make up tests.
4. The bell does not dismiss students; I do.
5. Do *not* touch any equipment unless I authorize you to do so.
6. If you are failing in your coursework or are not turning in assignments, I will notify your parents.
7. No student is prejudged. That is, I do not read student files beforehand to see who and what problems may be coming in. I assume all students are capable of A work. I also assume that no student is a behavioral problem. If there are any such problem students, those persons will have to show me and the class who they are. Problems, should there be any, will be dealt with accordingly.
8. These behaviors will result in points being subtracted from your grades:
   a. Excessive talking
   b. Disruptive/disrespectful behavior
   c. Failure to follow instructions
   d. Unexcused tardiness

Student Contract

I have listened to and read the classroom policies regarding citizenship, behavior, and coursework. I agree to adhere to this contract and understand that each violation will result in losing 5 points. This will be reflected in my final grade.

Signed: _____

Date: _____

Teeter-Tottering and Hydraulic Lifts

As was stressed earlier in the chapter, effective teachers create classrooms where students feel that they are loved, they belong, and there is a sense of community. Effective teachers not only exemplify a caring positive attitude toward each student, but also insist their students interact with one another in the same way. They teach their students how to treat one another with respect and genuine regard.

Put-down or harassment-type comments and behaviors can destroy the positive emotional climate of a school faster than almost anything else. How often have you heard comments such as "What an idiot!" "I hate her!" "That is so gay!" or "Get lost!" Children are obvious and to the point with their put-downs. As we grow older we become more subtle and sophisticated, but are equally cutting: "I'd never do that," "He is nice, but . . .". Sexual harassment, bigotry, bullying, giving the silent treatment, and excluding people are also pervasive forms of put-down behavior.

It is very important to understand why we and our students spend time and energy trying to undermine others: we do so in a futile effort to try and raise our own insecure sense of worth. This behavior can be easily understood by depicting it with a **teeter-totter** or see-saw (**Figure 1-3**). It is as though we were sitting on a teeter-totter and watching for someone to sit on the other end. We put others down to feel "up," or on a higher level. Feeling superior to others is a false "high" and very short lived. Have you ever been elevated on a real teeter-totter when the other person suddenly got off? You might

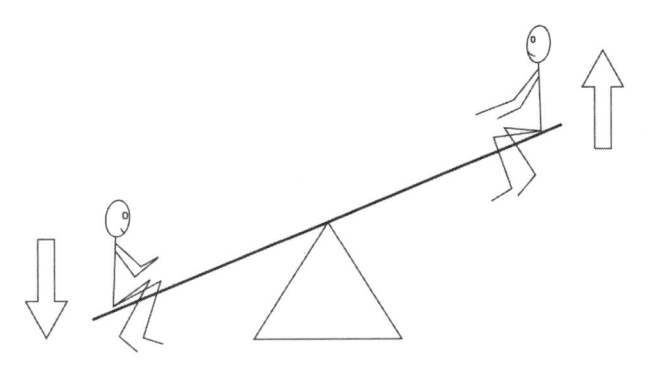

FIGURE 1-3 Teeter-tottering. Teeter-tottering is putting another down in an effort to feel better about yourself.

have skinned the inside of your ankles as you came crashing down. In the same way we "crash" when we figuratively teeter-totter. Then, we look around for someone else to put down, to once again raise our relative sense of worth. Teeter-tottering can become such a pervasive way of thinking, acting, and speaking that we do it with fanlike speed. Adolescence is typically a time of rapid change and insecurity. As a result, this stage of life is particularly vulnerable to frequent teeter-tottering.

Teeter-tottering can easily become epidemic at school—and teachers are not immune. This type of behavior naturally occurs because we have become a society that is very proficient at put-downs. TV programs often glamorize put-down behaviors, and "putting someone in their place" is depicted as very "cool." Young people mimic being "cool" by gossiping, spreading malicious rumors, and excluding the "noncool." In too many homes, put-downs are the predominant form of communication. Some children have become so calloused by this type of behavior that they don't even recognize it is wrong.

Reverse teeter-tottering is also harmful. In this behavior, people develop the habit of putting themselves down as they elevate others. In reverse teeter-tottering, toxic thought habits can erode a person's sense of worth and that individual's ability to reach his or her potential. Reverse teeter-tottering is often done by women in abusive relationships.

How do we break out of the **teeter-totter syndrome**? First, we have to recognize when we are caught up in it. Just as we take our temperature to see if we are ill, so we can check our emotional health by observing how often we teeter-totter. Be sure to take the time to do the application exercise found in **Box 1-3**. We have repeatedly been told that this is one of the most impacting assignments students have every completed in their lives.

You can help your students learn about the teeter-totter principle depicted in Figure 1-3 by drawing this simple diagram on the board and discussing how teeter-tottering works, or, more accurately, how it does not work. Assign students to do the Marks on You activity in Box 1-3 to help them become more aware of their teeter-tottering habits. This activity can easily be modified for younger children.

Students don't appreciate being put down and are very willing to give up teeter-tottering to create a classroom (school) where they feel emotionally safe and accepted. Your classroom (school) can be designated as a teeter-totter–free zone. This does not mean that teeter-tottering will immediately disappear, but it will greatly diminish. Then, whenever you overhear a put-down, you can just make a teeter-totter hand motion. Students appreciate this gentle reminder and will quickly comply with the rule because they want to be in an emotionally safe environment.

Behavior scientists tell us we cannot successfully eliminate a behavior without replacing it with something else. As we work at deleting put-downs, we need to replace teeter-tottering remarks with hydraulic lifts (**Figure 1-4**). A **hydraulic lift** is the act of raising someone else with kind acts or comments. When we are kind to another person, we cannot help but feel better about ourselves. It is as if we were sitting on a hydraulic lift. As we show kindness, we rise along with whomever we are trying to lift. This positive action creates a genuine "high" and a more lasting sense of self-worth.

FIGURE 1-4 Hydraulic lift. When you lift another, you too are lifted.

1-3 Application Exercise

Marks on You

The Marks on You activity was inspired by a very wise mother whose popular, bright teenage daughter was critically injured. Joni and her friends hopped a fence and ran across an interstate to get to a mall. Her friends made it, but Joni was hit by a car. By the time Joni got out of the hospital and was able to return to school, her friends had graduated. The once-popular cheerleader found herself in special education classes instead of honors courses. She became depressed and withdrawn. Her mother helped her become happy again by having her change her focus. She asked Joni to make a mark on the back of her hand every time she was able to make someone in the class smile. This helped Joni focus on lifting others. After school, Joni told her mother the story behind each mark on her hand and again experienced the joy of lifting others.

Doing the following will help you see yourself more clearly and help you identify your teeter-totter and hydraulic lift habits. For four days, make a small mark on your left hand for every "teeter-tottering" remark/act/thought you have. At the same time, make marks on your right hand for every "hydraulic lift" remark/act/thought you have. If you don't want to mark your hands, keep a tally on a 3 × 5 card. We know it is impossible to become aware of *everything* you say, do, or think, but the more you try to become aware of these things and record them, the more you will get out of this exercise.

At the end of each day, tally up both your teeter-totter and hydraulic lift marks and then write a summary paragraph of what happened that day. After completing the four-day tallies and summary paragraphs, write a one-page reaction paper about the entire experience—what you observed and learned by doing it.

Helping children learn self-control by replacing teeter-totters with hydraulic lifts is the single most effective way to create an emotionally supportive climate in a classroom or school. It also alleviates many discipline problems. Be sure to review the many ways teachers can assign students to practice being kind to each other in the activities at the end of the chapter.

Sensitivity to Diversity

We live in an exciting world where diversity of peoples and cultures abounds. In our public schools today, about half of the students are minority (Hispanic, African American, Asian/Pacific Islander, and American Indian/Alaska Native).[10] As educators, we must model sensitivity to diversity for our students and strive to view individuals from various cultures from their perspectives rather than from our own perspectives. We must be sensitive to students who are struggling to learn a new language and adapt to a new culture. How we treat each student affects our relationship with every other student in the classroom. Being respectful and positive creates a classroom climate of understanding and sensitivity to diverse cultures, ethnicities, races, and needs.

Ethnocentric, racist, or stereotypic attitudes held by teachers and students serve as critical barriers to learning and establishing sensitivity toward various cultures and ethnic groups. **Ethnocentricity** involves the attitude that one's own ethnic group or culture is better than others or failure to recognize the existence or validity of other ethnic/cultural groups and their customs, values, beliefs, and norms. **Racism** expresses an attitude that defines certain cultural or ethnic groups as inherently inferior to others and legitimately subject to exploitation, discrimination, and various types of abuse. **Stereotypes** reflect conscious or unconscious attribution of exaggerated characteristics or oversimplified opinions, attitudes, or judgments regarding members of a given ethnic group or culture. A **prejudice** is a negative attitude toward a specific group based on comparison using the individual's own group as a positive reference point. Teachers have a professional responsibility to not let their personal attitudes, stereotypes, and prejudices interfere with their teaching. For example, a teacher raised in one cultural group may have stereotypes or prejudices against another cultural group. This teacher would need to overcome these stereotypes and prejudices to teach students of this cultural group successfully. Of course, stereotypes and prejudices are not confined to just cultural or ethnic groups. For example, some people may have stereotypes of and prejudices toward impaired individuals, the aged, or a variety of other conditions or types of people.

Teachers can build cultural and ethnic sensitivity in numerous ways. They should strive to display appropriate interpersonal skills, including showing warmth, respect, sincerity, concern, and caring for people of all cultures. Beyond this, it is critical to develop cross-cultural understanding in the communities where we serve and live. Recognizing culturally determined viewpoints and standards of behavior, including specific knowledge of and respect for differences, is important. Beyond developing personal cross-cultural understanding, emphasis should be given in the curriculum to developing cross-cultural competency among students.

It is also important to pay attention to culturally/ethnically appropriate learning and problem-solving styles. This involves recognition that a variety of strategies and approaches can be employed to complete a given task. To some extent, learning and problem-solving styles are culturally determined; thus a broad array of approaches should be encouraged to improve learning. Learning is also facilitated by appropriate style, manner, and content of communication for a particular cultural group. This includes the use of ethnically and culturally appropriate nonverbal skills such as eye contact, body language, and physical closeness.

■ STUDENTS WITH SPECIAL NEEDS

It is easy to become overwhelmed when working with the many students who have special needs. Many of these needs are complex problems that pose multiple difficulties in the lives of the affected children and for the school systems of which they are a part. Schools often have various staff in place to help students with special needs, such as guidance counselors, psychologists, learning specialists, social workers, special education teachers, and school nurses. A key to success when working with students with special needs seems to be the ability of these personnel and teachers to work together in a supportive team approach. The support given to those with special needs also benefits the entire student body as they learn from the adults' modeled behaviors and attitudes.

Emotional Needs

An example of emotional needs present in schools and the way in which a supportive team approach can help comes from Francis Scott Key Elementary and Middle School in Baltimore, Maryland, where Melissa Grady works as a mental health therapist. Grady sees four dozen children every week, some for the first time and others whom she has been counseling for years. Some are victims of sexual or physical abuse, have witnessed domestic violence, or have dysfunctional parents who suffer from drug addiction or alcoholism. Others have been traumatized by family disruptions such as divorce or unstable living arrangements.

"The huge thing is a lack of parental guidance," says Grady. "It's symptomatic of society. The children are not getting enough of what they need at home, they're not being taught the coping skills, the social skills. So, of course, all that's spilling out into the school system and the children are unavailable to learn or are disrupting others."[11]

Grady set up a student-support team consisting of herself, a school psychologist, a counselor, a social worker, and teachers representing the elementary and middle schools. The team meets once a week to review the academic performance and special needs of the student body. They are proactive in looking out for students in need, such as those who are acting out, depressed, withdrawn, or displaying sudden changes in behavior or significant decline in grades or attendance. When a child with a special need is identified, the student-support team arranges one-on-one sessions with the student, parent meetings and counseling, and adequate follow-up. This consistent, vigilant student-support team effort is responsible for helping students improve their grades and cope with a variety of special needs. Teachers at the schools are thrilled that the student-support team is in place and have seen a reduction in the severity of the discipline problems they face in their classrooms. A seasoned teacher at the school, who has taught at seven other schools, commented, "You can really teach here."

In coming chapters you will read more about how to deal with various emotional concerns in your classroom, including depression, family stress, and divorce (the *Stress Management Skills* chapter); eating disorders (the *Promoting Healthy Eating and Physical Activity* chapter); substance abuse and addiction for individuals and families (the *Promoting a Tobacco-Free and Drug-Free Lifestyle* chapter); abuse and neglect (the *Violence Prevention and Safety Promotion* chapter); and suicide, self-injury, and terminal illness (the *Dealing with Crises and Critical Issues* chapter). Ideally, you will be able to set up student-support teams in the schools where you teach that will help you better meet the emotional concerns of your students.

English Language Needs

Students for whom English is a second language (ESL) have to learn not only how to speak English, but also how to read and write it. ESL students demonstrate large variations in their skill levels. Misbehavior and indifferent attitudes can be masks for students who don't feel confident in their ability to succeed in the classroom.

Teachers can help ESL students succeed by doing the same things that help all students learn. Show them you care by establishing a personal relationship with them and their family. Pronounce

Students with English deficiencies or learning disabilities can find simple learning tasks difficult and stressful.

their names correctly and demonstrate interest in their cultures. Come to know their individual levels of understanding. Make sure they know what is going on in the class through interviews and assessments. Assign them learning "buddies." Teach with energy and help make lessons relevant to them by bringing their culture into the class and telling stories that they can relate to. Obtain free health materials that come in Spanish and other languages from health agencies and governmental sources. Demonstrate patience and give extra time as needed for completing assignments and tests.

Learning Needs

A **learning disability (LD)** is a disorder that affects a person's ability either to interpret what he or she sees and hears or to link information from different parts of the brain. These limitations can show up in many ways: as specific difficulties with spoken and written language, coordination, self-control, or attention. They can impede the ability to read or write, do math, or learn other important skills. They can also affect how students behave, how students perceive themselves, and how students interact with classmates.

It is not exactly clear how many students experience learning disabilities. Some experts estimate that roughly 1 of every 100 school-age children has some form of learning disability; others estimate that this proportion is almost one-third of all school-age children. What is clear is that many more boys than girls are affected. Many kinds of learning disabilities exist, including speech and language disorders (difficulty in producing or interpreting communication), academic skills disorders (reading, writing, or arithmetic skill problems), and miscellaneous learning disabilities (fine motor skills problems, nonverbal learning disorder, and others).

Teachers can help children with learning disabilities by first recognizing the problem. All too often, children with learning disabilities are labeled as "dumb" or "unmotivated." It is essential that these children be identified early, before they begin to see themselves as stupid and failing. Be suspicious if a fairly bright child has trouble learning certain skills. In such a case, you can make a referral to a school counselor or special education instructor. Every school district has its policy for screening learning disabilities. With the right help, most children with learning disabilities can overcome them. It is helpful to remember the following famous people who had learning disabilities: Albert Einstein, Thomas Edison, Nelson Rockefeller, Ludwig van Beethoven, Winston Churchill, Bruce Jenner, George Patton, Leonardo da Vinci, and Woodrow Wilson. Be mindful that as you interact with students with learning disabilities that you are, in fact, teaching all of your students attitudes and behaviors that they will mirror. You can facilitate your students in learning compassion and understanding for individuals with learning disabilities by doing the activities found at the end of the chapter.

Attention-Deficit/Hyperactivity Disorder

Attention-deficit/hyperactivity disorder (ADHD) is a common, chronic behavioral disorder characterized by inattention, hyperactivity, and impulsivity. **Inattention** is described as failure to finish tasks started, easy distractibility, seeming lack of attention, and difficulty concentrating on tasks requiring sustained attention. **Hyperactivity** is described as difficulty staying seated and sitting still, and excessive running or climbing. **Impulsivity** is described as acting before thinking, difficulty taking turns, problems organizing work, and constant shifting from one activity to another.

ADHD is believed to affect 5% to 10% of all school-age children worldwide. On average, at least one child in each classroom needs help with this disorder. It is diagnosed three times more frequently in boys than in girls. Some controversies have emerged regarding the prevalence of the ADHD diagnosis and drug treatment. The diagnosis is commonly made by a health professional who "draws a line" on a continuum scale of normal behavior indicating that he or she perceives the child's behavior to be extreme. Many recommend additional psychological testing to look for and confirm cognitive impairment before making such a diagnosis.[12]

The cause of ADHD is unknown. Nevertheless, some evidence indicates that ADHD is the result of a developmental failure in the brain circuitry that controls attention, inhibition, and self-control, with dopamine playing a role. There is no known cure for ADHD. Hyperactivity and impulsivity decrease with age, but problems with inattentiveness persist. Approximately two-thirds of children with ADHD continue to exhibit significant levels of inattentiveness and impairment into adolescence.[12]

Helping Students with ADHD

Children with ADHD have a variety of needs.* Some children are too hyperactive or inattentive to function in a regular classroom, even with medication and a behavior management plan. Such children may be placed in a special education class for all or part of the day. In some schools, the special education teacher teams with the classroom teacher to meet each child's unique needs. However, most children are able to stay in the regular classroom. Whenever possible, educators prefer not to segregate children, but rather to let them learn along with their peers.

Children with ADHD often need some special accommodations to help them learn. For example, the teacher may seat the child in an area with few distractions, provide an area where the child can move around and release excess energy, or establish a clearly posted system of rules and reward appropriate behavior. Sometimes just keeping a card or a picture on the desk can serve as a visual reminder to use the right school behavior, like raising a hand instead of shouting out or staying in a seat instead of wandering around the room. Giving a child with ADHD extra time on tests can make the difference between his or her passing and failing, and it provides the student with a fairer chance to show what has been learned. Reviewing instructions or writing assignments on the board, and even listing the books and materials they will need for the task, may make it possible for disorganized, inattentive children to complete their work. Many of the strategies of special education are simply good teaching methods. Telling students in advance what they will learn, providing visual aids, and giving written as well as oral instructions are all ways to help students focus and remember the key parts of the lesson.

Students with ADHD often need to learn techniques for monitoring and controlling their own attention and behavior. For example, students can be taught alternatives for what to do when they lose track of what they are supposed to be doing—look for instructions on the blackboard, raise their hand, or quietly ask another child. The process of finding alternatives to interrupting the teacher makes a student more self-sufficient and cooperative. In addition, because there is less interrupting, a student begins to get more praise than reprimands. **Box 1-4** contains resources that can help you become more effective at teaching students with ADHD.

Drug Treatment for ADHD

Stimulant drug treatment has been found to be very effective at helping individuals with ADHD concentrate, but there are some questions about the efficacy of using these drugs over the long term.[12] Stimulants such as **Ritalin** (methylphenidate) and **Dexedrine** (dextroamphetamine) have been used for some time. Newer drug formulations, such as **Adderall** (a combination of four amphetamines, including Dexedrine) and **Concerta** (methylphenidate extended-release tablets), are popular because of their longer-acting properties. These pills can be taken by a child or adolescent once a day, instead of two or three times a day, eliminating the need for a dose to be taken at school.

As with all medications, there is the potential for side effects. While on these medications, some children may lose weight, have less appetite, and temporarily grow more slowly. Others may have problems falling asleep. Other side effects can include irritability, agitation, nervousness, and periods of sadness. Serious side effects include facial tics and muscle twitching. Most of the side effects that do occur can often be handled by reducing the dosage.

Data from National Institute of Mental Health, Attention Deficit Hyperactivity Disorder (NIH Publication No. 12-3572), 2012.

1-4 Internet Support

Internet Support for ADHD

Numerous online resources can help teachers be more effective while working with students with ADHD. Here are a few sites that provide many varied resources.

- HELPGUIDE.org has information on ADHD causes, diagnosis, and treatment; parenting tips; and ways to help children with ADHD succeed in school, which includes tips for teachers.
- ADD in School (http://www.addinschool.com) is a comprehensive website that provides teachers with classroom interventions and tips for working with youth with ADHD in elementary and secondary schools.

One important concern about stimulant drugs is their potential for abuse. When these powerful stimulant drugs are abused, abusers have suffered psychotic episodes, violent behavior, and severe psychological dependence on the stimulant. Stimulants used to treat ADHD are classified by the Drug Enforcement Agency (DEA) as Schedule II drugs, the most highly addictive drugs that are still legal. According to the DEA, drugs to treat ADHD rank among today's most-stolen prescriptions and most-abused legal drugs. Most abusers, DEA officials say, are children. Most dealers are children who are prescribed the drugs to treat ADHD. Parents of ADHD-affected children have also been found to abuse the stimulant drugs.

COMMON K–12 HEALTH PROBLEMS

Health problems that commonly show up in schools today include infectious and chronic health problems, accidents, and bullying. Teachers need to become well informed regarding student health problems and how to deal with them. We will now look at communicable and chronic health conditions. The *Violence Prevention and Safety Promotion* chapter deals with accidents and bullying.

Communicable Health Conditions

Common health conditions that can spread from one student to another include colds, strep throat, flu, conjunctivitis, diarrhea, impetigo, and lice. Teachers need to model and teach vigilant habits of hand washing and covering the mouth with something other than our hands when we sneeze or cough. Students need to understand that it is important to stay at home when they are sick so that they do not spread their illness to others. Teachers also need to develop the practice of disinfecting commonly touched items in the classroom and teach students not to share combs and hats.

The Centers for Disease Control and Prevention (CDC) has issued the following guidelines for precautions against the spread of viruses. Following and teaching these measures will minimize the spread of infectious diseases in schools.

- *Avoid close contact.* Avoid close contact with people who are sick; keep your distance from others to protect them from getting sick, too.
- *Stay home when you are sick.* If possible, stay home from work, school, and errands when you are sick. You will help prevent others from catching your illness.
- *Cover your mouth and nose.* Cover your mouth and nose with a tissue when coughing or sneezing. This behavior may prevent those around you from getting sick.

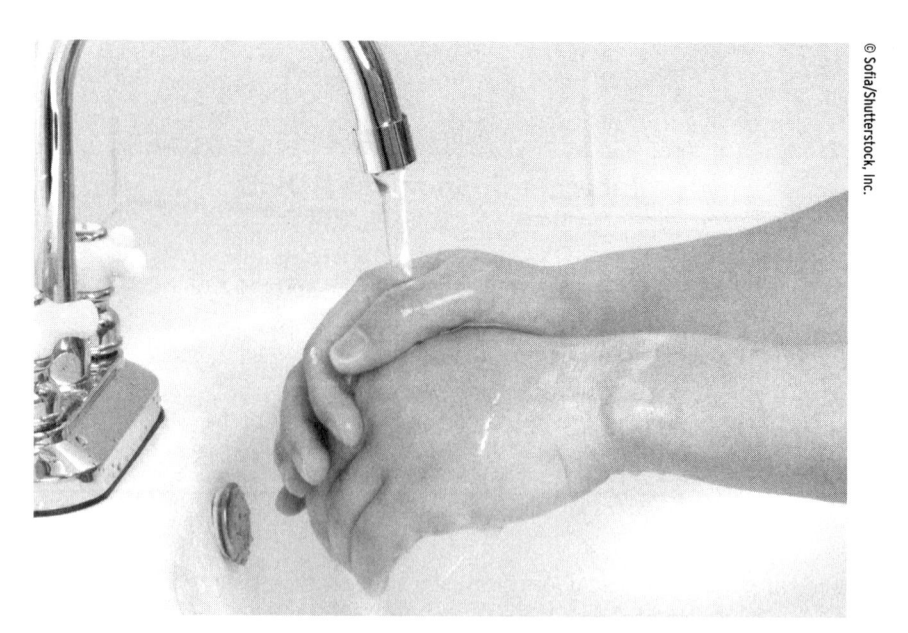

Students of all ages need to be reminded to frequently wash their hands.

- *Clean your hands.* Washing your hands often will help protect you from germs.
- *Avoid touching your eyes, nose, or mouth.* Germs are often spread when a person touches something that is contaminated with germs and then touches his or her eyes, nose, or mouth.
- *Practice other good health habits.* Get plenty of sleep, be physically active, manage your stress, drink plenty of fluids, and eat nutritious food.

Today we are grateful to have immunizations for many of the communicable diseases that debilitated and killed our ancestors, but we are still vulnerable. The H1N1 virus (swine flu) outbreak that originated in Mexico in April 2009 highlighted how concerned scientists are that a microbe will one day emerge that is as devastating as the 1918 virus flu pandemic, which killed 50 million people worldwide.[13] Influenza viruses and other microorganisms are constantly mutating. Every year scientists try to predict which new strains of flu viruses will be problematic and formulate flu shots to help us be prepared for our encounters with them. Unfortunately, indiscriminate use of antibiotics both in the United States and abroad creates a breeding ground for the growth of drug-resistant microorganisms, known as "super-germs." We need to be careful personally not to abuse antibiotics and to teach our students that antibiotics don't help when we are infected with viruses.[14]

As of 2013, the Department of Health and Human Services recommended that children receive the following immunizations by the time they enter school: hepatitis B, rotavirus, diphtheria/tetanus/pertussis (DTaP), *Haemophilus influenzae* type b (Hib), inactivated poliovirus (IPV), measles/mumps/rubella (MMR), and varicella. The following immunizations are recommended for certain high-risk groups: pneumococcal (PCV), hepatitis A, and meningococcal (MCV). Influenza vaccination is recommended yearly. For children age 11 or 12 and 13 to 18, the following immunization and boosters are recommended: tetanus/diphtheria/pertussis (Tdap), human papillomavirus (HPV), and meningococcal virus (MCV).[15]

Chronic Health Conditions

The term **chronic** refers to illnesses or conditions that are long-lasting. When a person has a chronic illness, the symptoms of the illness may be reduced or even go away for periods of time, but the person still has the same underlying condition.

Most teachers will encounter children with chronic health conditions in their classroom because more than 5 million school-age youth are affected by chronic health conditions.[16] The chronic health conditions most commonly seen in students are defined briefly here. **Asthma**, the most common chronic disease of childhood, periodically causes breathing difficulties that result from the constriction of the airways in the lungs. In **diabetes**, the body does not absorb the sugar in food as a result of the failure of the pancreas gland to produce the hormone insulin. **Epilepsy** is a general term used to describe different types of seizure disorders or temporary disruptions of electrical impulses in the brain that result in seizures. **Cerebral palsy** is a term used to describe a group of chronic conditions caused by damage to the brain that affects body movements and muscle coordination. Such damage usually occurs during fetal development or during infancy, but it can also occur before, during, or shortly following birth. **Congenital heart disease** is the result of a defect in the heart that is present at birth, whereas **acquired heart disease** develops during childhood, usually as the result of a viral or bacterial infection. **Cancer** refers to several diseases in which cells grow in an out-of-control manner, develop abnormal sizes and shapes, destroy neighboring cells, and can spread to other organs and tissues. Leukemia, lymphoma, and brain cancer are the most common childhood cancers. **Spina bifida** is a birth defect resulting from incorrect development of the spinal cord that can leave the spinal cord exposed after birth.

Children with chronic health conditions have special challenges and concerns. They want to be like everyone else and worry about being rejected by their classmates. They worry about being teased and excluded. In addition to these stresses, they must cope with the effects of the illness and the treatments that they undergo. Often these factors make it difficult to put all of their energy into schoolwork. For their part, teachers worry about these students and about their own competence in responding appropriately to any medical emergencies that might arise in the classroom. They ask themselves: What should I do if an epileptic child has a seizure in my classroom? What should I do if a diabetic child has a diabetic emergency? It is critical, then, that school personnel working with students with chronic health conditions have an understanding of the various health conditions and emergency management procedures of their students. The following are some tips:

◆ Your attitude of kindness, empathy, and acceptance toward others generates similar attitudes in the classroom. Your students will watch you and model your behavior.
◆ Know the protocol for possible emergencies. Make sure that the school nurse provides you with sufficient information about the medical conditions of students in your classroom.
◆ Be sensitive to when not to show concern, such as when a child with cystic fibrosis is coughing. The cough is important to clear the lungs. Paying too much attention to a symptom often makes it worse and reinforces a child's sense of shame.
◆ Children with medical problems are often overly sensitive. Don't perceive their behavior as babyish or immature or as a serious emotional problem. By reinforcing positive age-appropriate behavior, you are most likely to increase it.

When school personnel, parents, and health professionals work in partnership and in a creative manner, having children with chronic health conditions in the classroom can be a stimulus for the growth of everyone in the classroom environment. An example is a second-grade student with spina bifida who asked for classmates to receive orientation about his disease after classmates teased him when he had urine leakage. During the session, classmates asked many questions, including whether he would have children and whether he would live. Because of the careful preparation and support, he was not surprised by the questions and could answer them honestly. Once the children understood his condition, he was seen as "normal" and accepted with no further teasing.

1-5 Activities for Creating a Warm Emotional Climate

These activities and others found later at the end of Chapter 3 can help you create a warm caring classroom and school environment. Each activity can be embellished and modified to meet varying grade levels. We have identified the likely appropriate grade level(s) for use:

P: primary, kindergarten through third grade
I: intermediate, fourth through sixth grade
J: junior high
H: high school

Susan Boyle

Play a clip of Susan Boyle's performance on the TV show *Britain's Got Talent*. Discuss the audience's reaction before and after she sang—how and why their judgment of her changed. She touches us because we can all in some way identify with her. Discuss how we all might not be able to sing, but we all have talents, and that we all benefit when we encourage one another other to develop our unique talents. (P, I, J, H)

Admirable Graffiti

Wrap your classroom door with construction paper. Tell students that they can write on the door whenever they want to record an admired action or attitude they have observed in one of their classmates. (P, I, J, H)

Positive Tattle Telling

- Have students draw and display posters showing good things (helping, comforting, complimenting, being kind) that they catch somebody doing.
- Have students write good things that they catch classmates doing on pieces of paper and place the papers in a "tattle box." Read the papers at the end of the day or week.
- Include parents by having them catch and record their child doing good at home. Parents can then share through e-mail, letters, or phone interviews. (P, I)

Activities for Building LD Empathy

You can help your student acquire empathy for those struggling with learning disabilities by doing the following activities.

- Have students try to write a sentence with the hand they normally don't use for writing.
- Have students hold a piece of paper up to a mirror and try to write their names, a short story, or do a math problem while only looking in the mirror.
- Retype a story or text page with all the *b* and *d*, *c* and *e*, and *m* and *n* letters switched. Have students try to read it quickly.
- Give students a timed math quiz where all the numbers have been written on their papers in mirror image format. (P, I)
  (Additional hydraulic-lift-type activities can be found in Box 3-4 in Chapter 3.)

KEY TERMS

pyramid of influence 2
circle of concern 3
circle of influence 3
proactive people 4
reactive people 4
connectedness 7
self-fulfilling prophecies 7
discipline 8
teeter-totter 10
reverse teeter-tottering 11
teeter-totter syndrome 11
hydraulic lift 11
ethnocentricity 13
racism 13
stereotypes 13
prejudice 13
learning disability (LD) 15

attention-deficit/hyperactivity disorder (ADHD) 15
inattention 15
hyperactivity 15
impulsivity 15
Ritalin 16
Dexedrine 16
Adderall 16
Concerta 16
chronic 18
asthma 19
diabetes 19
epilepsy 19
cerebral palsy 19
congenital heart disease 19
acquired heart disease 19
cancer 19
spina bifida 19

KNOWLEDGE CHECK!

1. Define, differentiate, and discuss the key terms and their relative importance in this chapter.
2. Identify the three major areas of a teacher's pyramid of influence. Discuss each pyramid area by relating concepts discussed in the chapter that relate to it.
3. Discuss the principle behind the circle of concern and the circle of influence, and cite some examples from the chapter. What can you specifically do to enlarge your circle of influence?
4. Describe the characteristics of effective teachers, including the healthy and ethical behaviors they model. What do you exemplify and what do you need to work on?
5. What did Frank O'Malley do that made him such an effective teacher?
6. Which three key things did William Bennett find were characteristic of exemplary classrooms? What are "connected" students less likely to do?
7. Discuss how negative and positive labeling takes place at school and how labeling affects student behavior and learning. Discuss how teachers communicate their expectations for their students and how teachers can overcome negative scripting.
8. Explain why classroom policies and procedures are important, when they should be taught, and what a teacher can do when a procedure is not followed.
9. Explain why teacher self-discipline is important, and identify the Teachers' 10 Commandments.
10. Discuss how classroom rules should be enacted, communicated, and enforced.
11. Discuss the habits and effects of teeter-tottering and hydraulic lifts. Explain how teachers can make their classrooms teeter-totter–free zones.
12. Describe how you can celebrate diversity in your classroom and be ethnically sensitive.
13. Explain how schools can best meet the emotional needs of students.
14. Identify things that teachers can do to help ESL students in the classroom.
15. Describe the various forms of learning disabilities, explain how teachers can help students with learning disabilities, and describe how teachers can teach empathy for LD individuals.
16. Identify the signs of ADHD and explain what teachers can do to help children with ADHD.
17. Discuss ADHD drug treatment, including its controversies.

18. Identify infectious health conditions commonly found among K–12 students and the CDC's precaution guidelines.
19. Identify recommended immunizations for K–12 students.
20. Discuss the chronic health conditions that teachers are most likely to encounter in their students, and explain how teachers can help children with chronic health problems.

■ REFERENCES

1. Covey SR. *The eighth habit: from effectiveness to greatness*. New York, NY: Free Press; 2004.
2. Steinem G. The Royal Knights of Harlem. In: Canfield J, Hansen M, eds. *Chicken soup for the soul*. Deerfield Beach, FL: Health Communications; 1993:134–139.
3. Woodward KL. The life of a great teacher. *Newsweek*. October 21, 1998:60.
4. Glasser W. *The quality school: managing students without coercion*. New York, NY: Harper Perennial; 1998.
5. Bennett WJ. *The devaluing of America: fight for our culture and our children*. Colorado Springs, CO: Focus on the Family; 1994.
6. Centers for Disease Control and Prevention (CDC). School connectedness: strategies for increasing protective factors. Available at http://www.cdc.gov/healthyYouth/AdolescentHealth/connectedness.htm. Accessed April 12, 2013.
7. Rosenthal R, Jacobson L. *Pygmalion in the classroom*. New York, NY: Holt, Rinehart and Winston; 1968.
8. Hamachek DE. *Encounters with the self*. New York, NY: Holt, Rinehart and Winston; 1978.
9. Wong H, Wong RT. *The first days of school: how to be an effective teacher*. 4th ed. Mountain View, CA: Harry K. Wong Publications; 2009.
10. U.S. Census Bureau. School enrollment. 2011. Available at http://www.census.gov/population/www/socdemo/school/cps2007.html. Accessed April 12, 2013.
11. O'Conner HJ. The Cleavers don't live here anymore: some schools are facing up to their students' mental health problems. *ABCNEWS.com*. 1999.
12. Nauert R. Experts call for new approach to ADHD. *Psych Central News*. 2008. Available at http://psychcentral.com/news/2008/01/23/experts-call-for-new-approach-to-adhd/1825.html. Accessed July 15, 2009.
13. Morens DM, Taubenberger JK, Fauci AS. The persistent legacy of the 1918 influenza virus. *N Engl J Med*. 2009;361(3):225–229. Available at http://www.nejm.org/doi/full/10.1056/NEJMp0904819. Accessed April 12, 2013.
14. Centers for Disease Control and Prevention. Get smart: know when antibiotics work. 2013. Available at http://www.cdc.gov/getsmart. Accessed April 12, 2013.
15. Centers for Disease Control and Prevention. Immunization schedules. 2013. Available at http://www.cdc.gov/vaccines/schedules/index.html. Accessed April 12, 2013.
16. Perrin JM, Bloom SR, Gortmaker SL. The increase of childhood chronic conditions in the United States. *JAMA*. 2007;297:2755–2759.

Chapter 2
Teaching Today's Students

Courtesy of Lindsay Hansen.

Consider . . .

- A good teacher is like a candle—it consumes itself to light the way for others. —Author unknown
- A teacher affects generations yet unborn. —Author unknown

■ TODAY'S LEARNERS AND THE BRAIN

The world has drastically changed in recent years. As modern technology alters our world, teachers and their educational practices must keep up.

Today's learners are often referred to as "digital natives," "Generation M," or "millennials." Digital natives process and deal with information differently from members of earlier generations.[1] Rather than thinking linearly, they tend to jump around between multiple sources and piece information together. They are more visual and interpret and develop images with ease, having developed these skills with video and virtual games. Digital natives learn better through discovery rather than being told information. They can shift their attention rapidly from one task to another, and they often choose not to pay attention to things that don't interest them.

The brain's wiring is structured according to the stimuli to which it is exposed. Exposure to media and technology has literally "wired" today's kids differently than previous generations, which in turn affects how they process information. Today's learners generally are comfortable using new technology, like to be constantly connected to information and other people, expect immediate results, and enjoy connecting through social media.[2] Earlier generations were educated through a very hierarchical method in which teachers taught (told) students the information that they were to learn. Today's learners, however, prefer a more lateral approach to learning, in which they learn from peers and nontraditional sources such as the Internet and other media. Today's kids prefer to get their hands on things, figure out problems and processes on their own, and go through the "messy" process of learning from experience.[2]

Through brain-imaging studies, we have learned a great deal about how children's brains develop.[3] Even though the brain reaches adult size by age 11 or 12 (a 6-year-old's brain is 90% of its adult size), it does not become fully mature until individuals are in their 20s.[4] Extensive structural changes in the brain take place throughout adolescence. The brain's gray matter thickens until about age 12, but then begins thinning out until the early 20s. Conversely, the brain's white matter thickens (**Figure 2-1**). The **gray matter** contains nerve cells and dendrites that branch out and form connections with other nerve cells to send nerve signals (messages) throughout the brain. The **white matter** is made up of myelin sheaths, which cover and insulate the axons and make nerve signal transmissions faster and more efficient. Thus the "pruning away" of gray matter and the proliferation of white matter during the adolescent years mean fewer but faster nerve connections in the brain, or a more efficient brain.

Digital natives learn best through discovery and social interaction.

Teenage brains are immature and not fully developed. The last region of the brain to undergo the maturation process of proliferation and pruning of neural pathways is the prefrontal cortex. The **prefrontal cortex** is located behind the forehead (**Figure 2-2**). Here reasoning, planning, organization of thoughts, weighing the consequences of actions, suppressing impulses, and other "executive" functions take place. Adolescent specialist Laurence Steinberg stresses that some of these functions in the prefrontal cortex mature earlier than others. In the teen brain, for example, the systems that regulate logic and reasoning develop ahead of those regulating impulse and emotions.[5] As a result, according to Steinberg, adolescents are vulnerable to risky and dangerous behaviors. Unlike the adult brain, the prefrontal cortex of the teenage brain is unable to perceive that the negative outcomes of a risky behavior outweigh any potential thrill. This developmental characteristic makes teens prone to poor decision making.

The **limbic system** comprises a set of brain structures that sit under the cerebral cortex and on top of the brain stem. This part of the brain is sometimes called the emotive brain because emotions are processed here. The limbic system controls emotional responses and deals with motivation and behavior. It also plays a huge role in memory. The limbic system determines which stimuli are remembered and whether memories are stored in long- or short-term memory.

The **brain stem**, sometimes called the primitive brain, controls everything that keeps us alive, including breathing, blood circulation, and digestion. It coordinates everything necessary for

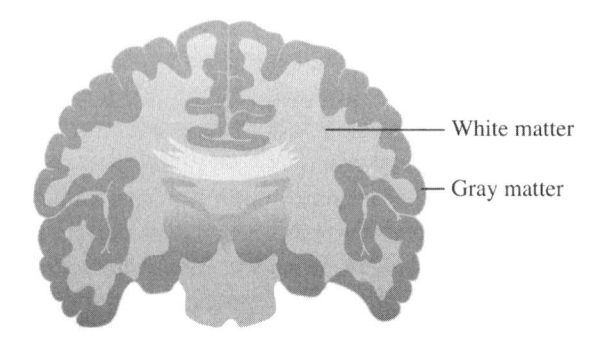

FIGURE 2-1 White and gray matter.

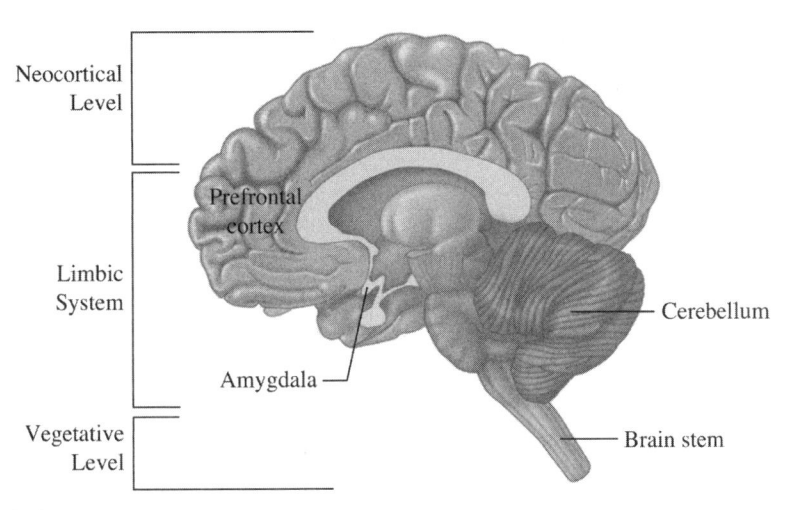

FIGURE 2-2 Levels of the brain.

survival without our conscious thought. The cerebellum coordinates movement, balance, and posture; it also stores motor memory (e.g., how to ride a bike.)

■ TEACHING WITH THE BRAIN IN MIND

Knowledge about how the brain learns is rapidly accumulating. Scientific tools such as magnetic resonance imaging (MRI), computerized axial tomography (CAT), and positron emission tomography (PET) have led to important discoveries. One of the most interesting findings is that learning changes the structure of the brain. In essence, the brain "rewires" itself in response to new stimulation and experiences. Learning experiences cause nerve cells in the brain to create new synapses or junctions through which information passes from one nerve cell (neuron) to another. A baby is born with only a small proportion of the trillions of synapses that he or she will eventually form as a result of learning. Other changes in the brain, such as increased capillary (tiny blood vessel) development and neuron-supported cell growth, are associated with learning.[6]

Our brains are designed to take in stimuli from our five senses. In response to the stimuli, we develop neural networks or connections among neurons through which the neurons communicate with one another. These neural connections, which are often described as neural pathways, are strengthened when they are frequently used or stimulated, much like a path worn into a field of grass. In contrast, when they are used only infrequently, they atrophy and cease to function, a process called **neural pruning**. New experiences (learning) cause new neural pathways to form—a process known as **neural branching**. Another term, **brain plasticity**, describes the ability of neural networks to continue to generate and to modify themselves throughout life.[7]

The important point here is that the brain's capacity to develop neural pathways depends critically on how much it is used. Changes in the brain occur as a function of use—use it or lose it, so to speak. Experiences early in life, when the number of connections between brain cells starts to increase rapidly, are important to optimal brain development.[8] Children need interactions with people and the environment to stimulate brain development. Children with stronger and more connected neural pathways are more likely to have greater learning ability, higher levels of motivation, and accelerated readiness to begin school.[9] Learning occurs at all ages, and the brain appears to maintain its plasticity for life.[10]

Learning is a natural and innate response to experience. Our brains are continually searching for meaning. The search for meaning occurs as the brain searches for patterns in an attempt to discern and understand events in its environment. The brain is constantly creating neural connections or associations with what is already known and found to be personally meaningful. Unless new information carries meaning for us, we are unlikely to make use of it.[11]

Relaxed Alertness

Emotions profoundly affect both the brain and learning. Positive emotions such as happiness, enthusiasm, hope, and optimism facilitate children's learning. Learning in a pleasant environment stimulates the flow of chemicals in the brain that stimulate those areas of the brain most responsible for learning.

Relaxed alertness is an optimal state of mind for student learning. In this state, students feel competent and confident, and they are interested or intrinsically motivated to learn.[12] In contrast, when students feel threatened, chemicals are released in the brain that cause the brain to **downshift**. When this occurs, students are less able to engage in intellectual tasks or form memories. Downshifting means that the lower and more primitive and emotional parts of the brain are in charge; these parts of the brain filter stimuli so that they cannot reach the cerebral cortex where learning occurs.

Teachers need to build classroom environments and relationships that maximize relaxed alertness and minimize threat and anxiety. Pay close attention to how you manage your classroom and interact with your students. Follow the Teachers' 10 Commandments and encourage the hydraulic lifts discussed in the *Teaching to Make a Difference* chapter. Help students who appear anxious or threatened to deal with their feelings. Recognize that students cannot simply turn on or off their emotions to learn better. Many students live in situations that are highly stressful and take a toll on their learning ability. Children with major threats need help. Consult counselors, school nurses, and other available professional resources. Follow school and district policies in seeking help for children who suffer from serious threatening conditions.

"So What?"

We have described how the brain innately searches for and construct's meaning. The brain responds differently to what it considers to be meaningless versus meaningful information.[13] Facts learned about various topics in isolation are soon forgotten by students, whereas information that has

The optimal tension level for learning is high challenge and low threat.

personal meaning is retained. Ask, "So what?" when preparing lessons. Make learning and the subject matter relevant, challenging, and fun for students. Focus less on everything that "needs to be covered" and more on making connections with what students already know.

To prepare meaningful lessons, envision one of your students sitting in class displaying a great deal of attitude in body language. He or she is physically screaming, "I don't care—this is boring!" Prepare your lessons with this student in mind. Find ways to make what you teach relevant and interesting for that student. For instance, if the student is interested in motorcycles, try to relate the lesson in some way to motorcycles.

You can also help your students learn how to answer "So what?" on their own. This is done by challenging them to search for meaning and to make connections on their own with what they already know and have experienced.

Active Learning

The notion that the brain is a sponge waiting to soak up information or an empty vessel waiting to have informative material poured into it is false. Learners are not passive recipients. In turn, learning requires more than the efficient delivery of information into students' minds (passive learning). The human brain is an information-processing organ, and it learns best through experience. **Active learning** engages students in doing things and thinking about what they are doing. It helps the brain learn more and remember more.

You can use many active learning strategies in your teaching to engage students actively. In class, you can use debates, role-playing, simulations, dramatizations, and learning centers. Outside of class, you can use service learning, health fairs, and several types of creative projects.

An important component of active learning is giving students time to process and think about what they have learned. Give them opportunities to reflect on what they are learning, what kind of value that information has, how they are learning, and what else needs to be learned. You can do this by creating opportunities for students to engage in self-reflection, such as writing in a journal, or to pair-share activities. Reflection and active processing create deeper understanding and meaning related to learning experiences.

Another active learning approach is **orchestrated immersion**.[12] With this technique, the key is for students to be "immersed" in rich and complex environments as a way of life, not just for a short time period. The teacher's role here is much different from the traditional scenario in which the teacher dominates by talking and holding the students' attention. Students who become immersed in learning experiences often become engrossed in learning without regard for time.

RAD Teaching

Judy Willis, a teacher and neuroscientist, proposes that we take into account three parts of the brain when preparing lessons and planning for instruction. She identifies these parts with the acronym **RAD**, which stands for reticular activating system (RAS), amygdala, and dopamine.

The **reticular activating system (RAS)** is located in the brain stem and has the job of filtering the various stimuli (sensory messages) that come into the brain. It determines which information goes to the conscious thinking brain, and which information is relayed to the autonomic response part of the brain. Billions of bits of sensory information are available to the brain every second, but only a few thousand can pass through this unconscious RAS filter. How does your big toe feel right now? The RAS gives priority to stimuli that are novel. Unless your big toe feels something novel (e.g., pain), you were probably unaware of it until we cued you to think about it. Because the RAS is geared to let things that are unexpected and novel capture our attention, novelty and surprise should be incorporated into teaching strategies. Think of a favorite lesson you had in high school. Did it contain something novel or unexpected? In addition to novelty and surprise, multisensory learning experiences are a great way to get and maintain students' attention.[14]

The **amygdala** is often likened to a switch because it determines whether information is sent to the "thinking brain" (prefrontal cortex) or to the "reactive brain" (lower autonomic brain). When a student is relaxed, information can flow more easily to the higher cognitive areas of the brain for processing and reflection. When students are stressed, bored, or frustrated, however, the amygdala directs the input to the unconscious, involuntary, reactive brain. In this state, no long-term memories are created.[14] This phenomenon explains why it is important to create an emotionally warm classroom setting.

Dopamine is a brain chemical (neurotransmitter) that is released during pleasurable experiences. Dopamine increases the brain's attention to the pleasurable activity and builds strong memories of the experience. The implication here is that when you incorporate pleasurable, joyful learning activities into the classroom, dopamine is released in students' brains that helps them pay attention and create long-term memories of what they learn.[14]

In the book *Made to Stick*, authors Chip and Dan Heath discuss why some ideas take hold while others are quickly forgotten. They explain that sticky ideas are things that we easily remember—things that we can't forget. The more "sticky" a teacher can make a concept, the more likely it is to be remembered. The six principles the Heaths propose make ideas sticky are in alignment with Judy Willis's RAD teaching concepts. Ideas are made sticky by using one, but preferably more, of the following principles:[15]

1. *Make it simple*. Strip the idea down to its most critical essence. The "golden rule" is a good example.
2. *Make it unexpected*. Use surprise, just as Judy Willis proposes.
3. *Make it concrete*. Explain it in terms of sensory information. The proverb, "A bird in the hand is worth two in the bush," makes an abstract truth become physical and touchable.
4. *Make it credible*. Provide a way for students to test the idea for themselves (e.g., ask, "How do you feel when you don't get enough sleep?").
5. *Make students feel something*. For example, the antismoking TRUTH campaign commercials create anger by exposing tobacco company lies and attempts to manipulate.
6. *Use stories to get students to act on ideas*. Stories act as driver simulators because they provide the brain with an opportunity to mentally practice behaviors. After story-based mental practice, the brain responds more quickly and effectively when it encounters similar situations.

Other Considerations

Because of space constraints, we mention only four more considerations for teaching with the brain in mind.

First, the brain learns better through social interaction than it does when working alone. Cooperative learning activities can help students learn communication and social skills at the same time that they are working toward a learning goal. Cooperative learning activities also foster a sense of being a member of a learning community and encourage meaningful discussion and reflection.

Second, the brain is poor at maintaining nonstop attention. It takes high levels of neural energy for students to concentrate and focus intensely, particularly for direct instruction. The attention spans of most students are brief. According to Jensen, author of *Teaching with the Brain in Mind*, the appropriate amount of direct instruction for children in grades 3 to 5 is 8 to 12 minutes; for those in grades 6 to 12, it is 12 to 15 minutes.[16] If students are not given time for rest or diversion, the brain loses its ability to focus and concentrate. Students need breaks, alternative learning strategies, and changes in topics to shift the emphasis of concentration. When you teach, be sure to change things up somehow every 10 or so minutes.

Third, one of the smartest things that teachers can do to facilitate learning is to keep students active.[11] Activity keeps students' energy levels up and provides the brain with the oxygen-rich blood needed for highest performance. Physical activity, either before or after learning, also releases chemicals that enhance long-term memory. Teachers who have students remain seated during the entire class period are not promoting optimal conditions for learning. Instead, use drama and role-plays, energizers, quick games, and stretching to physically invigorate students. If they are drowsy, students should be allowed to stand at the back of the room for a few minutes and do some stretching in a manner that does not distract other class members.

Fourth, Jensen encourages teachers to give students settling time and rest after a learning session.[16] This quiet period affords students a chance for the information to settle and for learning to take root.

TEACHING HEALTH LITERACY IN THE TWENTY-FIRST CENTURY

Success in the twenty-first century requires different skills than were required for successful living in previous centuries. The Partnership for 21st Century Skills was formed to create a model of learning for this millennium that incorporates the most up-to-date skills into our systems of education. The Partnership is a public–private collaboration of business, education, community, and government that serves as a catalyst to position twenty-first-century skills at the center of U.S. K–12 education. It presents a framework of teaching and learning that focuses on student outcomes and support systems to help students master these outcomes.[17] The outcomes comprise a blending of specific skills, content knowledge, expertise, and literacies that students will need to succeed in work and life. The Partnership advocates weaving themes, including health literacy, into core subjects.[17]

Simply stated, **health literacy** is the ability to read, understand, and use healthcare information to make decisions and follow instructions for treatment. It is a core element of the *Healthy People 2020* initiative of the U.S. Department of Health and Human Services.[18] Gaining health literacy can be problematic for non-native English speakers. School and community organizations can help with language barriers by providing health literacy materials in Spanish and other needed languages. These materials need to be culturally sensitive and relevant. To enhance learning in such circumstances, buddy systems can be created in which ELS individuals who are more fluent in English can assist those who are not as proficient. Measures also need to be established for helping ESL learners understand the U.S. healthcare system and culture.

Guide on the Side

Some have described the role of the twenty-first-century teacher as having changed from being a "sage on a stage" to being more of a "guide on the side." Teachers today need to facilitate students' involvement in learning through exploration and firsthand experience. Teaching approaches need to place less emphasis on memorizing and more emphasis on making connections, thinking through issues, and solving problems. Rodgers et al.[19] note that twenty-first-century learners prefer working in teams in peer-to-peer situations, performing visual and kinesthetic activities over reading and listening activities, learning things that matter, and being challenged to reach their own results and conclusion.

Innovative teachers are savvy about technological devices and the ways they can be used to enhance student learning. As part of their teaching approach, teachers can creatively use blogs, wikis, threaded discussion boards, chats, videoconferencing, cell phones, and new technologies that will continue to emerge. New technology creates exciting possibilities for student learning. It provides for infinite and rapid access to information and allows for students to be connected inside and outside of the classroom, to develop multimedia projects, and to learn experientially.

Learning Styles

Effective teachers strive to understand how their Generation M students learn best. They teach with the brain in mind and take into account their students' preferred learning styles and multiple intelligences. All students do not learn best in the same ways. One type of learning style relates to one's preference for taking in information—that is, via a visual, auditory, or kinesthetic learning style. A **visual learning style** means that a person has a preference for information presented in a visual format or through observation such as pictures, diagrams, demonstrations, displays, handouts, videos, and flipcharts. An **auditory learning style** means a preference for receiving information through listening to speech and sound, such as spoken instructions and songs. A **kinesthetic learning style** means a preference for learning through touching or manipulating things, through physical movement or practical hands-on experiences. Some students have a very strong preferred learning style for taking in information, but many people are multimodal, meaning they use a blend of two or all three of these learning styles. It is important for students to understand that there is no best learning style and that they can strengthen their ability to learn through any style.

Other types of learning styles relate to the manner in which individuals process the information that they receive. One dimension of processing information is global versus sequential. A **global learning style** is a preference or tendency for seeing the "big picture" before "putting all the pieces together." Once global learners have an overview or holistic sense of what is being learned and its relevance, they are then able to focus on details or smaller concepts related to the whole. A **sequential learning style** is a preference for "putting together the pieces" to understand the "big picture." Learning sequentially involves taking small steps and focusing on one task at a time. Learners who prefer to engage in this process are sometimes called linear learners.

Another dimension of processing information is abstract versus concrete. An **abstract learning style** is a preference for visualizing or conceptualizing ideas, which are intangible (cannot actually be seen). A **concrete learning style** is a preference for understanding things that can be seen, heard, or touched. A concrete learner is often excellent in processing factual information but may have difficulty understanding abstract ideas.

What is most important is for teachers to use a wide variety of instructional strategies to address the diverse learning styles of learners. Howard Gardner's theory of multiple intelligences[20] provides teachers with a framework that can help them avoid focusing too much on teaching only to students with high linguistic and mathematical abilities. Gardner notes that students who are not good at either linguistic or mathematical abilities have not traditionally received much attention from teachers, have been left behind, and have lost interest in learning. His theory suggests that people have different intelligences or abilities and that these unique ways of thinking and learning need to be given equal attention. The eight intelligences identified by Gardner that should be given attention by teachers are listed here:

- *Linguistic intelligence*: the ability to read, write, and communicate with words.
- *Logical-mathematical intelligence*: the ability to reason and calculate, to think things through in a logical, systematic manner.
- *Visual-spatial intelligence*: the ability to think in pictures and visualize future results.
- *Musical intelligence*: the ability to make or compose music, to sing well, or to understand and appreciate music.
- *Bodily-kinesthetic intelligence*: the ability to use one's body skillfully to solve problems, create products, or present ideas and emotions.
- *Interpersonal (social) intelligence*: the ability to work effectively with others, to relate to other people, and to display empathy and understanding.
- *Intrapersonal intelligence*: the ability to self-analyze and reflect or, in actuality, the capacity to know oneself—in other words, to be able to contemplate and assess strengths and weaknesses, to review behavior and feelings, and to make plans and set goals.
- *Naturalist intelligence*: the ability to find meanings and patterns in nature and the world.

Armstrong explains how to plan for teaching for the eight intelligences:

> To ensure you use a wide variety of strategies, develop the habit of doing the following. Write the core concept you are planning on teaching in the center of a blank page, then draw eight straight lines or "spokes" radiating out from the core concept. Label each spoke with a different type of intelligence. Try to think of one or more ways you can use each intelligence to teach the concept. Record your ideas between the spokes.[13]

DECIDING WHAT TO TEACH

Traditionally health education has been organized around 10 content areas: mental/emotional health; healthy eating and physical activity; personal health; substance use and abuse; family life/human sexuality; disease prevention and control; safety and first aid; consumer health; community health; and environmental health. Time constraints make it impossible, at both the elementary and secondary levels, for teachers to effectively address all 10 content areas. Effective health instruction emphasizes the National Health Education Standards and the risk behaviors identified by the **Centers for Disease Control and Prevention (CDC)**.

National Health Education Standards: Skills

The **World Health Organization (WHO)** advocates skill-based health education. WHO stresses that skill-based health education has been shown by research to reduce the chances of young people engaging in delinquent behavior and interpersonal violence; to delay the onset of using alcohol, tobacco, and other drugs; to prevent peer rejection and bullying; and to improve academic performance.[21]

The **National Health Education Standards (NHES)** are skill-based written expectations for what students should know and be able to do by grades 2, 5, 8, and 12 to promote personal, family, and community health. The NHES provide a framework for teachers, administrators, and policymakers to design or select health education curricula. Many state and local school districts use the NHES as a basis for creating their own local standards and curriculum documents. Seven of the eight national standards deal with life skill development.

Standard 1: Core Concepts

Students will comprehend concepts related to health promotion and disease prevention to enhance health. Curricula need to focus on the most important information and ideas that are essential to promoting health and preventing disease. In doing this, teachers build on what students already know and on what students want to know. Core health concepts can be integrated into other content areas, including language arts, social studies, and math. In coming chapters, we will discuss the core concepts that need to be taught in health education.

Standard 2: Analyze Influences

Students will analyze the influence of family, peers, culture, media, technology, and other factors on health behaviors. Students need to be taught how to analyze both external influences (those named in the standard) and internal influences (perceptions, emotions, values, beliefs, fears, likes/dislikes). Every chapter of this text will help you prepare to teach your students how to analyze influences.

Standard 3: Access Information and Products

Students will demonstrate the ability to access valid information and products and services to enhance health. This entails knowing which resources are reliable. Older students need to know how to assess the validity of information they find on the Internet. The *Media Literacy Skills* chapter explains how you can help your students analyze media messages and access valid health information and services.

Standard 4: Interpersonal Communication

> *Students will demonstrate the ability to use interpersonal communication skills to enhance health and avoid or reduce health risks.* Being able to effectively communicate helps students share their ideas and meet their emotional and physical needs. These skills facilitate empathy and relationship building. Being able to clearly communicate and resist peer pressure protects students from higher-risk behaviors. The *Life Skills* chapter addresses communication skills in depth and then subsequent chapters identify where communication skills need to be included in curricula.

Standard 5: Decision Making

> *Students will demonstrate the ability to use decision-making skills to enhance health.* Teachers need to help students learn age-appropriate processes for making decisions. Teachers can then coach students as they apply these processes to many different scenarios so that health-promoting decisions are made. The *Life Skills* chapter deals with this skill in depth as well as the skills called for in standards 6–8. Later chapters reinforce how to teach decision-making, goal-setting, self-management, and advocacy skills.

Standard 6: Goal Setting

> *Students will demonstrate the ability to use goal-setting skills to enhance health.* Teachers can teach the processes for working toward goals and then coach students as they apply goal-setting skills and work toward various health-related goals.

Standard 7: Self-Management

> *Students will demonstrate the ability to practice health-enhancing behaviors and avoid or reduce risks.* Students need many self-management skills, including self-awareness, self-control, willpower, anger and conflict management, stress management, disease prevention, and more.

Standard 8: Advocacy

> *Students will demonstrate the ability to advocate for personal, family, and community health.* When students advocate, they have to be able to clearly state their position if they are to educate and influence others. This facilitates their learning at a deeper level and reinforces the health behavior they are advocating. It also helps students support others and recognize that many people are making healthy choices.

CDC's Categories of Risk Behavior

Studying national data and trends helps teachers and school administrators identify what needs to be taught in the classroom. More than two-thirds of all deaths among youth and young adults aged 10–24 years result from only four causes. Can you name those causes? If you said motor vehicle crashes, other unintentional injuries, homicide, and suicide, you would be correct. But these deaths are only part of the picture. Almost two-thirds of deaths of those older than age 25 occur from cardiovascular disease and cancer. Many of these diseases are the result of behaviors that are established early in life, such as poor diet, lack of physical activity, and cigarette smoking. Additionally, many school-age youth suffer from nonfatal illness or injury, social problems, and lower quality of life as a result of their health-risk behavior choices. The CDC has identified that a high proportion of deaths, illnesses, and injuries in the United States result from six categories of risk behavior **(Figure 2-3)**.

Every teacher, regardless of teaching discipline and grade level, should understand how these risk behaviors adversely affect the lives of youth **(Box 2-1)**. Every teacher can be a part of his or her school's effort to educate youth about these risks and participate in school-based efforts to promote healthy lifestyles among students. Success in these endeavors requires participation from

CDC's six categories of risk behavior

Behaviors that contribute to unintentional injuries and violence

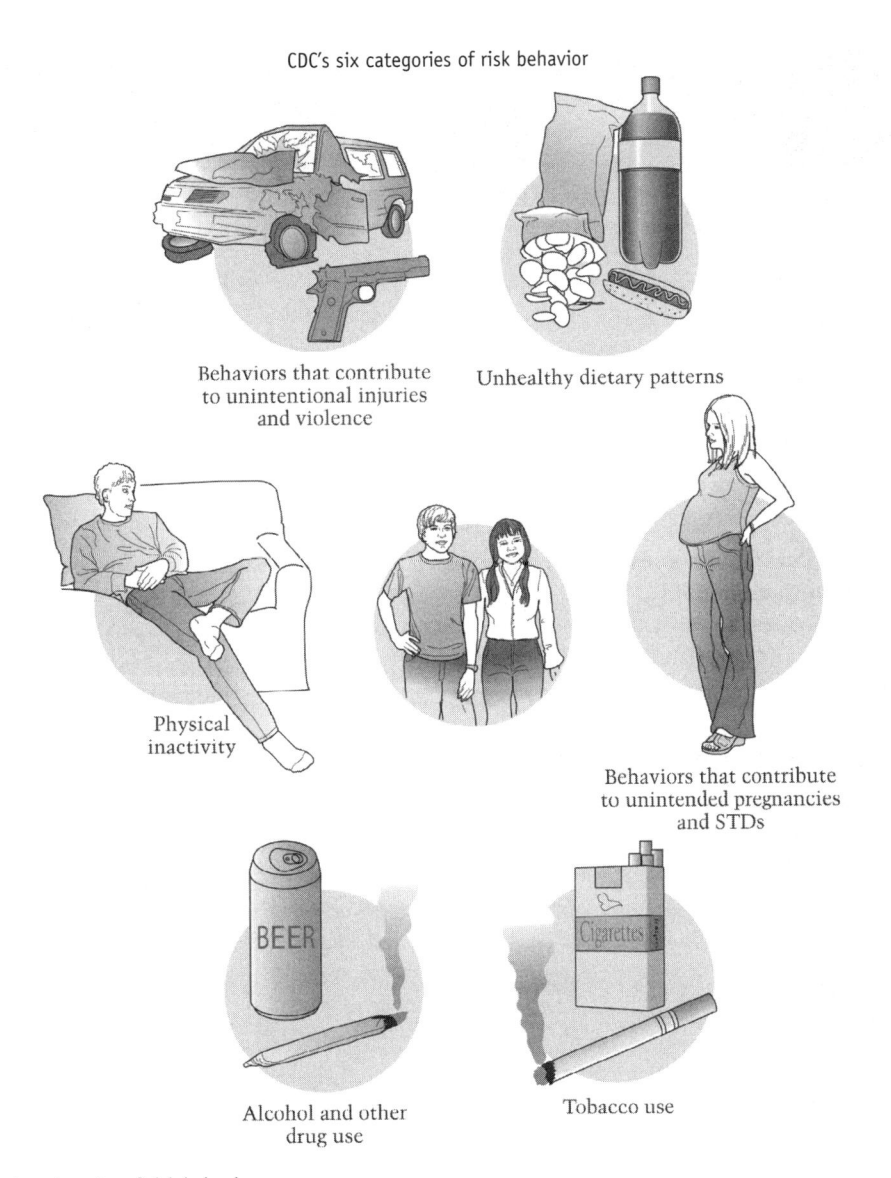

Unhealthy dietary patterns

Physical inactivity

Behaviors that contribute to unintended pregnancies and STDs

Alcohol and other drug use

Tobacco use

FIGURE 2-3 CDC's six categories of risk behavior.

educators representing all disciplines and all grade levels. Chapters 6–9 of this text address the CDC's risk behaviors in detail.

State and District Guidelines

In addition to taking into consideration the NHES and the CDC's risk behaviors, it is important to look at available state and local guidelines where you teach. These guidelines usually follow the NHES and are created with an awareness of the particular needs of the students in an area. Community attitudes and problems can play a part in the development of local guidelines.

Many states and school districts provide scope and sequence plans for health education that identify concepts and skills to be emphasized at different grade levels. Scope and sequence guides help teachers identify what they need to address and how their instruction might be reemphasized in coming years. You can find examples of state (e.g., New York) and local (e.g., Philadelphia) health education scope and sequences on the Internet. To do so, use search engines to search for health education "standards," "core curriculum," or "scope and sequence" in locations where you plan to teach.

> ### 2-1 Application Exercise
>
> ### Youth Risk Behavior Survey
>
> This exercise helps you become familiar with tools you can use in planning your health instruction. The Youth Risk Behavior Survey is a biannual school survey of students in grades 9–12 that is conducted by the CDC. Becoming familiar with your state's data and how they compare to national averages can help you identify what you need to emphasize in your classroom. Go to http://www.cdc.gov/HealthyYouth. On the Adolescent and School Health webpage, click on the Youth Risk Behavior Surveillance tab. On the YRBSS page, scroll down to the results and fact sheets for 2011. Study the 2011 results and answer these questions:
>
> 1. Which data surprised you the most?
> 2. How did your state compare to national data?
> 3. How can you use the Youth Risk Behavior Survey in your teaching?
>
> Snoop around the Healthy Youth website some more and identify at least five additional documents or resources that can help you teach health concepts.
>
> Adapted and condensed from Centers for Disease Control and Prevention. Adolescent and School Health. Characteristics of an Effective Health Education Curriculum. Available at http://www.cdc.gov/healthyyouth/sher/characteristics/index.htm.

Health Education Curriculum Analysis Tool

The **Health Education Curriculum Analysis Tool (HECAT)** is an assessment tool you can use to examine or plan your school health education curricula. It was developed by CDC and is based on the NHES, the CDC's categories of risk behavior, and the characteristics of effective health education curricula. The HECAT can help schools select or develop effective health education curricula and improve the delivery of health education. The following modules are available in HECAT and online:

- Module MEH: Mental and Emotional Health
- Module PHW: Personal Health and Wellness
- Module HE: Healthy Eating
- Module PA: Physical Activity
- Module T: Tobacco
- Module AOD: Alcohol and Other Drugs
- Module SH: Sexual Health
- Module V: Violence
- Module S: Safety

The HECAT Appendices provide lists of exemplar programs and aid in developing local health education scope and sequence. Upcoming chapters in this text discuss how to use the HECAT in curriculum design, including unit and lesson planning.

Characteristics of Effective Health Education Curricula*

Today's state-of-the-art health education curricula reflect the growing body of research that emphasizes the following issues:

- Teaching functional health information (essential knowledge)
- Shaping personal values and beliefs that support healthy behaviors

*The content in this section is adapted and condensed from Centers for Disease Control and Prevention. Adolescent and school health: characteristics of an effective health education curriculum. Available at http://www.cdc.gov/healthyyouth/sher/characteristics/index.htm. Accessed March 28, 2013.

- Shaping group norms that value a healthy lifestyle
- Developing the essential health skills necessary to adopt, practice, and maintain health-enhancing behaviors

Less effective curricula often overemphasize teaching scientific facts and increasing student knowledge. Reviews of effective programs have identified these **characteristics of effective health education curricula:**

1. *Focuses on clear health goals and related behavioral outcomes.*
2. *Is research-based and theory-driven* (e.g., built on social cognitive theory or other theories that have effectively influenced health-related behaviors among youth).
3. *Addresses individual values, attitudes, and beliefs.* Fosters attitudes, values, and beliefs that support positive health behaviors. Motivates students to critically examine personal perspectives, consider new health-promoting attitudes, and generates positive perceptions about protective behaviors, and negative perceptions about risk behaviors.
4. *Addresses individual and group norms that support health-enhancing behaviors.* Helps students accurately assess the level of risk-taking behavior among their peers (e.g., how many use illegal drugs), corrects misperceptions of peer and social norms, emphasizes the value of good health, and reinforces health-enhancing attitudes and beliefs.
5. *Focuses on reinforcing protective factors and increasing perceptions of personal risk and harmfulness of engaging in specific unhealthy practices and behaviors.*
6. *Addresses social pressures and influences.*
7. *Builds personal competence, social competence, and self-efficacy by addressing skills* (e.g., communication, refusal, assessing accuracy of information, decision-making, planning and goal-setting, self-control, and self-management skills).
8. *Provides functional health knowledge that is basic and accurate, and that directly contributes to health-promoting decisions and behaviors.*
9. *Uses strategies designed to personalize information and engage students* (e.g., group discussions, cooperative learning, problem solving, role-playing, and peer-led activities).
10. *Provides age-appropriate and developmentally appropriate information, learning strategies, teaching methods, and materials.*
11. *Incorporates learning strategies, teaching methods, and materials that are culturally inclusive* (e.g., considering ethnic foods in a nutrition unit).
12. *Provides adequate time for instruction and learning* (enough to promote understanding and practice skills).
13. *Provides opportunities to reinforce skills and positive health behaviors.* This can include "skill booster" sessions during the year or at subsequent grade levels. It also includes integrating skill application opportunities in other academic areas.
14. *Provides opportunities to make positive connections with influential others* (i.e., by engaging peers, parents, families, and other positive adult role models in student learning).
15. *Includes teacher information and plans for professional development and training that enhance effectiveness of instruction and student learning.*

Coordinated School Health Program

For health education to reach its maximum effectiveness, it needs to be supported by others. Families, healthcare workers, the media, religious organizations, community organizations that serve youth, and young people themselves also must be systematically involved. A **coordinated school health program (CSHP)** is recommended by CDC as a strategy for improving students'

FIGURE 2-4 Eight interactive components of the coordinated school health program.

health and learning in U.S. schools. CDC identifies the following interactive components of CSHP **(Figure 2-4)**:[22]

- *Health Education.* Health education curricula should address the National Health Education Standards and incorporate the characteristics of an effective health education curriculum. Health education assists students in living healthier lives. Qualified, trained teachers teach health education.
- *Physical Education.* The outcome of a quality physical education program is a physically educated person who has the knowledge, skills, and confidence to enjoy a lifetime of healthful physical activity. Qualified, trained teachers teach physical education.
- *Health Services.* These services are designed to ensure access or referral to primary healthcare services, or both; to foster appropriate use of primary healthcare services; to prevent and control communicable disease and other health problems; to provide emergency care for illness or injury; to promote and provide optimal sanitary conditions for a safe school facility and school environment; and to provide educational and counseling opportunities for promoting and maintaining individual, family, and community health. Qualified professionals such as physicians, nurses, dentists, health educators, and other allied health personnel provide these services.
- *Nutrition Services.* Schools should provide access to a variety of nutritious and appealing meals that accommodate the health and nutrition needs of all students. School nutrition programs reflect the U.S. Dietary Guidelines for Americans and other criteria to achieve nutrition integrity. The school nutrition services offer students a learning laboratory for classroom nutrition and health education and serve as a resource for linkages with nutrition-related community services. Qualified child nutrition professionals provide these services.
- *Counseling, psychological, and social services.* These services are provided to improve students' mental, emotional, and social health, and include individual and group assessments, interventions, and referrals. Organizational assessment and consultation skills of counselors and psychologists contribute not only to the health of students but also to the health of the school environment. Professionals such as certified school counselors, psychologists, and social workers provide these services.

- *Healthy and safe school environment.* A healthy and safe school environment includes the physical and aesthetic surroundings and the psychosocial climate and culture of the school. Factors that influence the physical environment include the school building and the area surrounding it, any biological or chemical agents that are detrimental to health, and physical conditions such as temperature, noise, and lighting. The psychosocial environment includes the physical, emotional, and social conditions that affect the well-being of students and staff.
- *Health promotion for staff.* Schools can provide opportunities for school staff members to improve their health status through activities such as health assessments, health education, and health-related fitness activities. These opportunities encourage staff members to pursue a healthy lifestyle that contributes to their improved health status, improved morale, and a greater personal commitment to the school's overall coordinated health program. This personal commitment often translates into greater commitment to the health of students and creates positive role modeling. Health promotion activities have improved productivity, decreased absenteeism, and reduced health insurance costs.
- *Family/community involvement.* An integrated school, parent, and community approach can enhance the health and well-being of students. School health advisory councils, coalitions, and broad-based constituencies for school health can build support for school health program efforts. Schools actively solicit parent involvement and engage community resources and services to respond more effectively to the health-related needs of students.

You might find yourself in a school where the coordinated school health program is only minimally established. Understanding the interactive components of the CSHP can help you see the possibilities for your school and enable you to enlist others in your school and community to become involved. Forming a SHAC can help you achieve this goal. A **School Health Advisory Council (SHAC)** is a group of individuals from various segments of the community who act collectively in advising the school district about aspects of the coordinated school health program. The members of a SHAC are usually drawn from the following groups of people: parents, teachers, school administrators, students, healthcare professionals, members of the business community, law enforcement representatives, and representatives of nonprofit health organizations or other community organizations.

NCATE Preparation Standards

For health education to be effective, it must be taught by well-prepared teachers. The National Council for Accreditation of Teacher Education (NCATE) is the teaching profession's mechanism for helping to establish high-quality teachers. The American Association for Health Education (AAHE) has been identified by NCATE as its specialty professional association for health education. AAHE has developed the **NCATE Health Education Teacher Preparation Standards**. These eight standards and their key elements can be found online.[23] In brief, they state that teachers must meet the following standards:

1. *Content knowledge.* Demonstrate the knowledge and skills of a health-literate educator.
2. *Needs assessment.* Assess needs to determine priorities for school health education.
3. *Planning.* Plan effective CSHE curricula and programs.
4. *Implementation.* Implement instruction using multiple strategies and technology while exhibiting classroom management and ability to adjust to changing needs.
5. *Assessment.* Assess student learning using instruments, and use assessment results to guide future instruction.
6. *Administration and coordination.* Plan and coordinate a school health program.
7. *Being a resource.* Serve as a resource person.
8. *Communication and advocacy.* Communicate and advocate for health and school health education.

■ TEACHING FOR BEHAVIOR CHANGE

Health education that provides information for the sole purpose of improving knowledge of factual information is incomplete and inadequate. It is important in health education to go beyond the cognitive level and address health determinants, social factors, attitudes, values, norms, and skills that influence specific health-related behaviors. Instruction that addresses the determinants of behavior is more likely to achieve longer-lasting results.[24]

The following sections briefly introduce some of the key health behavior theories and models that explain determinants of and influences on health-related behaviors among youth. Reviewing each of these models can give you great insights into how to help your students make needed health behavior changes.

Health Belief Model

The **Health Belief Model** was one of the first theories of health behavior and has been used extensively in public health practice. It was developed by social psychologists originally to understand why individuals failed to take advantage of public health services such as immunizations and screenings for tuberculosis. The model identifies six factors that influence individuals to act in ways that help improve their health:

- *Perceived susceptibility.* Belief that a person is susceptible to a disease, injury, or other poor health condition (e.g., lung cancer, motor vehicle injury, loss of teeth).
- *Perceived severity.* Belief that the condition has serious consequences (e.g., death, bodily injury, pain, suffering, loss of job, embarrassment or shame).
- *Perceived benefits.* Belief that taking an action (e.g., not smoking, participating in physical activity) will reduce personal susceptibility to the condition or its severity.
- *Perceived barriers.* The obstacles that get in a person's way of taking an action (e.g., not smoking, participating in physical activity).
- *Cues to action.* Factors that prompt action (e.g., seeing an antismoking television spot, an invitation from a friend to exercise).
- *Self-efficacy.* This sixth factor was later added to the model and is discussed in the following section on social cognitive theory.

You can design health education lessons to address each of these six factors. Lessons can help students to realize the seriousness of prevalent health conditions and the connection between the condition and personal behavior. Lessons can also stress the perceived benefits of various health behaviors. It is important to emphasize that the benefits often go beyond simply reduction of disease or injury risk. For example, you can stress the social and personal appearance benefits of not smoking cigarettes when discussing tobacco smoking. Health lessons that address perceived benefits and cues to action are helpful because they address important influences on health behavior.

Social Cognitive Theory

Social cognitive theory (SCT) is particularly valuable in explaining health behavior because it emphasizes social environment influences on personal behavior. SCT identifies that people learn and are influenced by watching what others do (modeling). Modeling, of course, can either be positive or negative. The modeling of health-enhancing behaviors by teachers, other adults, and peers is a positive force in young people's lives. Conversely, the modeling of health-risky behaviors such as cigarette smoking or weapon-carrying can exert a strong negative influence on behavior.

SCT introduces the concept that reinforcements (rewards) affect whether a person will repeat a behavior. Positive reinforcements increase a person's likelihood of repeating the behavior, whereas

Children learn from watching and imitating others. The importance of adults modeling healthy behaviors cannot be overemphasized.

negative reinforcements motivate a person to stop a behavior to eliminate the negative stimulus. An important point is that reinforcements can be either internal or external. Internal rewards are things that people do to reward themselves, whereas external rewards are provided by other people or the environment.

Self-efficacy is a component of many health behavior theories and is, according to SCT, the most important personal factor in behavior change. **Self-efficacy** comprises confidence in one's ability to perform a health action or behavior and to overcome barriers resistant to taking the action. Research shows that health behaviors such as not smoking, physical exercise, dieting, and condom use are highly associated with a person's level of perceived self-efficacy.[25] Self-efficacy is important in relation to behavior change because it indicates the amount of effort an individual is willing to make to change a health behavior and the person's persistence in continuing to strive for health despite obstacles, barriers, and setbacks. Margolis and McCabe[26] suggest that teachers focus on the following four areas to help their students develop a high state of perceived self-efficacy:

◆ Provide *mastery experiences* in which students experience success. Success boosts self-efficacy, whereas failures can destroy self-efficacy.
◆ Provide *vicarious experiences* for students to observe a peer succeed in performing an action or behavior. By observing a peer succeed, students can strengthen their belief in their own abilities.
◆ Provide *verbal persuasion* to encourage students to make their best effort while guiding the students in performing the behavior.
◆ Foster a *positive emotional state* for encouraging self-efficacy. Teachers can exude enthusiasm about engaging in health behaviors and help to reduce stress and anxiety surrounding the practice of these behaviors.

Theory of Planned Behavior

The **theory of planned behavior** examines the relationship between health behavior and beliefs, attitudes, and intentions. When teaching with this theory in mind, teachers must consider students' attitudes toward performing a behavior and their subjective norms about the behavior. A **subjective norm** consists of beliefs about whether key people approve or disapprove of the behavior. According to the theory of planned behavior, individuals behave in a way that gains approval from these key people. The theory also includes a factor called perceived behavioral control; **perceived behavioral control** is similar to self-efficacy and is the belief that one has, and can exercise, control over performing the behavior.

It is important to provide students with lessons that examine their subjective norms about various health behaviors. Subjective norms are largely determined by normative beliefs. **Normative beliefs** are an individual's perception of a particular behavior. Research shows that young people who simply overestimate the prevalence of smoking among their peers, as with other health risk behaviors such as alcohol and drug use, are more likely to engage in these behaviors.[27,28] Research also shows that media portrayals of smoking, which is often shown in a glamorous and positive light, contribute to false impressions of high smoking prevalence.[24] Teachers need to address normative beliefs to correct the misperception that many students have that risky behaviors, such as smoking, drug use, and early sexual activity, among their peers are normal and frequent. You can do this by highlighting survey data showing actual prevalence rates. Correcting misperceptions (e.g., overestimations) of the prevalence of risky behaviors is an important preventive strategy that teachers can implement in most classrooms.

Stages of Change Model

The basic premise of the **stages of change model** is that behavior change is a process, not an event. As a person attempts to change a behavior, he or she moves through five stages:

- *Precontemplation.* A person has no intention of taking action or making a behavior change within the next 6 months.
- *Contemplation.* A person intends to take action in the next 6 months.
- *Preparation.* A person intends to take action within the next 30 days and has taken some steps in that direction.
- *Action.* A person has changed behavior for less than 6 months.
- *Maintenance.* A person has changed behavior for more than 6 months.

The stages of change model has been applied to a variety of individual health behaviors. This model is circular, not linear. In other words, people do not systematically progress from one stage to the next, but instead may enter the change process at any stage, relapse to an earlier stage, and begin the process once more. They may cycle through this process repeatedly, and the process can stop at any point.

A key concept of this model is that people in different stages have different health education needs and benefit from different messages and interventions depending on which stage they are currently in.

■ INSTRUCTIONAL PLANNING

In this section, we discuss the developmental process of preparing to teach health in the classroom. Coming chapters will help you develop unit and lesson plans. Here we discuss the process in general terms.

Assessing Needs

Two main questions are at the heart of assessing needs. The first is "What do local, state, and national standards, curricula, and scope and sequence indicate needs to be taught at the grade level I am teaching?" These materials can be found on the Internet or obtained from school district offices. Study them to gain an overview of what needs to be addressed during the entire school year and then hone in on individual health units.

Next you want to try and ascertain your particular community's health education needs by asking, "Which health needs do *my students* and their families have?" This question is best addressed by creating a long list of unit-specific questions such as "Which healthy eating habits do my students need to change/develop?" Your students' needs can be identified by making observations and by talking to school personnel, parents, and community members. You can poll students or have them complete anonymous surveys. You can study state and local data available from government and nongovernment agencies such as health departments, the American Lung Association, and the CDC.

Setting Learning Goals

Having assessed needs, you are ready to set learning goals for what you want to accomplish while teaching. If we liken teaching to taking a trip, then learning goals are where you want to go. When you create your learning goals, you have a clear vision of the "trip" you will take with your students. An example of a learning goal is "I want my students to enjoy eating more vegetables and drinking water instead of soda." As you develop your learning goals, review the models and theories for behavior change. Consider those behaviors you might want to change, modify, or reinforce and figure out how to best go about doing that.

Instruction Mapping

Having determined needs and learning goals, you are ready for instruction mapping. Instruction mapping ensures that you get to the most important destinations on your "trip," and it helps you identify the best "route" to take. There never is enough time for everything. Determine how much time you will spend on various units and on concepts and skills within units. Mapping helps you see the best flow and understand how concepts and skills can be combined or built upon each other, and how they can be integrated into other subjects.

While mapping, consider what you want to teach at various times of the semester or school year. For instance, a teacher might have a unit on healthy eating and physical activity in the fall, encourage healthy habits throughout the winter, and then have a fun run in the spring. Mapping helps you identify how to reinforce concepts and practice skills throughout the semester or school year.

Coordinate with other teachers while you are creating your instructional maps. Synergistic ideas will emerge from this collaboration, and the scope and sequence of the map can be reviewed or developed.

Unit Planning

Objectives

Creating a unit plan involves writing learning objectives for that unit. You will want to write one or two main objectives for each class period or instruction session. Refer back to your instruction map to see how many days you have allotted for instruction. Your daily objectives need to be in alignment with your learning goals, characteristics of effective health instruction, and established curricula/standards. Writing objectives provides you with a clear idea of what you want to achieve during instruction. It also provides your students with a clear idea of what is expected of them, and gives you a clear basis for evaluation.

SMART is an acronym for good objectives. **SMART objectives** meet these criteria:

- *S*pecific: say exactly what students will be able to do.
- *M*easurable: can be observed by the end of the unit or lesson.
- *A*tta*inable*: realistically can be achieved by students.

- *Relevant*: to the needs of the students.
- *Time-framed*: achievable by the end of the unit or lesson.

Bloom's Taxonomy identifies three types of learning: (1) **cognitive**—mental skills and what we think of as knowledge; (2) **affective**—demonstrate emotional growth or improved attitude; and (3) **psychomotor**—deal with physical skills. Bloom's Taxonomy also divides objectives into **lower-order thinking skills** (remembering, understanding, applying) and **higher-order thinking skills** (analyzing, evaluating, and creating.) Effective instruction requires both lower- and higher-order objectives.

Perhaps the most helpful tool in writing objectives is having a list of strong verbs on hand. Do *not* use these verbs—*appreciate, believe, grasp, know, learn, understand*, and *realize*—because they are too nebulous and will not meet SMART criteria. Here are some strong verbs you can use for writing objectives at each learning level:

- *Remembering*: define, find, identify, list, name, record, show
- *Understanding*: classify, describe, explain, give example, match, outline
- *Applying*: act, adapt, determine, illustrate, predict, produce, solve, use
- *Analyzing*: analyze, categorize, differentiate, examine, distinguish, prioritize
- *Evaluating*: assess, choose, critique, defend, evaluate, justify, recommend
- *Creating*: compose, construct, design, formulate, invent, plan, produce

Assessments

After clearly identifying your learning objectives, you need to determine how you will assess student learning. There are three types of assessment: preassessment (what do students already know, feel, do?), formative assessment (done during instruction—are they getting it?); and postassessment (what have they learned?). **Preassessment** tools include pretests, knowledge surveys, self-reports, and attitude measurement scales. **Formative assessment** tools include teacher observations, embedded questions, classroom activities, and application exercises. **Postassessments** include tests (objective or essay), reports (written or oral), student self-assessments, and capstone experiences.

Grading assessments is much easier when you use a rubric. **Rubrics** are scoring guides that clearly identify the score given for each aspect of an assignment. Rubrics also clarify for students exactly what is expected of them, helping them to see that grades aren't "given," but rather earned based on the percentage of mastery achieved. Rubric templates can be easily found online and modified to meet your particular needs.

Unit Design

Now that you have determined needs and goals, written SMART objectives, and determined how you will assess student learning, you are prepared to design how you will teach your unit. Using a template like the one found in **Figure 2-5** can guide you in this process. First, indicate the objectives for each lesson. Then, to the right of each objective, identify correlating teaching activities that align with each objective—things you can do to help students meet each objective.

During each lesson, you will want to use a wide range of activities that address various learning preferences. Consider how to use RAD teaching to make ideas "sticky." Reflect on how students prefer to learn. Consider using attention getters, dramatization, group or pair work, stations, object lessons, demonstrations, games, case studies, stories, free writes, and music in addition to pictures, discussions, and lectures.

You will notice that the template in Figure 2-5 includes a column for technology use, which is intended to highlight the need for using technology in the classroom. In addition to using Power Point presentations, consider using other technology tools including search engines, desktop

Instruction Design Template			
Objectives	**Instructional Activities**	**Use of Technology**	**Adaptations for Learners**
Lesson 1:			
Lesson 2:			
Lesson 3:			
Lesson 4:			
Lesson 5:			

FIGURE 2-5 Instruction design template.

publishing, video development, and bulletin/message boarding. Mobile devices can be utilized and social media and networking can be harnessed as powerful learning tools. You can read more on using media in the classroom in the *Media Literacy Skills* chapter.

Also in the instruction design template, you will notice a column for possible adaptions for learners. Here you can record ways to help ESL and other students with special needs meet the learning objectives. You can also identify possible alternative activities you can revert to if those planned don't seem to be working.

How many activities you need for each lesson depends on your objectives and how much time you have. Secondary classes can last from 48 minutes to 1.5 hours with block scheduling. Elementary teachers need to identify how much time each lesson will take. Teachers should plan some sort of change-up in the lesson every 10 minutes or so. The first activity should create energy and motivation for the lesson (anticipatory set), and the last activity should help summarize and wrap up what has been learned.

Lesson Plan

Lesson plans can be simple or very detailed outlines that have been developed from the unit design template. **Figure 2-6** provides a worksheet identifying key elements in a lesson plan. Novice teachers need to create very detailed lesson plans. Doing so helps them think through every aspect of a lesson and mentally rehearse teaching it. We challenge student-teachers to develop lesson plans in sufficient detail that someone else can effectively teach the lesson plan without having to develop materials or ask clarifying questions.

Lesson Plan Worksheet

Unit:	Total time needed:
Lesson Title:	
For Grade Level:	Plan created by:

Key HBOs, Skills, or Concepts to be Taught:	**Characteristics of Effective HLTH Curriculum to be Included:**

Goal:

Lesson Objectives:

Assessments:

Materials Needed:

Before You Begin:

FIGURE 2-6 Lesson plan template.

Lesson Flow

   Top line: Identify Title of Activity   *Time Needed*
         Outline how you will do the activity. Include what needs to be stressed.
         List good questions you can pose.

1. **(Anticipatory Set)**

2.

3.

4.

5.

6. **(Summation)**

Remediation:

Extension Activities:

FIGURE 2-6 Lesson plan template. (*Continued*)

As you develop the outline of activities you will use in a lesson plan, be sure to indicate how long each activity will take. These times will likely be adjusted as you teach, but an initial time frame helps you pace your instruction. Also explain exactly how you will carry out each activity and identify things you want to remember to say or do and things you want to stress in your instruction.

You also want to create and record good questions that you might ask to facilitate discussions or assess student learning. **Factual questions** assess understanding and attention. **Probing questions** help students analyze and assess material. **Open-ended questions** require students to think and are nonthreatening because there is no clearly right or wrong answer. Avoid asking simple yes-or-no questions. Good questions take time to develop—which is why it is important to create them before you teach and to include them within the activities in your lesson plan.

Remediation activities are extra activities that students can do to help themselves meet an objective. Homework, for example, can be a remediation activity. **Extension activities** are intended for students who meet an objective faster than their classmates. They might include giving assistance to students who are struggling, opportunities for learning at a deeper level, or applying what has been learned in a unique way.

■ KEY TERMS

gray matter   23
white matter   23
prefrontal cortex   24
limbic system   24
brain stem   24
neural pruning   25
neural branching   25
brain plasticity   25
relaxed alertness   26
downshift   26
active learning   27
orchestrated immersion   27
RAD   27
reticular activating system (RAS)   27
amygdala   28
dopamine   28
health literacy   29
visual learning style   30
auditory learning style   30
kinesthetic learning style   30
global learning style   30
sequential learning style   30
abstract learning style   30
concrete learning style   30
Centers for Disease Control
   and Prevention (CDC)   31
World Health Organization (WHO)   31
National Health Education Standards
   (NHES)   31
Health Education Curriculum Analysis Tool
   (HECAT)   34

characteristics of effective health education
   curriculum   35
coordinated school health program
   (CSHP)   35
School Health Advisory Council (SHAC)   37
NCATE Health Education Teacher Preparation
   Standards   37
Health Belief Model   38
social cognitive theory (SCT)   38
self-efficacy   39
theory of planned behavior   39
subjective norm   40
perceived behavioral control   40
normative beliefs   40
stages of change model   40
SMART objectives   41
Bloom's Taxonomy   42
cognitive   42
affective   42
psychomotor   42
lower-order thinking skills   42
higher-order thinking skills   42
preassessment   42
formative assessment   42
postassessment   42
rubrics   42
factual questions   46
probing questions   46
open-ended questions   46
remediation activities   46
extension activities   46

KNOWLEDGE CHECK!

1. Define and explain the relative importance of each of the key terms in the context of this chapter.
2. Identify the various characteristics of today's learners and discuss the ways they prefer to learn.
3. Explain how the brain grows, develops, and changes. Explain the function of the cerebral cortex, limbic system, and brain stem in terms of learning.
4. Discuss how to teach with the brain in mind regarding relaxed alertness, "so what?", and active learning principles.
5. Identify and explain the components of RAD teaching, and explain how to make ideas sticky.
6. Discuss how the brain learns in relation to social interaction, attention span, physical activity, and settling time.
7. Discuss health literacy for the twenty-first century, and describe how teachers and the community can help ESL learners gain health literacy.
8. Explain how the role of a teacher has changed in comparison to what it was in the past.
9. Identify and discuss the various types of learning styles and the eight intelligences. Explain how teachers can plan instruction for learners who demonstrate various learning styles and intelligences.
10. Explain why skill-based instruction is important. Identify and discuss the eight National Health Education Standards.
11. Identify the CDC's six risk behaviors and explain why teachers need to address these behaviors.
12. Explain how teachers can use HECAT in developing health curricula.
13. Identify and discuss the characteristics of effective health education curricula.
14. Identify and explain each of the eight components of a CSHP.
15. Explain why NCATE standards exist and what they are.
16. Identify and discuss two behavior change models and two behavior change theories in terms of health curricula.
17. Explain how a teacher should determine what to teach, set learning goals, and create instructional maps.
18. Explain how to create SMART objectives using strong verbs that address both lower- and higher-order thinking. Explain why and how good objectives facilitate good assessment of student learning during and after instruction.
19. Explain the process of instructional design, including objective and activity alignment, multiple types of strategies, use of technology, and instructional adaptations.
20. Explain the key components of detailed lesson plan outlines.

REFERENCES

1. Oblinger DG, Oblinger JL. Educating the Net generation. EDUCAUSE; 2005. Available at http://www.educause.edu/educatingthenetgen. Accessed April 13, 2013.
2. National Association of Student Financial Administrators. *News from NASFAA: "Diana Oblinger details today's learners."* NASFAA; 2006.
3. Giedd JN. The teen brain: insights from neuroimaging. *J Adolesc Health*. 2008;42:335–343.
4. Wallis C. What makes teens tick. *Time*. September 26, 2008. Available at http://www.time.com/time/magazine/article/0,9171,994126,00.html. Accessed April 13, 2013.
5. Steinberg L. Adolescent development and juvenile justice. *Ann Rev Clin Psychol*. 2009;5:459–485.
6. Bransford J, Brown AL, Cocking RR. *Brain, mind, experience, and school*. Washington, DC: National Academy Press; 1999.
7. Cram HG, Germinaro V. *Leading and learning in schools*. Lanham, MD: Technomic Books; 2000.
8. Blakemore SJ, Frith U. *The learning brain: lessons for education*. Malden, MA: Blackwell; 2005.
9. Cram HG, Germinaro V. *Leading and learning in schools*. Lanham, MD: Technomic Books; 2000.
10. Blakemore SJ, Frith U. *The learning brain: lessons for education*. Malden, MA: Blackwell; 2005.
11. Christison M. Brain-based research and language teaching. *Engl Teach Forum*. 2002;40(2):2–7.
12. Caine RN, Caine G, McClintic C, Klimek K. *Twelve brain/mind learning principles in action*. Thousand Oaks, CA: Corwin Press; 2005.

13. Armstrong T. *Multiple intelligences*. Alexandria, VA: ASCD; 2009.
14. Willis JA. Information into knowledge: teacher and neuroscientist shares her RAD teaching strategies for bypassing the brain filters to increase student engagement, motivation, and memory as they turn information into knowledge. *CAIS Faculty Newslet*. Spring 2008:4–7.
15. Heath C, Health D. *Made to stick*. London, UK: Random House; 2007.
16. Jensen E. *Teaching with the brain in mind*. 2nd ed. Alexandria, VA: Association for Supervision and Curriculum Development; 2005.
17. Partnership for 21st Century Learning Skills. Framework for 21st century learning. 2009. Available at http://cell.uindy.edu/2009educationconference/resources/Kay-21stCentSkillsVisionEduEconomicDevelopment-Keynote.pdf. Accessed April 13, 2013.
18. HealthyPeople.gov. Health communication and health information technology. *20/20 Topics and Objectives*. Available at http://www.healthypeople.gov/2020/topicsobjectives2020/overview.aspx?topicid=18. Accessed April 1, 2013.
19. Rodgers M, Runyon D, Starrett D, Von Holzen R. *Teaching the 21st century learner*. Paper presented at the 22nd Annual Conference on Distance Teaching and Learning; 2006.
20. Gardner H. *Intelligence reframed: multiple intelligences for the 21st century*. New York, NY: Basic; 2000.
21. World Health Organization. *Skills for health* (Information Series on School Health Document 9). Geneva, Switzerland: WHO; 2003.
22. Centers for Disease Control and Prevention. Components of coordinated school health. Available at http://www.cdc.gov/healthyyouth/cshp/components.htm. Accessed March 28, 2013.
23. American Association for Health Education. AAHE standards. 2008. Available at http://www.aahperd.org/aahe/publications/HE-Standtard.cfm. Accessed April 1, 2013.
24. Centers for Disease Control and Prevention. Characteristics of an effective health education curriculum. 2013. Available at http://www.cdc.gov/healthyyouth/SHER/characteristics/index.htm. Accessed April 13, 2013.
25. Conner M, Norman P, eds. *Predicting health behaviour*. 2nd ed. rev. Buckingham, UK: Open University Press; 2005.
26. Margolis H, McCabe P. Improving self-efficacy and motivation: what to do, what to say. *Intervent School Clin*. 2006;41(4):218–227.
27. Juvonen SC, Martino PL, Ellickson DL. "But others do it!": do misperceptions of schoolmate alcohol and marijuana use predict subsequent drug use among young adolescents? *J Appl Soc Psychol*. 2007;37:740–758.
28. Moodie C, MacKintosh AM, Brown A, Hastings GB. Tobacco marketing awareness on youth smoking susceptibility and perceived prevalence before and after an advertising ban. Eur J Public Health. 2008;18(5):484–490.

Chapter 3
Life Skills

Courtesy of Sabrina Squires.

Teaching What Really Matters

On my very first day of teaching, a fight broke out. It was just before sixth-period sophomore slow-track English. As I entered my room, I found two boys tussling on the floor. "Listen, you retard!" yelled the kid on the bottom. "I didn't take your stuff!"

The fight was quickly broken up. After class I detained Joe, who had apparently started the fight. With a flat voice and dead eyes, he said, "Teach, don't waste your time on us. We're the retards of the school."

That entire night I couldn't get Joe's face and comment out of my mind. I tossed and turned in bed wondering if I really wanted to be a teacher. Finally, I knew what to do.

The following day I stood at the front of my sixth-period class and looked each student in the eye. I then turned and wrote DRAHCIR on the board.

I said, "That's my first name. Can anyone please tell me what it is?"

They laughed and said I had a really weird name. I then turned and wrote RICHARD on the board. A couple of students blurted out my name and several gave me a funny look. They were suspicious and wondered if I was playing a joke on them.

I said, "Yes, Richard is my first name. I have a learning disability—something called dyslexia. In elementary school, I had trouble writing my own name correctly. I couldn't spell and numbers got all jumbled up in my head. I was labeled retarded—RICKY RETARDED. I can clearly remember people calling me that and the way it made me feel."

"So how'd ya become a teacher?" asked a student in the front row.

I replied, "I hate negative labels. I love to learn and I'm not stupid. That's what my classes are all about, discovering just how smart you are and loving to learn. If you like the label 'retard,' you don't belong in here. Go see the guidance counselor and transfer out. But you have to know that I don't see any 'retards' in here. Now, this class isn't going to be a piece of cake. We're going to work hard, very hard. You're going to catch up and graduate and I'm sure some of you will go onto college. I'm not joking, and I'm not threatening you. I'm just making you a promise. I don't want to ever hear the word 'retard' again! Is that clear?"

No one transferred out and it wasn't long before the students began to believe more in themselves. As they came to expect more of themselves, they worked harder and harder, pushing themselves to catch up to their peers. We all learned a great deal about English literature that year, but so much more about life. While studying classics like The Grapes of Wrath *and* To Kill a Mockingbird, *we discussed the need for taking responsibility for our actions, choices, and consequences, and the need for setting life goals. We likened the characters' situations to similar problems they faced and practiced problem-solving methods, how to resolve conflicts, and other communication and relationship-building skills.*

We discussed various labels people carry, how those labels affect people's behavior, and how negative labels can be overcome.

All of them did graduate and five of them, including Joe, earned scholarships to college. I'm now in my twenty-third year of teaching. I laugh whenever I think back on my first day in the classroom and how, for a night, I wondered if I really wanted to be a teacher. What could I possibly do that would be more rewarding than trying to make a difference in young people's lives by teaching them the skills that really matter?

Source: Adapted from Connolly J. Don't waste your time with those kids. In: Kane PR, ed. *The first year of teaching: real world stories from America's teachers.* New York, NY: Walker; 1991.

There are thousands of skills that young people need today to help them successfully confront their problems, pressures, concerns, and challenges.[1] **Life skills** are abilities and behaviors that enable individuals to deal effectively with the demands and challenges of everyday life. This chapter addresses four major categories of life skills: self-awareness and self-evaluation; communication and relationships; goal setting and self-management; and decision making and problem solving. These skills, along with stress management skills (discussed in the *Stress Management Skills* chapter), serve as the framework for mental and emotional health units of study.

The **World Health Organization (WHO)** highlights the critical importance of life skills in the healthy development of young people. According to WHO, skill-based health education focuses on developing the knowledge, attitudes, values, and life skills that young people need to make and act on the most appropriate and positive health-related decisions. Individuals who possess these skills are likely to adopt and sustain a healthy lifestyle during their school years and throughout the rest of their lives. WHO stresses that skill-based health education has been shown by research to achieve the following:[2]

- Reduce the chances of young people engaging in delinquent behavior and interpersonal violence
- Delay the onset of using alcohol, tobacco, and other drugs
- Prevent peer rejection and bullying
- Teach anger control
- Promote positive social adjustment and reduce emotional disorders
- Improve health-related behaviors and self-esteem
- Improve academic performance

The United States' National Health Education Standards also call for life skills education. In fact, six of these eight national standards are skill based. This chapter provides the content and tools for teaching the seven skills called for in the national standards.

■ TEACHING LIFE SKILLS

Life skills development can be taught in all curricular areas in schools—English, social studies, science, math, and others. In addition, life skills are key components of all health education units of study. **Box 3-1** contains **HECAT** recommendations for teaching life skills as part of mental and emotional health. When teaching a life skill it is very helpful to include these steps:

1. *Sell it*. Create a desire in the students to become proficient in the skill and an appreciation for the value of the skill. Answer "So what?" questions by helping students understand why the skill is important in their lives and is useful to them personally. Explain how it can help prevent problems and what can happen when a person lacks the skill.

3-1 Internet Support

Instructional Planning for Mental and Emotional Health

The following are health behavior outcomes (HBOs) recommended by HECAT for the K–12 mental and emotional health curriculum. After reviewing these recommendations, check out the HECAT Mental and Emotional Health (MEH) module available on the Internet. Within this module you will find recommendations for all the content and skills to be taught at various grade levels.

- Express feelings in a healthy way.
- Engage in activities that are mentally and emotionally healthy.
- Prevent and manage conflict and stress in healthy ways.
- Use self-control and impulse-control strategies to promote health.
- Seek help for troublesome feelings.
- Express empathy for others.
- Carry out personal responsibilities.
- Establish and maintain healthy relationships.
- Get an appropriate amount of sleep and rest.

After reviewing the HBOs and the HECAT ME modules, try to ascertain mental/emotional health needs your students might have. You can do so by finding local/state data on the Internet (e.g., CDC's YRBS data) and by interviewing school staff or students. Find out if your state has guidelines for mental and emotional health instruction and if a scope and sequence or curricula exist for your school district. Continue your instruction planning by using the guidelines provided in the Teaching Today's Students chapter and the worksheets at the end of this chapter.

---

2. *Explain it.* Explain what the skill entails or the steps required to perform the skill. Use a simple visual aid to develop understanding of the skill.
3. *Demonstrate it.* Show how to do/perform the skill. If there are steps, demonstrate each one slowly and clearly so that the learners can easily follow you and gain confidence in their ability to practice the skill.
4. *Rehearse it.* Guide students as they practice the skill. Give feedback to help them feel comfortable and confident. Be especially sensitive to the fact that some students will need more time and practice to learn and demonstrate the skill.
5. *Apply it.* Help students apply the skill in a real-world setting. Assign students to demonstrate the skill to someone else so that they become the teacher.

Throughout this chapter, you will find numerous activities that can help you teach life skills to your students. Take the time to read these activities and choose which ones you would like to use. Consider how you can implement the steps just mentioned while teaching the activities you choose. Also, take the time to watch the YouTube film *The Butterfly Circus* identified in **Box 3-2**. Consider how this film can be used to help teach all of the life skills discussed in this chapter.

3-2 Application Exercise

Butterfly Circus

Locate and watch the YouTube short (20-minute) film *The Butterfly Circus*. You may also want to watch other video clips involving the lead actor, Nick Vujicic in the film. *The Butterfly Circus* can be used to teach many mental and emotional health concepts. Write a short reaction paper to the film; in it, describe at least three different ways you might use the film in your classroom.

Favorite Activities
Review all of the teaching activities in this chapter (Boxes 3-4, 3-5, and 3-6). Choose three or more activities from each of these boxes that you want to use while teaching. Record the names of the activities you choose, write down ways you can modify or embellish each activity, and indicate various health units you can use the activity in.

■ SELF-AWARENESS AND SELF-EVALUATION SKILLS

A foundational life skill is being self-aware. **Self-awareness** includes recognizing and understanding our perceptions, values, emotions, habits, and the impact our behavior has on others. Being self-aware is a progressive process that is tied to our cognitive development, our having skills to effectively see ourselves, and our willingness and desire to become self-aware. People who lack self-awareness fail to consider or understand their own emotions, do not reflect on their personal reactions, and do not recognize or acknowledge how their behaviors affect others.

How well do you understand your "selves"? This section defines, explains, and differentiates many *self* terms, including self-esteem, self-image, self-worth, ideal-self, Pygmalion-self, and self-efficacy. Understanding each of these selves will help you teach and personally apply self-awareness and self-evaluation more effectively. **Figure 3-1** provides an overview of our different selves. The three-way mirror illustrates two major influences on how we see ourselves. Also notice

Social Mirror

Ideal-self   Self-image   Pygmalion-self

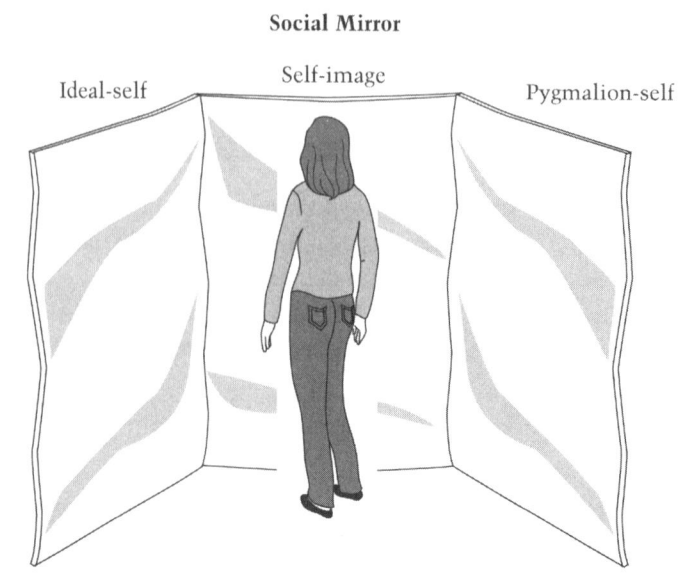

FIGURE 3-1 Understanding our "selves."

52   Chapter 3   Life Skills

the waves in the mirror; they represent our perceptions. On some occasions, our perceptions are more distorted than at other times, such as on "blue days." Consequently, how we view ourselves is dynamic and ever changing. **Self-esteem** is the evaluative component of self-image, or the positive or negative manner in which a person judges herself or himself. It is a product of what we perceive ourselves to be (**self-image**), how we want to be (**ideal-self**), and the expectations that we perceive others have for us (**Pygmalion-self**). Often our sense of worth is influenced by how competent we perceive ourselves to be, if we feel we belong in one or more groups that we esteem, and if we feel we have something we can contribute.

Self-Esteem

For 30 years, self-esteem curricula have been used to try and "inject" self-esteem into students to improve their scholastic performance. These curricula have included activities such as generously praising students for any effort they make and having students chant self-affirming statements such as "I'm great!" Unfortunately, these widespread educational efforts got the cart before the horse. Researcher and author Jean M. Twenge elaborates:

> There is a small correlation between self-esteem and grades. However, self-esteem does not cause high grades—instead, high grades cause higher self-esteem. Nor does high self-esteem protect against teen pregnancy, juvenile delinquency, alcoholism, drug abuse, or chronic welfare dependency. Several comprehensive reviews of the research literature by different authors have all concluded that self-esteem doesn't cause much of anything. Even the book sponsored by the California Task Force to Promote Self-Esteem and Personal and Social Responsibility, which spent a quarter of a million dollars trying to raise Californians' self-esteem, found that self-esteem isn't linked to academic achievement, good behavior, or any other outcome the Task Force was formed to address.[3(p.65)]

The belief that self-esteem can somehow be injected into students and the idea that self-esteem comes before accomplishment are two of the prominent myths generated by the self-esteem movement. Other self-esteem myths include the notions that narcissism and self-centeredness are self-esteem and that one should always feel good about oneself. The perpetuation of these erroneous and unhealthy ideas by teachers, parents, media, and society has fostered a generation that tends to feel good about mediocre performance, wants to be praised constantly, and is self-focused.[3] Teachers report that their students badger them for high grades and often have an unrealistic view of their performance (consider some of the contestants who try out for *American Idol*).

Research now indicates that self-control is a better predictor of success than self-esteem is. Self-control is correlated with earning better grades, finishing more years of education, and being less likely to use drugs and less likely to become pregnant.[3] Students experience a healthy increase in self-esteem when they exhibit self-control, do their very best work, and interact in positive ways with others. Teachers best nurture self-esteem by helping students learn self-discipline and by maintaining high academic and behavioral expectations for their students.

Self-Worth

The term **self-worth** is related to a person's self-esteem. Worth identifies the immense value and potential that every person has. Our "sense" of worth may vary, but not our potential or our value as a human being. Self-worth is best understood when we are "other" focused rather than "self" focused, when we see our own value because we recognize the value of those around us.

If we define our worth from a comparative view, we experience **conditional worth**—that is, we feel worthy only when we think we are somehow better than others. Consider what happens to the beautiful when beauty fades, is blemished, or is altered. Plastic surgery is currently used as a form of psychotherapy for individuals whose sense of self-worth depends on their appearance. The suicides resulting from the stock market crash of 1929 attest to the sensed loss of self-worth because of lost wealth. A common denominator among children and adolescents who are likely to attempt or commit suicide is a very low sense of self-worth. Young people who base their sense of self-worth on conditional factors are vulnerable to feelings of worthlessness when they experience failure or disappointment.

A classic example demonstrating **unconditional self-worth** is Ann Jillian. Jillian is a celebrated actress and singer who developed breast cancer. She was one of the first celebrities to publicly discuss her battle with breast cancer, and she did so to help others suffering from cancer or other life calamities. It took great courage to disclose the loss of her breasts from the cancer, especially when you consider that Jillian works in an occupation where a woman's figure is deemed as or more important than her talent. Unconditional self-worth, like that displayed by Jillian in her desire to help others, can help us meet life's challenges and gives us a firm foundation that allows us to work at achieving without fear of failure. Unconditional self-worth is nurtured when teachers and students interact with one another in positive building ways like the hydraulic lifts discussed in the *Teaching to Make a Difference* chapter and other activities in this chapter. Having and offering unconditional regard for every student is one of the most difficult, but most powerful, attributes a teacher can develop.

Ideal-Self

Ideal-self is our perception of what we want to be. Ideal-self involves every aspect of our being, including physical characteristics, mental abilities, emotional and social skills, and moral standards. Ideal-self is based on the expectations that we have for ourselves. These expectations are shaped through relationships and interactions with family members, peers, and others. The media also affect ideal-self through the messages and images to which we are exposed.

The aspect of ideal-self that youth—especially teenagers—tend to focus on most is their physical characteristics. Our *physical ideal* is what we perceive as the perfect body—our image of what we believe is the perfect height, weight, body build, coloring, facial features, and so forth. This ideal is tremendously shaped by the numerous media images we see of beautiful people, airbrushed to perfection, on television, in movies, in magazines, and on billboards. If we do not look like these people, it is easy to form the impression that we are less than ideal. Yet, the truth is that very few are capable of living up to these ideals. Even models report that there are some things they don't like about their bodies. The physical ideal that should be stressed, therefore, is having a physically fit and healthy body. This is a healthy, achievable physical ideal.

Although certain physical characteristics cannot be changed, moral characteristics can be attained. For example, everyone has the capacity to be honest, respectful, responsible, hardworking, and compassionate. These characteristics are not usually aspired to or sought after unless a young person receives guidance and nurturing from adults. Too many youths idealize low moral characteristics (e.g., disrespect, disregard for the law, cruelty). In other words, the ideal-self of many young persons (what they aspire to be) includes low moral character. How can we help youth want to incorporate moral characteristics into their ideal-self? The following sections on hero identification and character and values education address this question.

Hero Identification

Heroes are simply people whom we admire. The people we choose to admire shape our perception of what we want to be (ideal-self) by providing a standard against which to measure ourselves. Thus identifying one's heroes gives great insight into one's ideal-self. Think about who you truly admire. What is it that you admire about them? You will probably think of several heroes. Some may be people whom you know intimately, such as family members or friends. Others might be people whom you have come to "know" through books or media images. Consider how your heroes affect your life. How much do you attempt to emulate their traits that you find desirable?

How much do you think children and adolescents emulate the people whom they admire? If you ask children and adolescents who their heroes are, many will report celebrities—sports figures, actors, musicians, or other media stars. We are a culture fixated on celebrity status, and our appetite for reading about those individuals' extreme, chaotic, dysfunctional behavior is insatiable. Young people are constantly exposed to images of and news about celebrities through magazines, television shows, and social media. The drinking and drug use, wanton self-exposure, pornographic behavior, and revolving-door love lives of many celebrities provide unhealthy role models for our youth. Unfortunately, many young people's ideal-selves have been shaped by celebrity narcissism.[4]

Young people need to be exposed to heroes of high moral character in literature, history, and science, in our communities, nation, and world—heroes who have channeled their energy into positive activities that benefit the community, who have made healthy decisions to reach a constructive outcome.[5] Being exposed to many different types of heroes helps youth form ideal-selves with high character qualities. It prompts young people to ask themselves if they have the various traits exemplified by these role models and inspires them to develop these traits.

Share your heroes with your students. Highlight the admired characteristics of the heroes you discuss with your students. Explain why the characteristics are important to you and how the hero may have developed these characteristics. Ask your students to interview their parents, relatives, neighbors, or others about their heroes. Instruct your students to listen carefully and identify the admirable qualities these adults' heroes demonstrate. You can also have your students search local newspapers, the Web, and magazines for articles that might identify some individuals who have acted in heroic (admirable) ways. As you do these activities, make a large lettered list of the admirable character traits identified and display this list in a prominent location. In class discussions as the semester proceeds, continue to highlight admirable character traits that come to light in what your class reads or studies. The more exposure students have to examples of high character, the more likely they are to make those characteristics part of their ideal.

Character and Values Education

The very first readers (elementary-level books) used in public education in the United States were full of stories that taught morals—"the moral of the story is . . ." In the 1960s, however, educators stopped teaching morals. It was a time of cultural divide and distrust, and the sentiment was that values could not be taught because everyone's values were so different. In the absence of values education, a new approach of having students "clarify" their personal values became popular. In **values clarification**, students were not taught values, but rather were led through exercises that were supposed to help them clarify their own personal values. Perhaps you have been exposed to a values clarification exercise such as imagining you are on a lifeboat with 10 other people. You have water and food for only 4 people and are asked what you would do. In these types of values clarification exercises, teachers were instructed not to influence students' values by expressing their own. While conducting these exercises, it often became apparent that some students lacked moral values—they were amoral. Students would sometimes say things like, "Throw all the old people overboard—who needs them?"

The idea that values could not and should not be taught in the classroom persisted until the 1980s, when Tomas Lickona[6] helped educators recognize that respect and responsibility are two fundamental values necessary for any society to exist. We all share these values regardless of our political, religious, or social affiliations. The movement for character- and values-based curricula that emerged has since grown to the point where today many state educational standards require character/values education curricula. The political divide that once removed values education in schools has been replaced with one that calls for it. An example of this is President Barack Obama's inaugural address:

> Those values upon which our success depends—hard work and honesty, courage and fair play, tolerance and curiosity, loyalty and patriotism—these things are old. These things are true. They have been the quiet force of progress throughout our history. What is demanded then is a return to these truths. What is required of us now is a new era of responsibility.[7]

Character education is the deliberate effort to help people understand, care about, and act upon core ethical values—to incorporate those values into their ideal-self. Thomas Lickona explains that good character

> consists of knowing the good, desiring the good, and doing the good—habits of the mind, habits of the heart, and habits of action. All three are necessary for leading a moral life; all three make up moral maturity. When we think about the kind of character we want for our children, it's clear that we want them to be able to judge what is right, care deeply about what is right, and then do what they believe to be right—even in the face of pressure from without and temptation from within.[6(p.51)]

Therefore, character education consists of teaching students "the good," motivating them to desire "the good," and inspiring actions of good character. Lickona labels these three components of character education *moral knowing*, *moral feeling*, and *moral action*. Effective character education programs require intentional, proactive, and comprehensive approaches that promote core values in all aspects of school life. Schools that take a comprehensive approach to character education do the following:[8]

- Publicly stand for core ethical values, including respect, responsibility, trustworthiness, fairness, diligence, self-control, caring, and courage
- Define these values in terms of observable behavior
- Model these values at every opportunity
- Celebrate these values' occurrence in and outside of school
- Study these values and teach their application to everyday life, including all parts of the school environment (e.g., classrooms, corridors, cafeteria, playing field, school bus)
- Hold all school members—adults and students alike—accountable to standards of conduct consistent with the school's professed core values

Schools with effective character education programs provide students with repeated opportunities for moral action geared toward helping them develop their intrinsic motivation. To be successful, character education must take place in a school environment that is caring and academically challenging and supportive of all students. Parents and community members must be recruited by the school and made full partners in the character-building effort.

Pygmalion-Self

You may be familiar with the Greek myth of Pygmalion, a sculptor who created an ivory statue of a beautiful young maiden. His creation was so realistic and beautiful that he fell in love with it. In recognition of Pygmalion's strong affection for the ivory maiden, Aphrodite, the goddess of love, turned the statue into a live maiden. Using the theme from this myth, George Bernard Shaw wrote a play entitled *Pygmalion*, upon which the film *My Fair Lady* is based. The play and film portray the relationship between a young flower girl, Eliza Doolittle, and a professor. Professor Higgins's determination and expectations transform Eliza from a flower girl into a lovely lady of high society. The powerful influence of expectations of others on behavior and self-esteem has been dubbed the **Pygmalion effect**. A common expression illustrating the power of the Pygmalion effect goes like this:

> I am not what I think I am.
>
> I am not what you think I am.
>
> I am what I think you think I am.

Pygmalion-self is our perception of what we believe other people think of us. Thus Pygmalion-self is precisely what the preceding expression exclaims: "I am what I think you think I am." Eliza Doolittle became the lady Professor Higgins thought she could be. Take a moment to consider your Pygmalion-self. What perceptions do significant people in your life have of you? How are you affected and shaped by these perceptions? Pygmalion-self perceptions can be negative, positive, or even neutral. Can you think of ways in which you have been negatively and positively affected by your Pygmalion-self perceptions?

Relationships and interactions with many different individuals contribute to a young person's sense of Pygmalion-self, including family, teachers, peers, friends, coaches, and neighbors. However, Pygmalion-self is also highly specific to each relationship and interaction. For example, it is common for a teenager to feel low regard from certain peers but high regard from other peers.

Pygmalion-self-perceptions are prone to inaccuracy. Consider the following case. Melissa wholly believes that one of her teachers thinks she is "dumb" and incorporates this perception into her Pygmalion-self. In reality, the teacher considers Melissa to be a slightly above average student. Melissa's perception affects her schoolwork and her relationship with the teacher. Misperceiving the perceptions of others is a common problem associated with Pygmalion-self. The self-evaluation section in this chapter addresses how to help students accurately evaluate their Pygmalion-self.

All too often, individuals simply accept certain labels that have been "placed" on them. Students need to learn how to reject negative scripting imposed on them by others. Students and teachers also need to develop the habit of being Pygmalion positive to one another. Self-efficacy is fostered in a Pygmalion-positive environment. **Self-efficacy** is believing you can succeed at a particular task. Students who believe they can learn do so. Conversely, students with low self-efficacy for math find math very difficult. How a teacher and classmates interact with a student affects that student's self-efficacy for learning both in that setting and in the future. The *Teaching to Make a Difference* chapter also addresses the Pygmalion effect in the classroom in the section titled "Interacting with Students."

Self-Evaluation

Now that we have looked at our many "selves" and reviewed the importance of character and values, we are ready to look at self-evaluation. **Self-evaluation** includes reflecting on how we view and treat others, on our ideal-self and Pygmalion-self, on our strengths and weaknesses, and on our habits and values. A key in self-evaluation is the ability to take a nonemotive third-person view of ourselves—in other words, to see ourselves through the eyes of another person while maintaining a nonjudgmental state. This is a skill that can be learned. The following examples illustrate the need for more accurate self-evaluation.

Marie works hard in school and recently earned a 94% on a test. Upon reviewing her corrected test, she remarked, "I really messed up on the test!" Michael is very agile and proficient in sports, the "athlete of the family." He does moderately well in school but not as well as his older brother, the "brain of the family." Therefore, Michael feels that he is dumb. Both of these two young people have trouble evaluating themselves accurately. Being able to see oneself accurately is not an easy task, but it is an important life skill.

Teachers can assist students in evaluating themselves more realistically by first helping them develop an awareness of their ideal-self and Pygmalion-self. A variety of activities can help students answer the questions "How do I wish I were?" (ideal-self) and "How do others see me?"

(Pygmalion-self). Part of this awareness entails recognizing how our self-perceptions have been influenced over the years by the media, peers, parents, siblings, and teachers. Teachers can be especially effective in providing these kinds of insights through lecture, discussion, and learning activities. Once students recognize all of these influences, it becomes easier for them to evaluate the accuracy of their self-perceptions. They can also determine whether their ideal-self is what they really want it to be, and if they care to accept the Pygmalion-self imposed on them by others.

In the earlier example, Marie was able to accurately identify that she earned a high score on a test, but unrealistically evaluated her efforts as a failure because her ideal-self demanded perfection. Perfection is an unrealistic foundation for self-evaluation. One of the general characteristics of individuals with negative self-concepts is that they make unrealistically high demands of themselves, tending to judge themselves on the basis of unattainable goals of perfection. Marie can be helped to see how her ideal-self has demanded perfection and that it would be healthful for her change that aspect of her ideal-self.

In the case of Michael, he had accepted a label as part of his identity. He accurately assessed himself as talented in athletics but inaccurately believed he could not be both athletic and intellectual. Assigning labels and roles to relatives is common in families. Parents often place labels such as "the musician," "the brain," or "the athlete" on their children in an effort to reinforce talents they see in them. Unfortunately, parents don't realize that placing a label on one child sometimes discourages siblings from developing potential in the same area. Another unfortunate consequence of labeling is that it makes the labeled person focus on the labeled trait to the exclusion of other talents or interests that he or she might have. By coming to realize how his family label has affected his self-image, Michael is not likely to suddenly perceive himself as being smart, but he might wonder if he could be smarter than he had thought. In turn, he may challenge himself to see if he is capable of more than he had once believed.

Teachers are not in a position to counsel each student and individually review their self-perceptions. They can, however, help students become more aware of their "selves," question negative labels, foster Pygmalion-positive interactions, promote value development, give honest feedback and help students see their shortcomings, and challenge students to become all that they are capable of being. Helping students honestly and effectively complete self-evaluations of their schoolwork is one way teachers can promote self-evaluation skills. Carefully review the teaching activities at the end of the chapter for ideas on how you can help your students develop self-awareness and self-evaluation skills.

■ COMMUNICATION AND INTERPERSONAL SKILLS

Understanding the principles of effective communication is helpful in developing and maintaining interpersonal relationships. Communication skills consist of effectively sending and interpreting messages, including expressing your needs and being an advocate for others. Interpersonal relationship skills include communication skills and many additional abilities for establishing, building, and maintaining healthy relationships.

Sending and Interpreting Messages

We communicate in many ways. The saying "Actions speak louder than words" refers to the importance of **body language** in communication. Actors understand the importance of body language in communicating emotion. When happiness, disappointment, disbelief, or other emotions are displayed on the screen, they are done so primarily through body language. Body language includes facial expressions; posture while standing, sitting, and walking; closeness to (or distance from) to others; and the amount and type of eye contact made.

The tone of voice used is also an important part of sending and interpreting messages. Take a simple statement such as "You are really good at math" and see how many messages you can express changing your voice and inflection. Can you express praise, ridicule, and scorn without changing the wording of the statement?

When we send mixed messages, others have trouble interpreting our message. **Mixed messages** are sent when the spoken words and the body language or tone of voice do not match. For instance, a little boy said to his teacher, "You don't like fourth-grade boys, do you?" His teacher responded, "I love fourth-grade boys." The little guy then said, "I wish you would tell your face that." When we receive a mixed message, we tend to believe the nonverbal over the spoken message.

"I" Messages

Effective communication is enhanced when we take responsibility for our feelings. All too often we convey blame to others for our feelings ("You make me so mad!"). Instead, we should take responsibility for our emotions and convey them as such. For example, suppose a student who is upset with his father for forgetting to come to his soccer game shouts out in frustration, "You're so wrapped up in your work that you don't care about anybody else in this family!" The father may resent such a strong statement and an argument may ensue. Now assume that this student takes responsibility for his feelings and says, "Dad, when you didn't come to my game, I felt like you didn't care about me." This statement would encourage open communication because it describes true feelings and because the father is more likely to respond positively without becoming defensive. When we own our feelings and thoughts, we use **"I" messages**: "This is how I feel," "This is how I see it," "This is what I think."

Listening

Listening is the most powerful communication skill that most of us don't even consider. After all, as the saying goes, we were blessed with two ears and only one mouth. The most common listening mistakes include telling similar stories, giving unsolicited advice or solutions, and taking the message personally so that we aren't hearing objectively.

Listening is the most important communication skill.

Communication and Interpersonal Skills

Listening can be passive or active. In **passive listening**, an individual attentively listens without talking and without directing the speaker in any nonverbal way. Passive listening can be effective when you want the speakers to feel free to develop and express thoughts without concern for evaluation or intrusion from you as a listener.

Active listening requires a great deal more mental and physical effort and energy than passive listening. It involves giving complete attention to what an individual is communicating. Through active listening, a listener conveys understanding and caring to another person, using either verbal or nonverbal means. Active listening requires that you not think about the experiences and insights you want to add to a conversation, but instead "listen" with your eyes, ears, and heart. Verbal responses focus on what the other person is saying and convey sympathy, respect, acceptance, and encouragement—for example, "I understand," "What happened then?" "Is that right?" and "That's wonderful!"

You can also show you care and understand by using **reflective listening**. Reflective listening consists of paraphrasing ("Are you saying that . . . ?"), comparing ("Was it like . . . ?"), verbalizing unexpressed feelings ("Did it make you feel . . . ?"), and by seeking more information ("Tell me more about . . .").

Electronic Communication

Cell phones and the Web have greatly increased our opportunities to communicate with one another, but they have also created communication problems. Who hasn't been annoyed by someone's cell phone going off at an inappropriate time? Students need to be repeatedly taught cell phone etiquette and guidelines for appropriate use of the Web. Problems can arise even when these instruments are used correctly. Many have noted that young adults have largely lost the skill of conversation because most of their communication has taken place through mini-messages sent via text or e-mail. Maybe you, too, have seen young people sitting side by side texting each other rather than talking to each other. The lost art of conversation becomes very apparent when young people want to begin their lives together. Trying to work through the many needed adjustments is particularly difficult when the individuals have not had years of practice communicating and working out problems face to face.

Assertiveness and Advocacy

People tend to express opinions and feelings in one of three communication styles: passive, aggressive, or assertive (**Figure 3-2**). We act according to each of these three styles on certain occasions, depending on our situations. However, if we generally prefer to respond in one of these styles, then we can be classified as passive, aggressive, or assertive. As teachers, our goal is to model assertiveness and help our students become assertive. Persons who are **passive** tend to hold back their true feelings and go along with the other person or persons. They are timid, reserved, and unable to assert their rights. **Aggressive** individuals take charge of almost all situations and express their opinions, beliefs, and values with little or no regard for others. Their messages may be threatening or disrespectful. **Assertive** persons carefully express their true feelings in ways that do not threaten or make others feel anxious. They speak their minds and invite others to do likewise. Assertive individuals are especially skilled at using "I" messages and reflective listening. Assertiveness is also a key component to being able to say, "No." Many young people, as well as adults, find it difficult to say "no" to their peers when they are asked to do something they do not want to do. Resistance training teaches us how to say no without actually saying the word "no." For instance, if asked to do something you know you shouldn't do, you can say, "I can't do that," or you can excuse yourself by saying something like, "I promised ___ that I'd ___. I have to get going." If asked to do something you'd just prefer not doing, you can simply say, "I better pass" or "You go ahead and let me know how it goes."

	Assertive	Passive	Aggressive
Speaking Behaviors	Speaks clearly and confidently with eye contact	Mumbles, nervous, avoids eye contact	Yells or refuses to speak; points finger, glares, uses physical force
Evaluations	Expresses appreciation and respect	Criticizes self and is always apologizing	Criticizes, never compliments
Focus	Uses "I" messages to communicate	Hopes the other person will guess his or her feelings	Uses "you" messages to blame
Problem Solving	Seeks compromise	Gives in to others	Wants his or her own way
Listening Behaviors	Uses active listening skills	Silent, rarely speaks	Interrupts, is sarcastic
Emotions	Tries to understand other's feelings	Denies own feelings and makes excuses	Makes fun of others, uses name-calling

FIGURE 3-2 Communication styles.

The ability to recognize and appropriately communicate our emotions is an integral part of being assertive. Young children especially find it difficult to articulate what they are feeling and can act out aggressively when they are angry. A child might yell, "Mommy, I hate you!" when he truly loves his mother, but at that moment is frustrated and doesn't know how to express his emotion or his needs. Children and adolescents can learn to recognize what they are feeling, develop the vocabulary to express it, and then know how to communicate their message so that their needs will be met.

Advocacy comprises a group of skills that are built upon assertiveness and includes being able to make requests, encourage others, and express opinions. As students become more proficient at this skill, they are better able to influence other people's thoughts, attitudes, and actions. Advocates support other people in how they interact with them and in helping them express their needs. Students who develop the skill of advocacy are able to express and support a position with accurate information and to adapt and deliver a message to a specific target audience. Advocacy skills help students promote their own well-being and that of their family and community.

Empathy

Being able to recognize the emotions of other people is a fundamental people skill and a precursor to having empathy. **Empathy** is the ability to recognize emotions of others and have the sensitivity to understand how those emotions can make someone feel. People who are empathetic are more attuned to the subtle social signals of others. They have, so to speak, a social antenna. Individuals who can "read" others are often identified as "star" employees by coworkers. They are able to work well with others, cooperatively solving problems and creating synergistic energy. Conversely, those who have a hard time tuning into others find establishing and maintaining relationships difficult. They can become loners or bullies.

Another person's emotions are often displayed through body language, which serves as a means of communicating feelings. For example, in your mind you can probably picture the body language of someone who is sad or depressed. Other emotions invoke discernible body responses. Teach your students to recognize these responses. Through the use of video clips and pictures, students can learn to interpret the facial expressions and body movements of characters. You can also teach these concepts by having students role-play different emotions. Alternatively, you might have students play charades in which different emotions are acted out and the students guess which emotion is displayed. You can also teach empathy by discussing what people might have felt in historical settings, in fictional settings, or in real-life situations observed on the news or in daily interactions. Recognizing emotions and empathizing with others are skills that some children learn quickly, whereas others need considerably more help.

Relationship Building

Positive interpersonal relationships form the basis for filling many human needs. Relationships with significant others can alleviate loneliness, secure stimulation, establish contact for self-knowledge, and provide a means of sharing joy and pain. Young people often lack the skills to initiate and maintain satisfying relationships, resolve conflict, and deal with the deterioration or dissolution of relationships.

Intimate friendships do not develop immediately, but are built as they progress gradually through a series of stages. Understanding these stages and the skills necessary for their development and maintenance can help students build meaningful friendships. It can also help them strengthen family bonds.

In the first stage, initial **contact** is made and basic information is exchanged ("Hi, my name is Brittany"). Physical appearance often plays an important initial role in this interaction. Other important factors are personal qualities such as friendliness, warmth, and openness. Classroom activities can help students develop and refine skills in initiating conversation and relationships. Students should learn about their tendencies to label and make premature judgments based on physical appearance. This knowledge helps them to develop greater empathy and appreciation for their classmates and others. Learning about the processes of nonverbal communication helps students to analyze and interpret the messages they send and receive during the contact stage.

The **acquaintance stage** entails a commitment to get to know another person better and to become more open with this person. Feelings and emotions are shared, but only in a preliminary way. Relationships are often aborted during this stage when one person is unable to open up to the other, or opens up too much too soon. It is helpful for students to be aware of levels of communication. Communication ranges from a level of small talk ("That's a great shirt you're wearing") to the sharing of ideas ("Why don't we try doing it this way?") to self-disclosure ("I'm having trouble getting along with my mom").

The **intimacy stage** is characterized by a further commitment to another person. Becoming a best friend, boyfriend, or girlfriend are examples of this type of relationship. Intimacy is reserved for very few people at any one time. Children, for example, often have best friends to the exclusion of playing with others. Deep feelings and emotions are exchanged by intimates that are not shared with others outside this bond.

Having a best friend helps children learn intimacy skills. However, such strong bonding should not and does not mean excluding all others. Students can be taught how harmful cliques can be both to others and to themselves. Charity can be fostered among all class members as they are encouraged to interact with each other.

The **deterioration stage** is experienced when individuals begin to feel that the relationship may not be as important as they once thought or when the parties grow apart. Less time is spent together, awkward silences may occur, communication is not as open, and physical contact is not as frequent. Conflicts are more likely and reconciliation more difficult than earlier in the relationship. Indeed, conflicts often go unresolved because there is an inclination not to bother with reconciliation. When efforts are not taken to alter these events, deterioration can progress to dissolution of the relationship.

Deterioration is sometimes a natural, healthy way for individuals to grow apart. Children and adolescents need to learn how to gracefully stop being a best friend with someone or to "break up" with a girlfriend or boyfriend. Unfortunately, all too often youth become cruel in their efforts to end relationships. Role-playing and effective communication skills can help students learn to be kind in this stage.

Even though the deterioration stage is sometimes healthy, at other times relationships crumble that could and should have been maintained. Family ties and relationships are especially vulnerable if left in the deterioration stage. Coming to understand mixed messages by appropriately using "I" messages, engaging in active listening, and being appropriately assertive can assist individuals in resolving conflicts.

Students can be asked to take a good, long look at the health of some of their most important interpersonal relationships. They can ask themselves, "What needs to be improved? How can I make it better?"

A relationship **dissolves** when bonds are severed that once united individuals. Sometimes roles are redefined, such as from boyfriend or girlfriend to "just friends." At other times, so many negative emotions are present between individuals that they purposely avoid each other. Divorce is the outcome of a marriage that has reached this stage. Pain, bitterness, anger, rage, frustration, betrayal, and hurt are a few of the negative emotions that can result when a relationship dissolves. Many students have experienced some of these negative emotions as a result of dissolved relationships with peers or family members. Discussions of ways to handle these negative emotions or avoid them in future experiences can be helpful.

Young people need skills to build and maintain healthy relationships, resolve conflicts, and solve problems.

Relationship Bank Account

Covey gives great insight into how we can develop and maintain strong relationships.[9] He likens personal relationships to a **relationship bank account**. We have a different "bank account" with everyone we know, and we need to consciously make many deposits in these accounts if we want them to remain "fiscally sound." Whether our relationship with another person is at the low- or high-quality end of the relationship continuum depends on the amount of deposits and withdrawals we have made in that account. High-quality relationships have accounts with abundant funds. When a person makes an occasional withdrawal, such as being unsympathetic, not keeping a promise, or disciplining a child, the relationship survives the experience because there were enough "funds" to cover the withdrawal. Relationships at the low-quality end of the relationship continuum have minimal funds or have been run into bankruptcy; they are full of conflict and animosity. The only way to build up such accounts is to minimize withdrawals and make steady generous deposits over time.

Covey identifies six major types of deposits we can make: understanding the individual, demonstrating small courtesies and kindnesses, keeping commitments, clarifying expectations, showing personal integrity, and apologizing sincerely. We now take a closer look at each type of deposit. Monetary types of deposits have been linked to these relationship deposits in an effort to help us remember them.

1. *Understanding the individual* (showing *interest*) entails recognizing what is important to that person and taking interest in it. A teenage boy may not be interested in the stock market, but occasionally reading the financial section of the newspaper and discussing it with his father who is a stockbroker will make large deposits in their joint intimacy account.
2. *Demonstrating small courtesies and kindnesses* (small *change*) is often underrated, but the relationship funds banked by notes, winks, hugs, tired-feet massages, opening doors, and saying "thank you" quickly add up. These small acts demonstrate appreciation and acknowledge that the other person's physical and emotional states are important to us.
3. *Keeping our commitments* (*credit card*) means doing what we say we will, when we say we will. A boy who promises to attend his girlfriend's game, but doesn't, makes a withdrawal. A 12-year-old boy who promises to mow the yard when he comes home from school and does so without further reminders makes a deposit. A teacher who takes promised disciplinary action makes both a withdrawal and a deposit, thus breaking even.
4. *Clarifying expectations* (*check*) is critically important to avoid conflict and hurt feelings. We can easily encounter daily conflicts when we try to read others' minds or expect them to read ours. A mother's idea of a clean room may be much different from that of her child's. A newlywed woman's perception of sharing the housecleaning chores may be different from her husband's. A father picking up his daughter at the mall may expect her to be waiting somewhere different from where she is. A teacher's perception of an A-quality report may be different from his students. Clearly communicating our expectations helps us strengthen our relationships.
5. *Showing personal integrity* (*gold*) means demonstrating character in all our actions and relationships. For instance, if a person speaks ill of someone not present, we may wonder what that person says about us behind our back. How we treat one person can affect our relationship with 30 others. A young man once said to his youth leader, "You know how you are always telling us you love us? I didn't believe you until today." The leader asked what had made the difference. The young man replied, "I've always tried to be real good around you. I figured if you knew the real me, you wouldn't love me. Today Johnny messed up real bad and you wouldn't let the rest of us crawl all over him. You loved Johnny even when he didn't deserve it. That's when I knew you loved me."

6. *Apologizing sincerely (cash)* when we have intentionally or unintentionally made a mistake is one of the surest and fastest ways of strengthening a relationship. Unfortunately, our pride often holds us back from saying, "I'm sorry . . . ." Our mistake turns into a relationship deficit when it could have easily become a relationship asset.

At the end of the chapter you will find ideas on how to teach the relationship bank account in your classroom and activities for learning to better read people.

■ GOAL-SETTING AND SELF-MANAGEMENT SKILLS

Goal setting and self-management are key life skills needed for emotional well-being. In this section, we will first look at goal setting. Even very young children can be taught how to set and achieve realistic goals, thereby realizing the joy that comes from these experiences. Four-year-olds naturally set goals such as learning to tie their shoes and dressing themselves. As children grow and mature, they need direction in the kinds of goals they should set and in ways to reach their long-term goals.

Students can learn to see their academic progress in terms of goal setting and achievement rather than reactions to assignments given by teachers. All too often students are not involved in the setting of their academic goals. Teachers, curriculum committees, and others set standards for students to achieve. If students do not feel ownership for these standards, they can easily rationalize their lack of accomplishment (e.g., "The teacher expected too much," "The goal was set too high," or "No one should be required to do so much"). When students are involved in the goal-setting process, however, using such defense mechanisms is more difficult and accomplishments are personally felt, generating new motivation and enthusiasm.

Students can benefit from learning different types of goals to set, the process for setting them, and the process for reaching them. A key to setting goals is to base them on past performance and to differentiate between long-term and short-term goals. Individuals with negative self-concepts tend to set their goals either unrealistically low or unrealistically high. Either way, the results are perceived as failure. Children also tend to set unrealistically high goals; they don't feel comfortable with low goals. Teachers who have worked on goal-setting techniques have reported that children, when asked how many times they will try to respond correctly, usually set goals that are high in relation to past performance. The most reasonable type of goal setting is to make the goal slightly higher than previous performances. For many students, this may be at a level far below the long-term goal for which they and their teacher are aiming, but this shorter-term goal is attainable. Goals that are not attainable do not contribute to long-term commitment and performance. One way teachers can handle the tendency to set unrealistically high goals is by charting a child's goal as a long-term endeavor, with smaller, more easily achieved short-term goals identified as stepping stones. As the child focuses on and obtains the first short-term goal, a sense of competency is felt along with motivation for taking the next step.

As students work toward goals they have set, they need to evaluate their progress and deal with any failures. Students can be helped to see failure to meet a goal as an opportunity to learn more about how to set goals. With the teacher's help, they can ask and answer the questions "Was the goal unrealistic?" and "Should the goal have been set lower, and if so, what are some shorter-term goals that would lead up to it?" Students' efforts toward obtaining goals should also be part of the evaluation process.

The following steps are involved in setting and achieving goals:

1. *Identify your goal in writing.* If it is not written, it is just a wish.
2. *Identify resources* that can help you reach the goal.
3. *Map out goal achievement*—that is, the short-range goals necessary to achieve the major goal.

4. *Work toward the goal and adjust* your map as needed.
5. *Achieve and evaluate.* What did you learn? What went well? What could you do differently to be more successful when you purse your next goal?

Being Proactive

Taking responsibility for our lives, for our actions and choices, is another key life skill for living a happy, healthful life. Three prominent theories of determinism—genetic, psychic, and environmental—state that factors beyond our control are *responsible* for our behavior. Genetic determinism basically says, "It's your grandpa's fault"; it's in your DNA, it's in your nature. Psychic determinism says, "It's your parents' fault"; it's your upbringing, your childhood experiences, or emotional scripting that makes you who you are. Environmental determinism says, "It's your boss's, spouse's, or the economy's fault"; in other words, someone or something in the environment is responsible for your situation.

We do not deny the influence that genetic, psychic, and environmental factors have on human behavior. However, we want to bring to your attention the concept of **proactivity**, which rejects the view that people and organizations are *controlled* by genetic, historical, or environmental forces. As Covey explains, "As human beings, we are responsible for our own lives. Our behavior is a function of our decisions, not our conditions. We can subordinate feelings to values."[9] Highly proactive people "do not blame circumstances, conditions, or conditioning for their behavior. Their behavior is a product of their own conscious choice, based on values, rather than a product of their conditions, based on feelings."[9(p.71)] The concept of being proactive emphasizes taking personal responsibility for behavior.

A classic example comes from the life of Victor Frankl, a Jewish psychologist who was incarcerated in the Auschwitz concentration camp during World War II. While standing naked, alone, and stripped of all his earthly possessions and family, Frankl envisioned that he had only one freedom left: the freedom to choose his responses. This realization led to the choice to forgive his captors. His forgiveness was not the result of benevolence; rather, he knew that holding on to hatred and resentment would destroy him. He continued to develop his freedom of response as the weeks and months dragged on. While digging ditches, marching, and enduring countless persecutions, he envisioned himself in the future, lecturing to university students on the lessons he learned in the concentration camp. In time, Frankl developed more freedom than his captors. Although they had more liberty, he had more freedom.

Another classic example of being proactive comes from the courageous life of Christopher Reeve. He was an acclaimed, tall, athletic actor who won stardom for his role as Superman. In 1995, he was fully paralyzed after a fluke fall during an equestrian competition. At age 52, in October 2004, he died from a heart attack brought on by complications of his paralysis. During his years as a quadriplegic, Reeve displayed remarkable proactive behaviors. Rather than allow his situation to control him, he chose to take control over his life and to be happy. He reported that on most nights he would dream of walking, sailing, and playing with his children, and then awake in the morning to the reality of his paralysis. He would fight the anguish and sense of loss by immediately trying to shake it off and focusing on what he could do.

Reactive or Proactive

In every circumstance in life, we have the choice to be reactive or proactive. **Reactive** people are more or less controlled by circumstance or the environment. If they are treated well, they tend to feel and act "good." If they are treated badly, they feel bad and are defensive. Reactive people build their emotional lives around the behavior of others, believing that love is a feeling, bestowed upon them like Cupid's arrows. In contrast, proactive people such as Victor Frankl and Christopher Reeve "carry their own weather" with them. This means that they choose, to a large extent, how they will respond to the situations that they encounter. They are

Christopher Reeve was truly a "Superman" for the way he chose to live his life after becoming a quadriplegic.

value driven, having a carefully selected and internalized value code. Proactive people have the ability to subordinate an impulse to a value. This is the essence of proactivity—choosing how to act rather than being acted upon by circumstance, environment, or even impulse.

If you want to gauge your proactive versus reactive thinking, observe patterns in what you say to others. Reactive language contains statements such as "There's nothing I can do," "She makes me so mad," "That's just the way I am," "I have to do it," "I can't," and "If only . . .". Proactive thinking is identified with statements such as "I can . . . ," "I control . . . ," "I choose . . . ," and "I will . . .". You can help students replace "I can't" with "I will" and "I have to" with "I choose to."

We urge you to emphasize the powerful principle of proactivity as you teach students. Individuals do not happen to just "fall into" proactive thinking. It takes self-awareness, effort, and the building of character to achieve this way of thinking and living. You can help your students develop proactive living by modeling this behavior in your interactions with them. Insist that they take responsibility for their own actions; do not allow them to blame their behavior on someone else. Help your students develop a proactive thinking and speaking style.

Impulse Control and Delayed Gratification

Impulse control and **delayed gratification** are practiced by proactive people and lay the foundation for every accomplishment, from staying on a diet to pursuing a medical degree. Conversely, those persons having problems with impulse control and delayed gratification are more likely to

Goal-Setting and Self-Management Skills   67

drop out of school, become pregnant as teenagers, abuse drugs, and end up in jail. We live in a world saturated with advertisements whose messages tell us that we can have what we want *now*, that we deserve it and should have it *now*. This is not an environment conducive to helping us control our impulses and delay our gratification.

Teachers can help children learn self-discipline rather than act impulsively. Simple classroom structure such as not getting a drink of water until a designated time, not speaking in class until called upon, and staying seated until the teacher dismisses the class helps students learn self-management. Established procedures enable teachers to help students learn self-discipline. When a student doesn't follow an established procedure, the teacher just asks the student to identify the correct procedure and then do it. Some children need repetitive reminders and opportunities to practice correct procedures, but that is certainly acceptable. Each time the student practices getting it right, he or she is practicing self-mastery with the teacher acting as a coach. Classrooms can also offer opportunities to learn delayed gratification when students achieve a natural reward after hard work and effort.

Building Willpower and Self-Control

A great resource for learning how to increase self-control is the book *The Willpower Instinct: How Self-Control Works, Why It Matters, and What You Can Do to Get More of It,* by Kelly McGonigal. McGonigal explains how willpower is defined from a scientific standpoint and debunks many myths that hold us back from developing more of it. She explains how our brains respond to experience, much like a muscle growing in bulk, by becoming denser with more gray matter in the cerebral cortex. Committing to any small consistent act of self-control, such as opening doors with our nondominant hand, can "bulk" the brain. When we think before reaching for a door handle, we become more self-aware, and any increased self-awareness increases our willpower capacity.

Meditation is another fast and powerful way to increase willpower. It not only increases our perceived capacity for self-control, but actually changes our brain; these changes can be seen on imaging scans after accumulating just 11 hours of meditation.

Our willpower can become exhausted, again like a muscle, when we try to force ourselves to do too much all at once. Willpower is especially weak when we are physically exhausted, when we haven't gotten enough sleep, and when our blood sugar levels are low. McGonigal suggests that, if we want to make a big change or transform an old habit, we should find small ways to practice self-control so that we can strengthen our willpower without overwhelming it.[10]

Anger Management

We all experience anger, frustration, insecurity, and other negative emotions from time to time. Knowing how to deal with these emotions and being able to appropriately calm oneself are critical life skills. It is important to talk to young people about anger. Too often, children and adolescents come to believe that it is inappropriate to feel anger. Teachers can reinforce the notion that anger is a normal emotion that can be expressed in constructive ways. Stress to students that they are responsible for managing their anger.

To better manage their anger, students need to become aware of how they experience and traditionally express this emotion. They should recognize that anger generates a physical response—that it creates tension and stress. Building tension causes a release of hormones into the bloodstream that prepare the body to either fight or flee (the "fight or flight" response). The heart beats faster, the blood pressure increases, and breathing quickens. More blood is sent to the muscles, and these muscles become tense in anticipation of an emergency. Verbal responses to anger might include making sarcastic remarks, raising one's voice, and making put-downs.

Recognizing these physical and verbal signals is important so that students can make decisions about how to respond to their anger before it takes over. They also need to become aware of which thoughts and situations trigger them to feel anger.

Self-control is an important aspect of anger management. Teachers need to emphasize that everyone's behavioral response to anger is a choice, but that behavioral responses such as physical aggression and verbal explosions are destructive. **Box 3-5** contains many teaching strategies for helping students learn how to manage their anger as well as activities related to goal setting.

DECISION-MAKING AND PROBLEM-SOLVING SKILLS

Problem solving and decision making are very closely related. In this section, we first discuss problem solving as a whole and then take a closer look at decision making. Next, we look at negation and conflict resolution, resilience in a negative environment, and building assets to help students confront and overcome problems.

Problem-solving skills are, unfortunately, seldom seen modeled by young people. On television, they see complex problems easily resolved (often with violence) in a 30-minute to 2-hour program. Advertisements abound, convincing them that life should be pain free and enjoyed without any thought of the cost. Today few families eat dinner together more than one or two times per week. With so little family time, children are not in a position to observe their parents confront, handle, and overcome everyday problems. And sadly, in some homes, young people are told that they *are* the problem, not that they *have* a problem.

It is important for students to realize that life is filled with problems for people in all walks of life. Often youth feel they are the only ones with the burdens they carry. Simply discussing the universality of conflicts in people's lives can help students feel less isolated and overwhelmed by their problems. Such discussions help put one's own trials in proper perspective. Looking at other individuals' lives and the means by which they have overcome difficulties can help young people learn to solve problems and overcome obstacles.

Problem-Solving Steps

Problem-solving steps are quite simple. The greatest difficulty comes in the first step—differentiating the problem from the reality. Often we become sidetracked and waste a great deal of time and emotional energy bemoaning the "realities" of a problem and blaming others for its existence. For instance, how often do we yell about "spilled milk"? The milk on the floor is a reality; how to clean it up is the solvable problem. Being a pregnant teenager is a reality; securing the welfare of the mother and unborn child is a solvable problem. Once we clearly see what the problem is, we can move toward solving it.

Problem-solving steps include the following:

	Correlated Decision-Making Steps
1. Identify the problem and the reality	Describe the situation
2. Explore available resources	List possible decisions
3. Creatively look for alternative solutions	Seek counsel with a trusted adult
4. Judge the probable consequences of each solution	Evaluate possible consequences
5. Choose and then act on the chosen solution	Act on an appropriate, responsible decision
6. Evaluate the results	Evaluate

Making Decisions

Young people need help in recognizing how small and major decisions affect their lives both now and in the future. Small day-to-day decisions can have a great impact on their health—what they choose to eat, who they choose to spend time with, what they choose to do with their spare time, when they choose to go to bed, how they choose to express their emotions and needs.

It is also important for students to ponder the moral aspect of making decisions. Too often choices are made based on what feels good, what others might think of us, or what everyone else appears to be doing. It is important for students to consider the moral right or wrong of a decision. Getting in the habit of reviewing expectations set by parents, school, church, and community members can help young people make morally correct decisions. Asking "What would happen if everyone in the world did this?" also can identify the moral implications of a decision.

Split-second decisions are often made without thinking, almost like a reflex. Spontaneously deciding which flavor of ice cream to order can be fun, but acting spontaneously in risky situations is not helpful. Even when youth know what is right and wrong, they can make a split-second wrong decision if they have not previously decided what to do. Teachers can help students make clear, healthful decisions now and then recognize that they don't have to make that decision ever again because it has already been made. Risk-reducing decisions, such as what to do if someone who has been drinking offers you a car ride, can be made by students in class and then practiced by role-playing. Teaching students to choose their actions based on values rather than reacting to an impulse or circumstance helps them become proactive.

It also is helpful for students to see the thought processes that go into the countless decisions teachers make and the problems they solve each day in the classroom. Teachers can model problem-solving and decision-making skills by sharing with students some of the problems they face and the decisions they must make. In doing so, teachers can identify the steps they take in solving their problems and making their decisions. They can also ask their students to help them identify possible solutions and choices. Involving students in this way helps them feel more responsible and capable, and part of the solution rather than part of the problem.

Conflict Management

Children and adolescents need skills in negotiation and managing conflicts in an appropriate manner. Teaching conflict management skills to young people can help them reduce their risk of perpetrating or being a victim of violence and can help them establish nonviolent behavioral patterns.

Conflict management skills are best learned by children when they are not caught up in the heat of their own conflicts. To be meaningful, these skills must be practiced over a wide range of contexts. Young people also need ample opportunities to practice these skills in a trusting and supportive environment. Such an environment helps youth to talk about the conflicts they are having and provides a setting in which classmates can help one another with problem solving. With young children, puppets can be used for role-playing the range of conflict management skills. In teaching conflict management and having students implement it, teachers can help students with the following tasks:

- *Understand.*
    - Understand the problems or needs that caused the conflict.
    - See the two sides or viewpoints.
    - See the whole problem and how their behavior contributed to it.
    - Think of possible consequences if the conflict continues.
- *Negotiate* for a **win–win solution** (where both parties' needs are met).
- *Act with integrity* on the planned solution.
- *Reflect* on what was learned and give others ideas about solving conflicts.

Resilience

Resilience is a term that was originally used to define a material's ability to resume its shape after being bent, stretched, or compressed. Today **resilience** is commonly used to describe our ability to bounce back from adversity, to succeed despite facing serious challenges and adverse circumstances.[11] Life in the twenty-first century is filled with challenges and pressures that figuratively stretch, bend, and compress all of us. Teachers can facilitate students in developing more resilience.

Much can be learned from studies conducted to discover how resilient children thrive in spite of difficult circumstances (e.g., neglect, maltreatment, dysfunctional families, poverty, physical disability, trauma). Researchers have studied resilient children to see what they have in common—characteristics that are called **protective factors**. Masten points out that results from longitudinal studies of resilient children and youth show that the most important of all protective factors is a strong relationship with a competent, caring, prosocial adult.[12] She also lists the following as critical protective factors: normal cognitive development (average or better IQ scores, "street smarts," good attention skills), feelings of self-worth and self-efficacy, feelings of hope and meaningfulness of life, attractiveness to others (in personality or appearance), talents valued by self and others, and faith and religious affiliations.

When children grow up in a high-risk family environment (e.g., an alcoholic or drug-abusing family), studies suggest that they have a better chance of growing into healthy adulthood if they meet the following criteria:[13]

- Learn to do one thing well that is valued by themselves, friends, or community
- Are required to be helpful as they grow up
- Are able to ask for help for themselves
- Are able to elicit positive responses from others
- Are able to distance themselves from their dysfunctional families so that the family is not their sole frame of reference
- Are able to bond with some socially valued, positive entity such as a school, community group, church, or another family
- Are able to interact with an adult who provides consistent caring responses

You can foster resilience in your students by helping them develop the characteristics just described. In doing so, you can help them see that they are capable of coping with life's challenges and changes. Help them develop hope, and find meaning in life. Help them view their mistakes and weaknesses as opportunities to learn. Help them diminish perfectionism and accept that losing may precede winning. Guide them to focus on what they can do, rather than on what is outside of their control. Be patient with their mistakes. Encourage and praise their efforts rather than praising their accomplishments, and be sure to praise effort more than you correct.

Asset Development

Many communities have organized to help young people develop assets that will help them succeed in life. **Asset development** is a movement that focuses on combining life skills with family and community resources. It identifies by name and then tries to increase the positive building blocks in young people's lives. The Search Institute—the major force behind the asset development movement—has identified 40 different developmental assets that act as protective factors for youth. Research has shown that the more assets youth have, the fewer the risk patterns they demonstrate and the more positive behaviors they experience.

The Search Institute has divided these 40 assets into two different groups: 20 external assets and 20 internal assets. The **external assets** include actions that caring adults and communities can take to assist young people in three areas: supporting and empowering young people, setting boundaries and expectations, and fostering positive and constructive use of young people's time. The **internal assets** concern the positive internal growth and development of young people (life skills), focusing on positive values and identities, social competencies, and commitment to learning. A detailed listing and explanation of the 40 assets, along with a teaching curriculum and strategies for them, can be found at http://www.search-institute.org.

All too often we adults fail to do something about children's problems because we feel overwhelmed when we hear, see, and read about the extent of the problems facing young people today. Asset building says to everyone that we have a role to play, that we can say hello to a teenager, ask youth to help us help others, thank media when positive messages are broadcast about youth, and just smile more at young people. School professionals can help create a caring school climate, ensure there are plentiful after-school programs with lots of physical activity for all children, ensure that young people develop good goal-setting and decision-making skills, and provide opportunities for youth to contribute service and help others. Ideas on how you can teach decision-making and problem-solving skills in your classroom can be found at the end of the chapter.

■ ACTIVITIES FOR MENTAL AND EMOTIONAL HEALTH AND RISK BEHAVIOR

3-3 *Self-Awareness & Self-Evaluation Activities*

These activities can be embellished or modified to fit your teaching objectives, styles, and students. For instance, we observed a teacher very successfully modify and use activities indicated for the primary level in her high school class. As you review these activities consider how they can also be used in other units addressing healthy eating, drugs, sexuality, violence and safety. Each activity identifies likely appropriate grade level(s) for use.

P = primary, kindergarten through third grade
I = intermediate, fourth through sixth grade
J = junior high
H = high school

You can embellish or modify these activities to fit your teaching objectives, styles, and students. For instance, we have observed a teacher very successfully modify and use the activities indicated for the primary level in her high school class. She says teenagers like to act "cool" but are really little kids at heart.

Remember to use the suggested steps for teaching life skills when you develop these activities into lesson plans. Consider how you can use them as part of units addressing risky behaviors.

Getting to Know Me

Have students write endings to complete statements like the following as a self-awareness exercise. Encourage depth and honesty by assuring them that their answers are for their eyes only. (I, J, H)

1. I hate . . .
2. I wish . . .
3. I fear . . .
4. I love . . .
5. I want most to be . . .
6. I am most cheerful when . . .
7. I am interested in . . .
8. When bullied, I . . .

9. When I am the center of attention, I . . .
10. When I feel awkward, I . . .
11. When given responsibility, I . . .
12. When I want to show I like someone, I . . .
13. When I am angry, I . . .
14. When others put me down, I . . .
15. When I am under a lot of stress, I . . .

Reflective Writing

Have students keep a daily journal for a designated time period. Their journal entries could be about their feelings, perceptions, dreams, goals, decisions, habits, strengths, and weaknesses—you determine the prompts according to your teaching objective. (I, J, H)

Fingerprints

Help each child make a set of fingerprints. Have them compare their fingerprints with those of other children. Point out the differences and discuss how each person is unique and lovable. Students can also draw eyes, ears, hair, and so forth on their fingerprints and then compare their drawings. Have students frame their fingerprints and keep them on their desks as a reminder of their uniqueness. (P)

Classroom Stars and Sun Spots

Make a bulletin board of dark blue paper with a yellow moon in one corner. Have each student make a star, sign it, and write a positive personal quality. You may have to help them identify these qualities. Display all of the students' stars on the bulletin board.

A variation of this activity is to prepare or have students prepare one paper or cardboard sun (circle with perimeter lines for rays) for each student. Cut a hole in the center of each sun and have each student place one of their school pictures in their "frame." Then, you, the student, or classmates can write special things about each individual on the sun's rays. (P, I)

I Am Good at . . .

Have each student draw a picture to complete this sentence: "I am good at . . ." Ask students to show and explain their drawings to the class. Model and help the students give one another positive feedback, especially to any shy or insecure student. (P, I, J)

Eggs of Praise and Fortune Cookies

At Easter time, give every student in the class a plastic egg with a message in it that recognizes talents, abilities, or positive behavior you have observed. At Chinese New Year, give every student a fortune cookie that contains positive messages. The point of the activity is to enhance the student's Pygmalion-self. A modification of the activity that creates a hydraulic-lift exercise is to have students write the messages in the eggs or cookies. (P, I, J, H)

Who Is This?

Place a baby picture of a student on a bulletin board with the caption, "Who is this important person?" Highlight information about this student—place of birth, hobbies, number of siblings, favorite foods, and so on. Make efforts to spotlight students who need recognition or be sure to spotlight every student throughout the school year. Use this activity to help the students see one another's unique worth. (P, I, J)

(continues)

(*continued*)

Slide Show

Throughout the school year, take photographs of the students as they engage in various learning activities. Toward the end of the year, set aside time for students to view the slides, to give and receive positive comments, and to recall shared experiences. (P, I)

King/Queen for a Day

On birthdays or some other day, honor each student by having him or her wear a crown and cape and sit in front of the class. Have the other students write and/or illustrate some positive characteristic they have observed in the honored student. Make these writings and drawings into a "book" and place each student's book in the classroom library to be read by the class during free reading time. (P, I)

Pygmalion-Self

Have students complete each of the following phrases with at least two answers, preferably in paragraph form. (I, J, H)

1. My closest friend thinks I am . . .
2. My classmates think I am . . .
3. My parents think I am . . .
4. A stranger's first impression of me might include . . .

Me Inside and Out

Place on the floor a large sheet of paper that is folded so that it is double thick. Instruct students to lie down on the paper and then have someone trace around them. Cut out the figure. Have students color their figures to show how they look, both front and back. Put the two pictures together and staple around the figure, leaving part of one leg open. Request parents to make a list of all the good qualities they see in their child and have the students bring these lists to school. Create lists for those students whose parents did not comply. Have students write each characteristic on the back of a different piece of scrap paper, crumble the scrap papers and stuff them into the open leg and then staple the leg shut. Display everyone's paper dolls and discuss what the students are like inside and out. This activity can help you foster positive Pygmalion-self and character development. (P, I)

Evolution of Beauty

Have your students watch the YouTube video titled *Evolution of Beauty—Dove Campaign for Real Beauty*. Discuss male and female perceptions of beauty and explore how media shape unreal expectations. (I, J, H)

Labels I Wear

On slips of cardstock, write positive and negative labels that people "wear." Have a student stand in front of the class and tape one or more of the labels to his or her clothing. Discuss how a person might become labeled whatever you have indicated. Have other students come forward and "wear" the other cardstock slips. Discuss how we can choose to "wear" labels placed on us or we can choose to discard and disregard labels others try to give us. (I, J, H)

Coat of Arms

On drawing paper, ask students to draw a large shield and then design a personal coat of arms with symbols representing their personal talents, traits, values, and aspirations. Reassure students that this activity is not an evaluation of artistic ability, but rather an exercise to help them explore who they think they are and who they want to become. (I, J, H)

My Hero

Have students write papers identifying a person they greatly admire in the world and explaining why. Have the class share their heroes and make a cumulative list of their heroes' admirable attributes. Display this list and challenge the class to look for these attributes in one another. (I, J, H)

Ask your students to interview their parents, relatives, neighbors, or others about their heroes. Instruct your students to listen carefully and identify the admirable qualities these adults' heroes demonstrate. You can also have your students search local newspapers, the Web, and magazines for articles that might identify some individuals who have acted in heroic (admirable) ways. As you do these activities, make a large lettered list of the admirable character traits identified and display this list in a prominent location. In class discussions as the semester proceeds, continue to highlight admirable character traits that come to light in what your class reads or studies. The more exposure students have to examples of high character, the more likely they are to make those characteristics part of their ideal.

Repeated Pats on the Back

Have students pin a blank piece of paper on their backs. Every student is to write one positive thing about each classmate on his or her back. You should participate as well. When everyone has written on everyone else's backs, have the students return to their seats, take the papers off their backs, and quietly read the comments. Discuss how it felt to have others write on their backs and how the comments made them feel. (Comments may be shallow and superficial, such as "nice shoes.") Working as a class, create a list of admirable characteristics (e.g., hard-working, honest, loyal). Display these characteristics in large print on cardstock taped high around the perimeter of the classroom walls. Tell your students that they will be giving each other a "pat on the back" again in a couple of weeks or more. Challenge your students to look for the characteristics you have displayed on the walls in one another and be prepared to give each other more meaningful "pats." Be sure to follow through and repeat the activity. (I, J, H)

Me and Maslow

Have students draw Maslow's hierarchy of needs, label the levels, describe someone they have observed personally or otherwise at each level, identify where they believe they are, and identify things they could do to advance toward self-actualization. (J, H)

Strengths and Weaknesses

Discuss the Wise Man's Prayer: "God grant me the strength to accept the things I cannot change, the courage to change the things I can, and the wisdom to know the difference." Assign students to write a paper finishing the following sentences. (I, J, H)

1. My most important strengths are . . . (Consider health, creativity, common sense, good habits, natural ability, integrity, skills, and so on.)
2. My most serious handicaps are . . . (Consider bad habits, bad temper, moodiness, antisocial tendencies, poor ways of problem solving, and so on.)
3. Things I can change for the better are . . .
4. Things I am going to have to accept are . . .

3-4 Communication and Relationship Skills Activities

The following activities can help your students develop communication skills and strengthen their interpersonal relationships as well as help you assess how proficient your students are at these skills. As you modify and develop these activities in your lesson plans, be sure to remember the suggested steps for teaching life skills.

Understanding with Feedback

Draw a geometric diagram on a 3 × 5 card. Give the card to one student and have him or her describe the diagram to the class without using hand gestures or allowing for clarifying questions. Have the class members try to draw what they think was described to them. Compare the students' drawings with the original. Repeat the exercise with a different diagram and student describer. This time, encourage students to ask clarifying questions. This exercise illustrates the need for active listening. (I, J, H)

Gossip

Whisper a message into a student's ear. Have that student repeat the message by whispering it in another student's ear. Continue this process until the message has been passed through the class. Have the last student to hear the message repeat it out loud and check whether it is the original message. This activity illustrates how there can be problems with sending and receiving messages. (P, I)

Body Language

Introduce the concept of body language with music or video clip from *The Little Mermaid*. With the students, identify various types of nonverbal messages (e.g., arms crossed, sitting forward or lounging back, palms opened or clenched, direct or indirect eye contact, amount of space between participants, voice inflections). Discuss how mixed messages can be given when verbal and nonverbal language do not agree. (I, J, H)

Emotional Charades

Have students act out different emotions, utilizing only nonverbal language. This activity can be used to help younger children identify and then label different emotions, demonstrate how emotions affect behavior, and demonstrate concepts in nonverbal communication. (P, I, J, H)

Concentration

Have students mentally do a lengthy dictated arithmetic problem such as the following:

$$5 + 2 - 3 + 8 + 10 - 11 + 4 + 25 - 10 + 50 = ?$$

Make the point that listening in conversations takes concentration as well. Have students pair up, and then have one person listen while the other discusses a topic such as "the happiest moment of my life" or "the most important person in the world." Ask the listener to summarize what the speaker said. (I, J, H)

Sociogram

Have the class break into groups containing five to eight persons. Have the groups discuss a question (e.g., Why are some people constantly putting down others? or What are some things that cause communication to fail?). As the group discusses the topic, a ball of string is passed from one speaker to the next, unraveling as it goes. Only the person holding the ball of string can speak. When another person wants to speak, the ball is passed and the string unravels more. After a few minutes, a sociogram will be revealed to the group. Group members can see who is dominating the conversation and they can include those who have not yet spoken. Repeat this exercise with another topic and challenge the students to do a better job of including everyone who wants to speak. (I, J, H)

Pictures of Emotions

Have students cut out pictures of people showing various emotions. Make a bulletin board. Discuss possible reasons for the feelings that are expressed. You can also include animal pictures. (P)

No Sound Track

Play an unfamiliar TV or DVD clip in class with the sound turned off. Ask the students to provide the dialogue of the situation they see on the screen based on how they read the actors' faces and body language. Discuss the various emotions they saw the actors display. (P, I, J, H)

Faces of Emotions

Have students try to match these pictures with the following emotions, or have them play charades trying to depict each of the emotions:

Anger	Distrust	Frustration	Pride
Confusion	Embarrassment	Happiness	Sadness
Contentment	Excitement	Indifference	Satisfaction
Determination	Fear	Love	Worry

(continues)

(continued)

Emotional Log

Have students keep a 2-day log of the emotions they observe in the people around them. For each observation, have the students write how and why these people felt as they did. (I, J, H)

Show-and-Tell

For show-and-tell, have everyone share an incident such as their most frightening experience, their most embarrassing experience, or a time when they were really hurt. Sharing can help them realize that others sometimes feel as they do and can help them be empathetic to others' feelings. You can also discuss how to deal effectively with these and other situations. (P, I)

I Feel . . .

Have students complete sentences such as the following to help them recognize their own feelings and better understand others. (I, J, H)

When nothing seems to go right, I feel . . .
When someone laughs at me, I feel . . .
When I do a good job on something, I feel . . .
When I am afraid, I feel . . .

Relationship Bank Accounts

Make various relationship "banks" by wrapping empty cereal boxes in paper with a picture of different types of people on the front of each bank to represent who the account is with (e.g., parent, teacher, friend, sibling). Create deposit slips as described on pages 64 and 65, using the pictures depicted here. Divide the class into as many groups as you have banks. Give each group a sheet of deposit slips and have them write examples of "deposits" that could be made in their bank (e.g., show interest in Mom's hobby, tell her "thank you" for dinner, take the garbage out, check when Mom wants you home, not talk bad about Mom to friends, apologize for not cleaning up your mess). Have each group share their examples of deposits as they place them in their banks. Distribute a new sheet of deposit slips to each student, and then have them choose a family member and write deposits they can make to strengthen that relationship. (P, I, J, H)

Here are some examples of deposits a teacher can make for a student:

Showing **interest** (Asking about her hobbies)

Small **change**—acts of kindness (Thanking her for collecting assignments)

Good **credit**—keeping commitments (Looking up the answer to her question)

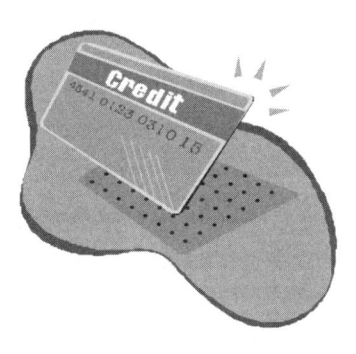

Checking expectations (Clarifying assignment grading criterion)

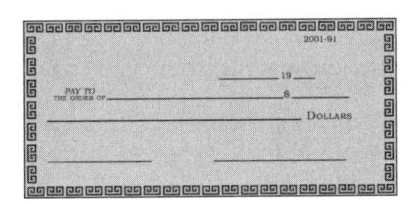

Pure **gold**—showing integrity (Not negatively talking about others)

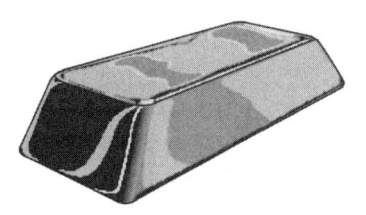

Cash—apologizing (Apologizing for making a grading error)

(continues)

(*continued*)

Good Friend Recipe

As a class, brainstorm the characteristics of good friends. Add those characteristics you want to emphasize. Have small groups create a "good friend recipe." Display the recipes on a bulletin board. (I, J, H)

Let's Do Dinner

Notify parents ahead of time, and then assign students to have a sit-down dinner with their family at least three times in one week. Instruct the families not to have any media on during the dinner and to eliminate any interruptions—mealtime is a time to eat and communicate with each other. Consider assigning topics for dinner conversation (world news, parents' experiences). At the end of the week, have students write a reflection paper on this activity. (I, J, H)

Random Acts of Kindness

Celebrate "Random Acts of Kindness Week" during the second week of February (or anytime). Discuss examples of random acts of kindness you and your students have experienced or given. Discuss how random acts of kindness for strangers are good, random acts of kindness for friends and family are better, and sustained acts of kindness for friends and family are best. (P, I, J, H)

Label Headbands

Carefully select four or more labels according to your classroom needs or your teaching objective (i.e., jock, popular, academic, Goth). Make headbands of these labels. Place your students into groups so that each group has one of each label. Don't let students know what their label says as you place headbands on them. Be sure to give students labels that are not characteristic of them. Instruct the students to do a group activity such as putting a puzzle together or discussing an issue. Tell them to interact with one another according to their labels. After the assigned activity, have students guess what their labels are, discuss how they felt with that label, explore why we stereotype people, and discuss how we can change the negative ways we interact with others into more supportive ways. (I, J, H)

I Do Care

Have students individually make a list of the most important people in their lives. Have them write down ways to show these people that they care about them (e.g., inquire about their activities, listen carefully, show appreciation and affection) and a list of things the students do that might make these people feel they do not care (e.g., don't listen, talk only about self, interrupt, criticize, break promises, never show appreciation or affection). Have students choose one person from their list and then keep a log of their interactions with that person for a week. Challenge students to make a conscious effort to increase the ways they show this individual that they care. (J, H)

3-5 Activities for Goal Setting and Self-Management

Let's Think About It

Display the following thoughts on bulletin boards to stimulate class discussions. (J, H)

- The poor man is not he who is without a cent, but he who is without a dream.
- What will I wish a month, a year, or 5 years from now that I had done today?
- No man has become a failure without his own consent.
- No man has ever climbed the ladder of success with his hands in his pockets.
- There are two kinds of people who never amount to much: those who can't do what they are told, and those who can do nothing else.
- Too many people itch for what they want without scratching for it.
- You can eat an elephant if you just eat him one bite at a time.
- Life by the inch is a cinch, but life by the yard is hard.
- Success comes in cans, not in can'ts.
- Success consists of getting up just one more time than you fall.

Stepping Stones

Teach goal setting by using the analogy of needing to cross a river. The other bank represents the goal you want to achieve. Stepping stones in the water represent steps needed to get to the goal. Identify several age-appropriate goals that students might have and the needed steps for accomplishing those goals. Draw a river with stepping stones. As you discuss each goal, write the steps to the goal on the stepping stones. Divide students into groups. Give each group two or more goals. Instruct the groups to draw a river for each goal and identify and label the stepping stones needed to reach each goal. (I, J, H)

Wishes to Reality

Have students write five things they wish to accomplish in the next 3 months. Ask them to choose one wish and work that wish through the first four of the six goal-setting steps included in this chapter. When they are finished, have students break into small groups and review one another's work for help in identifying aspects they may have overlooked. Challenge students to work toward their goals and support one another. Occasionally, have the small groups review their individual progress. At the end of 3 months, have students turn in a paper related to the project. (I, J, H)

Class Goal

As a class, set one or more class goals, either academic or behavioral. Help students write the goal, based on past performance, and have it be short range. Work through the goal-setting steps with the students, being sure to evaluate and then follow up with additional goals. (I, J, H)

Individual Academic Goal

Have each student, in conference or in writing, set a goal relevant to the class subject material. Review the goals set to see that they are based on past performance and that they are short range. If any goal does not meet these standards, help the student modify it. This is imperative if the student is to achieve the goal. (P, I, J, H)

(continues)

(continued)

Teach Study Skills

Sometimes the difference between the good student and the poor student isn't the amount of time spent studying, but rather the amount of effective time spent on this activity. Take time in class to teach study skills such as skimming, scanning, using parts of the text, previewing reading material, outlining, note taking, identifying key concepts, memorization techniques, and test taking. (P, I, J, H)

Bury the "I Can'ts"

Have each student list his or her "I can'ts" on a sheet of paper. Give students time to think and write until they have filled their paper with comments such as "I can't do long division," "I can't sit still very long," "I can't do a cartwheel," "I can't stand vegetables," and "I can't stay up late." Be sure and do this activity along with your students: "I can't get the school to give me more funding," "I can't get Justin to complete his homework," "I can't get Jennifer's mother to come in for a conference."

After 10 or so minutes, have the students put their pieces of paper into a shoebox that has been decorated to look like a coffin. Add your sheet of "I can'ts" to the box.

Lead your students out to the school yard and dig a grave for "I Can't." At the graveside, read the following eulogy. (If it is not possible to bury the box with your students present, modify this activity to meet your circumstances.)

> We have gathered here today to honor the memory of "I Can't." While he was with us on earth, he touched the lives of everyone, some more than others. His name, unfortunately, has been spoken in every public building—schools, city halls, state capitols, and yes, even the White House. We have provided "I Can't" with a final resting place and a headstone that includes his epitaph. He is survived by his brothers and sister, "I Can," "I Will," and "I'm Going to Right Away." They are not as well known as their famous relative and are certainly not as strong and powerful yet. Perhaps someday, with your help, they will make an even bigger mark on the world. May "I Can't" rest in peace and may everyone present pick up their lives and move forward in his absence. Amen.

After the funeral, cut out a large tombstone from butcher paper and write "I Can't" at the top, put "RIP" in the middle, and write the date at the bottom. Display this tombstone all year as a reminder for when a student forgets and says "I can't." When this happens, simply point to the tombstone and have your student rephrase his or her statement. (P, I, J, H)

Source: Adapted from Moorman C. Rest in peace: the "I Can't" funeral. In: *Chicken soup for the soul.* Deerfield Beach, FL: Health Communications; 1993.

Crisis

Ask each student to collect newspaper articles that describe how individuals have acted in crisis situations. Discuss whether these actions were reactive or proactive and why the students think the person acted as he or she did. (I, J, H)

Self-Actualization

Have students review Maslow's hierarchy of needs and examples of self-actualized individuals. Discuss the proactive characteristics these self-actualized people demonstrate. (J, H)

At the Top

Name and give a brief description of various successful individuals. Have students identify possible things these successful individuals had to work for and wait for—how they controlled their impulses and delayed their gratification. (I, J, H)

What Pushes My Buttons?

Ask students to think back over the last year and make a list of every incident they can remember when they got hot under the collar—not just the times they yelled, but all the times they were upset but did or said nothing. As a class, make a list on the board of "things that make me mad." This will help students recognize their anger triggers. Have them try to identify ways they can better cope with their anger triggers. (I, J, H)

What's My Anger Management Style?

Have students make a list of the last 10 times they were angry. Discuss the following anger mismanagement styles: (J, H)

- *Suppression:* swallowing the anger and acting passive. Research has shown that people who respond this way have a higher risk of developing migraines, ulcers, arthritis, hypertension, and breast cancer.
- *Punishing oneself:* feeling guilty or getting angry at oneself for being angry at others. People who do this may overeat or not eat, get too much or little sleep, or develop addictive behaviors such as alcoholism or over shopping.
- *Exploding:* going beyond appropriately expressing your feelings, often displacing the anger and using it to try to control others.
- *Sabotaging:* seeing oneself as the victim and trying to get even.

Suppress   Punish self   Explode   Sabotage

As a class, try to identify TV or movie characters who typically manage anger in these ways. Ask students to think of people they know who typically manage their anger in these ways. Have students think back to the last 10 times they were angry and see if they ever mismanaged their anger. Can they identify a pattern for how they typically manage their anger? Discuss healthy ways of dealing with anger, such as the following:

- *Express it.* Use "I" messages and active listening
- *Write a letter.* Express angry feelings but wait before mailing the letter.
- *Burn it off.* Jog, play basketball, chop wood, wash a car, or do some other physical activity.
- *Distract yourself.* Count to 10, sing a song, make a joke, pick up a magazine, and so on.
- *Look at negative thoughts.*

(continues)

(continued)

Letting off Steam

Show pictures of steam engines. Explain that steam can be both beneficial (fuel a steam engine) and harmful (burn you). Describe anger as emotional "steam." Discuss where it comes from and the proper and improper times and means of "letting it off." Have students make a simple poster illustrating both destructive and constructive methods of letting off steam. Discuss them and display them on a wall. (P, I, J, H)

Getting a Handle on Anger

Teach the following key anger management skills. The first set of skills concerns what to do long before you find yourself upset. The second group of skills concerns what you can do as soon as you find yourself getting upset. Have a rich class discussion on each skill. Provide examples from your own life and ask students to share as well. (I, J, H)

Before

- *Know yourself.* What makes you angry? What do you usually do with your anger? Which thinking patterns lead to your anger? (See the cognitive distortions discussed in the *Dealing with Stress* chapter.)
- *Develop a relaxation response.* The response could be counting to 10, doing a breathing exercise, singing a song to yourself, or visualizing yourself in a peaceful place—anything that helps you become calmer. (The *Dealing with Stress* chapter gives many more suggestions for managing stress.)
- *Practice using your relaxation response.* Practice looking at situations from other people's perspectives. Practice finding something funny in stressful situations. Practice asking yourself, "How big a deal will this seem a week, month, or year from now?"
- *Get connected.* When we feel isolated, we tend to get frustrated more easily and are more prone to hostility. Find a confidante, social group, or pet to spend time with.

During

- *Distract yourself.* Relaxation responses distract you from your anger trigger and negative thinking patterns. You can turn on the car radio if you get upset by traffic or pick up a magazine when aggravated by a long line in a grocery store.
- *Effectively communicate.* Explain your point of view using "I" messages.
- *Take 10.* Take a time-out, such as getting a drink of water or taking a walk, and use your extra energy in a productive way. During the time-out, look at your thoughts: Are they rational? Are there cognitive distortions? Try to look at the situation from the other person's point of view.

Anger Log

Have students keep a journal for a week or more of every time they were even a little bit upset. Have them record (1) what triggered the emotion, (2) what their thoughts were while they were upset, and (3) how they managed their emotions. (I, J, H)

Anger News

Share news articles about incidents in which anger was mismanaged. Have students identify the possible anger triggers in the incident. Have students identify what the persons involved might have been thinking at the time of the incident. Have students discuss how they could act to express their anger in a more healthy way if they were in the same situation. Mothers Against Drunk Driving (MADD) is a good example of positively using anger. (J, H)

Stop!

Have students pair up. Each student should take 2 minutes to tell the partner about a time when he or she was really mad, including every detail the student can think of. Halfway into the second student's time, yell "Stop!" as loudly as you can. Ask the students who had been talking what they were feeling when you stopped them. What caused them to feel this way? Ask them if their anger had been justified. Ask them to identify various positive ways they could express their anger in this situation. Explain that when they find themselves getting angry, it is helpful to yell "Stop!" and ask themselves these questions:

1. What am I feeling? (e.g., frustrated, threatened, insecure, afraid, mistreated)
2. What is causing me to feel this way?
3. Is my anger justified?
4. Am I still angry?
5. How can I positively express my anger?

Repeat the exercise with some volunteers at the front of the class telling about times when they were angry, the class yelling "Stop!" at your signal, and answering the five questions. (J, H)

Role-Play

Have students break into groups and write scenarios for role-play situations using a "top 10 things that make me mad" list. Have student groups take turns drawing a scenario, acting it out first using anger mismanagement styles, and then acting it out a second time using healthy anger management techniques. At appropriate times between the role-plays, have students identify irrational beliefs, cognitive distortions, or other perceptions that may be contributing to the anger. (J, H)

3-6 Decision-Making and Problem-Solving Activities

Decision-Making Styles

Display the following decision-making styles:

- *Reactive decision making:* allows others to overly influence or make decisions, lacks self-confidence and has a great need to be liked, gives control to others.
- *Inactive decision making:* fails to make choices, procrastinates, lacks self-control and direction in life, needs to take responsibility.
- *Proactive decision making:* follows decision/problem-solving steps; not driven by circumstances; not easily influenced by peers; guided by integrity, honesty, and dignity; in control.

(continues)

(continued)

Discuss examples of people who exemplify each of these styles and the consequences for each. Watch for examples to use from popular television programs or movies. You may want to show some clips. Challenge students to become proactive in their decision making. (I, J, H)

Apollo 13

Watch the movie *Apollo 13* and have students take note of the following: (I, J, H)

1. The realities—things that have happened that cannot be changed
2. The problems
3. How people act/react to realities and problems
4. How problems are solved (I, J, H)

What They Should Have Done

Collect newspaper articles about people who have made choices with negative effects (e.g., robberies, assaults, cheating, playing with guns). Discuss which early choices might have led to the major decision that resulted in tragedy. Discuss appropriate choices that could have prevented the negative outcome. (P, I, J, H)

"Dear Abby"

Request another class to write a "Dear Abby" letter about some problem they are having. Distribute these letters in your class to small groups and assign the students to answer the letters. Have groups exchange response letters and critique them for their helpfulness. Give the "Abby" letters to the class who wrote "her" about their problems. (I, J, H)

Recall Decision

Have each student write down one decision he or she made during the past 3 months. Have students list the alternatives and identify the decision. Have them evaluate the decision and rethink whether it is the same decision they would make today. (J, H)

Emotions and Decisions

Discuss how emotions can influence the decisions we make by giving several scenarios such as driving while angry or being afraid of what others will think. Ask students to relate their personal experiences. Discuss how emotions sometimes prompt people to make unhealthy choices. Discuss how good choices can be made in emotional situations. (J, H)

Thoughts on Thoughts

Make bulletin boards of the following quotes and discuss how our thoughts influence our ability to set and achieve goals, solve problems, make decisions, and resolve conflicts. (I, J, H)

Shakespeare: "There is nothing either good or bad, but thinking makes it so."
Milton: "The mind is its own place, and in itself can make a heaven of hell, a hell of heaven."
Ralph Waldo Emerson: "A man is what he thinks about all day long."
Norman Vincent Peale: "It has been said that thoughts are things, that they actually possess dynamic power. You can actually think yourself into or out of situations. Conditions are created by thoughts far more powerfully than conditions create thoughts."
Dale Carnegie: "Our thoughts make us what we are."
Hugh B. Brown: "You can't think crooked and walk straight."

Kids' Court

Have students brainstorm conflict scenarios that youth often face. From this list, select cases (scenarios) to try in kids' court. Select students to play the roles of the accused, defense attorney, prosecutor, witnesses, jury, and judge. Your role is to serve as moderator to assist students in their various roles. The jury decides on a win–win solution. (I, J, H)

Snow Ball: What Would You Do?

Have students anonymously write down a conflict they have observed or have had with someone. Have students wad up their papers and everyone throw them simultaneously and randomly in the air. Have students catch or retrieve a "snow ball," open it, and write how they would handle the problem on the paper. Share and discuss the varied conflicts and suggested win–win solutions. (I, J, H)

Problem-Solving Steps

Have students practice the problem-solving steps by giving them various scenarios and these visual clues. As a class or in small groups, assign students to different roles that represent each step. Have the "explorers" identify available resources for solving the problem. Have the "artists" look for creative alternative solutions. Have the "judges" look for probable consequences of the suggested solutions. Have the "warriors" role-play the solution. Be sure to help students first differentiate the problem from the realities of each scenario. Discuss what happens when we apply the steps in the wrong order. (I, J, H)

Identify the problem and reality.
© Timurd/Dreamstime.com

Explore available resources.
© James Steidl/Dreamstime.com

Creatively look for alternative solutions.
© Lepas/Dreamstime.com

(continues)

(continued)

Judge the probate consequences of each solution.
© Kasia Biel/Dreamstime.com

Choose and act.
© Dmitrijs Mihejevs/Dreamstime.com

Thinking Outside the Box

Here are two exercises that can help your students learn to think more creatively. The first one literally requires thinking "outside" the box. (I, J, H)

Draw the above dots on the board. Instruct your students to draw similar dots on a paper and then to connect the dots with four lines without lifting their pencils.

Instruct the students to draw a circle on their papers, pretend it is a pie, and "cut" their pie into eight pieces using only three cuts.

88   Chapter 3   Life Skills

Discuss how we get trapped into "boxed" thinking and need to be creative in looking at ways to solve problems.

Answers to the puzzles.

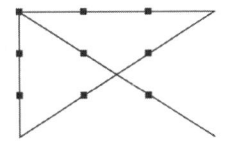

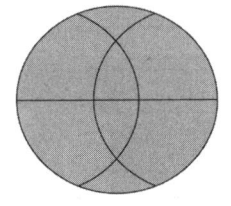

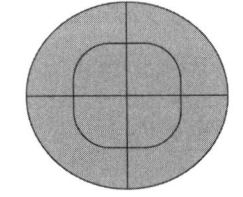

Activities for Mental and Emotional Health and Risk Behavior

■ **Additional Notes**

Instruction Plan Worksheet for Mental and Emotional Health

Use this worksheet to plan mental and emotional health instruction at the grade level you will be teaching. Refer to Chapter 2 for more information on how to complete each section in this worksheet.

■ Assess Needs

Identify topics and skills state or local curricula identify to be taught at ___ grade level.

Identify additional topics or skills the **ME HECAT Module** indicates for this grade.

Identify mental/emotional needs your particular students and their families have:
- What is the emotional climate of your classroom/school?
- What self-evaluation, communication, and relationship needs do your students have?
- What goal setting and self-management needs do your students have?
- What decision making and problem solving needs do your student have?

■ Set Major Learning Goal(s)

Identify your major learning goal(s)—what do you want to have happen?

■ **Develop Instruction Map**

Create a map (calendar or list of days) indicating the time frame you have/need to teach the curriculum, meet student needs and reach goal(s). For each day indicate the content/skills to be taught. Work to create a good flow.

■ Write SMART Unit Objectives

Write 1 or 2 major objectives for each day you will teach. Your objectives should be in alignment with your state/local curricula, your student's needs, and your major learning goal(s).

■ Identify Assessment Tools

Preassessment	Formative-Assessment	Postassessment
How will you determine what students already know or do?	How will you know if they are "getting it"?	How will you know if students master objectives?

Instruction Plan Worksheet for Mental and Emotional Health

■ **Develop Unit Plan**

Divide the chart into the number of days you will teach. Record each day's topic and objective key words. Identify activity names (in the book) that can help you meet each day's objective. Identify tech tools you can use and possible lesson adaptations you can make for special need learners.

Lesson Topic Objectives	Instruction Activities	Tech Tools	Adaptations for Learners

■ **Develop Lesson Plans**

Use the Lesson Plan Template found in Chapter 2 and this worksheet to create detailed lesson plans for your Mental and Emotional Health Unit.

KEY TERMS

life skills 50
World Health Organization (WHO) 50
HECAT 50
self-awareness 52
self-esteem 53
self-image 53
ideal-self 53
Pygmalion-self 53
self-worth 53
conditional worth 53
unconditional self-worth 54
values clarification 55
character education 56
Pygmalion effect 57
self-efficacy 57
self-evaluation 57
body language 58
mixed messages 59
"I" messages 59
passive listening 60
active listening 60
reflective listening 60

passive 60
aggressive 60
assertive 60
advocacy 61
empathy 61
contact 62
acquaintance stage 62
intimacy stage 62
deterioration stage 63
dissolves 63
relationship bank account 64
proactivity 66
reactive 66
impulse control 67
delayed gratification 67
win–win solution 70
resilience 71
protective factors 71
asset development 71
external assets 71
internal assets 72

KNOWLEDGE CHECK!

1. Define and explain the relative importance of each of the key terms in the context of this chapter.
2. Explain why WHO advocates life skills.
3. Describe the steps for teaching a life skill.
4. Describe a person lacking self-awareness. Describe what is necessary for a person to be self-aware.
5. Describe self-esteem myths and the problems these myths have generated. Identify the best predictor of success.
6. Explain how teachers can best nurture self-esteem and self-control.
7. Explain the different forms of self-worth, and explain how teachers can best foster a sense of worth in students.
8. Discuss influences on the ideal-self, and explain how teachers can help students develop character and values. Identify key aspects of character education.
9. Discuss the Pygmalion effect and provide examples of Pygmalion-positive and -negative scripting.
10. Discuss self-evaluation, and explain how teachers can help students review their self-perceptions.
11. Discuss important interpersonal communication skills identified in this chapter, and explain why students need assertiveness, advocacy, and empathy skills.
12. Identify and explain the various types of relationship bank deposits. Provide an example for each type of deposit in a teacher–student relationship.
13. Identify important components of goal setting, including the six steps involved.
14. Identify characteristics of reactive and proactive individuals, and explain how teachers can help students learn to be more proactive.
15. Discuss how impulse control and delayed gratification are related to health. Discuss how teachers can help students obtain these skills. Identify how to increase willpower and successfully make a big change.

16. Describe various anger management styles, and explain how teachers can help students learn anger management skills.
17. Identify and differentiate decision-making and problem-solving steps. Explain how teachers can teach problem-solving and decision-making skills.
18. Identify key concepts of conflict management, and describe how teachers can help students better manage conflicts.
19. Describe the attributes of resilient youth, and explain how teachers can facilitate resilience in youth.
20. Summarize how teachers can help students develop more assets.

■ REFERENCES

1. UNICEF. Life skills: which skills are life skills? 2004. Available at http://www.unicef.org/lifeskills/index_whichskills.html. Accessed April 17, 2013.
2. World Health Organization. *Skills for health* (Information Series on School Health Document 9). Geneva, Switzerland: WHO; 2003.
3. Twenge JM. *Generation me: why today's young Americans are more confident, assertive, entitled—and more miserable than ever before*. New York, NY: Free Press; 2006.
4. Pinsky D, Young SM. *The mirror effect: how celebrity narcissism is seducing America*. New York. MU: Harper Collins; 2009.
5. Borders MJ. Project hero: a goal-setting and healthy decision-making program. *J School Health*. 2009;79(5):239–243.
6. Lickona T. *Educating for character: how our schools can teach respect and responsibility*. New York, NY: Bantam Books; 1991.
7. Obama B. Inaugural address [transcript]. *New York Times*. January 20, 2009. Available at http://www.nytimes.com/2009/01/20/us/politics/20text-obama.html. Accessed April 17, 2013.
8. Center for the 4th and 5th Rs. What is a comprehensive approach to character education? 2002. Available at http://www2.cortland.edu/centers/character/. Accessed April 17, 2013.
9. Covey SR. *The seven habits of highly effective people*. New York, NY: Fireside; 1990.
10. McGonigal K. *The willpower instinct: how self-control works, why it matters, and what you can do to get more of it*. New York, NY: Penguin; 2012.
11. Fergus S, Zimmerman M. Adolescent resilience: a framework for understanding healthy development in the face of risk. *Ann Rev Public Health*. 2005;26:399–419.
12. Masten AS. Resilience in children at risk. *Research/Practice*. Spring 1997;5(1).
13. Center for Substance Abuse Prevention. *Making prevention work*. 1997.

Chapter 4
Stress Management Skills

Stress Journal

It's been a bad day. All of my teachers just dumped tons of homework, like they got together and decided now was the time to make life miserable for us. I swear, each of them thinks their class is the only class in the world, and most of the stuff is irrelevant and just a bunch of busy work. Err, and the test I took today, I studied my head off, but you'd never know by my grade. The questions were worded weird and Mr. Warrick asked stuff that wasn't even on his study guide!! Errrr, I'm really, really mad about that!!!! Then, there's the drama with my friends. . . . Katie is mad at Jennifer, Brad dumped Emily, and somehow I'm in the middle of it all, and no matter what I do someone's going to end up mad at me. Worst of all, I'm broke, like pockets turned inside out broke, and Mom won't give me any money. Uggggg.

Stress management is an integral part of promoting mental and emotional health. It, along with the life skills discussed in the previous chapter, is typically addressed in mental and emotional health units. Stress management skills are also integral components of units on nutrition, physical activity, drug, sexuality, violence prevention, and safety.

■ UNDERSTANDING THE NATURE OF STRESS

Stress is defined differently by different people. Eastern philosophies view stress as "an absence of inner peace." Western culture views stress as a loss of control and an inability to cope with problems. The term "stress" was first used by Hans Selye, a pioneer in the study of stress.[1] He simply defined **stress** as "the nonspecific response of the body to any demand made upon it." Selye coined the term **stressor** to refer to specific or nonspecific situations or demands that cause stress. Stressors may be specific (e.g., conflict between a child and teacher, giving an oral report in class, or nearly being hit by a car while crossing the street), but the response is a generalized physiological response. This generalized response, which is known as the **general adaptation syndrome (GAS)**, consists of three stages (also see **Figure 4-1**):

1. *Alarm.* The body initially responds to a stressor (whether real or imagined) by preparing for a physiologic emergency. This response has been referred to as the **fight-or-flight response**. The stress hormones cortisol, adrenaline, and noradrenaline are released to provide instant energy. Instantaneously respiration and heart rate increase, blood flow increases to the heart and skeletal muscles, pupils dilate, and fatty acids are released. The body is prepared to handle the emergency.
2. *Resistance.* With the source of the stress possibly resolved, the body attempts to restore balance, also known as **homeostasis**, and begins a period of recovery for repair and renewal. If stress persists, the body adapts by demonstrating continued resistance and arousal. When the body experiences alarm too often or maintains resistance too long, it enters the third stage.
3. *Exhaustion.* Long-term exposure to a specific stressor or a combination of stressors can deplete the body of the energy that it needs to return to homeostasis. The body then maintains a

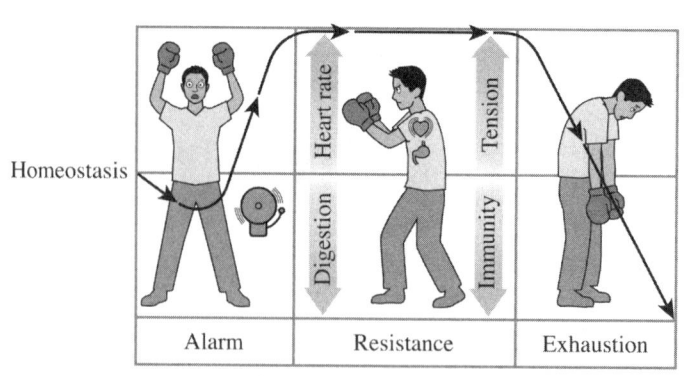

FIGURE 4-1 Three phases of GAS.

perpetual state of alarm, which runs the body into exhaustion. The exhaustion stage is the most hazardous stage to health.

We have all experienced alarm from time to time. Imagine yourself carelessly crossing a street when you suddenly realize that a speeding car is coming right at you. Your heart pounds, your muscles flex, and you find yourself jumping farther and running faster than you ever thought possible. Your body is in motion before you really have time to think, as it utilizes all its energies for survival. Once you are safely out of the car's path, you take a deep breath and over time your body returns to its former relaxed state. This is an example of **acute stress**, something that is intense and disappears quickly. **Chronic stress**, by comparison, is less intense but persists over prolonged periods of time. Poverty, learning disorders, and unstable home life can be forms of chronic stress. Three types of stress include **eustress** (happy stress, such as falling in love), **neustress** (neutral stress, such as calamity in a remote corner of the world), and **distress** (sad stress, such as losing your car keys).

Our autonomic nervous system, which is in charge of the fight-or-flight process, consists of the sympathetic and parasympathetic systems. If you think of your body as a car, the **sympathetic** nervous system is the gas and the **parasympathetic** system is the brakes. Both systems are partially active at all times, but with only one dominating at any given time. This means that you cannot be physically aroused and relaxed at the same time. The many stressors we experience today sometimes put us in a chronic state of alarm where we are constantly applying the gas and not taking the time to brake. All too often days, weeks, and even months pass without our relaxing—that is, returning to a state of homeostasis.

The endocrine system plays a major role in stress, with the pituitary, thyroid, and adrenal glands all secreting hormones that target certain organs. These hormones affect metabolism, blood pressure, gastrointestinal activity, sleep, and many other things. For example, cortisol is a hormone released from the adrenal cortex that facilitates the metabolism of fats for energy. During stress, increased levels of cortisol are produced, which in turn increases the amount of cholesterol in the blood. This cholesterol provides the energy needed for "fight or flight," but we usually don't "burn" it off because of our inactive lifestyles. Increased cholesterol levels can facilitate plaque buildup in the blood vessels.

■ DISEASE AND STRESS

Stress creates changes in our nervous and endocrine systems and then manifests itself in our bodies as tension headaches, backaches, insomnia, and heart disease. As was just noted, stress can elevate cholesterol, which in turn leads to plaque buildup in blood vessels and heart disease.

TABLE 4-1 Diseases and Conditions Caused or Aggravated by Stress

Accident proneness	Musculoskeletal disorders
Anorexia nervosa	Low back pain
Bulimia	Migraine headache
Cancer	Tension-type headache
Cardiovascular disorders	Muscle tension
Constipation	Obesity
Diabetes	Pain
Diarrhea	Psychological disorder
Gastrointestinal disorders	Respiratory disorders
Menstrual irregularities	Asthma
	Hay fever
	Skin disorders
	Ulcer

Stress can also play a role in the onset or aggravation of migraine headaches, asthma, hay fever, ulcers, diarrhea, constipation, eczema, allergies, influenza, and even the common cold. Cancer, lupus, and diabetes have also been found to be linked to stress (**Table 4-1**).

Stress causes physiological changes that tend to weaken the immune system. When the immune system becomes compromised, the body is vulnerable to disease. The **immune system** is a complex set of organs—highly specialized cells and the lymphatic system—all of which work together to clear infection from the body. Lymphatic vessels and lymph nodes carry **lymph**, a transparent fluid containing white blood cells, chiefly lymphocytes. Lymph bathes the tissues of the body, and the lymphatic vessels collect this fluid and move it back into the blood circulation. Lymphocytes are transported to tissues throughout the body, where they act as sentries on the lookout for foreign antigens. The two major classes of lymphocytes are B cells and T cells. **B cells** produce antibodies that circulate in the blood and lymph streams and attach themselves to foreign antigens to mark them for destruction by other immune cells. Certain **T cells**, which also patrol the blood and lymph for foreign invaders, can do more than mark the antigens: they attack and destroy diseased cells they recognize as foreign. T cells also orchestrate, regulate, and coordinate the overall immune response.

UNDERSTANDING YOUR STRESS

Before you read any further, take a few minutes to identify what things stress you right now and then rank order your stressors (see **Box 4-1**). After you do this, try and identify how you psychologically respond to your stress (become irritable, depressed, sullen, eat, . . .) and how you physically respond to your stress (get a headache, get tight neck or back muscles, unable to sleep, . . .).

If you are like most people, your top three stressors are related to time, money, and relationships. You may have discovered while doing the Marks on You exercise in the *Teaching to Make a Difference* chapter that you do a lot more teeter-tottering when you are under stress. Anger and resentment are two other common psychological responses to stress. Perhaps you "carry" your stress in tight neck, shoulder, or back muscles. Being self-aware of your stressors and your psychological and physical responses to stress can help you identify how you can better manage your stress.

New research indicates that men and women under stress fundamentally cope differently. Different parts of the brain become activated in men and women when they are faced with performance-related stress. Men's brain activity response is often characterized as "fight-or-flight,"

4-1 Application Exercise

Stress Management Plan

Before you can effectively help your students manage their stress, you need to assess and improve your own stress management skills. The exercise presented here is intended to help you identify your stress, discover how you deal with your stress, and figure out how you can better manage your stress. Do the following in order:

1. Make a list of your top three or four stressors.
2. Identify triggers for each of these stressors.
3. Identify how you physically respond to stress (e.g., muscle tension, headache).
4. Identify how you psychologically respond to stress (e.g., thinking patterns, moods).
5. Create a personal stress management plan:
    a. Identify specific things you will do to reduce stress.
    b. Identify stress coping skills you will practice.
    c. Identify relaxation skills you will practice.
6. Put your plan into action for a full week. Write a reaction paper that includes all of the elements in your stress management plan and discusses what you learned from doing this exercise.

---

whereas women's brain activity is characterized as "tend-and-befriend."[2] Perhaps you have noticed these differences. Women tend to want to reach out to others and talk through their stress; men tend to become quiet and withdrawn and cope with the stress on their own. Understanding these fundamental differences is helpful in maintaining good relationships.

Cognitive Distortions

Your thinking patterns play a major role in the amount of stress you experience. We experience stress when we perceive something as stressful. For instance, having a "bad hair day" may be perceived as terribly embarrassing by one teenage girl and mildly annoying by another. Uncooperative hair doesn't cause stress, but thinking that one's hair must be perfect does.

You are undoubtedly like most people and have some distorted thinking patterns that exacerbate the amount of stress you feel. Your students, particularly adolescents, are also prone to **distorted thinking patterns**. Review these categories of distorted thinking and see if any of them seem familiar—if they describe you or someone you know.[3]

- ◆ **All-or-nothing thinking.** Anything less than perfection is a failure. Evaluating in extreme black-or-white categories. "I spilled my glass of water—the dinner was a disaster." "I got a 93% on the test—I blew it!" "If part of me is bad, I'm all bad."
- ◆ **Jumping to conclusions.** Conclusions are not tested but are based on hunches, intuition, and experiences. There are two types: mind reading—"She did that on purpose!" or "My teachers don't like me"—and fortune telling—"Those parents wouldn't come if I asked them to" or "I'd blow it if I tried."
- ◆ **Overgeneralizing.** Thinking in a negative pattern. Key words are *always* and *never*. "I always make that mistake." "He never listens."
- ◆ **Filtering.** Dwelling on the negative details or aspects of a situation to the exclusion of all other details and concluding that the whole situation is negative. "That kid has ruined my whole day." "How can I concentrate when my hair looks terrible!"

- ◆ **Discounting the positive**. Accomplishments are the result of luck or are not really meaningful. "He got lucky." "Anybody could have done it."
- ◆ **Labeling.** Giving oneself or another person a label based on imperfections, as though a single word could completely describe a complex human being. "I'm so stupid." "He's an idiot."
- ◆ **Magnification**. Thinking that something is so horrible or so awful that one cannot bear it. In the process one feels helpless and pathetic. "I can't take this anymore!" "He's driving me nuts!"
- ◆ **Emotive reasoning**. Thinking that feelings are reality. "I feel inadequate, so I *am* inadequate."
- ◆ **Blaming**. Feeling that others are responsible when, in fact, we are. "She *makes* me so mad."
- ◆ **Self-blame**. Accepting responsibility for things we actually have no control over. "If I were a better mother. . . ." "It's all my fault my parents are getting a divorce."

Watch for the following red flag words to help spot irrational thinking patterns and beliefs: "must," "should," "always," "never," and "can't." Some of the most common irrational beliefs include feeling excessively upset over others' mistakes or misconduct, believing you have to be competent and successful in everything to be valued and worthwhile, believing avoiding difficulties and challenges will make you happier, and feeling that your happiness is dependent upon external forces outside of your control.[4]

Restructuring Your Thinking

Once we recognize we are having a distorted thought or are holding to an irrational belief, we can restructure our thinking. To do so, we can reevaluate the situation with a broader perspective (e.g., does he really "always" do that?), check and fine-tune our expectations (e.g., do I have to be perfect?), distract ourselves (look at a magazine) instead of focusing on the upsetting circumstance, or get quiet and listen for our own inner wisdom. Practicing just 5 minutes of daily meditation can profoundly decrease the amount of stress we feel and increase our self-control.[5] We can also "act ourselves" into new ways of thinking (e.g., smiling until we feel happy.)

Recognizing our negative thinking patterns can be a powerful means of gaining control over our emotions and soothing ourselves. By changing our thinking patterns, we can change what we feel. Take the example of Ann, a very conscientious young driver who drives her parents' new car to school. Ann is in the habit of swearing under her breath at inconsiderate drivers on the road. As a result, she often arrives at her destination exasperated, tense, and angry. In class, she learns how negative thoughts can produce negative emotions and takes the challenge to think positively of those she perceives to have wronged her. On her way home, a car pulls out in front of her and Ann has to slam on the brakes to avoid a collision. Just as she is about to burst forth with colorful language, she remembers her resolve and instead says aloud, "I . . . I . . . I . . . I bless you to get wherever you are going safely!" Immediately she starts laughing, feeling relaxed, calm, and even happy. Ann had been in the habit of thinking that others were thoughtless, self-centered, reckless drivers out to put a ding in her parents' new car and get her in trouble. In actuality, poor drivers like the one who pulled out in front of her might be confused, distracted, or ill. When Ann blessed the other driver, she in effect blessed herself.

UNDERSTANDING YOUR STUDENTS' STRESS

Once more, before you read any further, take a few minutes and try and remember what things stressed you in elementary school, in junior high, and in high school. What were you most concerned about? What made you mad? Which fears did you have? Perhaps your memories paint a picture of the "good ole days" where you had little stress, or maybe you recall painful events or interactions and vivid fears. Can you remember which stressors some of your classmates had in their lives? Your memories can help you recognize what might be causing stress for your students and give you insight into how to help them.

Although stress is a natural part of life and necessary for growth and development, it can be overwhelming, and young people can respond to it in negative ways. Some examples of less serious reactions are fatigue, headaches, stomach problems, mood swings, and poor attention span. More serious reactions include behavioral problems, depression, mental illness, unhealthy behaviors, and suicide.

Day-to-Day Hassles

It is important that educators acknowledge that it is not only major life events or highly stressful environments that take a toll on the lives of young people. Day-to-day problems and irritants have a cumulative effect and can be destructive as well. Examples of daily hassles that concern young people are physical appearance and peer acceptance, homework assignments and tests, and misplacing or losing things. Repeated minor hassles can add up to a major stress reaction.

Economic Stressors

The economic climate of the community in which young people grow up greatly affects the amount of stress they experience. Living in poverty or crowded housing, being exposed to a pervasive drug culture and periodic street violence, and attending poor schools are all highly stressful. Economic downturns can be very stressful for young people, especially when the adults in their lives encounter frustrations and do not have good stress management skills. Unemployment, debt, and diminished funds can put a family in a state of crisis. Bad economic news by itself can create stress for young people if they worry about things like their parent's job security, the possibility of friends having to move away, not being able to go to college, or not being able to get a good-paying job someday.

Immigration

One in five children in the United States lives in an immigrant family. These children have stressors that children of native-born parents do not have, including adapting to cultural norms that may differ from those of their parents and learning a language that may not be spoken at home. Poverty is another prevalent factor for these children, with a disproportionate number of them being the poorest of the poor. They may be ineligible for food stamps, and their families may experience a great deal of stress in obtaining and paying for food. Children in immigrant families are also less likely to receive public assistance, including Medicaid, than other low-income children. As a result, they may not seek out health care and may suffer from untreated health problems. Immigration poses additional stresses on children and families, including the loss of support systems; anxiety, depression, or grief associated with migration and acculturation; and trauma from events that preceded or occurred during their migration.[6]

Natural Calamities

Fires, hurricanes, tornadoes, earthquakes, and a host of other natural disasters can be very stressful for children, adolescents, and their families. Evacuating before or riding out a natural disaster is very stressful in and of itself. That stress is greatly compounded if a person's home, school, or community is damaged or destroyed. Following the devastation of a natural disaster, most young people are able to cope over time with the help of parents and other caring adults. The severity of a child's or adolescent's reaction to the disaster depends on the degree of exposure, personal injury, or need to relocate.

Teachers play a vital role in helping affected school-age children cope and recover. When natural disasters hit an area, teachers and schools can do several things to help meet students' needs:[7]

◆ Identify the unique needs of every student whose home has been destroyed or damaged and try and connect their families with supportive resource agencies.

- Create a list of phone numbers and addresses of students who have to relocate so that classmates can stay in contact with them.
- Listen—provide a variety of opportunities for students to discuss the event and how they are coping, understanding that it is normal for them to discuss it repeatedly.
- Use art, music, drama, and play to help students express their emotions.
- Integrate the natural disaster event into subject areas studied, such as science, math, and history.

Home-Based Stress

The home environment can give children a sense of belonging and structure, provide appropriate role models, and teach communication and social skills, all of which buffer the degree of stress children experience. In the home, youngsters initially learn stress-coping techniques that are modeled by parents, other adults in the household, and older siblings. Unfortunately, some young people's homes are stress-filled places where they see adults handle stress in unproductive and unhealthy ways.

Overscheduling

The American lifestyle is often characterized as being "on the go." It has almost become an American norm for parents to enroll their children in every extracurricular activity they can fit into their schedule. Some children are constantly on the go because their scheduled activities serve as baby-sitters for their working parents. From predawn until late at night, children and adolescents participate in team sports; take music, art, and dance lessons; attend school, scouting, and other youth group activities; and engage in community service.

Children and adolescents can benefit from the social skills often developed in play. When a child goes out to play, the child has to find someone to be with, convince that person to play, negotiate what to play, teach others how to play, help enforce the rules, and decide when to stop. Being overloaded with extracurricular activities prevents the child from engaging in these activities and can have a greater negative impact than the positive impact of the extracurricular program on development.[8]

Family life in the fast lane can leave both children and parents exhausted and irritable. Some schools have instituted "family nights" to try to give students and their parents time to relax and enjoy one another's company. On these family nights, no homework is assigned and no school activities are scheduled. Parents have also become proactive in some communities, stating that "enough is enough." These parents have organized themselves and taken petitions to local youth sports programs, schools, and community officials requesting that these institutions schedule their activities in a more family-friendly manner.

Lack of Sleep

Many Americans, both children and adults, get less sleep than they need. On average, we sleep 1 hour less than we need on weeknights and 30 minutes less than we need on weekend nights. By the end of the year, we are short 338 hours. **Sleep deprivation** is the result, and the lack of sleep can be very stressful. Stress is experienced when we don't have the energy and alertness we need to concentrate and interact effectively with others. Lack of sleep also causes physical stress on the body, especially when sleep deprivation becomes a way of life. Poor academic performance, unintentional injury, and obesity have been associated with shorter sleep durations.

Many adults and children become sleep deprived from staying up late at night watching TV programs or movies. Others become fixated on computer games or Internet surfing. Parents who let their children fall asleep in front of the television compound the problem.

Young people also become sleep deprived as they try to cram 28 hours of living into 24 hours. Many adolescents, in an effort to gain an edge in the competition to get into a highly rated university, sign up for every possible school sport and activity while trying to earn top grades and give community service. When these youth finally try to go to bed, they are often too wired to fall asleep.

Sleep experts say that first through fifth graders need to have 11 to 13 hours of sleep per night, but average only 10 hours. Preteens need 9 hours of sleep, but average only 8. Teenagers average

6 to 7 hours of sleep, but they need between 9 and 10. Students report their lack of sleep makes them tired in school, makes it hard for them to pay attention, contributes to their earning lower grades, increases their stress levels, and increases problems of getting along with others.[9]

School districts in a few states have shifted their schedules to give teens a little more time to sleep before school begins. Those who oppose such moves argue that a later starting time wreaks havoc on work, bus, after-school, and extracurricular activity schedules. The end result might be teenagers getting to bed even later, nullifying the desired outcome of more sleep.

Home Alone

Being home alone can be stressful for children. The number of children home alone without direct adult supervision has mushroomed in the last 20 years as the number of single-parent households and the number of families in which both parents are employed outside the home have increased dramatically.

Children left home alone are at risk for a variety of problems. Sometimes children who are routinely left to care for themselves are more fearful than those who receive adult supervision. Two prevalent fears are that someone will break into their home and hurt them while they are alone and that older siblings will harm them. Children home alone may also be more lonely and bored than supervised children are. Some evidence indicates that children who are unsupervised over large periods of time are at higher risk for having personality problems and depression during adolescence and adulthood. Children who are left unsupervised are also at increased risk of sexual abuse and accidents. Conversely, sometimes children who look after themselves achieve greater self-confidence and independence than those who are supervised by adults.

Media Exposure

We often think of relaxing in front of the television set, but viewing television programs and watching DVDs might not be as relaxing as we think. The amount and type of TV programming a young person watches influence the amount of stress he or she feels. Disturbing news reports of criminal activity, wars, natural disasters, and economic woes are stressful. Violent acts depicted in movies, TV shows, and video games can be distressful. Nightmares and night terrors can result from viewing troubling images. There is also evidence that heavy TV viewing is linked to depression, anxiety, and obesity.

Parental Conflict

Parental conflict can arise from numerous situations, including financial problems, alcoholism, adultery, abuse, and selfishness. Rarely is a child responsible for marital discord, but children almost always feel somehow responsible. Children experience high levels of stress as they deal with their parents' fights and their own misplaced guilt.

Separation and Divorce

Parental separation can be traumatic and creates stressful situations for children and adolescents. Separation can occur when a parent is deployed by the military or leaves to look for employment. Whatever the reason for separation, psychological separation is more traumatic for a child than physical separation from a parent. Separation from siblings can also create significant stress.

Approximately half the families in the United States have undergone the pain of marital separation, with 60% of those partings affecting children. In addition to the stress associated with separation, parental divorce has been linked in children to delinquency, psychological disturbance, hostility and acting-out behavior, low self-esteem, early home leaving, and poor self-restraint and social adjustment. When a parent remarries, children have to contend with a new series of adjustments, such as having a new parental figure in the home, feeling conflicting loyalties between biological parents and step-parents, and dealing with new routines, responsibilities, and personal space issues. All of these adjustments are intensified when stepsiblings are involved. Children of parents granted joint custody must also make the monumental adjustments of living in two different households. For many children of divorced families, school represents the only stable part of their environment. In such cases, educators and school personnel should be prepared to assess the student's behavior for signs of stress and recognize the signs of emotional problems.

Dysfunctional Families

Children reared in **dysfunctional families** are exposed to many childhood stressors, such as parental alcoholism or drug dependency, mental illness, ineffective parenting skills, and poor communication patterns. Alcoholic parents often place unreasonable demands upon their children, such as keeping secrecy about the alcoholic's behavior, taking responsibility for the alcoholic, neither acknowledging nor expressing their own feelings, accepting the blame for their parent's drinking, and providing emotional support and companionship for the alcoholic's spouse. (A detailed discussion of children of alcoholics is provided in the *Promoting a Tobacco-Free and Drug-Free Lifestyle* chapter.)

Poor Health and Death

Chronic or acute health problems experienced by a sibling or a parent can be stressful for young people. They worry about the future, the pain the loved one is experiencing, and their own health—will they get sick, too? Sometimes they become the caregiver and have nursing responsibilities. Often they take on additional household duties such as cleaning, cooking, and caring for siblings.

The death of a parent or loved one represents a tremendously stressful life event for a child or adolescent. Acceptance of the death often takes many months to a few years. Reactions depend largely upon the child's age and developmental level. Fortunately, most children survive a parent's death with only minor emotional scars, but effective coping is assisted greatly by supportive adults. (A more detailed discussion of children and death is provided in the *Dealing with Crises and Critical Issues* chapter.)

School-Based Stress

The school environment presents a number of conditions and situations that can evoke stress in children and adolescents. Examples of stressors encountered in the school environment include teacher attitudes, behavior, personality, and mannerisms; English being a second language; peer pressures and harassment; homework; grading and evaluation; competition and academic pressure; length of the school day; and extracurricular activities. Competitive stress occurs when teachers place emphasis upon competition in school situations. When teachers overemphasize competition and the need to finish first, unnecessary stress is created in the lives of students. Boredom is another school stressor. Polls taken often reveal that on a given day, half of teens surveyed in the United States say they primarily feel bored while in class. Bullying is a major stressor for far too many school-age youth. You can read more about bullying and how to prevent it in the *Violence Prevention and Safety Promotion* chapter 9. **Box 4-2** provides assistance in recognizing stress in students.

Early Grades

Children in kindergarten, first grade, and second grade often feel a great deal of stress about schoolwork, understanding work assignments, and completing creative projects correctly. After schoolwork stressors, the greatest source of worry for these youngsters is peer relationships. Peer relationship stressors include peer pressure, friendships, sharing, playing, and arguing. Other prominent stressors for children of this age are personal injury or loss (getting hurt, pushed, or kicked; theft; emergency drills; destruction or loss of personal belongings) and loss of personal

Physical activity helps release stress.

4-2

Recognizing Stress in Students

The following checklist may help you identify students who are experiencing excessive stress. Students with several of these signs or symptoms may need referral to appropriate counseling professionals. These signs appear in children who have experienced a loss (e.g., parental separation or divorce, death of a loved one) or are having difficulty at home or school (e.g., rejection by classmates, difficulty with schoolwork, parental drug dependency). The more signs or symptoms a child has, the greater the likelihood he or she is experiencing a stress-related or stress-induced problem. Children who are suffering great levels of stress exhibit it in their patterns of behavior. Often, they:

_____ Complain of headaches

_____ Complain frequently of an upset stomach

_____ Have out-of-control crying episodes

_____ Show evidence of not getting enough sleep

_____ Exhibit general tiredness

_____ Frequently appear irritable

_____ Appear restless

_____ Exhibit loss of appetite

_____ Have difficulty paying attention in class

_____ Tend to be physically aggressive with other children

_____ Easily become upset by changes

_____ Tend to quit tasks that are difficult

_____ Display difficulty concentrating

_____ Appear to lack emotion

_____ Seem depressed

_____ Lack self-confidence

comfort, space, or time (school schedule, homework interfering with personal time, loss of recess time, noise in lunchroom, changing classes, teacher not present or absent).

Middle and Upper Grades

Older children and adolescents also experience stress over schoolwork caused by being bored, not understanding the material, not having enough time in the day for homework, or worrying about grades. The more prominent school-related stressors for adolescents, however, are social rejection and fear of exposure in public. Losing friends, being ignored socially, feeling rejected, speaking in public, and making mistakes are examples of stress-provoking fears among adolescents. Anxiety over these fears can lead some students to develop regressive or self-destructive behaviors, school phobia, academic difficulty, and withdrawal. To counteract these tendencies, parents, teachers, counselors, and school administrators should assist adolescents in identifying and coping with these fears.

Teachers

Teachers can also experience stress in the school environment. Their stress is greatly intensified when they feel unsafe, unsupported, overworked, or out of control. Persistent long-term school-related stress can facilitate teacher **burnout**—a condition in which teachers become emotionally exhausted and ineffective. The *Teaching to Make a Difference* chapter gives insight into how to create a supportive school environment and effective classroom discipline. The stress reduction, coping, and relaxation skills in this chapter can help teachers as well as students better deal with the stress they experience at school. **Box 4-3** provides suggestions for reducing stress at school.

4-3

Reducing Stress at School

Teachers can do the following things to reduce the amount of stress they and their students experience in school:

- Establish and maintain classroom routines, procedures, and rules.
- Avoid using a harsh voice or screaming. When problems arise, handle them immediately and consistently. Try to correct students in private.
- Facilitate appropriate humor.
- Create a supportive culture by maintaining the class/school as a teeter-totter-free zone and facilitating hydraulic-lift experiences between students.
- Monitor hallway, schoolyard, and lunchroom activities.
- Use a variety of teaching methods and provide a break in concentration at least every 20 minutes.
- Remember that a degree of stress enhances academic performance, but that too much anxiety impairs functioning.
- Coordinate with other teachers and try to avoid giving major tests on the same days.
- Create a mechanism for students to obtain needed help for homework assignments.
- Institute family-friendly nights free of homework and during which parents are encouraged to keep media turned off and to participate in family-based activities.
- Contact the parents of any student who is persistently tired.
- Teach students stress-reducing, coping, and relaxation skills. Provide them with opportunities to practice these skills.

Unless otherwise indicated, the content from this section is adapted and condensed from the National Institutes of Mental Health.

STRESS AND MENTAL DISORDERS

Stress and mental disorders are strongly correlated. Stress can contribute to the onset of a mental disorder, and persons suffering from a mental disorder experience enhanced stress. The most common mental disorders include depressive and anxiety disorders.

Depressive Disorders

A **depressive disorder** is an illness that involves the body, mood, and thoughts. It affects the way one eats and sleeps, the way one feels about oneself, and the way one thinks about things. Depressed individuals experience persistent (2 or more weeks) symptoms including sad or irritable moods, appetite or sleep changes, loss of energy, trouble concentrating, feelings of worthlessness or inappropriate guilt, thinking about death or suicide, and lost interest in activities once enjoyed. Depression is not the same as a passing blue mood, and it is not a sign of personal weakness or a condition that can be willed or wished away. People with a depressive illness cannot merely "pull themselves together" and get better. Without treatment, symptoms can last for weeks, months, or years, but appropriate treatment, including learning stress management skills, can help most people who suffer from depression.

TVs, computers, and cell phones in the bedroom affect the quality and amount of sleep children get.

Only in the past 2 decades has depression in children been taken very seriously. Approximately 11% of adolescents have a depressive disorder by age 18. Girls are more likely than boys to experience depression. According to the World Health Organization, major depressive disorder is the leading cause of disability among Americans ages 15 to 44. Children and adolescents who have depression are more likely to have a family history of the disorder.

Because normal behaviors vary from one childhood stage to another, it can be difficult to tell whether a child who shows changes in behavior is just going through a temporary "phase" or is suffering from depression. The depressed child may pretend to be sick, refuse to go to school, cling to a parent, or worry that the parent may die. Childhood depression usually shows up in behaviors, not in verbal communication. Older children may sulk, get into trouble at school, be negative and grouchy, and feel misunderstood. Teachers can pay attention to the following signs in a child: cries easily, appears sad most of the time, doesn't seem happy with special activities or playthings, withdraws from friends and activities, becomes unusually sensitive and easily upset, has trouble concentrating and making decisions, pervasive negative attitude, low energy, and vague physical complaints.

Signs of depressive disorders in tweens and teens are often viewed as normal mood swings typical of a particular developmental stage. It can also be difficult to recognize depression in adolescents because they are likely to mask their feelings with behaviors not usually identified with depression, such as aggression, sexual promiscuity, academic failure, abuse of alcohol and other drugs, running away, and accident-proneness. Adolescents suffering from depression are more able to verbalize their sadness, if someone asks them about it, than are children.

Early diagnosis and treatment of depressive disorders are critical to healthy emotional, social, and behavioral development. Depression that occurs early in life often persists, recurs, and continues into adulthood. Depressed adolescents are at increased risk of substance abuse, suicide, and other mental disorders. Depression also increases a person's risk for heart disease, diabetes, and other diseases. Most youth can be effectively treated with medication or psychotherapy, or a combination of the two. Youth are more likely to respond to treatment if they receive it early in the course of the illness.

We now take a look at various forms of depression. **Major depressive disorder**, also known as **major depression**, is characterized by a combination of symptoms that interfere with a person's ability to work, sleep, study, eat, and enjoy once-pleasurable activities. Major depression is disabling and prevents a person from functioning normally. Some people may experience only a single episode within their lifetime, but more often a person has multiple episodes.

Dysthymic disorder, or **dysthymia**, is characterized by long-term (2 years or longer) symptoms that may not be severe enough to disable a person, but can prevent normal functioning or feeling well. People with dysthymia may also experience one or more episodes of major depression during their lifetimes.

Minor depression is characterized by having symptoms for 2 weeks or longer that do not meet the full criteria for major depression. Without treatment, people with minor depression are at high risk for developing major depressive disorder.

Not everyone agrees on how to characterize and define the following forms of depression. **Seasonal affective disorder (SAD)** is characterized by the onset of depression during the winter months, when there is less natural sunlight. The depression generally lifts during spring and summer. SAD may be effectively treated with light therapy, but nearly half of those individuals with SAD do not get better with light therapy alone. Antidepressant medication and psychotherapy can reduce SAD symptoms.

Bipolar disorder, also called **manic-depressive illness**, is not as common as major depression or dysthymia. Bipolar disorder is characterized by cycling mood changes—from extreme highs (e.g., mania) to extreme lows (e.g., depression). Bipolar spectrum disorder is rare in children but tends to manifest itself in adolescence and early adulthood.

You can read more about depressive disorders in children and adolescents on the American Academy of Child and Adolescent Psychiatry's webpage.

Assisting Young People Who Are Depressed

Schlozman presents the following advice for classroom teachers concerning childhood and adolescent depression.[10]

- ◆ Because teachers are on the "front lines," they may be the first to observe something is wrong. Suspected depression should be discussed with parents and a trained health professional such as a school counselor, psychologist, or nurse.
- ◆ Teachers need to be aware that depressed students often feel as if they have little to contribute. A teacher can help by showing confidence, respect, and faith in a depressed student's abilities and by not doing things in the classroom that would raise the student's anxiety. For example, when a teacher asks questions for which there is no clearly correct answer, a depressed student may be more likely to participate in a classroom discussion.
- ◆ Another way to increase a depressed student's confidence is to have the student assist younger or less able students in some way.
- ◆ Help young people who are depressed in forming a connection with a trusted teacher or other adult. This kind of relationship is often central to a young person's recovery from depression.
- ◆ When depressed students have difficulty discussing their feelings, it might be helpful for them to identify with literary or historical figures and use them as a proxy to explore their own feelings.

It is critical that educators recognize that none of the suggestions for helping depressed students in the classroom should substitute for the appropriate diagnostic evaluation and treatment of depression. Treatment for depressive disorders in children and adolescents often involves short-term psychotherapy, medication, or both, and interventions involving the home or school environment.[11]

Anxiety Disorders

Intense and unfounded fear is the common denominator in all anxiety disorders. We all experience fear. Six basic human fears include fear of failure, fear of rejection, fear of the unknown, fear of isolation, fear of losing control, and fear of death. **Anxiety** can be a normal reaction to a fearful stress, but when it becomes an excessive irrational dread of everyday situations, it constitutes a disabling condition. Symptoms of many anxiety disorders begin in childhood or adolescence. Approximately 8% of teens have an anxiety disorder, with symptoms commonly emerging around age 6. Imaging studies have shown that children with anxiety disorders have a typical activity in the fear-processing and emotion-regulating centers of the brain. Almost 20% of children are born with low levels of gamma-aminobutyric acid (GABA), a brain-soothing chemical. These children are in a constant state of fear even though they don't know they're anxious, because they have always felt that way. As a result, they are often shy, hang back, and act clingy.

Medications are sometimes prescribed for anxiety disorders, but effective cognitive psychotherapy and counseling techniques that teach relaxation, meditation, and positive self-talk have also been found to be very effective. The Anxiety Disorders Association of America has a very good website for teachers and parents of students with "worried brains." **Box 4-4** lists several Internet support sites related to mental health.

4-4

Internet Support for Mental Disorders

The following organizations have websites that provide helpful resources and teaching materials on mental disorders:
- American Academy of Child and Adolescent Psychiatry www.aacap.org/
- American Association of Sociology www.asanet.org/
- BAM! Body and Mind www.cdc.gov/bam/
- Anxiety Disorders Association of America www.adaa.org/
- Centre for Suicide Prevention suicideinfo.ca/

We now look at various anxiety disorders. **Generalized anxiety disorder (GAD)** is characterized by someone being extremely worried about many things, even when there is little or no reason to worry. Individuals with GAD are very anxious about just getting through the day and think things will always go badly. GAD develops slowly, but often starts during the teen years. Symptoms may get better or worse at different times, and often are worse during times of stress.

Someone with **obsessive–compulsive disorder (OCD)** feels the need to check things repeatedly. He or she has certain thoughts or performs routines and rituals over and over that get in the way of daily life. Frequent upsetting thoughts are called **obsessions**. As part of the effort to control these thoughts, a person will feel an overwhelming urge to repeat certain rituals or behaviors called **compulsions**. For many people, OCD starts during childhood or the teen years.

Stress in many forms can decrease a student's ability to learn.

Most people are diagnosed by approximately age 19. Symptoms of OCD may come and go, and be better or worse at different times.

People with **panic disorder** have sudden and repeated attacks of fear that last for several minutes, sometimes longer. **Panic attacks** can feel as if the person is having a heart attack and are characterized by a fear of disaster or of losing control even when there is no real danger. An attack can occur at any time, and people with panic disorder worry about when and where the next attack will take place. More women than men have this disorder, but not everyone who experiences panic attacks will develop panic disorder.

Post-traumatic stress disorder (PTSD) can occur after seeing or living through a dangerous event. People who have PTSD may feel stressed or frightened even when they're no longer in danger. Nightmares and flashbacks may be experienced.

Social phobia is a strong fear of being judged by others and of being embarrassed. Most people who have social phobia know that they shouldn't be as afraid as they are, but they can't control their fear. For some people, social phobia is a problem only in certain situations, whereas others experience symptoms in almost any social situation. Without treatment, social phobia can last for many years or a lifetime.

Teachers can help students with social phobias by being empathetic and by creating a warm, caring classroom environment where teeter-tottering is abolished and hydraulic lifts are encouraged. A life-line buddy can be assigned to a particularly shy student. Teaching students relaxation and meditation techniques can also help them deal with various forms of anxiety.

■ STRESS REDUCTION SKILLS

Managing stress is a little like being able to balance life on a three-legged stool (**Figure 4-2**). We need skills for coping while under stress, skills for being able to relax and help our bodies return to homeostasis, and skills for reducing the amount of stress we experience. If any one of these three skills is missing or inadequate, our lives will be very difficult to balance.

Stress reduction skills include all the things we can do to help us limit the amount of stress we experience in life. As noted earlier, most people's top stressors are related to time, money, and interpersonal relationships. Developing interpersonal communication skills, time management

FIGURE 4-2 We best manage stress and balance our lives by developing each of these types of skills.

skills, and money management skills are enormously beneficial for reducing stress. Activities for developing communication skills can be found at the end of the *Life Skills* chapter. We'll now take a closer look at time and money management. Activities for developing these skills can be found at the end of this chapter.

Time Management

Time management entails several skills, including the following:

- Prioritizing what you want and need to do with your time
- Organizing yourself
- Being self-disciplined

Prioritizing entails identifying and then doing the most important things first. Identifying what is most important is generally fairly simple—the difficulty comes in maintaining the self-discipline to accomplish what we know we should do first. Becoming organized can be a complex skill for students to learn. In an effort to help students be more organized, some schools provide them with day-planners that contain calendars on which students can record dates of tests and due dates for major assignments. These planners also provide students with an organized means of keeping track of daily assignments and homework. When planners are not provided, teachers can help students develop their own.

Teachers also can help students develop time management skills by teaching them how to break down a large assignment into steps with self-imposed due dates. For example, if a paper is due on February 20, a self-imposed rough draft due date of February 13 and a second draft due date of February 17 can be charted. Students who want minimal stress can also make their final due date one day earlier than that given by the teacher. Completing the work early prevents stress caused by rushing to complete an assignment at the last moment or from a computer or printer breakdown. Model the skill of time mapping for your students by displaying your unit plans or teaching calendar.

Money Management

The following are money management tips from financial experts. Following these recommendations will greatly reduce the amount of stress experienced in life. As you review the tips, consider how relevant they are in your life. Reflect on how you can teach and reinforce these principles in your classroom.

1. Pay yourself first—save!
2. Set financial goals and use a budget.
    - Budgeting is distasteful when used to keep us from what we want.
    - Budgeting is liberating when used to help us get what we want.
3. Avoid debt like the plague.
    - Perform plastic surgery (cut up credit cards).
    - Get out of debt.
    - Use debt only for things that grow in value over time.
4. Do without and use creativity.
    - Shop infrequently and avoid the mall.
    - Determine the "use cost" of an item before deciding to buy it. (A $5 shirt worn only once has a use cost of $5. A $30 shirt worn 30 times has a use cost of $1. Which is the better buy?)

- ◆ Do not expect to have what your parents have—now.
- ◆ Eat at home, buy in bulk, and cook from scratch.
- ◆ Help people move—you will recognize your junk better when you have to lift others'.

5. Have appropriate amounts of insurance (e.g., health, car, home, life).
6. Work toward home ownership. Buy modestly—not the maximum you can borrow.
7. Both partners in a relationship are responsible for finances.

- ◆ Set financial goals and make a budget together.
- ◆ Divide money management chores.
- ◆ Each person has a personal slush fund (amount determined by the budget) that can be spent any way that person wants and does not have to be reported to the partner.

Study and Test-Taking Skills

Students can read without gaining any meaning from what they read, missing the major and supporting ideas. Knowing how to read a textbook is an important study skill for all students to learn. Students can be taught to first scan a chapter's major headings and quickly identify the major concepts and important facts or principles. Younger students can practice this skill by first looking at pictures and trying to guess what the story is about. Students also need to develop the habit of reviewing key terms and questions before actually reading a chapter. Learning how to outline a chapter and use a glossary are other important study skills.

One of the best ways to learn how to take tests is to learn how to construct them. Having to write multiple-choice, matching, short-answer, and essay questions from given content helps students identify which material lends itself to the different kinds of questions. Constructing tests can also help students identify key concepts and facts. Reviewing good test-taking practices such as scanning the entire test, circling key words such as *not*, and eliminating obviously wrong possible answers are additional test-taking skills. It is also very helpful for students to learn how to relax during an exam by using diaphragmatic breathing (discussed later in this chapter); this practice can help them overcome anxiety-induced mental blocks.

Rest and Sleep

Getting adequate rest and sleep reduces the amount of stress an individual experiences and helps a person better cope with everyday hassles. Sleep also improves memory and learning, as during the sleep state the brain rehearses new information and works to create more stable neural circuitry. Encourage your students to remove all technology from their bedrooms when they sleep. Text messages can interrupt sleep cycles and create what is termed "**junk sleep**." Looking at television and computer screens before going to bed affects melatonin levels and can make it more difficult to fall asleep. Sleep specialists suggest not looking at a lighted screen for an hour before trying to go to sleep.

Giving and Serving

Those who give and serve are happier, experience less stress, have greater productivity, and live longer. The acts of giving and serving change us biochemically: we produce fewer stress hormones and more feel-good chemicals like dopamine. The **helper's high** is a euphoric physically measurable phenomenon. It makes people feel energized, like getting what some call a spiritual buzz. Donating our time or money seems to act as an antidote to stress, chronic pain, and insomnia. Giving has been shown to activate feel-good chemicals such as dopamine in the brain. Brain scans have shown that pleasure centers of the brain are more activated by giving than by receiving something. Just watching others give and serve can be stress reducing.[12]

STRESS COPING SKILLS

Stress **coping skills** are techniques that help us effectively deal with difficult circumstances or times in our lives. Children and young people can learn to be effective copers. Effective copers are likely to have role models whom they emulate and from whom they learn specific coping skills. In addition, effective copers have people they can turn to for support, encouragement, and advice. Children with effective coping skills are able to enjoy play, smile, and laugh. We now look at coping strategies and consider how teachers can help students develop coping skills.

Think About Thinking

Earlier in the chapter, we discussed distorted thinking patterns that bring about stress. One of the most powerful ways to cope with stressful situations is to become aware of what we are thinking in the moment. Writing down our thoughts or talking out loud can help us become aware of our inner monologues. The Marks on You activity in the *Teaching to Make a Difference* chapter can also help us become aware of our thinking patterns. As we pay close attention to what we are thinking, we can watch for "red flag" words including *should*, *must*, *always*, and *never*. We can also notice our emotions and ask ourselves questions such as "Why do I feel this way?" and "What am I telling myself about this situation?" Other things we can do when we find ourselves in a stressful situation include these options:

1. Reevaluate the situation. Step back and look at it with a broader perspective.
2. Check and fine-tune our expectations. Are they realistic? Are they shared?
3. Distract ourselves with music, exercise, reading, playing, laughter, ...
4. Get quiet and listen for our own inner wisdom that gives us insight.
5. Act ourselves into a new way of thinking, such as smiling first to become happy.

The old advice of counting to 10 in a frustrating situation can be very helpful, especially if during that time we evaluate why we are frustrated, check any thinking patterns that add to our frustration, and determine whether the situation is worth getting upset over. Humor can especially be helpful in a frustrating situation. One family has a rule that they can argue about anything, but when doing so they must lie down beside each other and sing their hostilities to one another. This family has discovered that arguments handled in this way soon turn into giggling sessions. Additional anger and conflict management skills are identified in the *Life Skills* chapter.

Humor

Perhaps nothing dissipates the stress response more quickly than humor. Humor can reduce pain, diffuse anger and anxiety, buffer the amount of stress experienced, and give one a sense of power in the middle of chaos.

Here is a true story that exemplifies this effect. A man we know was unexpectedly laid off and unable to find comparable employment for more than a year. Just 2 weeks after becoming unemployed, he awoke to discover his home was on fire. He was able to get his family out safely and retrieve his car from the garage, but nothing else was salvaged. A month after his home burned to the ground, his car—the one he had saved from the fire—was totaled. He and his entire family were in the car on a congested freeway when they were struck from behind by a driver who failed to slow down when the traffic came to a standstill. The family was propelled into a barrel pit and rolled several times in the car before it stopped with the tires in the air. Miraculously, no one was injured in either the car accident or the home fire. Equally miraculous is the fact that no one in the family developed a health problem as a result of all the stress experienced in the traumatic events and from battling insurance companies, hunting for new housing and employment, and grieving lost possessions. The fact that they continued to enjoy good health despite all their stress was in part a result of their use of humor. The father was in the habit of using humor to cope with stress. For instance, as the fire fighters were running toward the front door to try to save some of the house, he yelled out to them, "Don't forget to wipe your feet!"

Learning to not take life too seriously, to laugh at one's own shortcomings, and to look for humor in everyday situations is enormously helpful in managing stress. You can help your students enlarge their funny bone by studying and trying to use various types of humor. As you read through the following list, consider if you ever use these types of humor. Look for examples of each in the comics section of your newspaper. Create a "humor file" you can turn to when stress builds in your classroom.

- **Parody**: imitating something or someone for comical effect. This is the type of humor used at celebrity roasts.
- **Satire**: a written expression of personal or social inadequacies. Dave Barry is a popular satirist.
- **Slapstick**: physical humor such as being hit in the face with a pie or slipping on a banana peel.
- **Absurdity**: using two or more concepts that result in a stupid, ludicrous, or ridiculous perception. *The Far Side* comic strip was based on absurd humor.
- **Irony**: when two concepts or events are paired to mean the opposite of the expected outcome, such as ordering a highly caloric meal and then a diet drink.
- **Puns**: playing with words that have more than one meaning or connotation. Young children particularly like this kind of humor.
- **Black humor**: poking fun at death, often as a means of dealing with fears. Cancer patients and sometimes gravestone epitaphs provide examples.
- **Sarcasm**: a biting jab that is often followed by the remark, "I'm just kidding." It might be clever, but satire induces rather than reduces stress.

When teachers use humor in the classroom, it is important to help students differentiate humor from ridicule. Carefully review the differences contained in the *Healthy Laughter* activity in **Box 4-6.** Humor reduces stress and facilitates learning; laughing at someone else's expense does not. This truth can be emphasized by discussing the teeter-totter syndrome and hydraulic-lift principle addressed in the *Teaching to Make a Difference* chapter. Putting someone else down so as to elevate ourselves never makes us feel better for very long.

Journal Writing

Keeping a journal not only helps students develop writing skills, but also helps them identify and express their emotions. Encourage students to keep a stress journal, focusing on the stressors they encounter during the day. Writing such a journal can teach children to the following skills:

- To identify specific situations at home and school that are stressful
- To describe feelings and reactions to stressors
- To learn how to avoid certain stressors in their environment
- To gain insight into how to cope or confront stressors
- To provide feedback about efforts to avoid and control stress

Play

Play serves as an important stress management tool in the lives of children. Through play, they can symbolically reenact and solve problems as well as relieve tension. Preschool-and kindergarten-age children particularly need time to play to facilitate brain and emotional/social skill development. Play helps children learn natural consequences, and understanding natural consequences helps them develop what is often referred to as common sense.

Physical Exertion

One of the best ways to help students handle stress is to provide opportunities for regular physical activity. Sports, games, dance, and other activities can serve as a diversion from stressors. When students play hard, they forget about other things that are bothering them. Exercise also helps students relax by releasing excess muscle tension, by causing fight-or-flight stress hormones to be metabolized, and by encouraging the body to release endorphins. Endorphins, which are chemicals produced by the body, are closely related to opium and create a feeling of well-being. Exercise also increases the amount of oxygenated blood reaching the brain, thereby facilitating learning. There are many activities at the end of the chapter that you can use while teaching your students stress coping skills.

■ RELAXATION SKILLS

Relaxation skills are activities that help the body return to a relaxed state—that is, homeostasis. They can be used to deal effectively with an intense stressor or with the effects of cumulative stress. Although some relaxation techniques require special training or equipment (e.g., yoga, tai chi, biofeedback), those reviewed here are relatively easy to teach and are highly effective. People can use the various skills independently, but often combine them in relaxation exercises such as deep breathing and visualizing a restful scene while listening to music. We now describe various relaxation skills and many activities that can help you teach relaxation skills to your students.

Diaphragmatic Breathing

Diaphragmatic breathing is controlled deep breathing using the lower abdomen rather than expanding the upper chest area. It is exhibited by people deep in sleep when the stomach distends as the diaphragm expands. While awake, we often expand our chests rather than use our diaphragm to breathe. Expanding the chest area drives the sympathetic nervous system. When pressure is taken off of the thoracic area (chest), the sympathetic drive decreases and the parasympathetic drive overrides the sympathetic system, resulting in homeostasis. Diaphragmatic breathing to relax can be used in any setting and is particularly helpful in diminishing the amount of pain we experience. Learning to relax with breathing is a major part of the Lamaze natural childbirth method.

Normally, we breathe without thought, but diaphragmatic breathing requires concentration. When our minds wander, as they will, we simply bring our thoughts back to our breath. Noting what repeatedly pops into our thoughts while we are doing breathing exercises helps us become aware of our thinking patterns and facilitates **cognitive restructuring**. These are some exercises you and your students can practice:

1. While doing diaphragmatic breathing, notice which of your nostrils is dominant—one almost always is. Try and reverse it to make the other nostril dominate.
2. Place your hands on your abdomen and visualize your diaphragmatic breathing to be like riding a wave. The wave is the expansion and contraction of the stomach area.
3. Visualize yourself repeatedly inhaling clean, crisp mountain air and exhaling dark, cloudy smoke that represents all your stress, including frustration and other negative feelings.

Autogenic Training

Autogenic training entails learning to reverse or minimize the stress response using conscious thoughts. It is a means of exerting a degree of control over our respiratory, circulatory, and muscular systems. Your students can quickly learn the principles of this technique, but it might take a few weeks of practice for them to feel the effects fully. Two elements are key to autogenic training:

1. Learning to make your body feel heavy.
2. Learning to make your body parts, or your entire body, feel warm.

The feelings of heaviness and warmth are key indicators that our parasympathetic nervous system has taken charge and our bodies are beginning to return to a state of homeostasis. Do you remember what you did when you were little and your parents said it was time to go to bed, but you didn't want to go? Did you become limp whenever they tried to pick you up? Instinctively, you were trying to make yourself heavy—and this heavy sensation is what you want to feel in autogenic training. Warmth can be generated by simply thinking to yourself, "My arms and hands feel warm." Thoughts can direct our circulatory system to send more blood to a given area of our body or to the surface tissues of our entire body. The redirection of blood flow creates the sensation of warmth. Learning to warm parts of our bodies generally takes more practice than learning to become heavy.

Visualization/Imagery

Mental imagery allows us to forget about stressors and achieve a relaxed state by visualizing a pleasant situation. Visualized scenes that induce relaxation are quiet, peaceful, and warm. Imagined water in the form of a mountain stream, lake, river, or ocean also encourages relaxation. Visualizing oneself performing a physical task such as an athletic move to perfection can be relaxing as well.

It is often helpful for students with persistent test anxiety to practice mental imagery in combination with breathing and autogenic training. Have them get into a relaxed state and then imagine themselves taking a test while maintaining that relaxed state. They can also use mental imagery just before taking a test to help themselves become relaxed.

Progressive Muscular Relaxation

Progressive muscular relaxation is a technique used to help people become aware of the difference between relaxation and tension in the different parts of their body. Stress can cause muscle tension in various locations of the body, such as the neck, shoulders, and back. Young people can learn **progressive relaxation** by tensing and relaxing muscles in one set of muscles after another.

Music and Art

Music can alter our moods and either relax or excite us. Have you ever noticed the type of music played in elevators? This acoustic slow-tempo music is piped into elevators to help people better cope with the stresses of being with strangers in a small, confined space while rapidly ascending or descending. Young people usually prefer fast-paced energizing music, but teachers can help students identify more tranquil forms of music to listen to while coping with stress.

Drawing, painting, and creating other artwork in a relaxed setting can also facilitate a state of homeostasis. Some athletes find it therapeutic to color between events at major athletic competitions. Art can also be an effective tool for expressing thoughts, feelings, and perceptions. Teachers can use art to get a glimpse of what their students are thinking and feeling. Children may draw or paint their mental perceptions of school experiences, family experiences, and themselves. They draw what they know and feel, rather than what they see. A teacher cannot really understand a student's drawing, however, until the artist explains it. When you have students draw, do not praise any completed work (praise implies judgment of the worth or value of the student), instead say something like, "You've worked hard on this drawing" (to convey acceptance of feelings) and "Tell me about your drawing" (to gain insight). As a student responds, note what each part of the drawing represents according to what the student communicates about it (verbally and nonverbally). If a student draws a disturbing picture or pattern of pictures, and your impressions are supported by interactions with the student, relay your concerns to a school counselor or psychologist.

Psychological and emotional evacuation through art is very complex. **Table 4-2** provides some general guidelines for interpreting a drawing. **Figures 4-3**, **4-4**, and **4-5** provide examples of children's artwork for inspection. You can see additional children's artwork in the *Dealing with Crises and Critical Issues* chapter.

TABLE 4-2 Guidelines for Interpreting Artwork

Characteristics	Feeling Indicated
Colors Predominately Used (if child has choice)	
White	Overwhelming object or experience
Black or purple	Depressed feeling
Warm, light colors	Happy mood
Yellow	Cheerful
Red or orange	Excited or anxious
Green	Refreshed
Blue	Calm
Darker colors	Unhappy, sad
Overall General Impression	
Lightly or hesitantly drawn	Inadequacy
Darkly or heavily lined drawing	Unexpressed anger
Compartmentalized picture	Isolation, insecurity
Scribbling over or erasing part or all	Anxiety over what was revealed in drawing
Figures tiny in comparison to paper	Insecurity, withdrawal
Figures large	Competence, security
Significance of Figures or Parts of Drawing	
Shaded or omitted part(s)	Anxiety over function or symbolic importance of part(s)
Exaggerated or oversized part(s)	Feeling (e.g., power or lack of power) proportional to person or object drawn exaggerated or oversized; exaggerated or oversized object or person is more powerful
Omitted hands or legs	Painful or worrisome anxiety, inadequacy, insecurity
Indication of Family Relations	
Size of each member and order in which members drawn	Largest denotes most powerful
Position of members in relation to closest relationship	Those closest to each other denote those with each other
Omission of self or placement of one member far away from others	Does not feel part of family
Similarity of expressions or clothes of members	The more similar, the stronger the relationship
Family members without hands and/or not standing firmly on ground	Helpless or ineffective

Source: Adapted from Servonsky J, Opas SR. *Nursing management of children.* Sudbury, MA: Jones and Bartlett; 1987.

FIGURE 4-3 This drawing shows how a happy, adjusted 8-year-old boy saw his family.

FIGURE 4-4 A 10-year-old girl drew this picture when she was "feeling sad" one day. Note the detail and largeness of the figure.

FIGURE 4-5 A self-portrait by a 5-year-old. The child was very happy, yet chose to draw with black and brown colors, stating, "I like these colors on this paper. They show up!"

4-5 Activities for Reducing Stress

The following activities can be modified and embellished to meet many different objectives and be appropriate for many different grade levels. Stress management is often included in units studying mental and emotional health, nutrition, drugs, sexuality, violence, and safety.

Stress Reduction Activities

First Things First

Demonstrate the concept that we need to do the most important things first with the following demonstration. Display a wide-mouth glass, four or five large rocks, pebbles, sand, and a glass of water. Ask students what you should put into the jar first. Proceed to fill the jar (rocks, pebbles, sand, and water in order). Explain that time works the same way. If we don't do the most important things first, we won't find time. Have the class identify their "rocks." They might say homework, piano practice, or chores. Pass out a day or week time-planning sheet and have the students block out the time for their most important things first on their charts. (As a modification. you can use ping pong balls, marbles, and pellet balls to fill the jar.) (I, M, H)

Source: Covey SR, Merrill AR, Merrill RR. *First things first.* New York, NY: Simon & Schuster; 1994.

Where Does the Money Go?

Have students brainstorm a list of things they spend money on (e.g., food, clothes, entertainment, transportation). Make up and tell a story about a student who had a certain amount of money and how he unwisely overspent and didn't have enough funds for what he really wanted. Have students develop a budget for this fictional student. Have students identify something they really want but for which they need to save. Give each student a 3 × 5 card, and have the students draw or paste a picture of the thing they need to save money for. Instruct them to create columns on the other side of the card for categories of things they typically spend money on. Have them identify how much money they typically have each month and then determine how much they can afford to spend in each category and still save for what they want. Instruct them to carry their card and record on it every purchase they make for one month. At the end of the month, review the budget cards, evaluate students' progress toward their goal, and adjust the budget as needed. Reward the class's biggest saver. (I, M, H)

(continues)

(continued)

Book Chase

Help students learn textbook reading skills (scanning; skimming; using an index, glossary, and table of contents) by breaking students into groups. Be sure stronger-skilled students are included in each group. Tell students that they are going to have a competition to see which group can find the answers to questions in their text the most quickly. The first group to have every member with their finger on the page with the answer in their book raised high over their head wins that question. Group the questions so that the same text reading skill is repeatedly practiced. (I, M, H)

Surprise Quiz

Announce an unexpected pop quiz and proceed to give it. Stop after a number of questions and ask how the students feel. Discuss their physical and psychological reactions to learning about the quiz and then during the quiz. Discuss things they can do in the future to minimize stress (study and do homework) and relax (diaphragmatic breathing). (I, J, H)

Sleep Log Competition

Create a graphic like those used in telethons to raise money. Each day, have students "fill in" the number of hours of sleep they got the night before. Have a contest with another class to see who can "log" the most sleep in a week. The winning class can wear their pajamas to school as a prize. This activity helps create a positive social norm for getting a good night's rest. (P, I, J, H)

Spare Change

Help students experience the helper's high by having them choose a charity, family, or individual that they would like to help. Get a large jar or other container and encourage students to deposit their spare change in it. Have a delegation from the class deliver the raised funds. An example of this type of campaign is "Pennies for Peace," which you can read about at http://www.penniesforpeace.org. (P, I, J, H)

Secret Elves

As a class, do a "sub for Santa" or other similar activity for someone in need, such as raking a widow's leaves. Students could even do secret acts of service for each other or for members of their family. (P, I, J, H)

Volunteer

Research volunteer opportunities in your community and make a list of places where your students can donate time. Volunteer as a class or create incentives (i.e., assignment, extra points) for students to volunteer on their own or in teams. (I, J, H)

Altruistic Quotes

Post quotes like the following on bulletin boards and discuss them in class. (I, J, H)

- "Only a life lived for others is worth living."—Albert Einstein
- "Life's most persistent and urgent question is, what are you doing for others?"—Martin Luther King, Jr.
- "I don't know what your destiny will be, but one thing I know: The only ones among you who will be truly happy are those who have sought and found how to serve."—Albert Schweitzer

4-6 Stress Coping Activities

Marks on You

This activity is written as an application exercise in the *Teaching to Make a Difference* chapter. It provides great insight into negative thinking patterns. It can be adapted to check for various cognitive distortions. (I, J, H)

Rescript It

Play a video or TV clip(s) of a character demonstrating a cognitive distortion. Have your students rescript how that character could more healthfully look at the situation. (P, I, J, H)

Talk It Out

Talking about our stressors helps us cope better by helping us feel understood, cared about, and not isolated. It can also open the opportunity for others to share their healthful coping habits. Facilitate students talking about their stress by placing them in small groups and asking them to respond to statements such as "What stresses you out?" (J, H)

Lighten Your Load

Teach the importance of forgiving in stress reducing with this object lesson. Forgiving doesn't mean saying, "What you did was okay," but rather "I'm not going to waste any more time and energy on ...". Have students brainstorm examples of offenses or grudges that are hard to forgive. Write their ideas on rocks or cans of food. Fill a backpack with labeled rocks or food cans and have a student wear the pack for one day, including at recess or during physical education class. Have the student share how the pack affected his or her day. Discuss how forgiveness lightens your load—it's something you do for you. Take the rocks or cans out of the pack one by one and discuss how a person could go about forgiving each offense.

Fear and Shadow Games

Turn out the lights and use a spotlight to show the frightening shadows that ordinary objects can make. Involve students by asking them to suggest other objects that cast shadows. Discuss fear of the dark and how they have or might be able to overcome their fear. (P, I)

Healthy Laughter

Review the following chart in a class discussion where you identify how and when humor reduces stress levels and when it increases stress levels.

Laughing with
1. Going for the jocular
2. Caring and empathy
3. Builds confidence
4. Involves people in fun
5. Laughing at self
6. Amusing
7. Supportive
8. Builds bridges
9. Pokes fun at universal human foibles

Laughing at
1. Going for the jugular
2. Contempt and insensitivity
3. Destroys confidence
4. Excludes some people
5. Being the butt of a joke
6. Abusive, offensive
7. Sarcastic
8. Divides people
9. Reinforces stereotypes by singling out a particular group as the "butt"

(continues)

(continued)

Joke of the Day

After reviewing the various types of humor, encourage students to bring in examples they find to share in class. Be sure to instruct them first on what constitutes respectful, healthful humor. (I, J, H)

Caption That

Collect a series of funny baby pictures from off the Web. As you show your students each picture, have them try to come up with funny captions for it. (I, J, H)

Humor File

Have students create their own personal humor file of things that make them laugh. This file can contain stories or drawings about personal experiences, clipped cartoons, jokes, quotes, or pictures. Encourage students to use their file to help them when they need to lighten up. (P, I, J, H)

Mini-vacation

When stress builds in the classroom, have the students make a funny face or do a funny dance—anything to create a distraction or to add humor to the situation. Taking a "mini-vacation" can reduce the amount of anxiety the students feel. (P, I)

Keep a Journal

Have students keep a stress journal for a week or two. Have them record their various experiences, the emotions they felt, and what they were thinking at the time. Also have them keep track of how much sleep they got each night. This activity will give them great insight into what stresses them and how they handle it. Have them read their own journal entries and check for thinking distortions. Ask them to evaluate whether a lack of sleep is affecting how much stress they experience. (I, J, H)

Play It Out

Use role-play, puppets, or other imaginary play with stuffed toys to help students express their feelings and work through difficult situations. (P, I,)

Play with Me

Go outside with your students and play kickball or another organized game with them. As you play, teach your students about the benefits of physical exertion for coping with stress. (P, I)

Burn It Off

Provide appropriate ways for students to use up the energy created by the adrenaline released during stressful situations. This could be running in place, taking a walk, or having an early recess. (P, I)

Web Search

Many stress-coping resources can be found on the Web. Have a class competition to see who can find the best site.

4–7 Relaxation Activities

Meditative Relaxation

Move desks if necessary and have your students lie down on the floor. Play soft, tranquil music that does not have lyrics. Very slowly, instruct the students as follows:

> Close your eyes. Take a deep breath and let it out slowly. Imagine yourself lying someplace that is soft, quiet, and filled with sunlight. This sunlight is very yellow and pleasantly warm. Feel the warmth of the sunlight. Notice how this warm yellow light covers you like a blanket. The warm yellow rays warm your face, your arms, your body, your legs, and your feet. Stretch in the light and then totally relax. Your entire body is relaxed. You feel warm, heavy, and relaxed. (P, I, J, H)

Google It

You can access many simple relaxation/meditative exercises and soothing music you can use in your classroom by doing Google searches.

Progressive Relaxation

I. *Concentrate on breathing.* Instruct your students to sit quietly with their eyes closed and with one of their hands on their abdomen. Tell them to take a deep breath and try to completely fill their lungs by using their diaphragm muscle. Then have them exhale slowly. Instruct them to concentrate on their breathing for a few minutes, noticing the rhythmic flow of air as it enters and leaves their body. Have your students visualize that the air coming into their lungs is white, clean, and pure and that the air they are exhaling is dark and filled with any negative emotion they might be feeling. (I, J, H)

II. *Go limp.* After students have concentrated solely on their breathing, instruct them to turn their attention to the amount of tension they feel in their back, shoulders, and neck. Ask them to try to relax the muscles in this area of the body. Remind them of how, as a small child, they went totally limp when they didn't want someone to pick them up. Have them try to duplicate this feeling of going totally limp. (P, I, J, H)

III. *Progressive exercise.* Explain that we often do not realize the amount of muscle tension we have in our body. As we become more aware of it, we can relax more effectively. When we relax our body, our mind usually follows and relaxes as well. Follow the order outlined below to take your students through a progressive relaxation exercise. Instruct your students to tense the muscle group identified to 100% of their ability for about 5 seconds and then to relax for about 15 seconds. Then, tense the same muscle group to 75% and relax, 30% and relax, 10% and relax. This progressive approach will help students identify the amount of tension they are experiencing in each muscle group and the difference between the various degrees of tension and relaxation. Such a relaxation technique is especially helpful for "hyper" individuals who find it difficult to relax by just sitting still.

Follow this sequence:
1. Back, shoulders, and neck
2. Face and scalp

(continues)

(continued)

    3. Arms and hands
    4. Chest and stomach
    5. Legs and feet (I, J, H)

Sweet, Sweet Music

Have students close their eyes and use mental imaging while listening to soothing music. Discuss which types of music are truly stress reducing and why. Play soft music in the background while students work on assignments. (P, I, J, H)

Drawing How I Feel

Ask students to draw a picture of how they feel right now. When the pictures are completed, discuss the following questions: Which colors did you use and why? What is the size of the picture in relation to the paper? What were you thinking about as you were drawing? Have your feelings changed since completing the picture? If so, why? (P, I, J, H)

Instruction Plan Worksheet for Stress Management

Use this worksheet to plan stress management instruction at the grade level you will be teaching. It is often included in units on emotional/mental health, nutrition/physical activity, drugs, and violence prevention. Refer to Chapter 2 for more information on how to complete each section in this worksheet.

■ Assess Needs

Identify topics and skills state or local curricula identify to be taught at ___ grade level.

Identify additional topics or skills the ME HECAT Module indicate for this grade.

Identify stress management needs your particular students and their families have:
- What are your student's biggest stressors?
- How is stress impacting them?
- How prevalent is depression and anxiety disorders in the student body/community?
- How do students relax and cope with stress?

■ Set Major Learning Goal(s)

Identify your major learning goal(s)—what do you want to have happen?

■ Develop Instruction Map

Create a map (calendar or list of days) indicating the time frame you have/need to teach the curriculum, meet student needs and reach goal(s). For each day indicate the content/skills to be taught. Work to create a good flow.

■ Write SMART Unit Objectives

Write 1 or 2 major objectives for each day you will teach. Your objectives should be in alignment with your state/local curricula, your student's needs, and your major learning goal(s).

■ Identify Assessment Tools

Preassessment	Formative-Assessment	Postassessment
How will you determine what students already know or do?	How will you know if they are "getting it"?	Identify How will you know if students master objectives?

Instruction Plan Worksheet for Stress Management

■ **Develop Unit Plan**

Divide the chart into the number of days you will teach. Record each day's topic and objective key words. Identify activity names (in the book) that can help you meet each day's objective. Identify tech tools you can use and possible lesson adaptations you can make for special need learners.

Lesson Topic Objectives	Instruction Activities	Tech Tools	Adaptations for Learners

■ **Infuse Into Other Units**

Use this worksheet as you develop your mental health unit and possibly others.

■ KEY TERMS

stress 97
stressor 97
general adaptation syndrome (GAS) 97
fight-or-flight response 97
homeostasis 97
acute stress 98
chronic stress 98
eustress 98
neustress 98
distress 98
sympathetic 98
parasympathetic 98
immune system 99
lymph 99
B cells 99
T cells 99
distorted thinking patterns 100
all-or-nothing thinking 100
jumping to conclusions 100
overgeneralizing 100
filtering 100
discounting the positive 101
labeling 101
magnification 101
emotive reasoning 101
blaming 101
self-blame 101
sleep deprivation 103
dysfunctional families 105
burnout 107
depressive disorder 108
major depressive disorder (major depression) 109

dysthemic disorder (dysthymia) 109
minor depression 109
seasonal affective disorder (SAD) 109
bipolar disorder (manic-depressive illness) 109
anxiety 110
generalized anxiety disorder (GAD) 111
obsessive–compulsive disorder (OCD) 111
obsessions 111
compulsions 111
panic disorder 112
panic attacks 112
post-traumatic stress disorder (PTSD) 112
social phobia 112
stress reduction skills 112
junk sleep 114
helper's high 114
coping skills 115
parody 116
satire 116
slapstick 116
absurdity 116
irony 116
puns 116
black humor 116
sarcasm 116
relaxation skills 117
diaphragmatic breathing 117
cognitive restructuring 117
autogenic training 117
mental imagery 118
progressive relaxation 118

■ KNOWLEDGE CHECK!

1. Define, differentiate, and explain the relative importance of each key term in the chapter.
2. Describe GAS and explain the physiological changes that come with stress in the fight-or-flight response and during chronic stress.
3. Explain how disease and stress are linked and how stress affects the immune system.
4. Summarize the major stressors that most adults deal with.
5. Discuss common cognitive distortions that increase stress and provide an example of each.
6. Identify red flag words and common irrational beliefs.
7. Discuss things you can do to restructure your thinking.
8. Discuss the day-to-day hassles, economic stressors, and immigration-related stressors your students may experience.
9. Explain what a teacher can do to help meet students' needs following a natural disaster.

10. Discuss the eight home-based stressors students experience that are identified in the chapter. Explain what educators can do to help students appropriately deal with each of them.
11. Discuss school-based stresses that various age groups experience and identify ways teachers can reduce the amount of stress that both students and teachers experience at school.
12. Identify signs that may indicate a child is suffering from excessive stress.
13. Discuss the prevalence and signs of depressive disorders in children and adolescents. Explain why it can be difficult to detect such disorders in young people.
14. Describe what teachers can do to help depressed students.
15. Identify basic human fears and anxiety disorders. Explain what happens to the body during an anxiety attack.
16. Explain how and why time management, money management, study skills, rest and sleep, and giving and serving reduce stress. Describe ways teachers can help students learn these skills.
17. Explain the difference between humor and ridicule, and discuss how humor can be used effectively to cope with stress. Identify different types of humor and describe how teachers can effectively use humor in the classroom to reduce stress.
18. Explain how journal writing, play, and physical exertion can be used and taught as stress-coping skills.
19. Explain how diaphragmatic breathing is done and why it induces a relaxation response. Explain how the following are done and why they induce relaxation: autogenic training, visualization, and progressive muscular relaxation.
20. Describe the type of music that elicits a relaxation response. Explain why creating art is relaxing and identify what teachers need to do to understand their students' artwork.

REFERENCES

1. Selye H. *Stress without distress.* New York, NY: Signet Books; 1977.
2. University of Pennsylvania School of Medicine. Brain imaging shows how men and women cope differently under stress. *ScienceDaily.* November 20, 2007. Available at http://www.sciencedaily.com/releases/2007/11/071119170133.htm. Accessed April 17, 2013.
3. Schiaraldi GR. *Hope and help for depression: a practical guide.* Miami Beach, FL: Healthy People; 1993.
4. Ellis A, Dryden W. *The practice of rational emotive behavior therapy.* New York, NY: Springer; 1997.
5. McGonigal K. *The willpower instinct: why self-control matter and how you can get more of it.* New York, NY: Penguin; 2011.
6. Center for Health and Health Care in Schools. Children in immigrant families. *InFocus.* February 25, 2005. Available at www.healthinschools.org/ Accessed April 17, 2013.
7. National Association of School Psychologists. Helping children in the event of a tsunami: information for parents and teachers. 2005. Available at http://www.nasponline.org/resources/crisis_safety/tsunami.pdf. Accessed April 17, 2013.
8. Doherty WJ. *Parenting wisely in a "too-much-of-everything" world.* Guest lecture at Brigham Young University; February 23, 2009.
9. Noland H, Price J, Dake J, Telljohann S. Adolescents' sleep behaviors and perceptions of sleep. *J School Health.* 2009;79(5):224–230.
10. Schlozman SC. The shrink in the classroom: too sad to learn. *Educ Leadership.* 2001;59(1):80–83.
11. National Institute of Mental Health. *Depression in children and adolescents: a fact sheet for physicians* (NIH Publication No. 00–4844). Bethesda, MD: National Institutes of Health; 2000.
12. *ABC News 20/20.* Doing good and feeling better. August 20, 2007. Available at http://abcnews.go.com/2020/story?id=2685717. Accessed April 17, 2013.

Chapter 5
Media Literacy Skills

Maryland Seventh-Grader

In February of 2013 the world learned about a seventh-grader in Maryland who was bullied mercilessly at school and over the Internet. He began cutting himself and then posted a suicide note online, saying he was going to take his life on his thirteenth birthday. His mother found the posted note and acted quickly. She asked her friends to send letters of encouragement to her son. Those friends passed the cry for help along to thousands of others over the Internet. Letters began pouring into his mailbox, letting him know he was not alone and that a lot of people cared about him. His favorite letter was from his fourth-grade teacher, who told of his own similar experience and let the boy know that he was truly an amazing kid. By the boy's thirteenth birthday, his family's living room was filled with letters from all over the world. He will be reading the letters on his way to adulthood, and now knows how truly amazing the world is if you get past its dark side.

The world we live in today was unimaginable to most people 50 years ago. Modern technology makes it possible for us to communicate with people throughout the world, see news from around the globe in real time, access the answer to almost any question, and watch TV programs and movies in the palm of our hand. These technological powers, like fire, can warm and enrich our lives—but they can also "burn" us. Teachers and students need media literacy skills to appropriately harness and use the powers in modern media technology.

Media literacy refers to the skills needed to manage, analyze, evaluate, and create media messages. To be media literate is to be able to discriminately use and critically interpret one's media environment. Discussions of media should help students to recognize both the good and the bad regarding media consumption. Lynda Bergsma stresses that media literacy is not equivalent to media bashing. Youth culture, Bergsma acknowledges, is closely identified with media and pop culture. As such, she encourages adults to validate and acknowledge young people's experiences with their media culture. This will help youth accept and apply media literacy skills to the messages that they consume. Bergsma also makes the following recommendations for helping students develop media literacy skills:[1]

- Teachers and parents should develop familiarity with youth media and culture. Watch the movies that your students are watching, listen to their music, look at the websites they visit, and become familiar with the magazines that are popular among your students.
- Teachers and parents must become media literate themselves before they can guide the development of media literacy in their students and children.
- Start media literacy efforts as early as possible. Parents should start teaching media literacy as soon as children start watching TV. Media literacy should be introduced into school curricula in kindergarten.

- Media literacy efforts should be integrated into several curricular areas. Media literacy is especially appropriate in health, language arts, and social studies, but also has a place in math, science, geography, history, and other classes.
- Help students to become involved in media production. Media literacy skills are better internalized when students have opportunities to create and produce their own media.

Media literacy requires healthy skepticism—a questioning mind and the ability to look under every rock in an attempt to evaluate information in terms of its balance, bias, and accuracy. Media literacy also requires an awareness of the context and constraints in which media messages are created and consumed.[2]

MEDIA USE AND CONCERNS

The current generation of children and teenagers—sometimes called "Generation M," where the "M" stands for "media" instead of "millennials"—spends an unprecedented amount of time devouring media. Their media-saturated environment influences their attitudes, beliefs, and behaviors. School-age children spend, on average, 53 hours per week using various forms of media. That is more time than they spend with their parents, more time than they spend in class and doing homework, and more than a full-time job consumes! The following data give insights into media use of school-age youth (ages 8–18):[3]

- Every day children spend, on average, 7.5 hours using media—almost 11 hours, when multitasking is considered. They watch much of their TV through the Internet, cell phones and smart phones, and iPods. By the time they reach age 65, they will have spent more than 9 years of their life watching TV.
- Black and Hispanic children spend far more time watching TV. They average 13 total hours of media exposure per day.
- Heavy media users report getting lower grades. Heavy use occurs more often in homes where the TV is left on most of the time, where there are no family rules on media use, and where children have a TV in their bedroom.
- Approximately 70% of all U.S. children have a TV in their bedroom, and those who do average one more hour of media use per day. Approximately 50% of children have a video game player in their bedroom.
- Nearly half of children say they have rules about which TV shows and Internet sites they can view. Less than one-third have rules about how much time they can spend using media, which video games they can play, or which music they can listen to. Those who have rules average nearly 3 hours less of media use per day than those without any rules.
- Approximately 70% of children have some sort of cell phone and report spending more time listening to music, playing games, and watching TV on them than talking.
- Adolescents spend, on average, 1.5 hours per day sending and receiving texts.

This omnipresent media use raises many concerns. Media "sell" values, attitudes, beliefs, and behaviors. Some media messages are good and positive, but a great deal of what the media offer does not facilitate well-being, health, or character development. Consider how media promote, condone, and even glamorize the Centers for Disease Control and Prevention's (CDC's) six risk behaviors. This is especially troubling in light of the fact that the vast majority of children have televisions in their bedrooms where they can readily access violent and sexually explicit material.

Media messages shape how children see themselves, their parents, friends, and everyone they come in contact with. Media repeatedly tell them that they don't measure up unless they look and act in a certain way. Advertisements use female and male bodies to sell products in seductive manners,

Many young people have media-saturated lives with few rules on media use established by their parents.

which teach girls and boys what they are supposed to look like and how they are to treat each other. Media often reinforces stereotypes. Adults, particularly fathers, are often portrayed as incompetent or stupid. Cutting sarcasm and engaging in put-down behaviors are presented as funny, harmless, and very cool.

Culture is shaped and transformed by media. Twinge, in her book *Generation Me*, discusses how Generation M's perceptions of right and wrong are distinctly different from those of past generations.[4] Consider how often media messages in some way condone or glamorize killing, adultery, stealing, lying, coveting, swearing, disobeying parents, and worshiping people or things. Dysfunctionality is celebrated by making fun of the things that make civilized life possible: integrity, responsibility, and self-control. Often media producers opt for the dollar-laden low road to draw viewers' eyes, and their sleazy programs' promotional ads are repeatedly aired for everyone to see.

One example of how media can change culture is the television program *Friends*. It was the number one watched television show airing from 1994 to 2004 and is still in syndication. The program was developed to pull in and advertise to young single adults who have large amounts of discretionary money to spend. *Friends*, and other programs like it, helped promote the expansion of this demographic slice of our society. Today more young adults than ever before are choosing to "hang out" and remain single long after their parents and grandparents married and had children.

Another media concern is the consolidation of media producers. In 1980, 50 different corporations owned the media produced in the United States. Today, a mere 6 corporations own most of the media consumed in the entire world. This consolidation places a great deal of power in the hands of very few people, and many are concerned about the threat this poses to the free press and to democracy. News coverage is politically slanted, and stories that might offend advertisers are minimized or killed. For instance, when a TV special was aired about the top 10 things killing Americans, tobacco topped the list—but alcohol's role in traffic, murder, manslaughter, suicide, and drowning deaths was not even mentioned. Apparently network leaders were concerned about losing alcohol advertising revenues.

One way that media conglomerates maximize their profits is through cross-promotions between branded properties and products. Children's TV programs are created to sell toys, games, food, and other media products to kids. Guests appear on television talk shows to promote products (e.g., movies, music, books) created within the corporate family. The gigantic media corporations create an environment where no one dares question or challenge the merit and decency of what is produced anywhere within the corporate family.

Concerns about media use also go beyond what is in the actual programs. Today's young people experience very little, if any, quiet time—time they need for healthy mental and emotional development. Not having quiet time can prevent children from thinking deeply and getting to know themselves. Media devices also limit face-to-face communication—a means of interacting that is needed to learn how to read body language and become comfortable expressing feelings and needs in front of others. Media use can also isolate people from one another, even when they are in the same room. Parents and children may be gathered together, yet be so focused on watching television, surfing the Internet, texting, or playing video games that they do not interact with one another.

Be sure to do the application exercise in **Box 5-1**. This activity will most likely open your eyes to things you never noticed before.

Internet Use Concerns

Children today are digital natives, well versed in operating and navigating all kinds of media tools. However, most children are not as Internet proficient as they think. Too frequently they access inaccurate information and accept it as "truth." When writing reports, they all too often cut and paste rather than write original work from information they find, and they unknowingly cite sources that are highly biased.

Nearly three out of four parents say they think they know "a lot" about what their children are doing online. Most parents whose children are online say that they check their children's instant messaging buddy lists, review their children's profiles on social networking sites, and examine which websites their children have visited. About half of the parents who have children using the Internet at home say they use parental controls to block access to certain websites. Help these parents out by letting your students know that most parents have Internet use rules and that most parents monitor their children's Internet use. Unfortunately, studies indicate that many young people are accessing the Internet in an unsupervised manner. Many are online when their parents are not home, or gain access outside of their home, often on smart phones.

5-1 Application Exercise

TV Review

After reading this chapter and reviewing the questions below, watch an episode of a prime time (7–10 P.M.) television show that is popular among tweens/teens. Write a thoughtful reflection on the episode including the answers to these six questions. Be sure to include the name of the program and the date you watched it.

1. Why do children/teens like to watch this program?
2. Which healthy and which unhealthy (physical, mental, emotional, social) messages were included?
3. Which consequences of choices or behaviors were included or omitted (e.g., put-downs with no negative consequences, lying without getting into trouble, sexual involvement without consequences)?
4. Which lifestyles (e.g., rich, poor, ethnic, single, family) were depicted?
5. Which attitudes, values, or beliefs were depicted?
6. What was "taught" in—or better put, what could be "caught" from—this program?

Social media are a big part of young people's lives and can help them stay connected, find people with shared interests, and share good news, but such media also have a well-known down side. Students need to be warned that some websites try to pry into young people's private lives by using games and special promotions as bait to capture names, ages, and addresses. Youth need to be reminded to not put any information online that they would not mind having plastered on a billboard for everyone to see. Spending inordinate amounts of time online is another problem. Internet use can have addictive qualities, such that hours seem like minutes and problems arise from ignoring relationships and responsibilities. Chat rooms can be especially problematic in this way. Cyberspace bullying is another dark side of social media. This chapter's opening story about Noah Brocklebank highlights both the negative and the positive power that social networking can generate. Cyberbullying is discussed in great detail in the *Promoting Safety and Violence Prevention* chapter.

One of the most serious concerns about unsupervised Internet use by children and teens is the risk that they might become involved with a sexual predator who tries to "groom" them for sex. Grooming can involve flattery, sympathy, gifts, money, or offers for modeling jobs over extended periods of time. The predator tries to manipulate the victim to feel loved or just comfortable enough to want to meet the predator in person.

Another major concern is the easy, sometimes accidental, access to pornography. Wireless handheld devices such as smart phones, iPods, and video game consoles can be conduits for pornography available on the Internet. Sexting has become prevalent in recent years. Youth need to be educated about appropriate use of cell phones, e-mail, and social networking. They need to understand that once information or images are shared electronically, they cannot be retracted and can be passed on to an infinite number of people. Minors need to know that in many states they can be found guilty of a misdemeanor, or more serious charges, for sending pornographic materials electronically.

To understand the pervasiveness of pornography, you need to recognize that it is a big business—one driven by greed. This industry's revenue exceeds the combined revenues of all professional baseball, football, and basketball franchises along with the combined revenues of ABC, CBS, and NBC! Pornography is much more harmful than most people appreciate. Its sexual distortions can affect teenagers' attitudes about sexuality, and its products can be addictive, leading to the same devastating effects on relationships and families as other addictions. Many addicts report getting hooked at a very early age and note that kicking a pornography addiction is much like trying to overcome a cocaine addiction. All addictions change brain structures critical to decision making, learning and memory, and behavior control. This may help to explain the compulsive and destructive behaviors present in addictions.[5]

Recommendations for Media Use

Exposure to media usually starts early in life, often before age 2 years.[6] Many shows have been designed to gather infants and toddlers around the television screen. This has caused considerable concern about parents and caretakers using media as "electronic baby-sitters," and about the possible implications this practice has for baby and toddler brain development. The American Academy of Pediatrics has made the following recommendation:

> Pediatricians should urge parents to avoid television viewing for children under the age of 2 years. Although certain television programs may be promoted to this age group, research on early brain development shows that babies and toddlers have a critical need for direct interactions with parents and other significant caregivers (eg, child care providers) for healthy brain growth and the development of appropriate social, emotional, and cognitive skills. Therefore, exposing such young children to television programs should be discouraged.[7]

The American Academy of Pediatrics also advocates that healthcare professionals assess, as part of physician office visits, children's media exposure. For adolescents, physicians need to include questions about musical preferences and the meaning of that music to their patients. In addition to educating parents about the potential dangers of using the TV as an "electronic babysitter," the American Academy of Pediatrics recommends that physicians advise parents about three media dangers: having a television in children's bedrooms, prolonged time spent playing violent video games, and the risks of unsupervised Internet use.[7]

Encouraging parents to remove TVs from their children's bedrooms may be the most helpful thing an educator can do in regard to media literacy and a host of other health issues. The presence of a TV in the bedrooms of preteen youth has been found to be a stronger predictor of obesity than the amount of time spent watching TV.[8] Adolescents with a bedroom television spend more time watching TV, spend less time involved in physical activity, have poorer dietary habits, eat fewer family meals, get less sleep, and have poorer school performance.[9]

ADVERTISING POWER

On average, we see approximately 3,000 advertisements per day. These ads sell us much more than products—they influence our perceptions of ourselves and the world around us. They teach us attitudes, beliefs, and values without our noticing it, and they promote a culture of consumerism.

We have been conditioned into thinking that media programs (e.g., a television show) are brought to us by a sponsoring company ("Today's program is brought to you by Brand X"). The truth, however, is just the opposite. We, the potential consumers, are really the products being sold. Media (television shows, radio broadcasts, magazines, websites) exist to gather audiences to see and hear the advertisements. Noted advertising expert Jean Kilbourne explains it this way:

> Make no mistake: The primary purpose of the mass media is to sell audiences to advertisers. We are the product. Magazines, newspapers, and radio and television programs round us up, rather like cattle, and producers and publishers then sell us to advertisers, usually through ads placed in advertising and industry publications. "The people you want, we've got all wrapped up for you," declares *The Chicago Tribune* in an ad placed in *Advertising Age*, the major publication of the advertising industry, which pictures several people, all neatly boxed according to income level. Although we like to think of advertising as unimportant, it is in fact the most important aspect of the mass media. It is the point. As one ABC executive said, "The network is paying affiliates to carry network commercials, not programs."[10](p.34–35)

In this "ad-vironment," it is common to hear people say that they just ignore the ads. In reality, it is impossible to filter out all the ads we are constantly exposed to, especially when advertisements are carefully designed so that our brains process them in the "emotive brain" instead of in the critical thinking cerebral cortex. Every detail is planned, researched, and pilot tested. Have you ever wondered why so many people are willing to buy a bottle of water worth two cents and pay a dollar for it? More than buying the product itself, we buy the emotions that advertisers attach to the product. There is an old Madison Avenue saying, "You don't drink the beer; you drink the advertising."

Most advertising attempts to convey two fundamental messages. First, you should be dissatisfied with yourself. Second, purchasing this product is the only way to resolve your dissatisfaction. Ads try to make us feel insecure about everything—our weight, our appearance, our ability to attract lovers, and on and on. Buying a product is presented as the solution to these insecurities. Advertisements influence people to believe that their life and worth are defined by what they possess.

Companies may spend millions of dollars on a single commercial, and a great deal more on airing it. Because advertising is a business with billions of dollars at stake, advertisers do extensive research to be sure they are spending their money effectively. An ad is the end product of a complex and very costly process. Many specialists are involved, including researchers and psychologists. Everything is planned in detail—every image, word, scene, sound, camera angle, and background image—so that viewers will have an emotional response to the product. The following are common attention-getting devices and persuasion tactics, "hooks" that advertisers use to lure us in:

Humor	Warm fuzzy association
Sex	You deserve it
Surprise	Everyone does/has
Urgency	New and improved
Superiority	Scientific evidence
Slogan repetition	Celebrity endorsement

Ad Creep

Ad creep is a popular term used to explain the expansion of advertising into every aspect of our lives. Examples of ad creep include ads aired before movies, in airport waiting areas, in doctors' offices, and on public transportation, ATMs, and gas pumps. The selling of **naming rights** to sporting arenas, theaters, parks, schools, museums, and subway systems is another form of ad creep. **Digital (virtual) advertising** creates ad creep by using technology to superimpose logos on products that appear in scenes. TV coverage of sporting events digitally inserts ads onto billboards, sideboards, and playing surfaces in arenas and stadiums.

Product placement—a practice in which advertisers pay to have their product included in movies, TV shows, and museum exhibits—has become very pervasive. The product is usually placed in highly visible situations in the context of a program. This form of advertising is less expensive than buying air time to explicitly sell the product and more likely to slip by viewers' critical thinking processes. Concern has been raised that most product placements are inherently deceptive; most people do not realize they are, in fact, advertisements.

Undercover marketing is another form of advertisement where people do not realize that a product is being marketed to them. In one form of undercover marketing, a company pays an actor to use a product in a very visible way in a location where potential consumers are congregated. For example, a company marketing a new cigarette brand might employ an attractive-looking woman to go to a bar, strike up conversations with customers, hand out samples of the cigarette, and, in the process, extoll the virtues of the brand she is smoking. The people she talks to do not realize that she is a paid actor who is working to sell cigarettes; they view her as just another patron of the bar.

The goal of an undercover campaign is to generate **buzz**, or peer-to-peer word of mouth. Because buzz spreads from person to person in a seemingly spontaneous manner, buzz marketing is sometimes called **viral marketing**: somebody tells two friends, who then tell four friends, and so on, until the infection takes hold. Buzz marketing campaigns identify key influential young people, opinion leaders, and get them to spread information about a product to their peers through social media. An example of a successful buzz marketing campaign is Procter & Gamble's **Tremor**, which uses 280,000 teens as part of its "Tremor Crew." The Tremor Crew helps spread the word about Procter & Gamble brands through sleepovers, by social media, and at school.

The Tremor Crew perform these activities for free, and no parental consent is obtained during the application process. Coca-Cola, Valvoline, CoverGirl (cosmetics), shampoos, milk, Toyota (cars), and movies have also used Tremor's teens to generate buzz.[11]

The **Girls Intelligence Agency (GIA)** also uses buzz marketing. This campaign aims to attract girls aged 8 to 13 years. The marketing firm tells potential companies the value of having "40,000 secret agent influencers and their closest friends." Companies that contract with GIA use the girls to form focus groups, such as slumber parties, to show off their products. This approach raises controversial issues. Most important, do these girls understand that they are being used and that marketers are exploiting their personal friendships?

Mobile marketing is made possible today through smart and cell phones. Advertisers contact young people when they are near stores and restaurants with pitches that try to get them to come in and buy something spontaneously. Video sharing services such as YouTube also use mobile marketing to promote brands, sometimes overtly and sometimes in disguise.

Targeting Children

To the corporate world, children are big business. American companies spend $15 billion per year on marketing and advertising to children younger than the age of 12.[12] Advertisers aim not only to collect the billions of dollars that kids spend each year, but also the billions of dollars that adults spend on children—an amount that might be 10 times as high. The fact that children influence between 25% and 40% of household purchases has prompted all kinds of companies—from automakers to airlines—to aim their advertisements at youth.[13] Marketers also know that when brand allegiances are formed in childhood, the customer usually remains loyal to the product for many years to come. Thus marketers try to curry a child's favor so that they can enjoy that enduring loyalty. Children begin developing brand preferences in early childhood, even before entering school. The highly lucrative kids' market has spurred a proliferation of television channels (e.g., Nickelodeon, Fox Kids Network, Disney Channel, Cartoon Network) and websites to advertise products and services to children.

Vulnerability of Children

Parents and teachers need to be aware that children are particularly vulnerable to advertising. Very young children are unable to distinguish advertising from regular programs. By age 5 or 6, most children are able to comprehend the distinction between an advertisement and a program, but they may not necessarily understand that the purpose of an advertisement is to sell. Children consider the advertisements they view as entertaining or informational in nature. They also have a high degree of trust in advertisements. Around the age of 7 or 8, most children begin to understand the selling intent of advertisements. With the development of more conceptual thinking, children around age 12 can recognize the motivation of advertisers, the source of an advertisement, and the strategies used to persuade. Increasing consumer awareness allows most teenagers to become fairly critical and skeptical of advertising.[14]

School-Based Marketing

Advertisements abound in schools—on bulletin boards, scoreboards, book covers, and educational materials. School buses and school athletic fields are decorated with ads. Incentives, promotions, and contests are other frequently used in-school marketing devices. Channel One, a daily ad-bearing TV news program, airs in more than 12,000 schools. It contains 2 minutes of ads for every 12 minutes of programming. Channel One promises its advertisers "the largest teen audience around" and "the undivided attention of millions of teenagers for 12 minutes a day." Some communities, such as the Nashville, Tennessee, and Seattle, Washington, public schools, have expelled Channel One in an effort to reduce commercial intrusion in their schools.

Schools are vulnerable to allowing companies to cash in on children in an attempt to solve their financial difficulties. For example, Coca-Cola has entered into several "partnerships" with schools in which the company provides schools with large sums of money in exchange for a long-term contract giving Coca-Cola exclusive rights to school vending machines. Tax monies can be stretched only so far, and financially strapped schools are often willing to enter into ventures with generous commercial sponsors. These sponsors provide numerous enhancements (e.g., computers, educational materials, TV monitors) that a school might not otherwise be able to afford. Sadly, in the process, children gain more access to sugary drinks, are exposed to more advertisements, and learn from corporate-sponsored curricula.

School-based marketing campaigns carry implied school endorsement. Students are especially vulnerable to these marketing tactics because they believe that what they are exposed to at school is good for them. School-based advertising creates a blurred line between education and propaganda. In the future, ideally more schools will make efforts to become advertising-free schools. Doing so, however, requires significant, ongoing community commitment and involvement. It requires strict policies and the replacement of lost corporate contributions with large donations of time, talent, and money from parents and other community members.

Internet Marketing

Companies targeting children find Internet advertising an attractive and cost-effective way of reaching young people with their marketing messages. Internet advertising is inexpensive. Websites are relatively cheap to create, can remain online for months, and are not subject to the high costs associated with television advertising.

Young people are an ideal target group for Internet advertisers[15] because they stay online for longer periods of time than adults do, participate in a wider range of online activities, and are more likely to adapt quickly to new technology.[11] Internet marketing allows advertisers direct, usually unmonitored or parent-free access to children. In comparison to other forms of media, the Internet is the least regulated. As a consequence, websites directed at children may employ insidious and manipulative marketing techniques without fear of government-initiated repercussion.

A common online marketing strategy is the creation of **branded environments**, or websites designed specifically for children, with content that features a commercial product or brand.[10] These commercial websites entice children with such features as interactive games and activities, contests and competitions, prizes and other incentives, clubs, sports sponsorship, animated characters, "kids-only" zones, and online chat communities. Website marketing allows children to interact directly with a company and can be used to collect personal data from children (e.g., e-mail addresses for themselves and their friends) and extract marketing information (e.g., from having children vote on new flavors or packaging designs). Prizes or incentives are sometimes promised to children who share the e-mail addresses of their friends. Such sites may also feature online stores or links to websites that are created to make direct sales. Some websites have created "digital wallets" that allow a parent to use a credit card to place a set amount of money into a child's online account. Tobacco and alcohol companies have websites that are appealing and enticing to young people.

■ USING TECHNOLOGY IN THE CLASSROOM

Many forms of media can help teachers facilitate learning in the classroom. How effectively media are used determines whether such activities are a gimmick, a time filler, or an effective means for helping students learn content and skills.

Perhaps the most common error that novice teachers make is thinking that they can simply show a video. Teachers must be careful to not waste valuable classroom time by having students watch something that is "somewhat" related to the topic. Students might enjoy the class, but then leave with no idea of what the point of the lesson was. To be effective, video material must be carefully selected and edited so that it helps students reach learning goals and objectives, and time needs to be taken after showing clips to discuss and process them.

Music can be very a powerful and memorable means of teaching health concepts. Many classic popular songs contain messages about relationships and risk behaviors. Class discussions on topics can be facilitated with lyrics. Adding music to PowerPoint slides can create powerful and persuasive presentations (e.g., combining the song "Where Have All the Cowboys Gone" with a slide deck about the Marlboro man and smoking).

PowerPoint

PowerPoint is the most widely used technology tool in the classroom. The biggest problems with this Microsoft Office program are that it tends to be overused and its slides are too often overloaded because it is so easy to add content. PowerPoint slides are usually filled with too much information—long lists of bullet points, multiple charts, and distracting technofluff. We are all tempted to put everything we want to say on our slides so we can use them as teleprompters while we lecture, but doing so creates what many call "death by PowerPoint." Students experience cognitive overload when slides are overstuffed with information. Teachers may be able to put an unlimited amount of information on a slide, but students' capacity to receive that information remains limited. Cognitive overload causes students either to tune out and look bored, or to become highly agitated, especially if they think they will be held accountable for the material. To combat cognitive overload, many teachers post their PowerPoint presentations online. It would be much more effective for teachers to post their lecture notes online and then take advantage of PowerPoint to powerfully help their student's brains learn.

PowerPoint slides are "glance media." They should resemble a billboard, not a pamphlet. It takes only a second or two to process the message on a billboard. PowerPoint slides are most effective when they are designed to speed up the time it takes for students to grasp a message. Each slide should contain just one idea. To meet this goal, educators have to work at simplifying their slides. Less may be more, but it takes more effort to produce less on a slide.

Our brains are wired for decoding visual messages. Most of what we learn, in fact, is conveyed visually. Approximately 30% of our brain is devoted to visual processing, 8% to kinesthetic learning, and only 3% to auditory learning. We are incredible at remembering pictures, and our capacity for graphic memory is huge because images are stored in our long-term memory. Pictures evoke emotions, and emotions are processed in the limbic system. The limbic system, in turn, channels input into long-term memory. Well-chosen, highly pixilated pictures on PowerPoint slides can move us emotionally, which taps into this memory-making process. Such pictures can also be very persuasive—which explains why advertisers use images to sell their products. Inspire and persuade your students to engage in healthy behaviors by using powerful simple visuals. Such images will also help them remember the lessons you teach.

What about text on a slide—that's visual, right? Not quite. Text is processed in the cortex and, therefore, is stored in short-term memory. It also takes the brain much longer to process words than to process visuals because words are decoded linearly and sequentially. That is one reason why text should be minimized on PowerPoint slides—remember, you want your slides to speed up your message. Create them with a billboard in mind.

Sometimes teachers feel the need to project complicated slides that they want their students to study slowly. In this case, it is most effective to break the complex slide into many simpler slides and create a presentation where the slides "build" on each other. PowerPoint slides are free! It is better to have 20 simple slides than 1 complicated one.

Here are some additional hints for developing effective slides:

- Novel pictures or graphics can be used to capture students' attention, but teachers need to remember that it takes the brain some time to process novelty.
- To make an idea stand out, use contrast on a slide—color, size, shape, orientation, position, tone, and texture. Study magazine ads to see how they use contrast. Notice how much white space the ads include. Graphic designers use white space to direct the eye to where they want it to go. Using lots of white space helps keep slides simple.
- Lecture notes can be added to newer PowerPoint versions so that the lecturer can see the notes on his or her computer, but the notes are not projected onto the screen where the audience can see them.

Social Media in the Classroom

Social media entails the use of web-based and mobile technologies to turn communication into interactive dialogue. It is continually evolving as its uses change and expand. Many educators are excited about the possibilities that social media present for learning in the classroom. Their thoughts are in line with John Dewey, who said, "If we teach today's students the way we taught them yesterday, we rob them of tomorrow."[16]

When used effectively, social media can advance academic and social success, enhance peer-to-peer learning, and foster collaboration, critical thinking, and communication skills. Yes, cell phones and smart phones can be major classroom distractions, but they can also connect students with the world. The key for successfully using social media in the classroom is to establish and maintain firm, well-defined rules about when social media can be used and which sites can be accessed.

Using social media in the classroom offers many advantages, assuming some possible disadvantages can be overcome. First, social media are familiar to students and they enjoy using these sites. Teachers can use students' interest in and knowledge of social media to their advantage. In doing so, teachers can change entertainment tools into learning tools. Here are some additional advantages of using social media in the classroom:[17]

- The amount of free social media resources available is endless. Many of these resources can be adapted to enhance learning in the classroom.
- Improving student research skills, by teaching students how to find information on the Internet, is an important learning skill for them both in the classroom and in the workplace later.
- Teacher–student communication can be improved by using social media to post homework assignments, send reminders, organize projects, or ask for revisions.
- Student–student communication can be facilitated through the sharing of materials.
- Digital citizenship can be promoted as students learn how to conduct themselves appropriately online. Lessons about cyberbullying, privacy policies, and transferring data online can be learned in the context of appropriately using social media.
- Social media enable educators to appeal to different learning styles and to involve the shy student who might not otherwise participate.

Some possible disadvantages must be overcome to successfully use social media in the classroom. First, before accessing social media, schools must have Internet filters and use plans firmly in place to protect students from inappropriate communication or images. Second, teachers need to practice using social media tools and have clearly defined learning objectives before they attempt to use any social media with their students; otherwise, the activity becomes nothing more than a gimmick. Careful preparation also makes it possible for teachers to continually monitor their students' use of social media devices in the classroom.

Another possible disadvantage is exposing the "haves" and the "have nots" among students. Often schools do not have the resources to supply each student with access to the Internet, so students are asked to bring their own devices to school. Teachers can overcome possible embarrassment or teasing of students who do not have devices by either supplying these students with a device or by assigning students to work in groups where just one device is allowed per group.

The possibilities for using social media in the classroom are endless. Here are a few ideas to consider:

◆ Create a classroom blog or make assignments that mimic blogging. You can assign students to follow certain blogs or have them share favorite health-related blogs. Student work can be posted on blogs, through micro-blogging, or on Twitter, Facebook, or Pinterest.
◆ Tweet inspirational quotes or homework assignments to students.
◆ Use Twitter and Facebook like classroom bulletin boards.
◆ Use wikis for housing student portfolios.
◆ Use online content to spark discussion and explore international health issues.
◆ Use media production activities to review or process health issues and content.

If you want to use Facebook as a classroom tool, you must take several steps before doing so. Permission needs to be obtained from school administrators, and communication needs to take place with parents. Students need to understand the difference between personal and professional Facebook accounts. Students can then set up a professional Facebook account using only their first names or pseudonyms. An avatar—any picture other than their own—should be used. Teachers should set up a professional account as well. Teachers can then set up groups within Facebook for various purposes.[18]

ACCESSING VALID INFORMATION

Information literacy is the set of skills that allows us to find, evaluate, and use the information we need and filter out the information we don't need. What respected educator Alan November says in *Web Literacy for Educators* illustrates the importance of information literacy in the lives of students:

> The Internet is the most powerful, convenient, and potentially manipulative medium ever invented. It can give you any version of the truth you are looking for. Not only does information expand and change every day, the rules for finding information also change.[19(p.vii)]

One of the most important aspects of being a wise consumer is being able to determine if information is reliable—is it accurate and truthful? A key in determining the reliability of information is to ask if the purpose of those providing the information is to inform rather than to sell. If the information is provided to persuade people that they need to purchase a specific product or service, it is probably not reliable. Reliable health information is provided by individuals or organizations for the purpose of helping people make informed decisions and to encourage healthy behaviors.

The source of the information offers another clue about the reliability of the information. Be suspicious of organizations or individuals who might profit from the information they provide or who seems to have a particular "agenda." Any organization or individual with a vested interest in a particular product or service may present information that is biased toward that particular interest. For instance, which biases might be apparent in a brochure about nutrition and health created by the manufacturer of a line of vitamin and mineral products or by the owners of fast-food restaurants?

Reliable health information is based solely on scientific research and information and not on mere opinion. The information is more likely to be accurate if credible health professionals and health organizations agree with it. Unreliable information, in contrast, is sometimes presented in a way that attempts to convince us that it correlates with established medical knowledge. Headline news reports on health issues have often been criticized for calling small case study findings "breakthroughs" and for being alarmist, incomplete, or inaccurate. Be aware of health information that attempts to arouse feelings of fear or anxiety. Ask if the information or advice is plausible, if it makes common sense, or if it sounds like wishful thinking or sensationalism.

Evaluating Information on the Internet

The quality of information on the Internet ranges from highly credible to very poor. No one regulates the information on the Internet, and anyone can claim anything. Here are some good questions to ask when evaluating the reliability of Internet sites: Are advertisements mixed in with content? Does the site promise miracle cures or unbelievable results? Does the site ask you to give personal information, but not promise to keep that information private? Does the site fail to link to other reliable health information? Does the information on the site contradict what you have learned from a physician or a reputable health organization? Be very wary of information found on bulletin boards, in chat rooms, and in forwarded messages.

Tip-Offs to Rip-Offs

The **Food and Drug Administration (FDA)** has identified some tip-offs to health fraud rip-offs. The FDA suggests that you look for the following phrases and gimmicks used to catch your attention and gain your trust:[20]

- Quick fixes
- "Natural" or "nontoxic"
- Promises of easy weight loss
- "One product does it all" or claims that the product is an effective remedy for a wide range of ailments
- Personal testimonials
- Undocumented case histories of people who claim dramatic results
- Healthcare providers who may be unlicensed or lack other appropriate credentials
- Meaningless medical jargon
- "Satisfaction guaranteed" or "money-back guarantees"
- "Time-tested" or "newfound treatment"
- Claims of a "scientific breakthrough," "miraculous cure," "exclusive product," "secret ingredient," or "ancient remedy"
- Paranoid accusations
- Claims that the product is available from only one source

Sources of Reliable Health Information

Many federal, state, and local government agencies that focus on health-related issues are reliable sources of health information. The CDC is an excellent source on many topics. The FDA also serves as an information resource on numerous health topics. The **Consumer Product Safety Commission (CPSC), Federal Trade Commission (FTC),** and the **National Health Information Center (NHIC)** are other federal government agencies that provide valuable health information.

Other good sources of health information are voluntary health agencies and professional health organizations. Examples of voluntary health agencies include the American Cancer Society, American Heart Association, and American Diabetes Association. Examples of professional health organizations include the American Medical Association (AMA), American Public Health Association (APHA), and American Academy of Pediatrics. These organizations produce and circulate publications and also offer websites that provide sources of high-quality health information. Activities at the end of the chapter can help your students learn how to access valid information and evaluate what they find on the Internet. **Box 5-2** lists Internet sites offering free games, videos, and media literacy lesson plans.

> **5-2 Internet Support**
>
> ### Media Instruction Resources
>
> Games, videos, filmmaking resources, and lesson plans on media literacy are provided by these agencies on their websites:
> - Alliance for a Media Literate America
> - Media Literacy for Drug Prevention
> - Media-Smart Youth
> - National Association for Media Literacy Education
> - Privacy Playground: The First Adventure of the Three CyberPigs
> - The Media Awareness Network
> - The Media Literacy Clearinghouse: Resources for K–12 Educators

ANALYZING MEDIA AND TECHNOLOGY INFLUENCES

Questioning media lies at the heart of analyzing media messages.[21] Teaching students to ask five fundamental questions provides them with the tools they need to analyze media influences:

- **Who** created this?
- **Why** was it made?
- **What** is being "sold," and what has been omitted?
- Who does it **target?**
- **How** was it constructed?

Who Created This?

Students need to recognize that those who author messages make choices about the message they create. Their agendas, biases, and points of view are persuasively portrayed. Asking "Who wrote this?" and "Which personal biases, lifestyles, or agendas are evident?" helps students become more critical consumers.

Students also need to recognize that the media we consume are created by a handful of powerful corporate families—General Electric, Disney, News Corporation, Time Warner, and Viacom. Disney is more than a theme park and cable television channel: it also owns the ABC network; nine cable channels including ESPN, A&E, and Lifetime; six movie production and distribution companies; five music labels; five magazine publishing groups; sports teams; television and radio stations; and newspapers. Media conglomerates such as Disney create media products and then use all their media outlets to promote their products. We are usually totally unaware of this cross-promotion. Media conglomerates also own major food and beverage industries. This means that our mass media are not as diverse as it might seem on first glance.

The common profile shared by most program writers and producers must also be considered. These individuals are most likely white, single, male, relatively young, and very affluent. Their attitudes, behaviors, expectations, and agendas become part of what they produce—something that happens both intentionally and unintentionally. Students need consider this to uncover subtle messages about roles, stereotypes, fantasies, and expectations.

Youth need to get into the habit of analyzing media messages.

Why Was It Made?

Students need to understand that all media exist to make a profit. This is obvious for a music CD purchase, but is less obvious when we buy a magazine. We tend to think we are paying for the magazine when, in fact, more than 60% of the magazine production costs are covered by advertisements. Almost 100% of electronic media costs are covered by advertisements. As a consequence, the advertisements are the most important part of the media. Media messages, in whatever form, exist to gather an audience and put that audience in a receptive mood to hear/see the advertisements. This creates a culture driven by materialism and consumption.

Have you ever examined the amount of advertisements in a magazine compared with its editorial content? Most magazines are essentially catalogs of advertised products with a few stories sprinkled in, and those stories are often advertisements in disguise. This is particularly true of teens' and women's magazines. The stories contained in magazines are influenced tremendously by the advertisers. Magazines that carry tobacco advertisements do not run stories about the health effects of cigarettes, any more than magazines bearing alcohol advertisements carry stories about the tragedies of alcohol abuse.[22]

What Is Sold or Omitted?

Students need to understand that "What is being sold?" refers to much more than the products being advertised. Programs and advertisements "sell" attitudes, values, and behaviors. Questions that help identify what is being sold include these: "What lifestyles and attitudes are portrayed?" "What behaviors are modeled?" "What values are taught?"

Asking, "What was the moral?" can help identify values "sold" in media. One professor asked his class this question after showing them the classic movie *Butch Cassidy and the Sundance Kid*. When no one responded, he asked, "Wasn't it that they didn't have to kill anyone until they went straight?"

The class had to think about that for a moment, and then all agreed that they had absorbed this moral message without observing it. They had not consciously thought about it until the professor pointed it out. All media messages teach values, and we have to be careful about what we might be unconsciously "buying."

Students need to question what is portrayed—or not portrayed—in product advertisements. Help them question the validity of ad messages by asking things like, "If I buy this product, will imaginary playmates appear, making my life fun and exciting?" "Does this toy really do all the things it's shown to do, and do all the accessories come with it?" "Will this really make me beautiful and popular?"

Targeted to Whom?

Identifying the target population for a message helps students identify who advertisers are trying to round up. It also helps them watch for ways the media may be trying to "soften up" consumers and make them more receptive to advisements. Age, gender, economic, ethnic, political, and other demographics should be considered when trying to figure out who the target population is.

The actors chosen to be in a program or advertisement can give some clues about who the target population is. "Teen" magazines full of pictures of attractive teenagers are targeted to tweens who want to be like the teens. The Marlboro man targets men, especially teenage boys who long for macho independence. This ad campaign also appeals to women who want to be like, or with, a Marlboro kind of guy. Some ads feature animals, capitalizing on the large segment of the population who are animal lovers. Alcohol ads appeal to children, for example, by featuring horses, dogs, and other animals.

How Is It Constructed?

Students need to learn how carefully constructed media messages are. In advertisements, every detail is created first on a storyboard, where each second and each camera angle is mapped out. Directors take hundreds of takes for each segment to try to capture the perfect image that will entice us to buy the product. Messages are pilot tested to groups and reworked to be the most influential message psychological research and money can produce.

One of the best ways for students to understand how messages are constructed is to create their own media messages. Another way is to dissect commercials by asking questions such as these: "Which 'hooks' are used?" "How is the ad trying to create emotional transfer?" "How have lighting and special effects been used?" "Why is (every detail) included?"

The activities at the end of the chapter can help you teach your students how to question and analyze media messages. These activities can be incorporated into English and social study units. They can easily be modified to work within units on nutrition, drugs, sexuality, violence, or safety.

■ PRACTICING MEDIA MANAGEMENT

Both students and their parents need to be involved in establishing healthy practices for managing media use. Teachers can help parents by providing them with information and by helping their students understand the importance of viewing guidelines. Accessing, analyzing, and managing media literacy skills can be shared with parents at back-to-school night, at special events, or through school newsletters sent home. Most parents want help with putting parameters on their children's media use and find school-initiated programs and shared information very helpful. These parents appreciate being able to say to their children, "Your teacher told me about research that says you should not have a TV in your bedroom because . . ."

Parents also appreciate learning more about media control tools and research about media use. For instance, most parents would appreciate knowing that the American Academy of Pediatrics recommends that parents avoid TV viewing for children younger than the age of 2 years and that televisions should be removed from children's bedrooms.[6]

Limit Use

Several guidelines can help parents appropriately limit the amount of time their children spend in front of a screen. Of course, the ultimate goal is for students to develop good media habits and gain the self-control needed to limit their own media use. Parents also need to be encouraged to model this and all other media literacy skills. Here are some recommended guidelines for wisely limiting media use:

1. Create an electronic media-free environment in children's bedrooms.
2. Create a television (and computer, video game, MP3 player, and other electronic device) allowance. Determine the appropriate total hours per week for viewing and develop a media time budget for these hours.
3. Have cell phones turned off during school hours, and have a texting and talking time budget for after school.
4. Have a rule that children must finish homework and chores before watching TV or using other media devices.
5. Do not allow children to eat in front of the television set. The increased rate of obesity in childhood and adolescence is closely correlated with sedentary activities such as watching TV and eating the advertised junk food. Eating while watching TV is a double whammy that contributes to overweight and obesity.
6. Have media-free time each day at dinner time or other time to facilitate family members interacting more meaningfully with one another.

Online Safety Tips

Teachers can share the following online safety tips with students and their parents; these tips can be taken home as part of an assignment that generates family discussion.

- Place computers in an open, frequently accessed area of the home (i.e., family room) so that others can easily see the screen.
- Do not allow Internet access in bedrooms.
- Establish clear ground rules for Internet use (e.g., when, where, how long, which sites can or cannot be accessed).
- Tell parents all screen names, e-mail addresses, and addresses of blogs and profiles students use. Parents and students should frequently visit these sites together and discuss what is seen.
- Never make plans to meet an online acquaintance face to face.
- Post only information that you are comfortable allowing others to see (e.g., parents, future employers).
- Make sure screen names and sites do not say too much about you, such as your full name, age, home town, school, or job.
- Consider not posting photos of yourself. Such images can be altered or broadcast in ways you may not be happy about.
- Do not respond to dangerous or offensive communications (anything or anyone who has made you feel uncomfortable or scared).
- Do not send any communication in word or image that would make someone feel uncomfortable, offended, or scared.
- Immediately tell an adult if you ever feel threatened by someone or uncomfortable because of something online.
- Avoid flirting with strangers online, because you never know who you are really dealing with.
- Immediately turn off a computer if you accidentally access a pornographic site. Some pornographic sites disable the user's ability to escape when using normal key functions such as ESC (escape) and instead bring up additional windows containing pornographic images.

Make Positive Media Choices

Teachers can encourage and facilitate positive media choices by students and their families. They can talk about upcoming historical, scientific, geographic, and similar programs in class and can encourage students to watch these programs at home with their families. Classroom discussions can include research about the detrimental effects of viewing violent acts and the probable real-life consequences of unhealthy behaviors often glamorized on the screen. Here are a few guidelines for helping parents and children make positive media choices:

1. Preselect the programs to be viewed. Look for age-appropriate programs that are fair in their treatment of people, are not violent, do not display sexual images or themes, do not use vulgar language, and do not display other inappropriate behavior or messages.
2. Immediately turn off the TV at the end of a program. Have a reason for turning it on and lots of reasons for turning it off. Do not allow yourself to be sucked into watching the following program or to begin channel surfing.
3. Watch TV as a family, and analyze together the program and advertisement content by discussing the following:

    ◆ What is "real" and "unreal" in the scenes
    ◆ The actors' behaviors and dialogue, and what would be the real-life consequences of their actions
    ◆ Underlying messages or morals, including those that might not have been intended by the writers
    ◆ Why the advertisers chose to run their ads during that program

Select Creative Alternatives

Teachers can encourage parents and students to find creative alternatives to media consumption. Often parents need encouragement and good ideas to break television, video game, and computer use habits. Teachers can emphasize alternative activities such as physical activity, crafts, hob-

Cyberspace can be a dangerous place where media literacy skills are vital. Teachers can help families protect themselves by sharing safety tips with students and parents.

bies, and visits to museums. Teachers can encourage parents to be good role models by reading more and selectively limiting the media they consume. Some schools have promoted "screen-free" weeks where students and their families give up viewing television programs, watching movies, and playing video games for a week. This practice forces participants to discover alternative activities such as playing board games as a family.

5-3 Activities for Accessing Valid Information

Media Literacy is often taught in English, Social Studies, and Health classes as a unit in and of itself, or infused into other units. Many of these activities can help achieve learning objectives in mental health, nutrition, drugs, human development, violence, and safety.

Scavenger Hunt

Arrange for student Internet access at school; this may include asking students to bring their cell phones or smart phones to class. Divide students into teams, and have the teams compete to find answers posed on a subject you are currently studying. Teams can search the Internet, or call someone who can help. Review their sources for reliability. (I, J, H)

Website Evaluation

As a class, visit several websites on a topic. Have students evaluate the site by answering these questions: Is the information presented trying to sell anything? Is the source of the information biased? Does the source of the information stand to profit in some way? (J, H)

News Analysis

Review with students news articles (either online or in newspapers or magazines) that arouse fear or anxiety, that represent wishful thinking, that exhibit sensationalism, or that present something as truth based on just one study. Discuss why news sources contain this type of material and why we need to be wary of it. (J, H)

Hooked!

Collect an assortment of magazines. (Physician offices will often donate old ones.) Display a fishing pole with a huge hook in the front of the class. Identify and explain the hooks advertisers use to lure us in and buy their products. Tell the students they are going to "catch" advertisers. Pass out the magazines. Instruct students to search for ad hooks. When they find one, they are to yell, "Caught one!" and then show and explain what they found. (I, J, H)

Warning: Rip-Offs

Have your students evaluate Internet advertisements and branded websites while being on the lookout for "Tip-Offs to Rip-Offs." Have students print out the examples they find, and then post their examples on a bulletin board under a warning sign. (P, I, J, H)

Online Help

Assign students to review various government and health agency websites searching for information, products, or resources related to something they are studying. (J, H)

5-4 Activities for Analyzing and Monitoring Media

Be sure to get school administration approval before showing students any advertisements, video clips, or streaming videos. Consider how you could integrate these ideas into mental health, nutrition, drugs, human development, or violence units.

Media Apples

Insert a nail into the bottom side of a beautiful apple. Remove the nail and rub it on decaying fruit or vegetables. Reinsert the nail into the apple. A few days later, show the students the apple. Discuss the attractiveness of the apple. Cut the apple in half, exposing its unattractive insides. Ask the students, "How is this apple like some media?" Discuss the hidden negative messages contained in programs and commercials. (P, I, J, H)

Are the Top 10 Really Good?

Ask students to identify their favorite movies and TV shows. List the top 10 on the board. Ask students to identify healthy/unhealthy and moral/immoral behaviors that characters model in each. Chart these behaviors on the board. Ask students how they think watching these shows might influence them and whether they think watching each of these shows is a good idea or a bad idea for younger siblings. (P, I, J, H)

Did You Hear That?

Select a popular CD that contains objectionable material. Review this CD at a website, such as http://www.pluggedinonline.com/music. In a class discussion, ask students if they can identify all the objectionable material on the CD. Share with them what the review said and discuss why it found certain things objectionable. (P, I, J, H)

Talk Back

Identify unhealthy messages and modeling in programs by showing a TV or movie clip in class. While you are running the clip, talk back to the characters in the scene. For instance, during an action scene, you could say, "Yeah, right, like I'm going to believe you can do that and it's okay—nobody gets hurt." Show additional scenes and invite the students to yell things at the screen. Challenge students to talk back to their TV for a week whenever they see unhealthy behaviors modeled. (P, I, J)

Stuck in My Head

Divide students into small groups. Have them identify 10 different advertising jingles or slogans that have stuck in their mind. Sharing examples can help them get started. Have the small groups share their slogans with the class and have the class try to identify the products for each. (I, J, H)

TV Ad Analysis

Videotape television commercials. You might want to record only commercials aired after school, on Saturday mornings, during prime time, or during athletic events. Show these ads in class, and discuss which industries choose to run their ads at these various times and why. Dissect the ads looking for hooks, emotional transfers, untruths, attitudes, values, and behaviors taught. (P, I, J, H)

Magazine Analysis

Have students bring copies of favorite magazines to class. In groups, have students analyze the magazines by answering these questions:

1. *Hooks.* What did the magazine producers do to the cover to hook the audience into looking at and buying the magazine?
2. *Ad space.* What percentage of total space is devoted to editorial stories and how much to advertisements? Watch for stories that are really ads. How many ads are in the magazine? What are they for? What do these advertisements tell you about the magazine's target audience?
3. *Images.* Describe the major characteristics (gender, appearance, age, race, ethnicity, behavior, and other characteristics) of the people shown in the magazine's content and ads.
4. *Messages.* Which unhealthy or poor value messages are presented by the magazine? Were any contradictory messages given, such as an article on dieting placed next to an ad or recipe for high-calorie food?
5. *Overall.* What do you believe is the overall message portrayed by this magazine? (I, J, H)

Advertisement Log

Have students make a log of all the ads they see that are not on an electric screen (e.g., clothing, signs, naming rights) during a period of 1 to 3 days. Have students share their lists and create an inclusive list on the board. Discuss what they found, including the location and perceived effectiveness of the ads. (I, J, H)

Merchants of Cool

Show students "The Merchants of Cool," a Frontline PBS report on the creators and sellers of popular culture who have made teens the hottest consumer demographic in the United States. This program exposes motives and techniques of advertising. After showing it, be sure to help students process what they saw and learned. (I, H)

Product Placement Count

Assign students to count the number of product placements they can find in a popular movie or in a specified television viewing time period. Have them share what they find.

Ad Spoof

Have students take a printed ad and construct a spoof of the ad that reveals an untruth or half-truth in the ad. Alcohol, tobacco, fast food, beauty, perfume, and weight-control products are good materials for this assignment. Have students show and explain their spoofs to the class. (I, J, H)

Pull the Plug

Challenge students to give up TV and video games for 1 week. During the week, have students share fun alternative things they did the night before. At the end of the week, have students create a display of all the things they did instead of watching TV. (P, I, J, H)

Student Use Survey

Have students conduct a class or school-wide survey to determine how much time children spend watching TV, playing video games, on the Internet, listening to music, and texting or talking on cell

(continues)

(continued)

phones. Use this survey to facilitate parents and children talking about media use, things they need to change at home, and things they could do instead. (I, J, H)

Billboard Review

Have students create a list of all the billboards they see during a typical week. Make a chart or grid showing how many times each billboard is looked at by students in the class. Discuss the types of products advertised in this way in their community and why promoters might choose this form of advertising. Discuss the validity and persuasiveness of each billboard. (P, I, J)

Am I Influenced?

Have students identify what they have spent their money on in the past week or month. Here is how one hundred 9- to 14-year-olds filled out a survey on what they spent their money on:

- 74 bought food (mostly snacks).
- 17 bought clothes or accessories.
- 14 bought magazines or comics; toys, stickers, or games; movie tickets; or arcade games.
- 13 bought gifts.
- 12 bought music or movie rentals.
- 11 bought sneakers and footwear.
- 11 bought grooming products.

Discuss how various forms of advertisements might influence how students spend their money. (I, J, H)

Advocate Letter

Have students write and send an e-mail message or letter to the producer of a movie, TV program, or advertisement that they find offensive. The letter could do any or all of the following: clearly express their opinion, document any supporting evidence for their position, and make one or more requests of the producer. (I, J, H)

Instruction Plan Worksheet Media Literacy

Use this worksheet to plan media literacy instruction at the grade level you will be teaching. It needs to be infused into all health education units. Refer to Chapter 2 for more information on how to complete each section in this worksheet.

■ Assess Needs

Identify topics and skills state or local curricula identify to be taught at _____ grade level.

Identify additional topics or skills the ME, HE, PA, SH, V, and S HECAT Modules (Standard 2) indicate for this grade.

Identify media literacy needs your particular students and their families have:
- How much time do your students spend using various forms of media each day?
- How many have smart phones, iPads, or TVs or computers with internet access in their bedrooms?
- What are their favorite TV programs, video games, websites, music genre?
- What family rules do they have for their media use?

■ Set Major Learning Goal(s)

Identify your major learning goal(s)—what do you want to have happen?

■ **Develop Instruction Map**

Create a map (calendar or list of days) indicating the time frame you have/need to teach the curriculum, meet student needs and reach goal(s). For each day indicate the content/skills to be taught. Work to create a good flow.

■ **Write SMART Unit Objectives**

Write 1 or 2 major objectives for each day you will teach. Your objectives should be in alignment with your state/local curricula, your student's needs, and your major learning goal(s).

■ **Identify Assessment Tools**

Preassessment	Formative-Assessment	Postassessment
How will you determine what students already know or do?	How will you know if they are "getting it"?	How will you know if students master objectives?

■ Develop Plan

Divide the chart into the number of days you will teach. Record each day's topic and objective key words. Identify activity names (in the book) that can help you meet each day's objective. Identify tech tools you can use and possible lesson adaptations you can make for special need learners.

Lesson Topic Objectives	Instruction Activities	Tech Tools	Adaptations for Learners

■ Develop Lesson Plans

Use this worksheet as you develop your other health education units and lesson plans..

KEY TERMS

media literacy 133	Girls Intelligence Agency (GIA) 140
ad creep 139	mobile marketing 140
naming rights 139	branded environments 141
digital (virtual) advertising 139	social media 143
product placement 139	information literacy 144
undercover marketing 139	Food and Drug Administration (FDA) 145
buzz 139	Consumer Product Safety Commission (CPSC) 145
viral marketing 139	Federal Trade Commission (FTC) 145
Tremor 139	National Health Information Center (NHIC) 145

KNOWLEDGE CHECK!

1. Define, differentiate, and discuss the key terms and their relative importance in this chapter.
2. Discuss youth media use, including technologies used, time spent, and heavy users.
3. Identify media use concerns regarding health risk behaviors, character and emotional development, quiet time, sleep needs, culture, stereotyping, and big media.
4. Identify six different concerns associated with Internet use.
5. Discuss the American Association of Pediatrics recommendations regarding children and adolescent media use.
6. What is the most important aspect of media? What are the real products sold?
7. What are the fundamental messages of all advertisements?
8. Discuss what goes into producing and airing an advertisement.
9. Identify advertisement hooks and persuasion tactics.
10. Describe why, where, and how ad creep takes place.
11. Explain why and how corporations target children with advertising and the many concerns about advertising to children.
12. Describe why and how school-based marketing takes place and the concerns it raises.
13. Describe Internet marketing prevalence and tactics, and the concerns it raises.
14. Explain how teachers can make videos, music, and PowerPoint slides effective teaching tools.
15. Identify the advantages of social media and the disadvantages that need to be overcome, and explain how to set up Facebook for classroom use.
16. Discuss how the reliability of information can be determined. Identify key questions to ask. Identify "Tip-Offs to Rip-Offs."
17. Identify federal agencies, voluntary agencies, and professional organizations that are reliable sources of health information.
18. Identify and discuss the five fundamental questions for analyzing media.
19. Discuss limiting use, online safety tips, making positive choices, and selecting alternatives as part of media management.
20. Identify activities that can be used to help teach media literacy skills.

REFERENCES

1. Bergsma L. Media literacy and prevention: going beyond "just say no." *Thinking critically about media: school and families in partnership*. Alexandria, VA: Cable in the Classroom; 2002. Available at http://www.medialit.org/reading-room/thinking-critically-about-media-schools-and-families-partnership. Accessed April 27, 2013.
2. Considine D. Media literacy across the curriculum. Available at http://www.medialit.org/sites/default/files/551_CICML-Considine.pdf. Accessed March 14, 2013.

3. Henry Kaiser Family Foundation. Available at http://www.kff.org/entmedia/entmedia012010nr.cfm. Accessed March 14, 2013.
4. Twenge JM. *Generation Me: why today's young Americans are more confident, assertive, entitled—and more miserable than ever before*. New York, NY: Free Press; 2006.
5. Recovery Connection. Sex addiction and substance abuse. Available at http://www.recoveryconnection.org. Accessed March 14, 2013.
6. Villani S. Impact of media on children and adolescents: a 10-year review of the research. *J Am Acad Child Adolesc Psychiatry*. 2001;40(4):392–401.
7. American Academy of Pediatrics, Committee on Public Education. Media education. Available at http://pediatrics.aappublications.org/content/104/2/341.full. Accessed March 1, 2013.
8. Adachi-Mejia A, Longacre M, Gibson J, et al. Children with a TV in their bedroom at higher risk for being overweight. *Int J Obes Relat Metab Disord*. 2007;31(4):644–651.
9. Barr-Anderson DJ, VanDenBer P, Neumark-Sztainer D, Story M. Characteristics associated with older adolescents who have a television in their bedrooms. *Pediatrics*. 2008;121(4):718–723.
10. Kilbourne J. *Can't buy my love: how advertising changes the way we think and feel*. New York, NY: Touchstone; 1999.
11. Kotler P, Armstrong G. *Principles of marketing*. Upper Saddle River, NJ: Prentice Hall; 2006.
12. Wolcott J. Hey kid—you wanna buy a . . . ? *Christian Science Monitor*. April 28, 2004.
13. Chamberlain L, Wang Y, Robinson TN. Does children's screen time predict requests for advertised products? *Pediatric Adol Med*. 2006;160:363–368.
14. Strausburger VC, Wilson BJ. *Children, adolescents, and the media*. Thousand Oaks, CA: Sage; 2002.
15. Hawkes C. *Marketing food to children: the global regulatory environment*. Geneva, Switzerland: World Health Organization; 2004.
16. Public Broadcasting System. Digital media: new learners of the 21st century. Available at http://www.pbs.org/parents/digital-media. Accessed March 14, 2013.
17. Osborne C. The pros and cons of social media in classrooms. April 10, 2012. Available at http://www.zdnet.com/blog/igeneration/the-pros-and-cons-of-social-media-classrooms/15132. Accessed March 14. 2013.
18. Kist W, Sheninger E. Creating learning connections: effective use of social media in the classroom. *Education Week Webinar*. Available at http://www.edweek.org/media/2012-08-29-creatinglearningconnections.pdf. Accessed March 14, 2013.
19. November A. *Web literacy for educators*. Thousand Oaks, CA: Corwin Press; 2008.
20. Kurtzweil P. How to spot health fraud. *FDA Consumer Magazine*. 1999.
21. Jeong S, Cho H, Hwang Y. Media literacy interventions: a meta-analytic review. *Journal of Communication, 62(3)*. 2012.
22. Williams R. The making of a media literate mind. *Mothering Magazine*. November–December 2004;127.

Chapter 6
Promoting Healthy Eating and Physical Activity

Courtesy of Cherry Mann.

Prevalence* of Self-Reported Obesity Among U.S. Adults
BRFSS, 2012

*Prevalence reflects BRFSS methodological changes in 2011, and these estimates should not be compared to those before 2011.

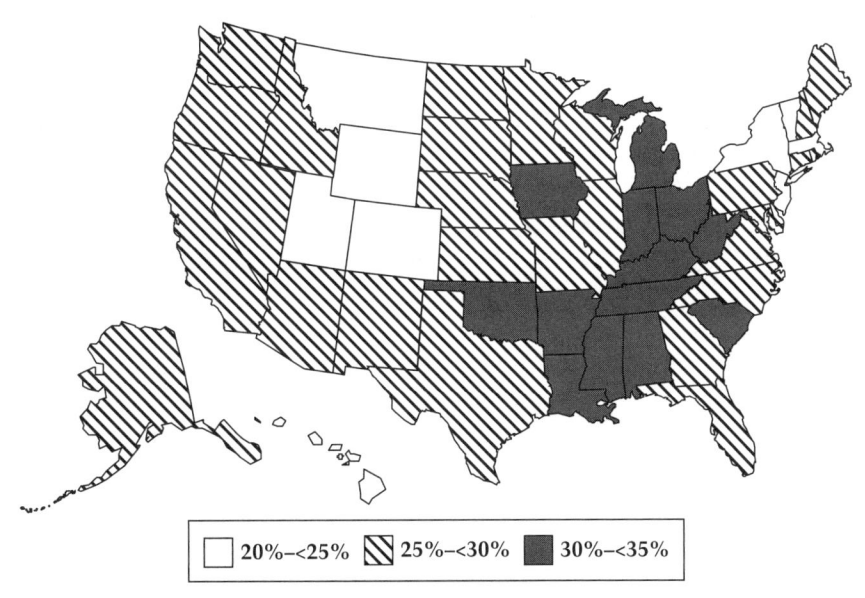

☐ 20%–<25% ▨ 25%–<30% ■ 30%–<35%

Source: Courtesy of the Centers for Disease Control and Prevention.

How Fat Are We?

This map indicates the prevalence of adult obesity in the United States. An animated map on the Centers for Disease Control and Prevention's (CDC's) Internet site graphically displays how U.S. state obesity rates changed between 1985 and 2010. This map and 31 PowerPoint slides of historical maps can be downloaded to help students conceptualize how the United States has become fat. These resources can be located at http://www.cdc.gov/obesity/data/adult.html.

Healthy eating patterns and regular physical activity promote optimal health, growth, and development in childhood and adolescence and reduce the risk for chronic disease in adulthood (e.g., coronary heart disease, cancer, stroke). This chapter is intended to help teachers optimize their potential in helping students adopt and establish lifelong healthy eating behaviors and physical activity patters. It examines how patterns of eating and physical activity contribute to health and well-being and explains what teachers can do to help young people establish these healthy habits.

TRENDS AND INFLUENCING FACTORS

Obesity levels in the United States have increased dramatically since 1990. Today more than one-third of all U.S. adults are obese, and approximately 17% of U.S. children and adolescents are obese. Since 1980, obesity prevalence has almost tripled among children and significant racial and ethnic disparities have become apparent. Hispanic boys and black girls are significantly more likely to be obese than their white counterparts. Black adults have the highest adult obesity prevalence at nearly 50%, and Mexican American adults have the second highest prevalence at 40%. Low socioeconomic status is also a risk factor for obesity. One in seven low-income preschool-age children is obese.[1,2]

To comprehend weight-related statistics, it is important to have a clear understanding of the terms *overweight* and *obese*. **Overweight** often is defined in health studies as having a **body mass index (BMI)** of 25 to 29.9, and being **obese** as having a BMI of 30 or higher. BMI is used in these definitions because, for most people, it correlates with their amount of body fat. For example, an adult who is 5'9" tall and weighs 125–168 pounds (BMI 18.5–25.9) is considered healthy weight. That same individual would be considered overweight at 169–202 pounds (BMI 25–29.9) and obese at 203 or more pounds (BMI 30 or higher). Because BMI is computed by a mathematical equation and not by directly measuring body fat, some people, such as athletes, may have a BMI that identifies them as overweight even though they do not have excess body fat. Many websites offer BMI calculators for adults and children, including http://www.ChooseMyPlate.gov.

Youth today are not eating as well as they should and are not getting all the physical activity they need. These behaviors bring about obesity and other health problems. Research indicates that most children and adolescents do not meet the recommendations for eating fruits and vegetables, whole grains, and limiting sodium intake.[3] Almost half of their caloric intake comes from eating empty calories in the form of added sugars and solid fats found in soda, fruit drinks, dairy desserts, grain desserts, fast food, and whole milk.[4] Black youth are more likely to not eat fruits, not drink milk, not eat breakfast, not be physically active, and be sedentary while watching television or using computers 3 or more hours per day.

Unfortunately, the American diet and lifestyle that have led to our nation's weight gain are spreading around the world, creating a pandemic often referred to as **globesity**. The dramatic increase in the prevalence of overweight and obesity among both children and adults has prompted health organizations and officials to warn of coming health problems and rises in healthcare costs (**Figure 6-1**). A former U.S. Surgeon General, David Satcher, said, "Left unabated, overweight and obesity may soon cause as much preventable disease and death as cigarette smoking."[5] We now look at other trends and factors that led to and continue to promote overweight and obesity in children and adults.

Physical Inactivity

Children today do not get as much incidental physical activity as their predecessors did. In past generations, children were likely to run to the store on errands, walk to school, or bike to sports team practices. Forty years ago, half of all children walked to school, but today only 10% do. One reason for this trend is that walking to school is not safe for some children. In many areas where children live, sidewalks—if they exist—end at the entrance to a subdivision or housing area. Modern suburban design often brings subdivision streets to connect to high-traffic roadways, which makes walking and biking dangerous. Many schools are located on busy highways or in areas that are dangerous for children to travel by foot or by bicycle unassisted.

The prevalence of overweight among adolescents has nearly tripled in the past 20 years

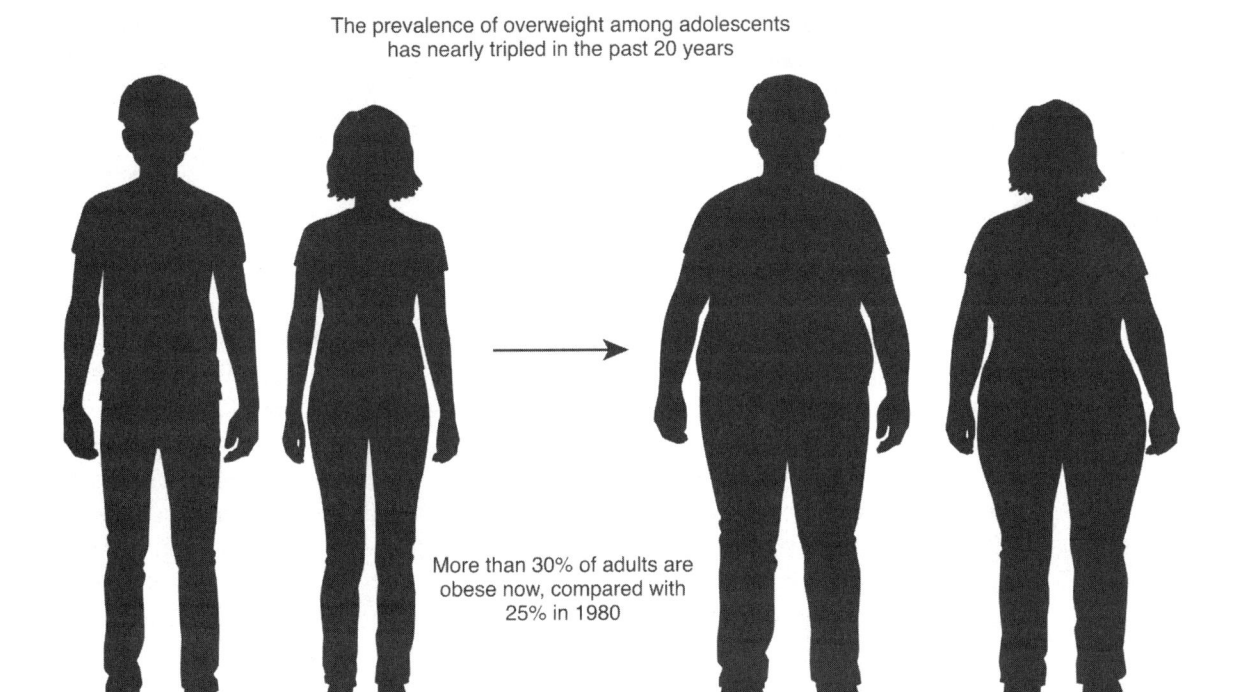

More than 30% of adults are obese now, compared with 25% in 1980

FIGURE 6-1 Problems associated with being overweight.

Today's children spend more time being sedentary indoors using electronic entertainment devices than they do in play or physical activity (**Figure 6-2**). Parents' worries about children's safety keep many children indoors instead of outdoors playing games or sports, walking, or biking. This is particularly true in inner cities, where youth have higher overweight and obesity rates than those in other areas.

The number of students enrolled in daily physical education classes and the percentage of time students spend in moderate or vigorous physical activity during physical education classes have also decreased over the past 20 years. This decline is largely attributed to the emphasis on testing and giving more time to core subjects. The childhood obesity epidemic, however, has made many people recognize the need for increased physical education in schools. Changing school policies to promote physical activity to prevent obesity in youth has been called for by *Healthy People 2010*,[6] the Institute of Medicine,[7] the Council on Sports Medicine, and the Council on School

FIGURE 6-2 This bike is broken . . . its motor is inside watching TV.

Health.[8] Unfortunately, limited fiscal resources often impede needed changes. In 2011, only 29% of high school students surveyed had participated in at least 60 minutes per day of physical activity on all 7 days before the survey, and only 31% attended physical education class daily.[9] Black high school students are almost twice as unlikely to not participate in physical activity on any day as white students.

Too Many Calories

Today we consume many more calories than our ancestors did. In part, this trend reflects the fact that inexpensive food is abundantly available. Portion sizes today are often double to four times the size considered normal 30 years ago, creating a phenomenon known as **portion distortion**. For instance, bagels today are typically 6 inches in diameter and contain 350 calories. Thirty years ago, they were only 3 inches in diameter and contained 140 calories. Portions have ballooned at restaurants, in grocery stores and bakeries, and at home. Cookbook recipes provide much larger serving portions than in the past, and the plates and bowls we use are larger than the ones our grandparents used.

We not only eat more, but also eat more calorie-dense foods both at home and when dining out. Restaurants know what sells best, and that, unfortunately, is calorie-dense food. For instance, when Burger King introduced its Enormous Omelet Sandwich, which consisted of two slices of cheese, two eggs, three strips of bacon, and a sausage patty, its breakfast sales jumped by 20%. When Pizza Hut got cheesier with a triple-cheese stuffed-crust pizza, that item alone accounted for 20% of the chain's business within 4 days.

Poor eating habits play a role in weight gain and can cause health problems even for those who do not become overweight. Poor dietary habits often displayed by young people include skipping meals (especially breakfast); dieting; avoiding nutritious foods such as milk, fruits, or vegetables; and frequently eating fast food and other low-nutritive, high-energy foods and drinks. Less than one-third of youth say they eat the recommended amounts of fruits and vegetables in a day.[9] In addition, many kids today prefer drinking soda pop over drinking milk (**Figure 6-3**).

Like it or not, as an educator you will be modeling your personal eating and physical activity patterns for your students. Take the time to complete the self-analysis in **Box 6-1**. As you review your diet and activity record, analyze the factors in your life that influence your healthy and unhealthy eating and activity habits.

Family and Social Factors

Children and adolescents today frequently decide what to eat with little adult supervision. The availability of convenience foods and fast-food restaurants in the community and in the school cafeteria inhibit the ability of parents to monitor their children's eating habits. The desire for

We have become used to supersized portions.

Teen (ages 12–19) consumption of milk and soft drinks

1970s   Today

FIGURE 6-3   Liquid candy. A 12-ounce can of nondiet soda has about 10 teaspoons of sugar, 150 calories, and no nutritive value.

independence and identity, concern for appearance, and peer acceptance all play roles in youths' food choices. Family background, increased independence and mobility, and money for discretionary spending on food products also influence eating habits.

About half of the money Americans spend on food today is spent at restaurants. We eat out more for three main reasons: our fast-paced lifestyle; the relatively low cost of fast food; and our appetite for fatty, salty, and sweet food. Eating out has become such a way of life that many young adults have minimal to no cooking skills. Even poor people living in inner cities eat a great deal of cheap fast food. McDonald's, Burger King, and other fast-food outlets are much more plentiful in inner cities than are grocery stores. Often the only options for buying groceries in "rough" neighborhoods are small convenience stores that offer limited or no fruits, vegetables, and other healthy food items.

Media Use

Numerous international studies show that media use is contributing to the current epidemic of obesity worldwide.[10] Sedentary activities take time away from participation in energy-expending physical activities. Television viewing is also associated with snacking on high-energy, low-nutrient foods. Food marketing to children is a massive enterprise that is composed almost entirely of messages promoting consumption of nutrient-poor, calorie-dense foods. Food advertisements targeting children encourage preferences for high-fat, high-sugar foods and are considered a factor contributing to childhood obesity.

6-1 Application Exercise

Diet and Activity Analysis

For 3 days, keep a detailed record of everything you eat, including the amounts you eat and the triggers that prompted you to eat (e.g., smell, sight, time, hunger). For the same 3 days, also keep track of how much time you spend doing moderate activity (e.g., walking) and vigorous activity (e.g., jogging.) Keeping records tends to motivate us to do better, but try to maintain your usual habits for this analysis. When your record is compete, go to the http://www.ChooseMyPlate.gov website and analyze your diet and activity record using the SuperTracker tools. Determine your BMI. Write a summary of what you have learned about your habits and indicate changes you would like to make.

The U.S. food industry is the second largest advertiser in the American economy, and it targets children and teenagers because of their vulnerability and spending power. Food advertisements are now much more prevalent and sophisticated than in the past. Ads often include a push to a website and tie-ins to games, toys, and TV and movie characters. Advertisers know that children and teens spend billions of dollars of their own money on snacks, beverages, and fast food each year. It is also estimated that children influence almost three-fourths of their families' food and beverage purchases. In turn, advertisement campaigns have been designed to help children know how to pester their parents into buying what they want. Ads are also designed to create brand loyalty. For instance, McDonald's has run ads suggesting that children can be started on fast foods (e.g., hamburgers, fries, shakes) at a very young age.

Unhealthy food choices are also marketed to children at the point of sale. Product package design constitutes a $100 billion per year industry. Walking down the cereal aisle of a grocery store reveals the various advertising appeals used to create visual appeal, attract children's attention, and build brand loyalty. Retail studies have shown that as many as 85% of all consumer purchases are made on impulse, and packaging design has a great deal to do with impulse purchases made by or influenced by children.[11] Restaurants represent another venue for points of sale to children by offering playgrounds, cartoon characters, and kids' meals that include toy giveaways.

The Internet also markets food to children. Companies sponsor websites with online games where branded food products are embedded features. Identification characters or spokes-characters are the main focus of the games. Players spend their time focused on the embedded product without being aware that they are staring at an advertisement the entire time they are playing a game.

One common tactic in TV-based food marketing directed toward children is to depict food as having a drug-like property. Eating the product is associated with exaggerated pleasure (euphoric highs), kaleidoscopic colors (visual hallucinations), taking extreme measures to obtain the food (needing a fix), and loss of control over the food product (addiction). Making connections or associations of food and mood alteration and addictive behavior to sell products to children is seen by many as irresponsible and potentially harmful.[12]

Energy Drinks

Energy drinks such as Red Bull, Monster, 5-Hour Energy, and Full Throttle are one of the United States' fastest-growing markets and have some health professionals worried about their health implications. These drinks often contain controversial ingredients, including Guarani, taurine, ginseng, and caffeine. Although these substances may be harmless when taken in low doses, they can do major damage when consumed in large amounts. The amount of caffeine in a single can of most energy drinks is more than three times the physician-recommended daily limit for caffeine intake. Small "energy shot" drinks contain even more. The Food and Drug Administration does not regulate these drinks. Also troublesome is the fact that some products contain both caffeine and alcohol. A trend of mixing alcohol and energy drinks has emerged. Those who drink alcohol combined with an energy drink often feel wide awake and less impaired than they really are; in turn, they are more likely to be drunk when they drive after consuming such mixed drinks.

Food in Schools

Many schools today provide a variety of food options: foods are for sale in vending machines, school stores, and snack bars, and á la carte foods are for sale in the cafeteria. Students also bring foods into schools and often exchange food items. Food allergies are a particular concern in the school environment. A **food allergy** is an abnormal immune response to a certain food that the body reacts to as harmful. Although the reasons for this trend are poorly understood, the prevalence of food allergies and associated anaphylaxis appears to be on the rise. School personnel need to be ready to effectively manage emergency needs. One-fourth of all anaphylaxis reactions that occur in schools happen among students with no previous food allergy diagnosis.[13]

The availability of low-nutritive foods at schools appears to be a major cause of poor eating habits in youth.[14] Faced with the challenges of increasing financial pressures and limited resources, schools often put nutrition at the bottom of their priority list. Many schools have compensated for lost funds from budget cuts by increasing the sale of á la carte foods and fast-food options. Other schools have entered into contracts with food or beverage marketers to generate additional income. Some school districts have negotiated exclusive "pouring contracts" with soft drink companies and receive a percentage of profits when sales volume increases. Such arrangements offer a substantial incentive for schools to promote soft-drink consumption by adding vending machines, increasing the times they are available, and marketing the products to students.[14]

In spite of these incentives, there are many examples of schools making wise nutrition changes for their students. On the CDC's website, **Make It Happen—School Nutrition Success Stories** can be accessed. The theme of these case studies is that students will buy and consume healthful foods and beverages and that schools can make money from healthful options.

Media's Influence on Body Image

It is pretty hard not to be affected by the media's constant message that "Thin is in!" By the time a girl reaches age 17, she is likely to have seen 250,000 commercials that emphasize the importance of beauty and physical attractiveness. The women portrayed in almost every ad are not typical of normal, healthy women. Fashion models weigh substantially less than the average women, and

Young girls "buy" media messages about beauty, love, success, and acceptability.

it has been estimated that a young woman in the United States has only a 1% chance of being as thin as a supermodel.

Advertisers purposefully normalize unrealistically thin bodies in ads to create an unattainable desire that drives product purchase and consumption. In other words, when individuals realize that their own bodies are not in line with the desired or ideal body shape, they become anxious, frustrated, and disappointed. The overriding message is that we need to change something about ourselves to be accepted, loved, or successful, and that the correct change is to buy the advertised product.

Being able to analyzing media messages is a vital skill for young people today—and a skill identified in the National Health Education Standards. At the end of the chapter you will find some teaching activity ideas for helping your students learn how to analyze media food messages and how to make healthy eating choices.

■ PROBLEMS RELATED TO UNHEALTHY EATING AND INACTIVITY

There are many problems and consequences of unhealthy eating and physical inactivity for school-age youth. Risk factors for heart disease, such as high cholesterol and high blood pressure, occur with increased frequency in overweight children and adolescents. The consequences of being overweight go beyond disease. Children who are overweight or obese feel tremendous psychological pain as a result of their condition. They are likely to suffer from a poor self-image and feelings of inferiority and rejection. They are often teased, ridiculed, and left out of games, athletics, and other activities. The rejection and isolation that result from this treatment are a source of intense frustration and may cause a child to withdraw, act out, and overeat.

Substantial weight gain in very young girls can sometimes trigger premature puberty—as early as age 8 or 9 years in some girls. Puberty then triggers additional weight gain. Approximately 2 years later, a young girl begins menstruation and soon reaches full height. If her extra weight gain triggers premature puberty, a young girl often loses inches in height that she would otherwise have achieved, missing the opportunity for her height to catch up or for her to "grow into" the added weight.

Undernutrition also causes problems. Many students start school with no breakfast or an inadequate breakfast. Skipping breakfast is not limited to children who live in poverty. Many children who can afford breakfast go to school without eating breakfast. Even those children who eat before leaving the house may become hungry long before lunch time. Starting the school day hungry puts students at a disadvantage. Physical, emotional, and psychological effects of hunger interfere with students' ability to learn and to perform academically and socially. Over time, undernutrition can have lasting effects on children's cognitive development and school performance. Chronically undernourished children attain lower scores on standardized achievement tests, especially tests of language ability.

Adolescent girls are at higher risk of failing to meet nutritional requirements than are boys. The overwhelming desire of many adolescent girls to be thin can create energy and nutritional inadequacies. Adolescent boys on the whole consume greater amounts of food than girls and are less likely to suffer nutritional deficiencies. Adolescent girls, by comparison, are at high risk for **iron-deficiency anemia** because of inadequate intake of foods high in iron and vitamin C, which helps the body absorb iron. Lacking sufficient iron, the young person's body has reduced ability to produce hemoglobin. Hemoglobin is needed to carry oxygen in the blood, so girls with iron-deficiency anemia have difficulty paying attention and suffer from fatigue. They are also vulnerable to infections.

Unsafe Weight-Loss Methods

Being overweight, fearing weight gain, and feeling pressure to be thin lead many young people to practice unsafe weight-loss methods. Such dieting attempts often begin in elementary school. The **unsafe weight-loss methods** of skipping meals, fasting for long periods of time, taking diet pills, using laxatives, inducing vomiting after meals, and going on crash diets can be problematic. Deliberately restricting food intake over long periods can lead to poor growth, delayed sexual development, and eating disorders.

Eating disorders are food-related means by which individuals attempt to relieve emotional problems, such as low self-esteem, lack of social acceptance, fear of rejection, and inability to express feelings in appropriate ways. Often, eating disorders begin as youth use unsafe weight-loss methods and then keep using those methods to try to solve their emotional problems. Young girls are especially susceptible to eating disorders just before or just after puberty. The emergence of an eating disorder may be an unconscious effort to delay physical maturing of the body. Stress may also trigger eating disorders. Stressful life events that may trigger eating disorders include moving, parental divorce or death, a broken love relationship, or ridicule by others that the individual is fat or becoming fat.

Smoking is an unsafe means that some young people use to regulate weight. Concern about weight gain is a major issue among young women smokers. Because slenderness is highly prized, adolescents may be willing to overlook the very serious long-term consequences of smoking (e.g., emphysema, lung cancer) to achieve or maintain a desirable body weight.

Teachers of all grade levels need to have a clear understanding how to safely lose weight, because students at even early elementary levels may be dieting. **Box 6-2** describes the elements found in safe weight-loss programs. **Box 6-3** details an activity that can help you teach key weight-loss principles that children can understand and that everyone will remember.

6-2

Safe Weight-Loss Programs

Safe and effective weight-loss programs should include the following components:

- Healthy eating plans that reduce calories but do not forbid specific foods or food groups.
- Tips to increase moderate-intensity physical activity.
- Tips on healthy behavior changes that also keep your cultural needs in mind.
- Slow and steady weight loss. Depending on your starting weight, experts recommend losing weight at a rate of 0.5–2 lb per week. Weight loss may be faster at the start of a program.
- Medical care if you are planning to lose weight by following a special-formula diet, such as a very-low-calorie (1,200 calories or less) diet.
- A plan to keep the weight off after you have lost it.

To take off 1 pound per week, you will need to reduce calories (the amount of food you eat) by 500 per day. (One pound of body fat equals about 3,500 calories.) Try eating 250 calories less per day and exercising enough to burn 250 calories—by walking about 2.5 miles each day. The easiest way to cut back on calories is to watch your portion sizes.

> ### 6-3
>
> **Fat Burning Analogy**
>
> Help students understand that losing fat is a lot like burning logs. Show students the following items:
>
> ◆ A picture of a wood-burning stove. (It is like our muscles where our calories are burned.)
> ◆ A large log. (It is like fat, full of potential energy.)
> ◆ A long paper chain. (The chain is like a complex carbohydrate, and one link is like glucose.)
>
> Discuss how you cannot start a log on fire without some kindling, and explain that our bodies cannot burn fat without glucose. Tear off one paper chain and explain how it is like a molecule of glucose, the log is like fat, and the stove is like our muscles. Describe how our muscles burn protein (themselves) when glucose is not available to "ignite" fat.
>
> Discuss how we need to eat complex carbohydrates to ensure that we have a steady stream of glucose available to help burn our fat. This consideration is especially important when we diet so that we can burn our fat instead of our muscles. If we lose muscle while dieting, we will have a more difficult time burning calories because we do not have as much muscle to burn fat in.
>
> Describe how when we eat something full of simple sugars, such as a cookie or candy bar, our blood sugar levels spike, and then our pancreas releases insulin to bring the levels back down. With little sugar in our blood, we are soon craving more sweets. In contrast, when we eat complex carbohydrates, such as brown rice and vegetables, digestion slowly breaks these large molecules into glucose. This slow process makes our blood sugar levels only slightly elevated, keeping us feeling satisfied and not hungry, and it slowly produces the glucose our muscles need to burn fat. (I, J, H)

Anorexia Nervosa

Anorexia nervosa is a serious psychological disorder that affects many more females than males. This disorder is characterized by having a body weight at least 15% below normal weight for age and height, an intense fear of gaining weight or becoming fat, and body image distortion. Also, menstrual periods are often absent in females with anorexia. A central feature of anorexia nervosa in adolescents is the issue of control. By controlling her weight through obsessive dieting, an anorexic female feels she is able to gain greater control over her life. Anorexia nervosa can be fatal, however, owing to its tendency to produce kidney failure or heart shrinkage. It is sometimes necessary to hospitalize patients in severe cases to prevent death.

Anorexics do not lack appetite, but refuse to eat, whether they are hungry or not. For anorexics, the idea of becoming fat creates intense fear and disgust. As the self-starvation progresses, these individuals frequently experience behavioral and mood changes. Normal perception of what their bone and skin frames look like becomes distorted. Even though they are emaciated, they typically feel too fat. This misperception arises in part because of where females lose weight first—in the upper body. As their chests shrink, their hips appear to grow. Individuals with anorexia also mistake the sensation of food in their digestive tract as fat. They suffer fatigue and may be sensitive to cold. Their skin becomes dry and grayish. In advanced stages of the disease, a fine, downy covering of hair appears all over the body; it represents the body's attempt to provide a thermal padding for lost fat layers.

Persons with anorexia come from all socioeconomic levels and are frequently high achievers. Nevertheless, it is common for grade-point averages and other signs of high achievement to decline as the anorexia progresses. Individuals with this eating disorder have an overwhelming need to please their parents and teachers. Parents are often shocked at their child's starvation tactics because they are contrary to the usual good behavior and obedience that are characteristic of the child. Anorexic children usually conform to rules at home and outside of the home. This conforming is often to the point of losing self-esteem and the capacity for independent thought.

Bulimia

Bulimia is an eating disorder that consists of gorging on food, followed by self-induced vomiting or purging. This behavioral disorder may be part of anorexia nervosa or it may constitute a distinct, separate disorder. As with anorexia nervosa, most persons with bulimic behaviors are female. Unlike anorexia nervosa, which typically emerges during early and middle adolescence, bulimia is most likely to occur during the late teenage years or early twenties.

Bulimic people are usually aware of their abnormal eating habits and fear not being able to control their eating. Food-binging episodes are followed by efforts to control weight through dieting, fasting, or purging. These efforts may include vomiting, compulsive exercising, or the use of laxatives, diuretics, enemas, and weight-reducing drugs (e.g., amphetamines). Food binges often represent responses to intense emotions such as depression, anger, loneliness, stress, and feelings of inadequacy; they serve to tranquilize or calm these negative feelings. Bulimics may consume as many as 1,000 to 10,000 calories or more per binge. Self-induced vomiting produces a sense of relief and often a feeling of euphoria. Vomiting episodes are often described by bulimic persons in sexual terms, ascribing to the vomiting an orgasmic quality. The resulting relief and euphoria are often associated with a sense of calmness, relaxation, and tiredness. These feelings, however, are short lived and replaced by disgust, guilt, shame, and self-condemnation. A progression to more serious feelings of depression, hopelessness, and suicidal ideation is also common.

Although most bulimics maintain normal body weight, bulimia carries the risk of serious medical complications. Kidney impairment and heart irregularities may develop. In addition, the stomach or esophagus may rupture in response to binging or purging episodes. Chronic hoarseness, premature facial wrinkles, electrolyte disturbances, and hemorrhages in the conjunctiva of the eye are other complications. Tooth decay and erosion may result from regurgitation of acidic gastric contents. Syrup of ipecac, an over-the-counter drug used for inducing vomiting in poison victims, is sometimes abused by bulimics to purge after food binges. Repeated use of syrup of ipecac can cause irreversible heart damage. One famous victim of syrup of ipecac abuse was Karen Carpenter, a popular singer and performer during the 1970s.

■ DISEASES RELATED TO UNHEALTHY EATING AND INACTIVITY

The eating practices that contribute to disease are established early in life. Young people who have unhealthy eating habits tend to maintain these habits as they age. For this reason, it is critical that children and adolescents are taught healthy eating patterns before poor habits become firmly established. Health experts note that the number of deaths from obesity, overweight, and lack of physical activity in the United States exceeds the number of persons killed annually by pneumonia, motor vehicle accidents, and airline crashes combined. Overweight and obesity are associated with type 2 diabetes, heart disease, high blood pressure, certain types of cancer, stroke, arthritis, breathing problems, and psychological disorders such as depression. Unhealthy eating patterns are also associated with osteoporosis, dental decay, anemia, and poor academic performance. The good news is that many of these health problems and disease symptoms can be minimized and occasionally overcome when individuals diagnosed with them build healthy eating patterns and effectively manage their weight. **Box 6-4** outlines both the immediate effects and possible chronic diseases a person can experience from unhealthy eating and inactivity.

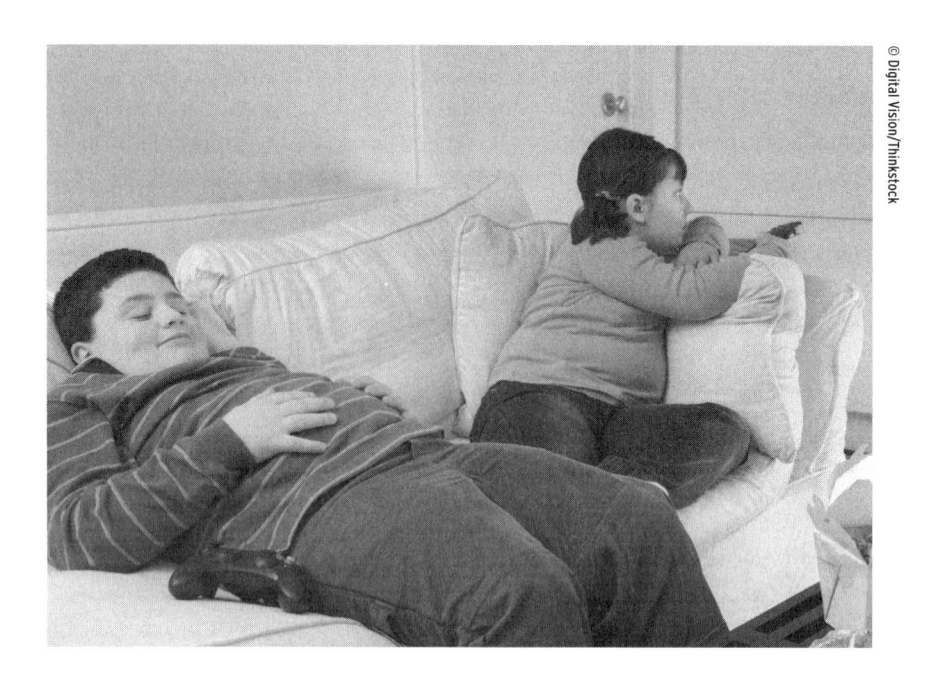

Diabetes

The United States is experiencing an epidemic of diabetes, and health experts attribute this epidemic to the rising obesity rates among adults and children. Rates of diabetes are particularly high in the southeastern states of the United States and among minority populations.[15] The CDC warns that one in three U.S. children born in 2000 risks becoming diabetic unless people start eating less and exercising more.

Type 1 diabetes, which was previously called insulin-dependent diabetes mellitus or juvenile-onset diabetes, accounts for about 5% of all diagnosed cases of diabetes. **Type 2 diabetes** is a diet-related chronic disease that can develop during childhood or adolescence. In the past it was called adult-onset diabetes because it occurred mostly in men and women older than age 50. Now

6-4

Effects of Unhealthy Eating Patterns

Chronic Disease Risks
- Diabetes
- High blood pressure
- Coronary health disease
- Stroke
- Cancer
- Osteoporosis
- Arthritis

Immediate Possible Effects
- Dental caries
- Poor concentration
- Overweight/obesity
- Psychological pain
- Premature puberty
- Iron-deficiency anemia
- Eating disorders

type 2 diabetes is showing up at an increasing rate among children, especially those who are obese and physically inactive.

In type 2 diabetes, the pancreas is usually producing enough insulin, but for unknown reasons the body cannot use the insulin effectively, a condition called **insulin resistance**. After several years, the insulin production decreases. For this reason, healthy eating, physical activity, and blood glucose testing are the basic therapies for type 2 diabetes. Basic therapies for type 1 diabetes include all of these measures plus insulin injections.

Uncontrolled blood sugar can injure blood vessels, leading to serious health problems and even life-threatening conditions such as blindness, kidney disease, nerve damage, and heart disease. Children and adolescents diagnosed with diabetes have a longer time span in which to develop these complications than individuals who develop the disease later in life. It appears that type 2 diabetes is a more aggressive disease when it occurs at a young age, increasing the individual's risk of complications, but there is hope. People with diabetes can take steps to control the disease and lower their risks of complications. People with prediabetes who lose weight, eat right, and increase their physical activity can prevent or delay diabetes and return their blood glucose (blood sugar) levels to normal.

Cases of diabetes have occurred in early childhood, but the peak age for diagnosis is usually after the onset of puberty. Changes in hormone levels during puberty can cause insulin resistance and decreased insulin action. Nearly 215,000 people younger than 20 years had diabetes (type 1 or type 2) in the United States in 2010.[15]

The symptoms of type 2 diabetes develop gradually; they are not as sudden in onset as the symptoms of type 1 diabetes. These symptoms may include fatigue or nausea, frequent urination, unusual thirst, weight loss, blurred vision, frequent infections, and slow healing of wounds or sores. Some people, however, have no symptoms.

Coronary Heart Disease

Poor eating habits and obesity are known to contribute to the development of coronary heart disease, high blood pressure, and stroke. Heart disease is the leading cause of death for both men and women in the United States—responsible for 1 in every 4 deaths. The correlation between weight, diabetes, and heart disease is easily seen by looking at maps depicting heart disease death rates, obesity rates, and diabetes rates. All three of these rates are highest in the southeastern portion of the United States and are higher among minority populations.[16] Non-Hispanic blacks also have higher rates of high blood pressure. **High blood pressure** is called the "silent killer" because it often has no warning signs or symptoms, so people may not realize they have it. About 1 in 3 U.S. adults is estimated to have high blood pressure, and this condition increases the risk for heart disease and stroke.[17]

Heart disease is caused by narrowing of the coronary arteries that feed the heart. Like any muscle, the heart needs a constant supply of oxygen and nutrients, which are carried to it by the blood in the coronary arteries. When the coronary arteries become narrowed or clogged by cholesterol and fat deposits—a process called **atherosclerosis**—and cannot supply enough blood to the heart, the result is coronary heart disease. Atherosclerosis can begin in childhood.

Cholesterol is a waxy, fatlike substance that occurs naturally in all parts of the body. Our bodies need cholesterol to function normally. In fact, this lipid is present in cell walls and membranes everywhere in the body, including the brain, nerves, muscle, skin, liver, intestines, and heart. Our bodies use cholesterol to produce many hormones, vitamin D, and the bile acids that help to digest fat—but it takes only a small amount of cholesterol in the blood to meet these needs. If a person has too much cholesterol in the bloodstream, the excess becomes deposited in arteries (including the coronary arteries), where it contributes to the narrowing and blockages that cause the signs and symptoms of heart disease.

If not enough oxygen-carrying blood reaches the heart, the individual may experience a type of chest pain called **angina**. If the blood supply to a portion of the heart is completely cut off by total blockage of a coronary artery, the result is a **heart attack**. A heart attack is usually the result of a sudden closure of the artery by a blood clot forming within a previous narrowing.

Cancer

Researchers agree that poor diets and sedentary lifestyles are among the most important factors contributing to cancer risk. A poor diet can increase the risk for lung, esophageal, stomach, colorectal, and prostate cancers. At least one-third of all cancer deaths are linked to poor diet, physical inactivity, and carrying excess weight.[18]

Except for quitting smoking, the best way to cut your risk of cancer is to achieve and maintain a healthy weight, to be physically active on a regular basis, and to make healthy food choices. Being active helps with weight control and can also reduce your cancer risk by influencing hormone levels and your immune system. Eating *at least* five servings of vegetables (including legumes) and fruits each day, especially those with the most color (a sign of high nutrient content), provides antioxidants and many other substances that work together to lower risk of several cancers, including cancers of the lung, mouth, esophagus, stomach, and colon. Eating whole grains adds fiber to the diet that helps prevent constipation, dilutes hazardous carcinogenic substances, and provides an environment conducive to "friendly" bacteria. Cutting back on processed meats such as hot dogs, bologna, and luncheon meat and red meats such as beef, pork, and lamb may help reduce the risk of colon and prostate cancers.[19]

Osteoporosis and Arthritis

Osteoporosis is a disease in which bones become fragile and more likely to break. It is often called a silent disease because the bone loss occurs without symptoms. The first symptom may be a fracture or a collapsed vertebra in the spine. When vertebrae collapse, the result is severe back pain, loss of height, or spinal deformities and stooped posture.

The risk of osteoporosis increases with age if you are female and may be, in part, hereditary. Caucasian and Asian women are more likely to develop osteoporosis than are African American and Hispanic women. Small-boned and thin women are at the greatest risk, and early menopause increases the risk of developing osteoporosis. Smoking cigarettes, drinking alcohol, consuming an inadequate amount of calcium, and getting little or no weight-bearing exercise are lifestyle factors that increase risk.

Consuming enough **calcium** is particularly important during childhood, adolescence, and young adulthood to reduce one's risk of osteoporosis. Adolescent females tend to consume less calcium than the amount recommended by health experts—namely, at least 1,200 mg of calcium per day. An adequate calcium supply helps bones to reach their maximum density. To meet the calcium recommendation, girls need to consume a minimum of three servings daily of milk or yogurt. Given that almost half of an adult's bone mass is formed during the teen years, inadequate calcium intake among children and adolescents is a serious concern. Young females who consume inadequate amounts of dietary calcium are at increased risk for osteoporosis in later life.

Young people need to understand that their bones become stronger and denser when the demands of physical activity are placed on them. **Weight-bearing exercises** are those in which your bones and muscles work against gravity, such as jogging, walking, climbing stairs, dancing, and playing soccer. **Resistance exercises** use muscular strength to improve muscle mass and strengthen bone, such as the use of free weights and weight machines. The National Osteoporosis Foundation recommends both types of exercise for building and maintaining bone mass and density.

Arthritis is another bone-related disorder. It involves painful inflammation in one or more joints of the body. There are over 100 different forms of arthritis that are the result of joint trauma, infection, or age. Carrying extra body weight is hard on body joints and can cause the protective cartilage between bones to wear down creating arthritis. As obesity rates have climbed, so have the number of people dealing with both obesity and arthritis. These individuals need to be physical active to help improve both their weight and their arthritis, but fear of pain can get in the way of their motivation to become more active.

Dental Decay

According to the CDC, **dental decay** is one of the most common chronic infectious diseases among U.S. children. This preventable health problem begins early. By the age of 8, approximately 52% of children have experienced decay, and by the age of 17, dental decay affects 78% of children. Among low-income children, almost 50% of tooth decay remains untreated and may result in pain, dysfunction, underweight, and poor appearance—problems that can greatly reduce a child's capacity to succeed in the educational environment.[20]

Dietary habits often contribute to the development of dental caries in children. Sticky, sweet food is very bad for teeth because it maintains high sugar levels in the mouth and is very likely to cause tooth decay. There is also a positive correlation between soft-drink consumption and dental decay. In many carbonated beverages, the sugar content can equal 10 teaspoons per 12 ounces. Most carbonated beverages contain phosphoric acid, citric acid, and carbonic acid, all of which lead to chemical erosion of teeth.

■ SCHOOL HEALTH GUIDELINES TO PROMOTE HEALTHY EATING AND PHYSICAL ACTIVITY

The CDC has established the following **School Health Guidelines** to serve as the foundation for developing, implementing, and evaluating school-based healthy eating and physical activity policies and practices for students. Each of the nine guidelines is associated with a set of implementation strategies that were developed to help schools work toward achieving it; these implementation strategies can be found on the CDC's website.[21]

1. Use a coordinated approach to develop, implement, and evaluate healthy eating and physical activity policies and practices.
2. Establish school environments that support healthy eating and physical activity.
3. Provide a high-quality school meal program and ensure that students have only appealing, healthy food and beverage choices offered outside of the school meal.
4. Implement a comprehensive physical activity program with high-quality physical education as the cornerstone.
5. Implement health education that provides students with the knowledge, attitudes, skills, and experiences needed for livelong healthy eating and physical activity.
6. Provide students with health, mental health, and social services to address healthy eating, physical activity, and related chronic disease prevention.
7. Partner with families and community members in the development and implementation of healthy eating and physical activity policies, practices, and programs.
8. Provide a school employee wellness program that includes healthy eating and physical activity services for all school staff members.

9. Employ qualified persons, and provide professional development opportunities for physical education, health education, nutrition services, and health, mental health, and social services staff members, as well as staff members who supervise recess, cafeteria time, and out-of-school-time programs.

Supportive School Environment

The availability of healthy and appealing foods in school cafeterias, vending machines, school stores, and at school functions is critically important in supporting positive behaviors. These health messages are undermined, however, when teachers use food or physical activity as rewards or punishments. Some teachers give candy or other sweets as a reward for good behavior or as prizes for games and competitions. If food is served in classrooms, teachers should see that healthy snacks and treats are served and that consideration is given to possible food allergies, religious prohibitions, and safe food handling. Making students who misbehave or fail to meet expectations run laps or do other exercises can lead young people to create negative associations with physical activity.

Teachers and school personnel need to serve as positive role models for students. Health promotion programs can foster healthy habits among school personnel and students and create many benefits. Teachers who participate in them are absent from work less and report higher levels of job satisfaction. Participating in health promotion programs improves levels of physical fitness, lowers levels of body fat and blood pressure, and reduces stress.

A supportive school environment provides adequate time for both health education and physical activity. Curricula need to include sufficient time for students to be able to master concepts and become proficient in behavioral skills.

School Personnel Collaboration

The efficacy of good nutrition and fitness education is enhanced when teachers and other school personnel coordinate their efforts and collaborate with one another. Foodservice personnel can serve as guest speakers in classes focusing on nutrition topics. Physical education teachers are great resources for promoting physical fitness. Counselors can give guidance for teaching behavioral skills associated with healthy lifestyle issues. Many schools plan health fairs, and school nurses and other professionals mentioned in this section are wonderful resources when it comes to planning such an event or similar activities.

Parental Involvement

Helping parents modify their children's eating behaviors may be one of the most effective ways to improve the eating behaviors of students; the same is true for physical activity. Here are a few ideas on how schools can involve parents in promoting healthy eating and physical activity:

- Send nutrition and physical activity education materials and cafeteria menus home with students.
- Ask parents to send healthy snacks to school.
- Invite parents to periodically eat with their children in the cafeteria and participate in recess, ball games, fun walks/runs, dances and other health promotion activities.
- Invite families to attend exhibitions of student nutrition projects at health fairs.
- Offer nutrition education workshops and screening services.
- Assign homework that students can do with their families (e.g., reading and interpreting food labels, reading nutrition-related newsletters, preparing healthy recipes).
- Request that parents serve as volunteers, coaches, or leaders of extracurricular physical activity programs and for community sports and recreation programs.

Community Involvement

Students are most likely to adopt healthy behaviors if they receive consistent messages through multiple channels (e.g., home, school, community, media) and from multiple sources (e.g., parents, peers, teachers, health professionals, media). Schools should establish community links with qualified public health and nutrition professionals who can provide screening, referral, and counseling for nutrition problems; inform families about supplemental nutrition services available in the community, such as WIC (Women, Infants, and Children), food stamps, and local food pantries; and implement nutrition education and health promotion activities for school faculty, other staff, school board members, and parents.

Community resources can also be used to create healthy eating incentives. For instance, local farmers markets can help promote the idea of eating fresh local foods, local grocery stores can provide samples of fruits and vegetables that students may have not tasted, and extension agencies can demonstrate healthy meal planning and preparation. Jamie Oliver serves as an example of how major changes can take place in a community when schools work in tandem with community leaders—check out his "Food Revolution" on the Internet.

HEALTHY EATING CURRICULA

Education about healthy eating should aim to help students develop the knowledge, attitudes, and behaviors they need to establish and maintain patterns of healthy eating. The curriculum needs to focus on the relationship between personal behavior (diet and physical activity) and health. Care must be taken to not embarrass or offend overweight or obese students. This can be done by emphasizing healthy choices and by discussing how to help those who struggle with weight issues. Creating a warm, supportive environment facilitates students in sharing their struggles and triumphs while encouraging classmates to be empathetic and supportive.

Lessons are most effective when active-based strategies are used, and when they emphasize the positive, appealing aspects of healthy eating rather than the negative consequences of unhealthy eating. It is important to emphasize the benefits of adopting healthy choices and to tie these benefits to students' present aspirations—for example, by emphasizing short-term benefits such as improved physical appearance, sense of personal control and independence, and an improved capacity for physical activities.

Healthy eating can be integrated into many school subjects. For example, math lessons can analyze nutrient intake or calculate exercise heart rates. Reading lessons can feature material about many topics relating to eating and physical activity. Social studies lessons can examine topics such as how obese people are often treated poorly in society or how changes in our society in the past century have contributed to a more sedentary way of life and differences in the kinds and amounts of food available.

Cultural dietary and physical activity patterns in community ethnic groups need to be included in curricula. Emphasis should be placed on the many healthy ethnic food choices available and on the way in which a person's culture can help him or her become more physically active.

The following sections and **Box 6-5** identify the content and skills that need to be included in healthy eating and physical activity curricula. The Internet sites mentioned in Box 6-5 also provide resources that can be used in creating unit and lesson plans.

Dietary Guidelines

Every five years the **U.S. Department of Agriculture (USDA)** and the U.S. Department of Health and Human Services (HHS) publish *Dietary Guidelines for Americans*.[22] These guidelines recommend a diet rich in fruits and vegetables, whole grains, and fat-free and low-fat dairy products

6-5 Internet Support

Health Behavior Outcomes and Instructional Planning

The following are **health behavior outcomes (HBOs)** recommended by the **Health Education Curriculum Analysis Tool (HECAT)** for K–12 healthy eating and physical activity curriculum. After reviewing these recommendations, check out the HECAT models available on the Internet for healthy eating (HE) and physical activity (PA). Within these modules you will find recommendations for all the content and skills to be taught at various grade levels.

- Eat a variety of whole-grain products, fruits and vegetables, and fat-free or low-fat milk or equivalent milk products every day.
- Eat the appropriate number of servings from each food group every day.
- Choose foods that provide ample amounts of vitamins and minerals.
- Eat the appropriate amounts of foods that are high in fiber.
- Drink plenty of water.
- Limit foods and beverages that contain large amounts of added or processed sugars.
- Limit the intake of fat, avoiding foods with saturated and trans fats.
- Eat breakfast every day.
- Eat healthy snacks.
- Eat healthy foods when dining out.
- Prepare food in healthful ways.
- Balance caloric intake with caloric expenditure.
- Follow a plan for healthy weight management.
- Brush and floss teeth daily.
- Practice behaviors that prevent foodborne illnesses.
- Engage in moderate to vigorous physical activity for at least 60 minutes every day.
- Regularly engage in activities that enhance cardiorespiratory endurance, flexibility, muscle endurance, and muscle strength.
- Avoid injury during physical activity.

After reviewing the HBOs and the HECAT HE and PA modules, try to ascertain the eating and physical activity needs in your particular community. You can do so by finding local/state data on the Internet (e.g., CDC's YRBS data) and by interviewing school staff or students. Find out if your state has guidelines for healthy eating or physical activity education and if a scope and sequence or curricula exist for your school district. Continue your instruction planning by using the guidelines provided in the Teaching Today's Students chapter and the worksheets at the end of this chapter.

These organizations provide related material and lesson plans on their internet sites:

- Media-Smart Youth
- A to Z Teacher Stuff
- Discover Education
- National Dairy Council

---

for persons aged 2 years and older. The guidelines also recommend that children, adolescents, and adults limit their intake of solid fats, cholesterol, sodium, added sugars, and refined grains. Unfortunately, most young people are not following these recommendations.[23] The 2010 guideline recommendations are organized in these four categories:

1. Balancing calories to manage weight
2. Foods and food components to reduce
3. Foods and nutrients to increase
4. Building healthy eating patterns

MyPlate

To help people of all ages make healthful food choices, the USDA created the **MyPlate** educational tool (**Figure 6-4**). The traditional food guide pyramid was abandoned in favor of a place setting as a means to prompt people to make their meal plates healthier. MyPlate emphasizes that a meal should be half fruits and vegetables paired with lean proteins, whole grains, and low-fat dairy products.

The USDA also created an interactive educational website to help promote MyPlate and the 2010 *Dietary Guidelines*. This website, which can be accessed at http://www.chooseMyPlate.gov, is filled with resources for teachers, parents, and students to use:

◆ MyPlate videos
◆ Printable materials
◆ Healthy eating tips
◆ Healthy eating on a budget
◆ Sample menus and recipes
◆ Daily food plan

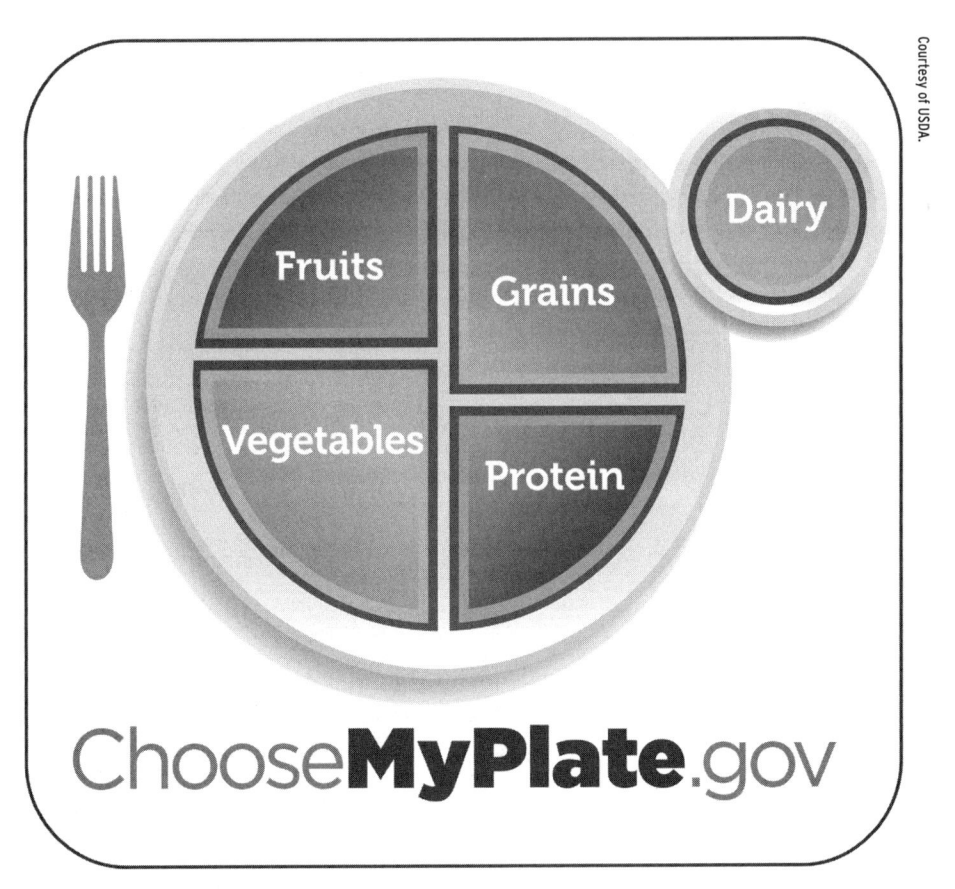

FIGURE 6-4 MyPlate.

Healthy Eating Curricula   179

FIGURE 6-5 SuperTracker.

The site also provides many tools that you can use in your classroom:

- Daily food plans
- Calories Burn chart
- Calories Count chart for mixed dishes
- Portion distortion
- Food labeling
- SuperTracker

SuperTracker is an especially helpful tool (**Figure 6-5**). It can help students track their foods and physical activities to see how they stack up, get a personalized nutrition and physical activity plan, and get tips and support to help them make healthier choices and plan ahead. Tools available on SuperTracker include the following:

- Food-A-Pedia: Look up nutrition information for more than 8,000 foods and compare foods side by side.
- Food Tracker: Track the foods you eat and compare to your nutrition targets.
- Physical Activity Tracker: Enter your activities and track your progress as you move.
- My Weight Manager: Get weight management guidance; enter your weight and track your progress over time.
- My Top 5 Goals: Choose up to five personal goals; sign up for tips and support from your virtual coach.
- My Reports: Use reports to see how you are meeting goals and view your trends over time.

National Standards

National Standard 1: Concepts Students need to gain an understanding of key nutrition concepts if they are to make healthy food choices. Carefully review the health behavior outcomes for healthy eating and physical activity identified in **Box 6-6**. Consider the concepts students need to master to achieve these behavior outcomes. Here is an abbreviated list of the concepts included in the HECAT modules:[24]

- Explain the importance of choosing healthy foods and beverages.
- Identify a variety of healthy snacks.

- Identify the benefits of drinking plenty of water.
- Identify nutritious and non-nutritious beverages.
- Describe the benefits of eating breakfast every day.
- Describe the type of foods and beverages that should be limited.
- Describe body signals that tell people when they are hungry and when they are full.
- Identify eating behaviors that contribute to maintaining a healthy weight.
- Identify the number of servings of food from each food group that a child needs daily.
- Identify foods and beverages that are high in fat and low in fat, and high in added sugars.
- Describe methods to keep food safe from harmful germs.
- Explain that both eating habits and level of physical activity can affect a person's weight.
- Explain various methods available to evaluate body weight.
- Identify healthy and risky approaches to weight management.
- Identify foods that are high in fiber and examples of whole-grain foods.
- Identify how to make a vegetarian diet healthy.
- Differentiate between a positive and negative body image, and state the importance of a positive body image.
- Describe the signs, symptoms, and consequences of common eating disorders.

National Standards 2–8

Students also need the skills in the National Health Education Standards 2 through 8. Here are those standards applied to healthy eating, along with examples of related skills:

Standard 2. Analyze family, peer, culture, media, and technology influences on food choices. *Dissect food commercials and explain how they influence food choices.*

Standard 3. Access valid information about nutrition and weight management and healthful products and resources. *Access accurate information about healthy dieting practices on the Internet.*

Standard 4. Demonstrate communication skills for obtaining healthy foods and beverages and for avoiding unhealthy choices. *Request that healthy snack choices be available at home for after-school snacks.*

Standard 5. Demonstrate decision-making skills for making wise food choices. *Demonstrate how to select healthy—rather than unhealthy—foods on a fast-food restaurant menu.*

Standard 6. Demonstrate goal-setting skills for effectively making dietary changes. *Identify barriers to eating healthy meals.*

Standard 7. Demonstrate personal management skills for identifying, describing, and analyzing personal eating practices and demonstrating improvement. *Plan and prepare a healthy meal.*

Standard 8. Demonstrate advocacy skills for encouraging peers and others to make positive food and beverage food choices. *Lobby for healthy choices to be made available in school vending machines.*

Activities at the end of the chapter can help you teach the content and skills called for in the national standards.

PHYSICAL ACTIVITY CURRICULA

Regular physical activity in childhood and adolescence is imperative to maintain healthy weight and emotional well-being both during those periods of development and in later years. Physical activity improves strength and endurance, builds healthy bones and muscles, helps control weight, reduces anxiety and stress, increases self-esteem, and may improve blood pressure and cholesterol levels.[25] More physical education and physical activities are needed at school to offset today's sedentary lifestyle and to promote many other benefits. Students who participate in interscholastic sports are less likely to be regular or heavy smokers or to use drugs and are more likely to stay in school and have good conduct and high academic achievement than are nonparticipants. Sports and physical activity programs can introduce young people to skills such as teamwork, self-discipline, sportsmanship, leadership, and socialization. Lack of recreational activity, in contrast, may contribute to making young people more vulnerable to gangs, drugs, and violence.

One of the main goals of school physical education is to help students develop an active lifestyle that will persist into and throughout adulthood. Curricula should emphasize knowledge about the benefits of physical activity and the recommended amounts and types of physical activity. Physical education should help students develop the attitudes, motor skills, behavioral skills, and confidence they need to engage in lifelong physical activity.

Physical fitness is another main goal of physical education. **Physical fitness** is a state of well-being that allows individuals to perform daily activities with vigor, participate in a variety of physical activities, and reduce their risks for health problems. Five basic components of fitness are important for good health: *cardiorespiratory endurance*, *muscular strength*, *muscular endurance*, *flexibility*, and *body composition* (percentage of body fat). A second set of attributes, referred to as sport- or skill-related physical fitness attributes, includes *power*, *speed*, *agility*, *balance*, and *reaction time*.

We will now take a look at some resources available for effectively making physical activity a viable part of a curriculum. **Box 6-7** lists some activities you can use in your classroom to promote both healthy eating and physical activity.

Physical Activity Guidelines

The *Physical Activity Guidelines for Americans*, issued by the U.S. Department of Health and Human Services, recommend that children and adolescents aged 6–17 years should have 60 minutes or more of physical activity each day.[26] As part of their 60 or more minutes of daily physical activity:

- Most of the time should be either moderate- or vigorous-intensity *aerobic* physical activity, with vigorous-intensity physical activity being included at least 3 days a week.
- Activities should include *muscle-strengthening* physical activity on at least 3 days of the week.
- Activities should include *bone-strengthening* physical activity on at least 3 days of the week.

To promote the guidelines and support youth physical activity, the CDC and several partner organizations developed the **Youth Physical Activity Guidelines Toolkit**. This toolkit highlights strategies that schools, families, and communities can use to support youth physical activity. It contains fact sheets, PowerPoint presentations, posters, and videos and can be accessed on the CDC's website.[27]

Here are the national standards applied to physical activity with examples of related skills:

- Analyze influence: Describe how television, computer, and video games can influence an individual's level of physical activity.
- Access valid information and products: Identify places where young people and families can be physically active.
- Communication: Demonstrate interpersonal skills for dealing with peer influence to be physically inactive.
- Decision making: Identify physically active alternatives to watching television or playing video games.
- Goal setting: Monitor progress in attaining a physical activity goal.
- Self-management: Analyze precautions for physical activity in weather and climate conditions such as very high or low temperatures and direct sunlight.
- Advocate: Advocate for increased physical activity for students and school personnel.

A **Physical Education Curriculum Analysis Tool (PECAT)** has also been developed by the U.S. Department of Health and Human Services in conjunction with the CDC. The PECAT takes an in-depth look at a complete Physical Education curriculum, whereas the HECAT Physical Activity Module considers physical activity as part of a Health Education curriculum.

ACTIVITIES FOR HEALTHY EATING AND PHYSICAL ACTIVITY

These activities can be modified and adapted for use at many grade levels (as indicated in previous chapters). Check out the activities in Chapter 3 regarding self-concept and self-management, in Chapter 4 regarding stress management, and in Chapter 5 regarding media influences. Many of the activities in these other chapters can help meet objectives for healthy eating and physical activity.

6-6 *Activities for Analyzing Eating and Activity Influences*

Commercial Analysis

Record and then play food commercials aired on TV during Saturday morning or after school. Have students analyze each ad looking for hooks and untruths. Watch for the drug-like effects often depicted in such ads (e.g., highs, rushes, energy surges, hallucinations.) (P, I, J, H)

Couch Potato Count

Have students keep a record of the time they spend watching television during a week and a log of all the food commercials they see during that time. Have them determine what percentage of the food commercials promoted consumption of foods that are high in fat and sugar. Also have them identify the times of day when the most food ads were aired. (I, J, H)

Portion Distortion

Have students prepare PowerPoint presentations on how much food servings have grown and how many calories are contained in common foods. (Do a Google image search for "portion distortion" or "portion size.") Display various sizes of bowls and plates, and ask students what size they like to use and why. Provide examples of the size of plates in China produced at the turn of the 20th century. (P, I, J)

Magazine Look

Have students do an analysis of all the people pictured in a magazine. Have them count the images by gender, race, weight, physical attractiveness, and perceived socioeconomic status. Have students discuss the attitudes, values, beliefs, and lifestyles projected by these images, and ask them to consider how they have been influenced by similar images over time. (I, J, H)

Double Messages

Have students look in magazines and on magazine covers for double messages, such as a picture of a fattening dessert right next to an article on dieting. Discuss why editors place double messages side by side. (I, J, H)

(continues)

(continued)

Real Beauty

Have a healthy body image ad campaign competition in which students create their own slogans, public service announcements, and postures. Review Dove's "Campaign for Real Beauty Worldwide" website, but be sure to identify that this site is also a marketing tool. (I, J, H)

Fad Diets

Assign student groups to research various fad diets and evaluate how safe, healthy, and effective they are. Also ask them to research the amount of money generated by diets, and discuss why magazines touting diets really don't want their readers to lose weight (i.e., readers would stop buying the magazines). As a culminating activity, have students name and create a healthy diet based on safe weight-loss methods. (I, J, H)

Popcorn!

Bring something into class that smells delicious, like hot popcorn. Ask students to identify all the things that prompt them to begin eating, such as smells, time of day, or feeling blue. Discuss how those prompts can be helpful and harmful. (P, I, J, H)

6-7 Activities for Healthy Eating and Physical Activity

Healthy Food Selection

Lunch Sack

Place three different foods into three lunch sacks and label the sacks 1, 2, and 3. For instance, put a box of pectin in sack 1, dog food in sack 2, and a cup of soup in sack 3. Let students know exactly what is in each sack by showing them the lists of ingredients in each food, but not the food, and ask students which lunch they want. Have students identify which sack they want and try to guess what is inside. This is a good activity to introduce the question "Do you know what you're eating?" (I, J, H)

Label Match

Teach students how to read a food label and then play a matching game where students have to match food labels with products. Students can provide the labels from packages of foods they commonly eat at home. A variation of this activity is Nutrient Match, where students match vitamins and minerals with their functions or rich food sources. (I, J, H)

Label Dissection and Comparison

Discuss each part of a food label (http://www.cfsan.fda.gov/~dms/foodlab.html), and then have students compare food labels of similar foods such as various cold cereals, different types of milk, snack foods, and various juices. Make a game of identifying the most healthful food products. (I, J, H)

Serving Size?

Ask a student to pour the amount of cold cereal he or she typically eats into a bowl. Measure the amount poured in a measuring cup. Compare the student's serving size to that indicated on the food label. Display pictures of portion distortion found on an image search on the Web. Discuss how package labels sometimes indicate abnormally small serving sizes to conceal calorie, fat, and/or sugar counts. (P, I, J, H)

Food Court

Divide students into groups and have each group find out how much fat and sugar is contained in the class's top 10 favorite fast-food items. Create a "food court" by having students display pictures of these 10 food items. Beside each picture, place a paper plate. Instruct students to measure out and place on the plates the amount of fat contained in the food pictured to its side (1 tablespoon of shortening = 12 grams of fat). Have students also indicate how much sugar is in the food by placing sugar cubes on the plates (1 cube = 4 g of sugar). They will be excited to discuss their food court findings with one another and with their families. This activity can be a springboard for making changes. (P, I, J, H)

Sugar Stack

A slight alternative to the previous activity is for students to indicate how much sugar is contained in various beverages, and in various containers. Various sizes of cups can be obtained from 7-11 or other fast-food outlets. Measure into cans, bottles, or cups the amount of sugar contained in each, or you can stack sugar cubes beside each container. It can be fun to surprise students by pouring just sugar out of a can they thought contained soda pop. (P, I, J, H)

Good Menu Choice

Collect restaurant menus (in person or from the Internet). Have students make good menu selections based on prompts you give them (i.e., for a 1,800-calorie diet, to get more fiber or other nutrients). (P, I, J, H)

SuperTracker Assessment

Have students analyze their own or a fictional student's diet and physical activity using the MyPlate SuperTracker tool. You can access this tool at http://www.ChooseMyPlate.gov. (I, J, H)

BMI Calculator

Have students calculate the body mass index for fictional students, themselves, or family members by using the BMI calculator found at http://www.ChooseMyPlate.gov or another website. (I, J, H)

House Analogy

Discuss the various sizes and styles of homes and the common materials they are built from. Discuss the various healthy sizes of bodies and the common nutrients they are built from (wood/bricks = proteins; fuel = carbohydrates; chemical compounds = vitamins and minerals). Discuss what happens when not enough of the right materials are available for building first a home and then a body. (P, I, J, H)

A to Z

In teams, have students try a fruit that begins with every letter of the alphabet. This same exercise can be done with vegetables. Have students identify which of the foods on their lists they have eaten. A great resource for this activity is provided by the CDC at http://www.fruitsandveggiesmatter.gov/. (P, I, J, H)

(continues)

(*continued*)

Top 10

Generate a list of fruits, vegetables, and fruit juices. Have students try to identify the top 10 nutritious fruits (or veggies or fruit juices). Have students research which are the most nutrient dense using the Web at http://www.whfoods.com/foodstoc.php. (P, I, J, H)

Fear Factor

Have a fun new-food tasting challenge somewhat like the TV show *Fear Factor*. Contact the produce sections of local grocery stores to see if they will provide you with samples of fruits and vegetables. (P, I, J, H)

Grow a Garden

Follow Michelle Obama's example and plant, harvest, and eat vegetables from a garden your class grows. Recruit the PTA to help with this project. (P, I)

MyPlate Fill-In

Have students record everything they or their family eat on a laminated MyPlate chart hung on their refrigerator. (P, I, J, H)

Marketing Competition

Have students compete in developing a marketing campaign for healthy eating or increased physical activity (i.e., eating more fruits and vegetables, drinking less pop, walking to school more). Encourage students to study and use marketing techniques. (I, J, H)

Menu Planner

Have students plan a day or more of menus to meet their healthy eating goals using the SuperTracker tool. (I, J, H)

Recipe Alterations

Have students' families experiment with healthy alterations to their favorite recipes. This is fun to do for Thanksgiving dinners. (P, I, J, H)

Cookbook

Have students work with their parents to come up with healthy recipes for foods they love to eat. Create a classroom cookbook. (P, I, J)

Cafeteria Tour

Tour the school's cafeteria and learn about all the precautions those who work there must take to ensure food safety. Discuss how school menus are planned. (P, I)

Restaurant Inspection

Check the Web for restaurant alerts in your area. Invite a restaurant inspector to be a classroom guest speaker. (J, H)

Food Drive

Sponsor a school or community food drive for a local food bank. Have students be physically active as they collect and deliver the food. (P, I, J, H)

Physical Activity Enhancers

Map Quest
Make a class goal of walking/running to a given location such as the state capitol building. Each day, have students add up how far they collectively walked or ran. Mark their mileage on a map on the classroom wall showing the total distance from your school to your goal location. (P, J)

Fun Run/Walk
Sponsor a school-wide fun run. Ask parents and the PTA to participate. Invite local high school track team members to run with and encourage individuals as they participate. Have preparation "training" activities. Have participants make their own time goals for the course and celebrate each participant's involvement. (P, I)

Let's Move
Have students use the tools and resources found on the Let's Move website (http://www.LetsMove.gov). (I, J, H)

President's Challenge
Have students use the tools and resources for obtaining the Presidential Youth Fitness Award at https://www.presidentschallenge.org/. (I, J, H)

PSA Benefits
Have students create public service announcements (PSAs) for the radio that highlight the benefits of physical activity. (I, J, H)

Energizers
Search the Web for classroom energizers that will get your students moving, grab their attention, and increase their concentration and long-term memory. (P, I, J, H)

Extension and Integration Activities

Cultural Fair
Work with your school's PTA and sponsor a school food fair highlighting healthy ethnic foods found in your area or from around the globe. Have the fair celebrate various cultures and "tastes." Highlight favorite physical activities enjoyed in these cultures. Invite parents and local ethnic restaurants to participate. (P, I, J)

Make It Happen!
Have students read the *School Nutrition Success Stories* posted on the CDC's website and the *Plant a Garden*, *Success Stories*, and *Community Leaders* sections of the Let's Move website. Have students in small groups outline proposals for something they would like to see their school or community do. Discuss and analyze these proposals as a class. Choose one they can make happen. Create a plan with steps to help them achieve their goal. Work toward the goal and evaluate and make adjustments along the way. (P, I, J)

(continues)

(continued)

Math Ideas (I, J, H)

- Do math story problems using food labels.
- Calculate family food budgets and savings from eating at home and cooking from scratch.
- Compare costs of eating fruits versus eating other dessert choices.
- Calculate the yearly cost of habitually drinking soda or eating some junk food items.
- Do heart rate and breathing rates at rest and after exertion, and then calculate norms, means, and averages.

Language Arts Ideas (I, J, H)

- Create brochures or blogs on dieting tips.
- Write poems or songs about healthy food choices.
- Write stories, case histories, or mini dramas about physical activity.

Social Studies Ideas (I, J, H)

Discuss and/or research

- globesity
- culture and food
- war and food
- food production and distribution
- government farm subsidies
- world food trade and embargos
- historical perspectives on physical activity and food including its availability, preparation, and preservation

Instruction Plan Healthy Eating and Physical Activity

Use this worksheet to plan Healthy Eating and Physical Activity instruction at the grade level you will be teaching. Refer to Chapter 2 for more information on how to complete each section in this worksheet.

■ Assess Needs

Identify topics and skills state or local curricula identify to be taught at ___ grade level.

Identify additional topics or skills the HE and PA HECAT Modules indicate for this grade.

Identify eating and activity needs your particular students and their families have:
- What, where, and when do they eat?
- What are their activity patterns?
- How prevalent is overweight and obesity?
- What diet/activity related disease risks are prevalent in the community?

■ Set Major Learning Goal(s)

Identify your major learning goal(s)—what do you want to have happen?

■ Develop Instruction Map

Create a map (calendar or list of days) indicating the time frame you have/need to teach the curriculum, meet student needs and reach goal(s). For each day indicate the content/skills to be taught. Work to create a good flow.

■ Write SMART Unit Objectives

Write 1 or 2 major objectives for each day you will teach. Your objectives should be in alignment with your state/local curricula, your student's needs, and your major learning goal(s).

■ Identify Assessment Tools

Preassessment	Formative-Assessment	Postassessment
How will you determine what students already know or do?	How will you know if they are "getting it"?	How will you know if students master objectives?

Instruction Plan Worksheet Healthy Eating and Physical Activity

■ **Develop Unit Plan**

Divide the chart into the number of days you will teach. Record each day's topic and objective key words. Identify activity names (in the book) that can help you meet each day's objective. Identify tech tools you can use and possible lesson adaptations you can make for special need learners.

Lesson Topic Objectives	Instruction Activities	Tech Tools	Adaptations for Learners

■ **Develop Lesson Plans**

Use the Lesson Plan Template found in Chapter 2 and this worksheet to create detailed lesson plans for your Healthy Eating and Physical Activity Unit.

KEY TERMS

overweight   162
body mass index (BMI)   162
obese   162
globesity   162
portion distortion   164
food allergy   166
Make It Happen—School Nutrition
   Success Stories   167
undernutrition   168
iron-deficiency anemia   168
unsafe weight-loss methods   169
eating disorders   169
anorexia nervosa   170
bulimia   171
type 1 diabetes   172
type 2 diabetes   172
insulin resistance   173
high blood pressure   173
atherosclerosis   173
cholesterol   173
angina   174

heart attack   174
osteoporosis   174
calcium   174
weight-bearing exercises   174
resistance exercises   174
arthritis   175
dental decay   175
School Health Guidelines   175
U.S. Department of Agriculture (USDA)   177
Dietary Guidelines for Americans   177
health behavior outcomes (HBOs)   178
Health Education Curriculum Analysis Tool
   (HECAT)   178
MyPlate   179
SuperTracker   180
physical fitness   182
Physical Activity Guidelines for Americans   182
Youth Physical Activity Guidelines Toolkit   182
Physical Education Curriculum Analysis Tool
   (PECAT)   183

KNOWLEDGE CHECK!

1. Define and explain the relative importance of each of the key terms in the context of this chapter.
2. Discuss overweight and obesity trends in the United States. Which populations and locations have higher rates? How are children and adolescents doing on meeting recommendations for eating and physical activity?
3. Identify and discuss various factors that have led to young people getting less physical inactivity than past generations.
4. Identify and discuss various factors that have led to our consuming too many calories.
5. Identify and discuss various family and social factors that contribute to poor eating habits.
6. Identify how media use is associated with poor eating choices, how food is marketed to children and youth, and how food marketing has changed.
7. Discuss foods available in schools, incentives for providing junk food, and findings from case studies of schools' food changes.
8. Explain why advertisers use very thin actresses and models and how these choices can affect females.
9. Identify and discuss the physical, psychological, and developmental problems children and adolescents experience from being weight or obese and from being undernourished.
10. Describe unsafe and safe weight-loss methods.
11. Describe signs, triggers, and risks of eating disorders.
12. Discuss the epidemic of diabetes, including the types of diabetes, risk factors, complications, diagnosis, and symptoms.
13. Explain the connections between diet and coronary heart disease, cancer, osteoporosis, and dental decay.
14. Identify the School Health Guidelines to promote healthy eating and physical activity.

15. Discuss how schools can provide a supportive environment for healthy eating and physical activity, how school personnel can collaborate to produce it, and how parents and the community can become involved.
16. Discuss the needs, goals, and guidelines for healthy eating curricula.
17. Discuss the *Dietary Guidelines for Americans* and the recommendations for children and youth.
18. Identify the components of the MyPlate guidance system, including http://wwwChooseMyPlate.gov website features and food-group portion size recommendations.
19. Identify the many different teaching resources and activities that can help you teach to the recommended HECAT HBOs for healthy eating and physical activity.
20. Discuss the goals, needs, and guidelines for physical fitness curricula.

■ REFERENCES

1. Ogden C, Carroll M. Prevalence of obesity among children and adolescents: United States, trends 1963–1965 through 2007–2008. Division of Health and Nutrition Examination Surveys (NCHS HEalth E-Stat). Available at http://www.cdc.gov/nchs/data/hestat/obesity_child_07_08/obesity_child_07_08.htm. Accessed January 24, 2013.
2. Anderson SE, Whitaker RC. Prevalence of obesity among U.S. preschool children in different racial and ethnic groups. *Arch Pediatr Adolesc Med*. 2009;163(4), 344–348.
3. U.S. Department of Health and Human Services. *Report of the Dietary Guidelines Advisory Committee on the Dietary Guidelines for Americans, 2010, to the Secretary of Agriculture and the Secretary of Health*. Washington, DC: U.S. Department of Health and Human Services; 2010.
4. Reedy J, Krebs-Smith SM. Dietary sources of energy, solid fats, and added sugars among children and adolescents in the United States. *J Am Diet Assoc*. 2010;110:1477–1484.
5. Office of the Surgeon General. *The Surgeon General's call to action to prevent and decrease overweight and obesity*. Rockville, MD: U.S. Department of Health and Human Services, Public Health Service; 2001. Available at http://www.cdc.gov/nccdphp/dnpa/healthyweight. Accessed January 24, 2013.
6. U.S. Department of Health and Human Services. *Healthy people 2010: with understanding and improving health and objectives for improving health*. Washington, DC: U.S. Government Printing Office; 2000.
7. Jeffery P, Liverman C, Karrak V. *Preventing childhood obesity: health in the balance*. Washington, DC: National Academies Press; 2005.
8. Council on Sports Medicine and Fitness. Active healthy living: prevention of childhood obesity through increased physical activity. *Pediatrics*. 2006;117(5):1834–1842.
9. Centers for Disease Control and Prevention. Youth Risk Behavior Surveillance System. 2011. Available at http://www.cdc.gov/HealthyYouth/yrbs/index.htm. Accessed January 24, 2013.
10. Strasburger VC. Why do adolescent health researchers ignore the impact of the media? *J Adolesc Health*. 2009;44:203–205.
11. Page R, Montgomery K, Ponder A, Richard A. Targeting children in the cereal aisle: promotional techniques and content features on ready-to-eat cereal product packaging. *Am J Health Ed*. 2008;39(5):272–282.
12. Page RM, Brewster A. Depiction of food as having drug-like properties in televised food advertisements directed at children: portrayals as pleasure enhancing and addictive. *J Pediatr Health Care*. 2009;23(3):150–157.
13. Centers for Disease Control and Prevention. Food allergies in schools. Available at http://www.cdc.gov/HealthyYouth/foodallergies/. Accessed May 31, 2013.
14. U.S. Department of Agriculture. Foods sold in competition with USDA school meal programs: a report to Congress. 2001. Available at http://www.cdc.gov/mmwr/pdf/wk/mm58e1005.pdf. Accessed January 24, 2013.
15. Centers for Disease Control and Prevention. Diagnosed and undiagnosed diabetes in the United States, all ages, 2010. Available at http://www.cdc.gov/diabetes/pubs/estimates11.htm#4. Accessed January 24, 2013.
16. Centers for Disease Control and Prevention. Heart disease facts. Available at http://www.cdc.gov/heartdisease/facts.htm. Accessed January 24, 2013.
17. Centers for Disease Control and Prevention. High blood pressure. Available at http://www.cdc.gov/bloodpressure/. Accessed June 1, 2013.
18. Kushi L, Byers T, Doyle C, et al. American Cancer Society guidelines on nutrition and physical activity for cancer prevention: reducing the risk of cancer with healthy food choices and physical activity. *CA: Cancer J Clin*. 2006:56:254–281.

19. American Cancer Society. Heart healthy foods your whole body will love. Available at http://www.cancer.org/cancer/news/expertvoices/post/2012/02/09/heart-healthy-foods-your-whole-body-will-love.aspx#continue. Accessed January 24, 2013.
20. Centers for Disease Control and Prevention. Youth Risk Behavior Surveillance—United States, 2007. *MMWR.* 2008;57(SS-05):1–131.
21. Centers for Disease Control and Prevention. School health guidelines to promote healthy eating and physical activity. Available at http://www.cdc.gov/mmwr/preview/mmwrhtml/rr6005a1.htm. Accessed January 2013.
22. U.S. Department of Agriculture, U.S. Department of Health and Human Services. *Dietary guidelines for Americans, 2010.* 7th ed. Washington, DC: U.S. Government Printing Office; 2010.
23. Reedy J, Krebs-Smith SM. Dietary sources of energy, solid fats, and added sugars among children and adolescents in the United States. *J Am Diet Assoc.* 2010;110:1477–1484.
24. Centers for Disease Control and Prevention. HECAT: module HE. Healthy eating curriculum. Available at http://www.cdc.gov/healthyyouth/hecat/pdf/HECAT_Module_HE.pdf. Accessed June 1, 2013.
25. U.S. Department of Health and Human Services. *Physical Activity Guidelines Advisory Committee report.* Washington, DC: U.S. Department of Health and Human Services; 2008.
26. U.S. Department of Health and Human Services. *Physical activity guidelines for Americans.* Washington, DC: U.S. Department of Health and Human Services; 2008.
27. Centers for Disease Control and Prevention. Your physical activity guidelines toolkit. Available at http://www.cdc.gov/healthyyouth/physicalactivity/guidelines.htm. Accessed June 1, 2013.

Chapter 7
Promoting a Tobacco- and Drug-Free Lifestyle

Once Upon a Time... My Story

The following was turned in by a university student in a personal health class. The assignment was to write a short story about a family suffering from alcoholism.

Once upon a time there lived a family of six—a mom, an alcoholic (Dad), and four children. The mother was kind of crazy trying to keep up with her alcoholic husband. She loved him, so in her eyes she had to drink along with him to prove her love to him.

Out of the four kids there was only one family hero. She was 16 at the time, but she had to grow up a lot faster than she ever expected. She took care of the two younger children and covered up the alcoholic's mistakes constantly. She took care of everything because she had to become the mother and father and still keep up with her own life.

The other two girls in the family were labeled somewhere between a scapegoat and the family mascot or clown. They were the reason the alcoholic dad lost four jobs and was drinking his life away. Yet, at times they brought relief to the family due to their humor.

The youngest child was the lost child of the family. He fit all the classic characteristics of a lost child. He died at age 15 due to someone choosing a life in the bottle over his family.

This is a true story. It's my story.

Alcohol and other drugs are facts of life in most communities. The use of psychoactive substances by children and adolescents is a national problem that demands the attention of all professionals who work with young people. Substance use poses many problems for young people. Youthful substance users are vulnerable to life-threatening accidents and injuries. Indeed, substance abuse is the major cause of most of the premature lives lost and morbidity seen in adolescents in the United States and many other nations. The Centers for Disease Control and Prevention (CDC) reports that three-fourths of unintentional injuries (the leading cause of death in adolescents) among adolescents are directly or indirectly related to substance abuse.

Substance users are often impulsive and engage in risk-taking behavior and illegal activity that increases their risk of injury and serious medical consequences. Young people who use drugs often expose themselves to sexually transmitted diseases, including HIV infection. The effects of psychoactive drugs erode emotional, social, and cognitive development in youth, making it difficult to face developmental challenges during adolescence and in later stages of life. Involvement with substances interferes with school achievement and contributes to school dropout and truancy. School systems are also adversely affected by substance use. Students under the influence of psychoactive substances cannot learn, and teachers cannot teach such students. Substance-using students alter the learning environment for everyone in a school.

Compared with non-substance-using youths, teenage substance users:

◆ Have a greater chance of getting into trouble with parents, friends, and teachers
◆ Have a greater chance of engaging in problematic behavior, such as truancy, vandalism, petty theft, and property damage

- Have a greater chance of not learning many of the emotional and social skills necessary for a safe and productive life
- Have a greater chance of causing an accident or injury to themselves or others
- Have a greater chance of engaging in sexual behavior that can put them at risk of unintended pregnancy and sexually transmitted diseases
- Have a greater chance of progressing to heavy use and drug dependency

MONITORING SUBSTANCE USE TRENDS

Three major national surveys provide data on substance use among youths. Websites make the data from these surveys readily available, allowing you to follow trends in substance use. There are some limitations to the data available. First, it takes a great deal of time to collect and analyze the information, so the data are usually 1 to 2 years old by the time they become available. Second, the data do not represent every young person. For instance, individuals who have dropped out and students not in school on the day a survey is conducted will not be represented in the data set. Even with these limitations, you can learn a great deal by monitoring substance use trends.

The **Monitoring the Future (MTF)** study is an annual survey funded by the National Institute on Drug Abuse that measures the extent of drug use among high school seniors, tenth graders, and eighth graders. The goal of the survey is to collect data on 30-day, annual, and lifetime drug use among students in these grade levels. This survey has been conducted every year since 1974 and its results can be found online.

The **National Survey on Drug Use and Health (NSDUH)**, sponsored by the Substance Abuse and Mental Health Services Administration (SAMHSA), is the primary source of statistical information on illicit drug use in the U.S. population aged 12 years and older. Formerly known as the National Household Survey on Drug Abuse, this survey collects data through household interviews, currently using computer-assisted self-administration for drug-related items.

The **Youth Risk Behavior Survey (YRBS)**, part of the CDC's Youth Risk Behavior Surveillance System, is a school survey that collects data from students in grades 9 through 12. This survey includes questions on a wide variety of health-related risk behaviors, including tobacco, alcohol, and other drug use.

The following key summary findings from the 2011 MTF and YRBS studies illustrate drug use trends and data available on the Internet. Data are available for each state and for some large metropolitan areas.[1,2]

- *Cigarettes.* Nearly half (45%) of American young people have tried smoking. Approximately 10% tried smoking a whole cigarette before turning age 13. About 1 in 5 is a current smoker. Smoking among youth peaked in the late 1990s and then steadily declined through 2004. In recent years, the rates have basically leveled off.
- *Smokeless tobacco.* Approximately 8% of youth have chewed tobacco or used snuff or dip in the past month. This rate is about half of what it was at peak levels.
- *Alcohol.* Alcohol use among teens is at historic lows, but use remains widespread. A little more than 20% of youth say they drank alcohol for the first time before the age of 13, nearly 40% said they drank in the past month, and more than 20% report they binge drank (consumed five or more drinks at one time) in the past 2 weeks.
- *Marijuana.* Since 2008, marijuana use has increased, in contrast to the gradual decline of use noted in the preceding decade. Almost 40% of students say they have used marijuana one or more times during their life, and 23% say they used it at least once in the past month. That means more youth are smoking marijuana than are smoking cigarettes.

- *Psychotherapeutic drugs.* Almost 1 in 5 students has taken a prescription drug (e.g., OxyContin, Percocet, Vicodin, codeine, Adderall, Ritalin, or Xanax) without a doctor's prescription.
- *Inhalants.* Modest declines in inhalant use have been noted since the mid-2000s. Approximately 11% of today's students report having sniffed glue, breathed the contents of aerosol spray cans, or inhaled paints or sprays to get high.
- *Illicit drugs.* Over the past decade, reported illicit drug use has remained fairly level. More than 25% of students say they have been offered, sold, or given an illegal drug by someone on school property within the past year. By twelfth grade, nearly 25% have tried one or more illicit drugs (50% if marijuana is included). Only about 3% have used heroin and 4% methamphetamines, but almost 7% have used some form of cocaine. There is also concern about Ecstasy. After a several-year decline in perceived risk and disapproval of Ecstasy use, use of this drug appears to be rebounding, primarily among older teens.
- *Race/ethnicity.* Contrary to popular assumptions, African American students have substantially lower rates of drug use than whites. Half as many smoke cigarettes (10% versus 20% of whites). Likewise, relatively fewer African American students drink alcohol (30% compared to 40% of whites) or use illicit drugs (2.6% versus 3.7% of whites). However, they report using marijuana more (25% of African Americans versus 22% of whites). In contrast, Hispanic students smoke cigarettes a bit less than whites, but drink alcohol and use marijuana and other illicit drugs at higher rates compared to whites. Asian students have the lowest reported use rate for all substances.
- *Location.* You can obtain YRBS data for individual states and districts (e.g., Boston, Milwaukee, Seattle) and see comparisons between selected states or districts and national data. Go to http://www.cdc.gov/healthyyouth/yrbs/factsheets/index.htm.

Despite the considerable progress made in the past decade in curbing youth substance use, educators, parents, and the entire nation should not be lulled into complacency. To some degree this happened in the early 1990s, after the considerable improvements in youth substance-use rates in the 1980s. In the 1990s, attention to the problem of drug use nearly disappeared from national news coverage, and many governmental and nongovernmental institutions withdrew attention and programmatic support, which likely helped to set the stage for the costly relapse in the drug epidemic of the 1990s.

Take the time to do the application exercise in **Box 7-1**. It helps turn the data just presented into something more meaningful and personal.

7-1 Application Exercise

How Many in My Class?

Make the statistics in this chapter have greater meaning by calculating how many students in your classroom are likely to be affected by tobacco, alcohol, and drugs. For instance, if 18% of high school students in your state smoke, then in a class of 33 students 6 will likely become smokers before leaving high school. Computations might be easier for you to do in your head if you think in terms of fractions: if your average class size is 33 students, that is one-third of 100, so you simply take one-third of the reported percentage to discover the number of students likely affected in your classroom. Visit the YRBSs website at http://www.cdc.gov/healthyyouth/yrbs/factsheets/index.htm to find data specific to your state or metropolitan area.

MEDIA PROMOTION OF ALCOHOL AND TOBACCO USE

Alcohol and tobacco companies spend billions of dollars each year promoting their products through advertisements and other means. These industries proclaim that they do not target children and adolescents and that they are not in the business of recruiting new users. In your mind, do the following facts refute or support their claims?

- Beer and tobacco companies need young consumers because they would suffer enormous financial losses if underage drinking and tobacco use stopped.
- The alcohol industry does not really want everyone to drink "responsibly" because if a magic wand could cure alcoholism, the alcohol industry's revenues would be cut in half. Advertising campaigns encourage young people to drink to foster brand loyalty and because it takes much less time for an adolescent to develop alcoholism than for an adult to do the same.
- The alcohol industry advertises heavily on youth-oriented programming—that is, on programs with disproportionately large audiences of 12- to 20-year-olds.
- Beer and liquor companies deliberately target young people by sponsoring "extreme" sporting events that appeal to youths and in which many of the contestants are teenagers. Alcohol companies also sell related sport paraphernalia with beer company brand logos.
- Alcohol and tobacco companies design websites that are particularly attractive to underage audiences, featuring popular music, games, contests, animations, and downloads.
- Nearly 90% of teen smokers smoke one of the three most heavily advertised brands of cigarettes: Marlboro, Camel, and Newport.
- Tobacco and alcohol companies have developed products that hold special appeal to youths, such as sugary alcoholic beverages that resemble soda pop.

Our "ad-environment" is full of messages designed to influence young people.

These points highlight the fact that the alcohol and tobacco industries do target kids and use the media as a major tool to do so. One of their main tactics is to make use behavior look like "everyone is doing it." They pay TV and movie producers large sums of money to have actors hold, talk about, and consume their products on screen. These are clearly advertisements. Some actors further promote drug use by engaging in such behavior in their personal lives, which are then talked about on media outlets.

Research clearly indicates that young people are susceptible to media and celebrity modeling, especially given that adolescents are three times more likely to go to the movies than adults are. In an effort to combat this influence, the World Health Organization and the CDC have recommended that films featuring smoking be given an adult (R) rating.[3]

Television is another medium that routinely portrays the use of alcohol and tobacco in the programs shown. A recent study showed that 7 of 10 prime-time TV programs contain scenes of alcohol use, averaging 3.5 scenes per hour, and the music videos most popular with teens show 4.2 drinking episodes per hour.[4] Television shows also frequently feature smoking at high levels. And, of course, most movies eventually show up on cable and network television. In turn, young people view thousands of media depictions of alcohol and tobacco use in their own homes and, increasingly, on their own bedroom TV sets and smart phones.

In addition, abundant research attests to the impact of alcohol and cigarette advertising on teenagers' use. Advertisements and product placements for alcohol and tobacco often use the following untruthful appeals: happiness, maturity, sex appeal, healthy athletic appearance, slim body, freedom, social acceptance, romance, and escape. Alcohol and tobacco actually promote the exact opposite. Advertisers know this, so they sell a lie. Another disturbing practice is to depict behaviors associated with alcoholism (e.g., lying, stealing, hiding, hitting, having alcohol as more important than family relationships) in such a way that they seem funny and entertaining. We laugh and without conscious thought take in the message that hitting someone, lying, stealing, and jeopardizing our loved ones' safety so as to consume alcohol is okay, normal, and even "cool."

The media can also be employed to effectively curtail tobacco and alcohol use among minors. In 2000, the American Legacy Foundation began its very successful "truth" ad campaign. The first "truth" ads included media images of young people placing 1,200 body bags at the door of a cigarette company office building and cowboys leading horses with body bags over the saddle. Teenagers exposed to the "truth" countermarketing ads showed an increase in antitobacco attitudes and beliefs. "Truth" campaign video clips can be found on many social networking sites, including YouTube.[5]

SUBSTANCE ABUSE PREVENTION EDUCATION

It is vital that schools assume some responsibility for substance abuse prevention. As noted earlier, substance abuse interferes with school goals by disrupting the educational process. Schools, however, employ personnel who have the necessary skills to plan and implement programs to prevent substance abuse. Schools also provide important access to youths.

Of course, substance abuse is also a family and community problem; therefore, it is unrealistic to expect the schools alone to solve drug abuse problems. The responsibility for ensuring the well-being of children and for assisting in substance abuse prevention is shared by all individuals and institutions affected by substance abuse: parents, students, school staff, communities, professional organizations, colleges, businesses, policymakers, the media, social services, healthcare professionals, and mental health agencies. Effective prevention programs evolve only with the collaboration of these groups in developing coordinated and comprehensive efforts.

School-Based Programs That Work

The drug education that students receive in schools varies considerably from school district to school district. Drug education is sometimes delivered as early as kindergarten; in other districts, however, it may not be delivered until late elementary, middle school, or junior high. Sometimes drug education is designed to stand alone as a course; at other times, it is integrated into a health education, family life, or life skills course. It may be taught by the school's own teachers or by outside personnel (e.g., police officers). Some school districts purchase drug education curricula from commercial vendors, whereas others develop their own curricula and materials.

The most widely used drug education program is Drug Abuse Resistance Education (DARE). DARE began in 1983 and is found today in more than three-fourths of all school districts in the United States, despite the fact that researchers have consistently found that it is ineffective and sometimes actually counterproductive. For this reason the U.S. Department of Education strictly prohibits the use of any of its funding to support DARE in any school.

Many other evidence-based programs are available for schools. In fact, the federal agency SAMHSA has identified more than 60 model programs. The National Institute on Drug Abuse publication *Preventing Drug Use among Children and Adolescents: A Research-Based Guide*[6] identifies what research has found to be the principles of effective substance abuse prevention. These principles state that prevention programs should have the following characteristics:

- Enhance protective factors and move toward reversing or reducing known risk factors.
- Target all forms of drug abuse.
- Include skills to resist drugs when offered, strengthen personal commitments against drug use, and increase social competency (e.g., in communications, peer relationships, self-efficacy, and assertiveness).
- Include interactive methods, such as peer discussion groups, rather than didactic teaching techniques alone.
- Be family-focused prevention and include a component for parents or caregivers that reinforces what the children are learning.
- Be long term, over the school career, with repeat interventions to reinforce the original prevention goals.
- Reach all youth populations and specific subpopulations at risk for drug abuse, such as children with behavior problems or learning disabilities and those who are potential dropouts.
- Be adapted to address the specific nature of the drug abuse problem in the local community. The higher the level of risk of the target population, the more intensive the prevention effort must be and the earlier it must begin.
- Be age specific, developmentally appropriate, and culturally sensitive.

Information-Based Strategies

In the 1960s and 1970s, education programs often used scare tactics in an effort to change attitudes and behavior regarding substance use and abuse. It was common practice for local police to tell stories about drug abusers and the troubles that drug abuse made in their lives or to invite former addicts to explain how easy it is to get hooked on drugs and to describe the horrible life that results from addiction. Research, however, shows that such scare tactics and testimonials are not the most effective means of changing attitudes and behaviors. Listeners tend to quickly forget negative information and often disregard warnings by convincing themselves "that doesn't apply to me" or "they're just trying to scare me."[7]

Information-only-based strategies assume that if students understand that drugs are harmful, they will avoid experimentation and drug use. Information-only approaches are ineffective because information is just one of the many factors that govern an individual's decision to use or not use substances. However, sound information about drugs and their effects and consequences is fundamental to substance abuse prevention efforts. Information provides the foundation for effective substance prevention programs.

Information about how specific substances produce immediate effects (e.g., yellow stains on teeth, bad breath from cigarette smoking) is more effective than information about the possible long-term consequences (e.g., lung cancer, emphysema). Regardless of the focus or strategy of a program, any information presented in a substance abuse prevention program must be accurate.

Normative Education

Young people typically overestimate the prevalence of tobacco, alcohol, and other drug use among their peers. Consequently, a critical component of a substance abuse prevention program should be clearing up misconceptions—often prevalent in the media—that "everybody is drinking, smoking, or doing drugs." This approach is sometimes referred to as **normative education**. Students gain more accurate perceptions when they are provided with information concerning drug use prevalence rates among their peers from national and local surveys. This information can then be compared with their own estimates of drug use. Misconceptions can also be cleared up when students organize and conduct surveys of drug use in their school and community. Research shows that normative education, which posits that drug use is not the norm, is an effective strategy in diminishing substance abuse behavior.[8] The same research has also shown that refusal skills and enhancing competence in personal and social skills are effective strategies in reducing drug use among youths.

Resistance Strategies

Peer group acceptance and identification are major concerns of young people. Peer pressure to use various substances or engage in other health-risky behavior can be great for many young people. Therefore, teaching upper-elementary–specific, middle-school–specific, and high-school–specific skills to resist peer pressure may be effective in deterring substance use and abuse. A typical refusal skills technique includes a film or video depicting the various social pressures students are likely to encounter from peers, media, and others. After "inoculation," or exposure to these anticipated pressures ("germs"), students brainstorm and discuss possible refusals to the pressures. Role-play is then used to practice and rehearse these skills. These skills can assist young people not only in refuting pressure from peers and others, but also in resisting the persuasive influence of advertising. Students are then better able to recognize the appeals in ads and formulate counterarguments to them.

Personal and Social Skills Training and Enhancement Approaches

In addition to peer and media pressure, factors such as poor self-concept, anxiety, low social confidence, external locus of control, impulsivity, and low assertiveness increase the risk of substance use. The recognition that problem behaviors, including substance abuse, result from the interplay of these personal and social factors has led to the development of effective prevention programs such as the Life Skills Training program. The Life Skills Training program deals directly with the interpersonal and social factors that promote drug use by teaching general self-management and social competence skills. It includes teaching the following skills:[9]

- ◆ General problem-solving and decision-making skills
- ◆ Critical thinking skills for resisting peer and media influences
- ◆ Skills for increasing self-control and self-esteem (e.g., self-appraisal, goal setting, self-monitoring, self-reinforcement)
- ◆ Adaptive coping strategies for relieving stress and anxiety through the use of cognitive coping skills or behavioral relaxation techniques

♦ Skills for communicating effectively (e.g., how to avoid misunderstandings by being specific, paraphrasing, asking clarifying questions)
♦ Skills for overcoming shyness
♦ Skills for meeting new people and developing healthy friendships, including conversational skills, complimenting skills, and general assertiveness skills

Skills training requires instruction, demonstration, feedback, and reinforcement. Adequate classroom time must be devoted to practicing the skills (behavioral rehearsal) as well as to providing extended practice outside of class through behavioral homework assignments. The Life Skills Training program has been shown to be effective in reducing drug use behavior, especially when the training is followed by booster sessions to reinforce retention of personal and social skills. **Box 7-4** indicates where to locate activities in this text that help teach social skills.

Peer Approaches

Many youth substance abuse prevention programs utilize exemplary peer leaders. The rationale for using peer leaders is that they often have higher credibility with young people than do teachers or other adults. Peer leaders may lead discussions in classroom or group settings or serve as facilitators of skills training by demonstrating skills taught in prevention programs (e.g., refusal skills). Peer leaders also serve as role models who do not use drugs. They can be about the same age as prevention program participants or may be older students who work with younger students. **Peer tutors** are usually older students who teach younger students about drugs, including how to resist pressures to use them.

Peer counselors are exemplary students who have received specific training in how to listen, avoid making judgments, maintain confidentiality, and be supportive of others. Peer counselors make themselves available to their peers who need to discuss problems, and then refer students with serious problems to an appropriate professional or school staff member.

Some sources suggest that peer-led programs are more effective in preventing and reducing high-risk behavior than teacher-led programs are. This may be explained by the fact that peers have more social information than teachers and other adults do. Further, modeling appropriate behaviors outside of school, where youths actually use substances, may explain the effectiveness of peer-led programs. To ensure successful implementation of peer approaches, it is imperative that school administrators and personnel provide extensive support, guidance, and training.

Drug-Free Activities and Alternatives to Drugs

We can assume that some children and adolescents take drugs to achieve an altered state of consciousness. As a result, some substance abuse prevention programs teach and/or provide youths with opportunities to achieve "natural highs" or altered states of consciousness through drug-free activities. Stimulating, relaxing, creative, or growth-enhancing activities such as meditation, exercise, sports, or performing arts have all been used as alternatives to drugs. Service projects in which youths volunteer to assist people in need may also serve as alternatives to substance abuse activities.

Student Assistance Programs

Student assistance programs provide professional counseling to students at risk for substance abuse or other problems. In addition, these programs can provide interventions for students already abusing substances and can refer students and their families to outside agencies and professionals as needed. Student assistance programs are partnerships among people inside and outside of schools (e.g., substance abuse and mental health treatment professionals, businesses, law enforcement personnel) and can serve communities in the following ways:

- Provide substance abuse education to teachers, students, and parents
- Help identify youths with problems
- Accept self-referral of students and referral by teachers, parents, and peers of youths needing evaluation or services
- Help students and families find and use community resources
- Conduct discussion groups to allow youths troubled by substance abuse (or other problems) to talk about their concerns
- Conduct reentry groups for students returning to school after receiving treatment for substance abuse

Parent Approaches

A variety of parent approaches has been used in substance abuse prevention programs. Information programs strive to give parents basic information about drugs and the impact they have on health and society. Programs on parenting skills assist parents in learning and developing personal and interpersonal skills that may serve to prevent drug abuse in the family. For example, parents refine their skills in communicating with children, decision making, setting goals and limits, and even how and when to say no to their children. These important skills can improve weak family relationships and poor family communication, which are often found in families where youths use drugs.

Parent support groups help parents cope with drug problems in their homes and neighborhoods. Parents meet to gain mutual support by discussing problem solving, communication skills, parenting and child-management skills/strategies, and ways to take action against drug problems. These groups often provide supervision for young people's activities that are free of alcohol and other drugs.

Some of the most promising drug prevention programs are those in which parents, students, schools, and communities join together to send a firm, clear message that the use of alcohol and other drugs will not be tolerated. Parents can help their children to remain drug free

Children who eat with their families are less likely to smoke, drink, or use drugs.

by supporting community efforts to give young people healthy alternatives to substance use. Alcohol- and drug-free proms and other school-based celebrations are growing in popularity around the country. Parents can help to organize such events, solicit contributions, and serve as chaperones.

SUBSTANCE ABUSE PREVENTION CURRICULA

The content and skills that need to be taught in tobacco, alcohol, and drug-free curricula are identified in **Box 7-2**. Detailed lists of core concepts for various grade levels can be found on the HECAT website within the Tobacco-Free (T) Module and the Alcohol and Other Drug-Free (AOD) Module available online.[10] Module T and Module AOD also contain multiple examples of skills for each of the national standards. Here are some examples:

- *Analyze influences*: Explain why friends ask friends to use alcohol.
- *Access valid information and products*: Demonstrate the ability to access school and community resources to help if someone is affected by the alcohol or drug use of another person.
- *Interpersonal communication*: Demonstrate effective refusal skills when pressured to use tobacco, alcohol, or other drugs.
- *Decision making*: Predict immediate and long-term consequences of using alcohol or other drugs for oneself, for one's family, and for the community.
- *Goal setting*: Discuss how personal goals can be affected by alcohol and other drug use.
- *Practice behaviors*: Express intentions to avoid riding in a motor vehicle with a driver who has been drinking alcohol or using other drugs.
- *Advocate*: Demonstrate how to effectively persuade and encourage others not to use alcohol or other drugs.

Later in this chapter in Boxes 7-3, 7-6, and 7-7, you will find teaching activities that will help you teach these skills to your students. As you prepare your curriculum, be sensitive to the specific needs of your local school and community in terms of cultural appropriateness and local substance abuse problems.

Developmental Considerations

Age and developmental abilities play a role in being susceptible to abusing substances and able to understand associated dangers. Educators need to consider their students' developmental levels as they prepare teaching strategies and curricula for promoting a drug-free lifestyle.

Grades K–3

The knowledge gained in grades K–3 should be the foundation for all future substance abuse prevention education. Much of the early health education experience for children should emphasize **wellness**. Wellness is an approach that stresses the positive physical, social, and emotional benefits of being healthy and acting safely. It is a key concept in developing young children's determination to avoid drugs. At this age, children should also begin to develop a sense of responsibility toward themselves and others, including the responsibility to tell adults if something is wrong.

Substance abuse prevention education for this age group should discuss alcohol, tobacco, marijuana, cocaine, Ecstasy, and methamphetamine. Children should also be introduced to

7-2 Internet Support

Instruction Planning Resources

The following are health behavior outcomes (HBOs) recommended by HECAT for K–12 drug-free lifestyle curricula. After reviewing these recommendations, check out the HECAT models available on the Internet: Tobacco Free (T) and Alcohol and Other Drug Free (AOD). Within these modules, you will find recommendations for all the content and skills to be taught at various grade levels.

Tobacco-Free HBOs

- Avoid using (or experimenting with) any form of tobacco.
- Avoid secondhand smoke.
- Support others to be tobacco free, including supporting a tobacco-free environment.
- Seek help for stopping the use of tobacco by oneself and others.
- Quit using tobacco if already using it.

Alcohol and Other Drug-Free HBOs

- Use over-the-counter and prescription drugs properly and safely.
- Avoid experimentation with alcohol and other drugs.
- Avoid the use of alcohol.
- Avoid the use of illegal drugs.
- Avoid driving while under the influence of alcohol and other drugs.
- Avoid riding in a car with a driver who is under the influence of alcohol or other drugs.
- Quit using alcohol and other drugs if already using them.
- Seek help for stopping the use of alcohol and other drugs by oneself and others.

After reviewing the HBOs and the HECAT T and AOD modules, try to ascertain the tobacco, alcohol, and drug use risks in your particular community. You can do so by finding local/state data on the Internet (e.g., CDC's YRBS data) and by interviewing school staff or students. Find out if your state has guidelines for tobacco, alcohol or drug education and if a scope and sequence or curricula exist for your school district. Continue your instruction planning by using the guidelines provided in the Teaching Today's Students chapter and the worksheets at the end of this chapter.

These organizations provide related materials and lesson plans on their internet sites:

- Media Literacy for Drug Prevention
- National Institute on Drug Abuse
- Center for Substance Abuse Prevention
- A to Z Teacher Stuff
- Discovery Education
- Truth: Smoking Prevention Campaign
- American Lung Association
- U.S. Drug Enforcement Administration
- NIDA for Teens
- It's My Life
- The Cool Spot
- National Association for Children of Alcoholics
- Center for Substance Abuse Prevention

Unless otherwise noted, the facts and statistics cited in this section are from the CDC's Smoking & Tobacco Use website (http://www.cdc.gov/tobacco/data_statistics/fact_sheets/).

the dangers of inhalants, because inhalant abuse may be one of the first forms of drug abuse with which children experiment. A special effort should be made to counter the myths that marijuana and other substances are not harmful. K–3 students should learn how to identify a responsible adult through homework assignments involving parents and through classroom presentations by police officers, school nurses, doctors, clergy, and human services professionals. Parents can participate in homework assignments by identifying family rules for behavior, conducting safety checks, and helping with class assignments. Having parents sign homework assignments is a good way to involve them and keep them informed of what is going on in class.

At the early elementary level, instruction may include both formal curricula and other types of classroom activity, including songs and skits and the use of character props such as puppets, cartoon characters, and clowns. These approaches are particularly useful for relaying messages about safety, personal health, and dangerous substances. Skits enable children to practice resistance skills by acting out scenarios in which they encounter dangerous substances or situations. Songs encapsulate important information in an easily remembered form. Some packaged curricula incorporate standardized songs and skits; teachers often enjoy creating their own.

Grades 4–6

In grades 4–6, peer influences continue to grow. Because of an expanding world of friends and experiences, older elementary school children have a particular need to deal with increased pressures. Some in this age group may experiment with tobacco, alcohol, and other drugs. For this reason, they need more information, more analysis of why people use drugs, stronger motivation to avoid drugs, and specific skills for avoiding drug use. In particular, children in the upper elementary grades need specific strategies for resisting pressure, including knowing how to say "no." Planning ahead can be very helpful. Here are a few examples for how to say "no":

- ◆ "Everybody drinks!"—"I think plenty of people don't drink. Anyway, it's not right for me."
- ◆ "Pot will make you feel good."—"I already feel pretty good, and I don't want to mess that up."
- ◆ "If you're my friend, you'll get high with me."—"I really like you. I just don't like drugs."
- ◆ "No one will know."—"I'm not taking any chances. I'd be grounded for life if I got caught."

Curricula at these grade levels should emphasize personal safety. Children in grades 4–6 have more freedom than younger children do, may travel alone to and from school and other local destinations, and may be left alone for part of the day. Personal safety lessons can include how to use the "buddy" system of always traveling in groups or at least in pairs, why to avoid certain routes, how to get help (such as through the local emergency telephone number), and how to answer the telephone or door.

It is important to help children at this age level understand rules and laws. They should learn about society's interest in protecting people from dangerous substances and behavior. They need to understand that they have certain rights—the right to be safe, the right to learn, and the right to say no. Along with these rights come duties and responsibilities.

Within the classroom, students in the upper elementary grades benefit from hands-on learning experiences. Students can build models to illustrate health lessons, such as showing how drugs affect the circulatory or respiratory system. Teachers can assign independent research projects that promote critical thinking about substance use. Students can prepare class projects that reflect real-life events, such as mock television interviews or press conferences. These are just a few examples of hands-on learning experiences. Can you think of others?

Middle/Junior High School (Grades 7–9)

The onset of adolescence creates new challenges for substance abuse prevention. The natural desire for peer acceptance may become a significant cause of anxiety and concern for the adolescent. As a result, the influence of peer pressure to use drugs may become intense. The desire to appear mature and independent rapidly emerges during the middle/junior high school years. Access to tobacco, alcohol, and other drugs is often readily available to many members of this age group. Also, changing bodies and developing minds are very vulnerable to the damaging effects of psychoactive substances.

Adolescents often possess a sense of personal invulnerability ("It can't happen to me"), together with a great insecurity about personal attractiveness and social responsibility. For these reasons, emphasizing that alcohol, tobacco, and other drug use can immediately affect their appearance, coordination, thinking, and behavior can be an effective teaching strategy. Nothing gets the attention of junior high school students like knowing that they may look ridiculous, smell bad, not be capable of playing sports, become unattractive, or not develop physically and sexually. Suggestions that drugs can impair one's chances of getting into college and succeeding in a career begin to have a powerful impact at this age. In addition, and particularly in view of the many other strains on today's families, young teenagers are likely to pay close attention to discussions of how drug use impairs family relationships.

Most adolescents understand that they are gradually gaining freedom; they should also understand that this means greater accountability for their actions. Accordingly, at this grade level, curricula should emphasize personal responsibility, awareness of the law, and penalties for law-breaking. As students begin dating, contemplate colleges and careers, and anticipate getting a driver's license and entering into other aspects of adulthood, the time is right for introducing training for adult responsibilities.

Because middle and junior high school students will probably be exposed to people who use drugs and who pressure them to do so, they need to be familiar with support resources. The curriculum should make students aware of what these services are and how they function. Students should learn that they are not responsible for creating or curing another's problem, but that they can turn to responsible adults and services for help in such situations.

Middle and junior high school students often become involved in school-sponsored social events and activities. The organization and supervision of these activities (such as bands, athletics, clubs, and student organizations) should focus on making and keeping them drug free. Students at this age also benefit from field trips, guest presentations, and research assignments. For example, students in these grades might visit a hospital, hear presentations from personnel working with drug addicts, and cooperate on developing class-wide research projects involving different media.

High School (Grades 10–12)

Students in these grades are beginning the transition to adulthood, which can be a confusing time for them. Even though they are obtaining licenses to drive and preparing for work and postsecondary education, most high school students are still minors under the law. Use of alcohol and other drugs is illegal for them. Substance abuse prevention education faces the dual challenges of motivating these students to continue resisting illicit substances and of helping them behave responsibly as they prepare to assume new roles in society.

Students in high school are in the process of establishing themselves in the world. In turn, it is essential that the lessons of substance abuse prevention education carry over into students' lives outside of class. Among the aspects of increasing responsibility that should be stressed are the importance of serving as positive role models for younger children, realizing one's responsibility in the workplace, and understanding how substance abuse affects personal growth and professional success.

Some curricula use high school students as peer leaders. Peer leaders make presentations to students in lower grades and serve as "buddies" to younger children. Peer leadership can be very effective in motivating older students, but peer leaders need close supervision and monitoring by teachers and school personnel. Student leaders should be drug free and well trained. They should be taught to refer any problems to teachers or other school officials. When properly supervised, peer leaders can help maintain communication and reduce the likelihood of tragedy during a critical period in students' lives.

Special Education Students

Physically and mentally, special education students may be more susceptible to pressure to use drugs than other children are. They are vulnerable to exploitation, may have low self-esteem, and may feel an intense need for acceptance. For all these reasons, they may not appreciate the risks associated with substance abuse without careful instruction. It is incumbent upon school personnel to teach them sound prevention principles and to make sure that they get their full share of prevention education.

Educators also need to recognize that many physically and mentally impaired students must rely upon medicines to treat their health conditions. They are psychologically sensitive to implications that there is something wrong with them because they rely on medication. They may also be very sensitive to substance abuse prevention education when their impairment is the product of, or is affected by, their parents' use of dangerous drugs.

High-Risk Students

High-risk students are those who are at high risk of becoming substance users or who are already abusing drugs. High-risk students include students in the following situations:

◆ Drop out of school or suffer academic failure
◆ Become pregnant
◆ Are economically disadvantaged
◆ Are children of an alcohol or other drug abuser
◆ Are victims of physical, sexual, or psychological abuse
◆ Have committed violent or delinquent acts
◆ Have attempted suicide
◆ Have substance-abusing friends

Curricula for high-risk students should present drug education early and in a form appropriate for their age and experience. Resistance training and lesson plans should pay attention to the total environment in which such children live. If they have not begun using drugs, prevention-oriented education can be useful. Recovering users can also benefit from a positively presented message about drug-free lifestyles. Children who are using drugs, recovering, or dealing with the addictions of family members and friends need to learn and be constantly reminded that addiction does not end when formal treatment ends; addiction cannot be cured, but it can effectively be treated and controlled.

Both children who are recovering and those who are exposed to high-risk environments need support services outside the curriculum. **Support groups** are an effective method of in-school or out-of-school assistance for students and staff. These confidential discussion and counseling sessions are led by professionals or trained volunteers. Nonusers may find such groups helpful in dealing with friends who use drugs and with home problems such as the addictions of parents or siblings. For recovering users, support groups can reinforce their determination to stay off drugs, while helping fulfill the terms of their conditional reentry to school.

Infusion of Substance Abuse Prevention Education into the Curriculum

Schools often have limited time for prevention education in the curriculum. One solution to this problem is to infuse substance abuse prevention into other curricular subjects. Substance abuse prevention education can be integrated into almost every other subject in the curriculum. For example:

- *Math* classes can use statistics to describe the financial and human costs of substance abuse.
- *Science* classes can explore the chemical characteristics and physiological effects of specific drugs.
- *Visual arts* and *English* classes can discuss media pressures and advertising techniques and explore ways to resist these pressures.
- *Social studies* classes can discuss the effects of substance abuse on society and individuals.
- *Physical education* classes and coaches can discuss the effects of anabolic steroids.

TOBACCO

Even though data indicate a decrease in smoking rates among teenagers in recent years, there is always the threat of another epidemic outbreak, and current smoking levels are still not acceptable. Most cigarette smokers begin smoking during their teen years.* In fact, 80% of adult smokers started smoking before the age of 18. Every day of the year, more than 3,600 youth younger than 18 years of age smoke their first cigarette and an estimated 900 kids become daily cigarette smokers (**Figure 7-1**). Many of these youth will become addicted before they are old enough to understand the risks and will ultimately die too young of tobacco-related diseases.

Both federal and state tobacco laws have been enacted to try to protect young people from tobacco. The FDA has issued a broad set of federal requirements designed to significantly curb access to and the appeal of cigarettes and smokeless tobacco products to children and adolescents. These requirements include prohibiting the sale of cigarettes or smokeless tobacco to people younger than 18; prohibiting the sale of cigarette packages with fewer than 20 cigarettes; banning distribution of

FIGURE 7-1 Early onset of smoking.
Data from Centers for Disease Control and Prevention. Smoking and Tobacco Use Fact Sheet. Available at http://www.cdc.gov/tobacco/data_statistics/fact_sheets/.

*Unless otherwise noted, the facts and statistics cited in this section are from the CDC's Smoking & Tobacco Use website (http://www.cdc.gov/tobacco/data_statistics/fact_sheets/).

free samples of cigarettes and smokeless tobacco; and prohibiting tobacco companies' brand-name sponsorship of any athletic, musical, or other social or cultural events. The American Lung Association has posted reports on the Internet that grade states' key tobacco control policies.

Nicotine

When a person inhales cigarette smoke, the **nicotine** in the smoke is rapidly absorbed into the blood and starts affecting the brain within 7 seconds. In the brain, nicotine activates the same reward system as do other drugs of abuse, such as cocaine or amphetamine, albeit to a lesser degree than those illicit drugs. Nicotine's action on this reward system is believed to be responsible for drug-induced feelings of pleasure and, over time, addiction. Nicotine also has the effect of increasing alertness and enhancing mental performance. In the cardiovascular system, it increases heart rate and blood pressure and restricts blood flow to the heart muscle. The drug stimulates the release of the hormone epinephrine, which further stimulates the nervous system and is responsible for part of the "kick" from nicotine. It also promotes the release of the hormone beta-endorphin, which inhibits pain.

People addicted to nicotine experience withdrawal when they stop smoking. This withdrawal involves symptoms such as anger, anxiety, depressed mood, difficulty concentrating, increased appetite, and craving for nicotine. Most of these symptoms subside within 3 to 4 weeks, except for the craving and hunger, which may persist for months.

Health Consequences of Smoking

Smoking damages nearly every organ in the human body. It causes heart and lung disease. It is linked to at least 15 different cancers, and accounts for some 30% of all cancer deaths. In the United States, cigarette smoking is responsible for about 1 in 5 deaths annually, or approximately 443,000 deaths per year. An estimated 49,000 of these deaths are the result of secondhand smoke. In total, cigarette smoking causes more than 1,200 deaths per day (**Figure 7-2** and **Figure 7-3**). This clearly makes cigarette smoking the leading preventable cause of death in the United States. Cigarette smoking kills more people than do AIDS, alcohol abuse, illegal drug abuse, car crashes, murders, suicides, and fires—combined (**Figure 7-4**). On average, smoking reduces a person's life by 13 to 14 years.

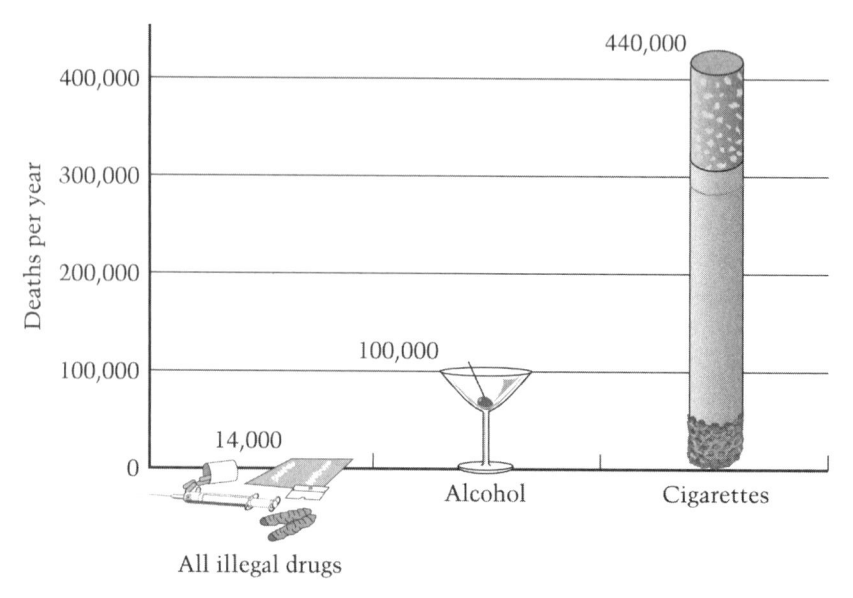

FIGURE 7-2 Deaths per year from substance abuse.

The number of Americans dying each year from cigarette-related diseases is the equivalent of three fully loaded 747 aircraft crashing daily for 365 days a year with no survivors.

FIGURE 7-3 Daily deaths from cigarettes.
Data from Centers for Disease Control and Prevention. Smoking and Tobacco Use. Available at http://www.cdc.gov/tobacco.

Cigarette smoking kills more Americans each year than the combined total of the following:

Suicide   Murder   Alcohol

AIDS   Car accidents   Illegal drugs   Fires

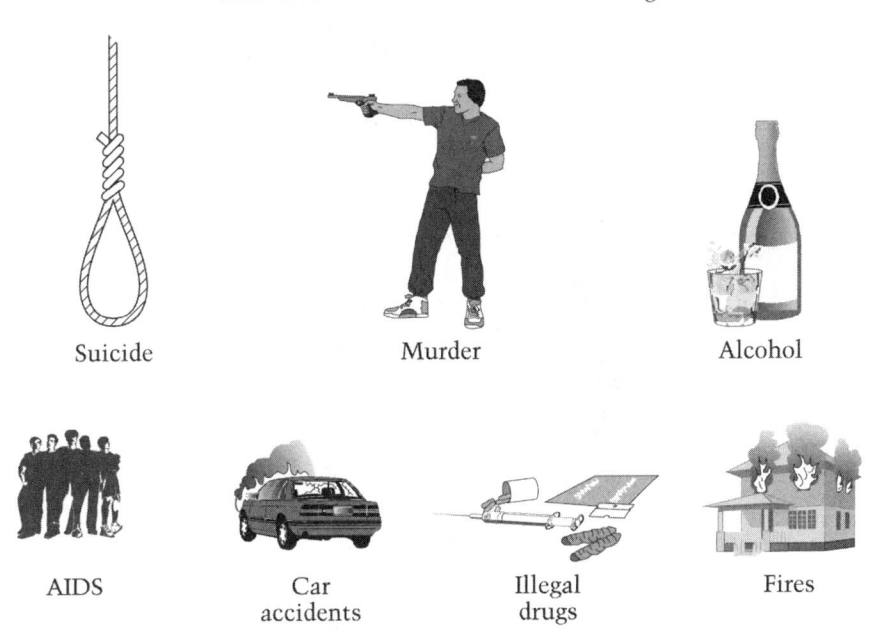

FIGURE 7-4 Cigarettes kill . . .
Data courtesy of the FDA.

Researchers have identified more than 4,000 chemical compounds in tobacco smoke; of these, at least 43 cause cancer in humans and animals. Each year, because of exposure to environmental tobacco smoke, an estimated 4,000 nonsmoking Americans die of lung cancer, and 300,000 children suffer from lower respiratory tract infections.

Smoking also has short-term consequences for young people. These include both respiratory and nonrespiratory effects, addiction to nicotine, and the associated risk of other drug use. Health effects of cigarette smoking for young people include the following consequences:

- Cigarette smokers have a lower level of lung function than nonsmokers, and smoking reduces the rate of lung growth.
- Smoking affects young people's physical fitness, in terms of both performance and endurance.
- Smoking is responsible for coughs and increased frequency and severity of respiratory illnesses. Teenage smokers suffer from shortness of breath almost three times as often as teens who do not smoke do, and they produce phlegm more than twice as often as do nonsmoking teens.
- Teens who smoke are at increased risk of engaging in other risky behaviors, such as abuse of other substances, fighting, and unprotected sex.
- Smoking may be a marker for underlying mental health problems, such as depression, among adolescents. Teenage smokers are more likely to have seen a doctor or other health professionals for an emotional or psychological complaint.

Smoking and Girls

Lung cancer, which was once rare among women, surpassed breast cancer in the late 1980s as the leading cause of female cancer death. Data consistently show that cigarette smoking is even more problematic for women than for men. Females appear to be more susceptible to the addictive properties of nicotine and might clear nicotine at a slower rate from their bodies than males do. In addition, females seem to be more susceptible to the effects of tobacco carcinogens than men are.

Women who smoke or who live with a smoker face unique health effects related to reproductive health, including problems related to pregnancy, oral contraceptive use, menstrual function, and cancers of the cervix and bladder. Young women need to be alerted to the facts that smoking can impair fertility and the production and implantation of ova and that it can contribute to early pregnancy loss. Further, smoking appears to cause irregular menstrual cycles and increased menstrual discomfort. Women who smoke experience menopause at a younger age, which may increase their risk of osteoporosis, heart disease, and other conditions for which estrogen provides a protective effect.

Girls who take up smoking often hope this behavior will help them lose weight or keep them from getting fat.

Cigarette smoking also increases the risk of pregnancy complications. Women who smoke are more likely to experience bleeding and to have low-birth-weight babies. The risk of sudden infant death syndrome (SIDS) is also increased when a woman smokes. Women who smoke and who have children put them at risk of serious health problems. Children exposed to their mother's secondhand smoke have more frequent infections, including colds and flu, ear infections, and lower respiratory infections such as bronchitis and pneumonia. Secondhand smoke has been shown to cause new cases of asthma, as well as to make existing cases of asthma worse.

Smoking affects a woman's appearance as well. Long-term smoking causes the skin to age prematurely and lose its elasticity, the nails and teeth to turn yellow, and the breath to smell foul.

Smokeless Tobacco

The use of **chewing tobacco** and **snuff** delivers nicotine to the central nervous system. Although nicotine is absorbed more slowly through the mouth than through the lungs, the blood nicotine levels in smokeless tobacco users are similar to those in cigarette smokers. Like cigarette smoking, smokeless tobacco use can lead to dependency on nicotine and result in withdrawal symptoms when the user attempts to quit.

Some youths and adults believe that smokeless tobacco is a safe alternative to smoking cigarettes because it is not likely to cause lung cancer. In fact, chewing tobacco and snuff contain potent carcinogens. Oral cancers occur several times more frequently in smokeless tobacco users than in nonusers. Inspection of a snuff dipper's or tobacco chewer's mouth often reveals abnormally thickened, wrinkled, and whitish patches of tissue. These **oral leukoplakias** occur at sites where the tobacco is held in the mouth as a result of direct irritation and contact with tobacco juice. Some leukoplakias transform into precancerous and cancerous lesions in the mouth, throat, or esophagus, or on the tongue or lip.

Smokeless tobacco use can lead to serious dental problems because the gums tend to recede from the teeth in areas near where the tobacco is held in the mouth. The bare roots are then more susceptible to decay and more sensitive to cold, heat, air, certain foods, and chemicals. Smokeless tobacco also contains sugar, which can increase tooth decay. Abrasion of the enamel of teeth, as well as staining of teeth, may occur as a result of tobacco use. Bad breath is another problem of chewing and "dipping."

Hookahs, Bidis, and Kreteks

Hookah cafes have been gaining popularity among youth around the globe and in parts of the United States. **Hookahs**, sometimes called water pipes, are used to smoke specially made tobacco in a variety of flavors (e.g., chocolate, cherry, watermelon). Many users think—erroneously—that hookah smoking is less harmful than smoking cigarettes. In reality, hookah smokers are at risk for the same diseases caused by cigarette smoking. In a typical 1-hour smoking session, a participant inhales 100 to 200 times the volume of smoke inhaled from a single cigarette.

Bidis are thin, unfiltered cigarettes produced in India that are wrapped in brown leaves and tied with a short length of thread. They come in different flavors, including strawberry, chocolate, almond, and root beer. The cigarettes are sold in tobacco specialty stores and in some health food stores. Although some people claim that bidis are a safe alternative to regular cigarettes, this is not true. Bidi smoke contains higher levels of carbon monoxide, nicotine, and tar than cigarette smoke does. The fact that bidis lack a filter also means that more of the cancer-causing agent, tar, goes directly to the smoker's system.

Kreteks are clove cigarettes that are sometimes mistaken for bidis. They are made in Indonesia and contain tobacco and clove. The clove deadens sensation in the lungs, making it easier to inhale smoke deep into the lungs.

Tobacco Use Prevention and Cessation Programs in Schools

Successful programs to prevent tobacco use (as well as other substance abuse problems) address multiple psychosocial factors related to tobacco use among children and adolescents. The psychosocial factors that need to be addressed include the following:

◆ *Immediate and long-term undesirable physiologic, cosmetic, and social consequences.*
◆ *Social norms regarding tobacco use.* Decrease the social acceptability of tobacco use, highlight existing antitobacco norms, and help students understand that most adolescents do not smoke.
◆ *Reasons that adolescents say they smoke.* Some adolescents smoke because they believe it will help them be accepted by peers, appear mature, or cope with stress. Help students develop other more positive means to attain such goals.
◆ *Social influences that promote tobacco use.* Help students develop skills in recognizing and refuting tobacco-promotion messages from the media, adults, and peers.
◆ *Behavioral skills for resisting social influences that promote tobacco use.* Develop refusal skills through direct instruction, modeling, rehearsal, and reinforcement, and coach students to help others develop these skills.
◆ *General and personal skills.* Develop necessary assertiveness, communication, goal-setting, and problem-solving skills that may enable students to avoid both tobacco use and other health-risky behaviors.

Schools should address these psychosocial factors at developmentally appropriate ages. Specific instructional concepts should be provided for students in early elementary school, junior high or middle school, and senior high school.

Successful tobacco use prevention programs develop and enforce a school policy on tobacco use. Such a school policy must be consistent with state and local laws. Further, the CDC recommends that a policy should include the following elements:[11]

◆ Prohibitions against tobacco use by students, all school staff, parents, and visitors on school property, in school vehicles, and at school-sponsored functions away from school property
◆ Prohibitions against tobacco advertising in school buildings, at school functions, and in school publications
◆ A requirement that all students receive instruction on avoiding tobacco use
◆ Provisions for students and all school staff to have access to programs to help them quit using tobacco
◆ Procedures for communicating the policy to students, school staff, parents or families, visitors, and the community
◆ Provisions for enforcing the policy

To ensure broad support for school policies on tobacco use, representatives of relevant groups, such as students, parents, school staff, and school board members, should participate in developing and implementing the policy. Clearly articulated policies, when applied fairly and consistently, can help students decide not to use tobacco.

Effective cessation programs for adolescents may already be available in the community through the local health department or a voluntary health agency (e.g., American Cancer Society, American Heart Association, American Lung Association). Schools should identify available resources in the community and provide referral and follow-up services to students. If cessation programs for youth are not available, such programs may be jointly sponsored by the school and the local health department, voluntary health agency or other community health providers, or interested organizations (e.g., churches or civic clubs). At the end of the chapter you will find activities you can use to teach the content and skills students need to be empowered to live a tobacco-free lifestyle.

ALCOHOL

Alcohol is a central nervous system depressant. Alcohol hinders coordination, slows reaction time, dulls senses, and blocks memory functions. It affects almost every organ in the body, and chronic use can lead to numerous preventable consequences, including serious injuries, alcoholism, and chronic disease. Heavy drinking can increase the risk for certain cancers, especially those of the liver, esophagus, throat, and larynx (voice box). It can also cause liver cirrhosis, immune system problems, brain damage, and harm to the fetus during pregnancy. **Box 7-3** discusses problems children experience that are caused by drinking mothers. **Figure 7-5** identifies how drinking increases the risk of death from automobile crashes, recreational accidents, and on-the-job accidents, and how it increases the likelihood of homicide and suicide.

Although it is illegal for anyone younger than the age of 21 to purchase, possess, and consume alcohol, many young people do drink. In addition to breaking the law, these youth are particularly vulnerable to the various problems that alcohol can cause. Among young people, alcohol use is linked to troubles with law enforcement authorities and academic organizations, property destruction, physical fighting, and a host of other problems. Alcohol lowers inhibitions and impairs judgment, which can lead to risky behaviors, including practicing unprotected sex. This behavior, in turn, can lead to acquiring HIV/AIDS as well as other sexually transmitted diseases and unwanted pregnancy. Driving ability is seriously hampered when combined with alcohol use. Approximately 40% of motor vehicle fatalities among teenagers are alcohol related. Many drownings and other injuries among young people are also alcohol related.

Alcoholism

Alcoholism is best explained as a complex, progressive disease. It involves a progressive preoccupation with drinking that leads to physical, mental, social, and/or economic dysfunction. The complexity of alcoholism results from various causes and factors—genetic, psychological, familial, and social—many of which are not clearly understood. Alcoholism usually has the following characteristics:

- *Craving*: a strong need, or compulsion, to drink.
- *Loss of control*: the frequent inability to stop drinking once a person has begun.
- *Physical dependence*: the occurrence of withdrawal symptoms, such as nausea, sweating, shakiness, and anxiety, when alcohol use is stopped after a period of heavy drinking. These symptoms are usually relieved by drinking alcohol or by taking another sedative drug.
- *Tolerance*: the need for increasing amounts of alcohol to get "high."

7-3 Internet Support

FAS and FAE

Fetal Alcohol Syndrome (FAS) is a result of high doses of alcohol consumption during pregnancy. It is the leading known cause of mental retardation in the western world and affects all the systems of the body. Babies with FAS have characteristic features that can fade as they grow, but FAS effects persist for life. **Fetal Alcohol Effects (FAE)** are the results of moderate drinking during pregnancy. The more alcohol consumed the greater risk to the developing baby for mental and behavioral impairments and body malformations.

You will likely teach students with FAS or FAE. The ABC's of FAS/FAE is a teacher's guide and resource booklet available on the Internet. It contains information, signs/clues, checklists, referral forms, and materials for teaching these students. It can be accessed at http://www.lcsc.edu/education/fas/.

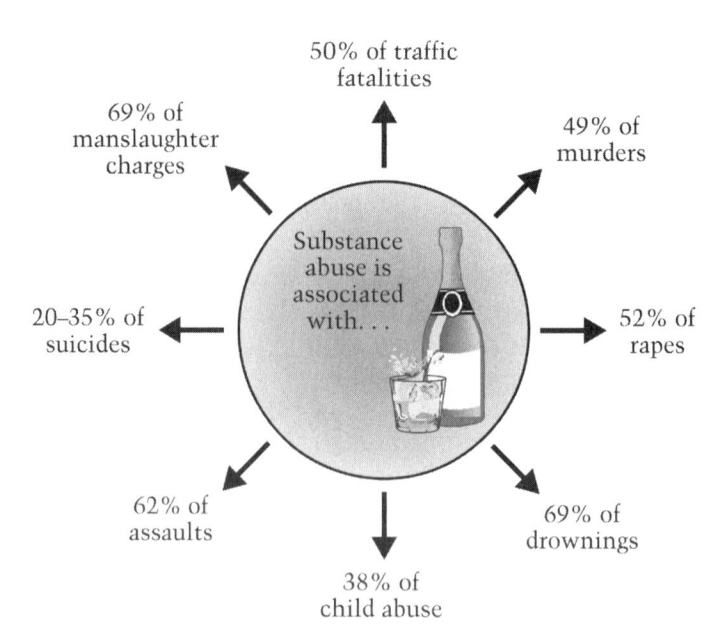

FIGURE 7-5 Problems associated with alcohol use.

Substance abuse is associated with...
- 50% of traffic fatalities
- 49% of murders
- 52% of rapes
- 69% of drownings
- 38% of child abuse
- 62% of assaults
- 20–35% of suicides
- 69% of manslaughter charges

Adolescents, in comparison to adults, appear to be more susceptible or vulnerable to alcoholism. In addition, the disease of alcoholism shows a more accelerated progression in adolescents than that observed in adults. By the time parents, health providers, or school personnel become aware of the problem, an adolescent may have a serious drinking problem.

It is important for educators to be aware of and teach students the signs and symptoms of problem drinking and alcoholism, which include the following:

◆ Drinking in secret or hiding levels of consumption
◆ Drinking in response to worry, depression, tiredness, and so forth
◆ Increasing tolerance
◆ Blackouts (periods of alcohol-induced amnesia)
◆ Increased frequency and amount of drinking, and continuing to drink after others have stopped
◆ Lying about one's drinking
◆ Preoccupation with getting and maintaining a supply of alcohol
◆ Gulping drinks
◆ Early-morning drinking
◆ Difficulty managing money
◆ Changes in eating behavior
◆ Withdrawal symptoms

In addition to these warning signs, young alcoholics often demonstrate indirectly related behaviors that are observable by teachers and parents:

◆ Impulsive behavior
◆ Declining grades, decreased attention span, and difficulty completing projects and assignments
◆ Absences from and tardiness in school
◆ Inability to cope with frustration and irritability with others
◆ Change from one peer group to another or rebelliousness

Addiction in the Family

Addiction to alcohol or other drugs has tragic effects not only on the addict, but also on the children of addicts. About one in five adult Americans live with an alcoholic while growing up. An average of five students in every classroom come from a home with a parent who has a substance addiction. Some of those students are physically affected by their mother's substance abuse. Box 7-3 provides information and resources for teachers working with FAS or FAE students.

Children raised in substance-abusing families have different life experiences than children raised in non-substance-abusing families. Excessive parental substance abuse contributes to a family environment of chaos, unpredictability, anxiety, tension, and denial, in which the primary needs of children are not met. Children of addicts often feel great responsibility and guilt for their parents' substance abuse behavior. They are told by parents or given subtle messages that "if they were better, dad (or mom) wouldn't be so angry and drink so much."

The unpredictability in such an environment arises because children are confused by the difference between the intoxicated and sober behavior of a parent. Promises made by an intoxicated parent are likely to be forgotten when the parent is sober, and vice versa. Confusion and unpredictability also result when a certain action is praised one day and then ignored or punished the next.

Parental substance abuse breeds a host of negative emotions, including insecurity and anger: "If mommy really loved me, she wouldn't drink." Children may also be angry with a non-substance-abusing parent who does not protect them from the violent, addicted parent. They may have concerns about being in an accident when driving with an intoxicated parent or of having the home catch on fire because a parent passed out while holding a lit cigarette. They realize that a frequently intoxicated parent could lose control of the car while driving or become seriously injured in many other ways. Children are also terrified of the arguments that typify the addict home. They may have suffered abuse at the hands of an addicted parent or fear that they will become victims of abusive behavior.

Effects of Growing Up in an Alcoholic Family

Three rules characterize an alcoholic family: "don't talk," "don't trust," and "don't feel." Children learn to not talk about the alcoholism in the family to anyone outside and, therefore, they "don't talk." Because the reactions of the alcoholic parent cannot be predicted or trusted, they "don't trust." Finally, as children see painful feelings avoided or numbed through the use of alcohol, they learn to "not feel" and use denial to escape emotional pain.

Teachers can help children of an addicted parent hear the following important messages:

- *Alcoholism/drug dependency is a sickness.* You didn't cause it and you can't control it.
- *You can't make it better.* You can't cure it.
- *You deserve help for yourself.*
- *You are not alone.*
- *There are safe people and places that can help.*
- *There is hope.*

Family Hero

To cope and survive in their alcoholic environments, children may assume roles that represent particular and rigid ways of relating to other family members and the outside world. The **family hero** is often the eldest child and tries to make up for the deficits in the family. These individuals often assume unfulfilled parenting responsibilities. They are often very responsible with a drive or compulsion to achieve in schoolwork, athletics, music, or other pursuits. Family heroes are usually well-behaved children but may seem bossy or parental in their relationships with other children, often being labeled "teacher's pet." They tend to "take charge" in group activities and may volunteer often and have a strong need for attention and approval from adults.

Three rules that characterize an alcoholic family: "don't talk," "don't trust," and "don't feel."

As adults, family heroes are prone to becoming compulsive overachievers, workaholics, and perfectionists. They often suffer physical problems that come from constantly striving to achieve, but not knowing how to relax or play after spending years attending to the needs of others. They often rely on drugs and alcohol to sustain their straining lifestyle. Family heroes who are not substance dependent often marry spouses who are chemically dependent, weak, sick, or otherwise dependent and become the chief enabler of the chemically dependent partner. Despite all their achievements, family heroes often feel a deep sense of failure because their accomplishments and brilliant performances did not make the alcoholic parent stop drinking. A sense of failure also arises with the realization that the hero is continually meeting other people's needs while ignoring his or her own, is often taken advantage of, and does not know how to stop it.

Teachers can help family heroes learn how to ask for help, follow and negotiate, identify their own needs, relax and have fun, and balance work and play by doing the following:

◆ Limit classroom responsibilities of the child.
◆ Give positive attention at times when the child is not achieving.
◆ Give attention to the child when he or she participates as a follower rather than as a leader in an activity.
◆ Help the child understand that it is all right to make mistakes.

- Suggest to the child that he or she pay attention to his or her own needs.
- Teach relaxation techniques such as progressive relaxation, imagery, exercise, and biofeedback.
- Do not allow the child to monopolize class discussions or always be the first to volunteer or answer a question.
- Validate the child's worth based on being himself or herself, not on doing or achieving.
- Help the child balance work and play by organizing and participating in social and recreational activities.

The Scapegoat

The child playing the **scapegoat** role is blamed for the alcoholic's shortcomings. He or she refuses to compete with the family hero and develops the attitude, "I'd rather be hated than ignored." The scapegoat often displays rebelliousness, irresponsibility, breaking rules, talking back, and acting out. Acting out may take the form of substance abuse, but may also occur through other delinquent or problem behaviors (e.g., criminal activity, sexual promiscuity, high-risk activities). The scapegoat relies heavily on peers and tends to blame others. These individuals' substance abuse and other high-risk behaviors make them vulnerable to early pregnancy, accidental death, suicide, disease, and trouble with the law.

The scapegoat needs to learn how to express anger in a constructive manner, to forgive himself or herself, and to take responsibility for his or her mistakes but not those of others. In addition, the scapegoat needs to learn activities that will bring positive attention and social skills that will allow friendships. Teachers can assist the scapegoat by doing the following:

- Stress the importance of personal responsibility for the child's actions and not allow the child to blame others.
- Give affirmations to the child when he or she takes responsibility.
- Apply logical consequences when the child misbehaves.
- Develop an understanding of the child's behavioral and attitudinal patterns, to avoid getting angry at the child's behavior.
- Provide suggestions for developing social skills, and work with the school counselor to provide this training.
- Do not treat the child in a special manner.
- Do not take the child's behavior personally.
- Do not agree with the child's blaming and complaints about others.

The Lost Child

The **lost child** is often shy, quiet, and withdrawn. Cliff Evans in the story that opens the *Teaching to Make a Difference* chapter is a lost child. Lost children have few friends and seldom cause problems. They typically daydream and fantasize to escape painful reality. They like to work alone and are often creative in nonverbal ways, such as art, music, and writing. Teachers frequently overlook lost children because they do not demand attention and rarely misbehave.

As adults, lost children tend to attach to things rather than people. Their lack of social skills and self-worth typically lead to dissatisfying interpersonal and marital relationships. Loneliness makes them vulnerable to substance abuse. They often die early in life.

Teachers want to make a difference in the lives of their children, and perhaps the greatest difference they can make is recognizing and reaching out to lost children. This can be done in the following ways:

- Take an inventory of students in your classroom who are lonely or whose name you cannot consistently recall.
- Make efforts to notice and attend to the child.

- Find out more about the child's interests and talents.
- On a one-to-one basis, encourage the child's creativity, talents, and academic progress.
- Assist the child in developing relationships with other children in the classroom.
- Have the child work in small groups frequently to build social trust and confidence.
- Make a point of calling on the child in class, not allowing him or her to remain silent.
- Do not allow other children in the class, siblings, or parents to take care of the child by talking and answering for him or her.
- Redirect fantasy and daydreaming activities into appropriate and creative channels, such as writing or artwork.
- Do not be overly sympathetic to the child.

The Mascot or Clown

The **mascot** or family clown diverts attention from the alcoholic parent and reduces family tension by being cute or funny. In school, this child makes repeated and constant attempts to be funny or get attention and is often suspected of hyperactivity. Consequently, such a child comes to the attention of the school counselor or nurse.

The "job" of mascot becomes a full-time role that mascots do not seem to outgrow even as adults. There is the constant need to be the clown, yet unhappiness underlies the continual attempts to be humorous or funny. Unfortunately, many mascots turn to alcohol and other drugs to deal with their deep feelings of sadness and depression.

The mascot needs to learn how to receive attention, praise, and help from others in an appropriate manner, how to deal with conflict and solve problems, and how to recognize and accept feelings. Classroom teachers can assist the mascot by doing the following:

- Give attention to the child when he or she is not attempting to be funny or exhibiting attention-getting behaviors.
- Reinforce to the rest of the class the importance of not paying attention to the child's misbehavior.
- Give the child classroom jobs or tasks that require responsibility.
- Discuss the importance of appropriate behavior with the child in brief, one-to-one discussions.
- Encourage an appropriate sense of humor.
- Do not laugh at the mascot's attempts to be funny.
- Remember that the mascot's behavior is an effort to mask fear and depression.

Al-Anon and Alateen

Al-Anon is a fellowship of people who have been affected by the alcohol abuse of someone. Al-Anon members meet in small groups to harness the strength and hope of others who have lived with alcoholism. This organization provides an opportunity for individuals to learn from the experience of others who have lived in similar situations.

Alateen meetings are similar to Al-Anon meetings except that Alateen is restricted to people younger than age 20 who live, or have lived, with someone who abuses alcohol. Alateen meetings include one or two Al-Anon sponsors. Young people who are living with a person with an alcohol problem, or who have lived with an alcohol abuser in the past, should be encouraged to attend an Alateen meeting. They will find other young people who have faced similar experiences.

You can obtain further information about Al-Anon and Alateen from the Al-Anon/Alateen website at http://www.al-anon.alateen.org/meetings/meeting.html. You can identify local Al-Anon contact information and meeting schedules at http://al-anon.alateen.org/how-to-find-a-meeting.

Teaching activities are located at the end of the chapter that can help you teach the content and skills needed for living an alcohol-free lifestyle.

MARIJUANA AND CANNABIS

Between 1996 and 2012, 18 states and the District of Columbia enacted laws that remove criminal sanctions for the medical use of marijuana, define eligibility for this use, and allow some means to access "medical marijuana." Many additional states have pending legislation to follow suit. Marijuana cannot cure anything, but it has been used to relieve symptoms of the following diseases: AIDS, glaucoma, neuropathy, and nausea and vomiting associated with cancer chemotherapy. All states that have removed the criminal sanctions for medical use of marijuana require a doctor's diagnosis authorizing marijuana treatment, but this is not an effective safeguard to prevent abuse. Instructions for how to fake medical conditions to get medical marijuana cards are easily found on the Internet.

Many individuals and groups fear that legalizing marijuana for medical use is a slippery slope. In some states, people already joke about the ease of getting medical cards for recreational use. The following questionable medical conditions have been used to get such medical cards: hair loss, dry skin, ligament or tendon pain, anxiety, muscle spasms, loss of appetite, arthritis, and migraine headache. Medical use laws have also increased the market for marijuana. Proposals for legalizing commercial production, retail sale, and taxation of marijuana are put forward by those eager to cash in on the expanding market. Their adoption could result in dependence upon tax-generated revenues from the sale of marijuana and the launch of advertising campaigns aimed at adolescents, much like those undertaken by the alcohol and tobacco industries to increase consumption of their products.

As the number of states with medical use laws has increased, the perception that smoking marijuana is fairly safe has likewise increased.[1] Between 2002 and 2008, the states with medical marijuana laws had higher rates of adolescent marijuana use.[12] Today almost half of adolescents say they have tried marijuana, and one-fourth say they have smoked it in the past month.[2]

We will now take a closer look at what marijuana is and how it affects the body. **Marijuana** is the dried, shredded flowers and leaves of the hemp plant *Cannabis sativa*. It usually is smoked as a cigarette (called a *joint* or *nail*), or in a pipe or bong. In recent years, it has appeared in **blunts**, which are cigars that have been emptied of tobacco and refilled with marijuana. Some users mix marijuana into foods or use it to brew tea.

THC (which is short for delta-9-tetrahydrocannabinol) is the chemical that accounts for the major psychoactive effects of marijuana. THC is found most abundantly in the upper leaves, bracts, and flowers of the resin-producing variety of the plant. The dried leaves (marijuana) average from 3% to 5% THC. However, through special breeding, marijuana may be manipulated to yield greater amounts of THC (7% or higher). **Hashish**, which is the dried and pressed flowers and resins, contains as much as 12% THC. **Hashish oil**, a crude extract of hashish, contains as much as 60% THC. THC tends to remain stored for long periods of time in the body. Complete elimination of THC can take up to 30 days.

A typical marijuana high may last 2 to 3 hours. The user experiences an altered perception of space and time. Marijuana adversely affects judgment, complex motor skills, and physical coordination. These effects make driving a car dangerous and increase the possibility of many types of accidents. Using marijuana can also impair one's judgment regarding decision making about sex. Sexual activity places young people at risk for unplanned pregnancy and sexually transmitted diseases, including HIV infection. Marijuana users are also likely to experience difficulty in thinking and problem solving. There is concern that regular use of marijuana by young people may impair psychological and physical maturation and development. Apathy, lack of concern for the future, and the loss of motivation have been seen in some heavy users.

Many education campaigns have been designed to inform the public about the dangers of driving under the influence of alcohol, but it is equally important to recognize that driving under the influence of drugs can be just as dangerous as driving drunk—and "drugs" in this sense includes use of both marijuana and prescription drugs. THC, the active ingredient in marijuana, negatively affects coordination, memory, and judgment. As a result, a driver high on marijuana may not be able to react appropriately to unpredictable traffic conditions. Young drivers are particularly at risk for a number of reasons. Simply because teens are less experienced drivers, they have a higher risk of being involved in an accident. When lack of experience is combined with the use of marijuana or other substances that affect cognitive and motor abilities, the results can be tragic.[13]

The effects of smoking marijuana on the lungs have raised concern because this drug is usually taken through smoking. A marijuana smoker is likely to experience many of the same respiratory problems that tobacco smokers have. Compared to tobacco smoke, however, marijuana is typically inhaled more deeply and held in the lungs for a longer period of time. These inhalation practices are likely to increase the risk of respiratory problems. As a result, marijuana smokers may have daily cough and phlegm, symptoms of chronic bronchitis, and more frequent chest colds. Concerns have also been voiced that marijuana smoke contains carcinogens that could increase the risk of lung cancer.

Several thousand people are treated each year for marijuana dependency. Marijuana's effects on the brain and those produced by such highly addictive drugs as alcohol, heroin, cocaine, and nicotine are quite similar. Marijuana seems to affect the brain's reward systems in much the same way as these other addictive substances. These actions in the brain keep users desiring to repeat the use of marijuana. When heavy users of marijuana abruptly stop taking the drug, they are likely to feel anxiety and other negative emotions. In turn, individuals may keep using marijuana in an effort to avoid these feelings. Many teenagers who seek treatment for drug dependency report being addicted to marijuana.

OTHER DRUGS OF ABUSE

Any drug, legal or illegal, can be abused. Using a substance for purposes other than those intended by the manufacturer is considered **drug abuse**. Teen substance abuse overall has declined since the 1990s, but abuse of prescription painkillers is a notable exception. In particular, the rate of abuse of addictive narcotic painkillers that imitate morphine has grown. Clearly, educators, parents, and others can never become complacent about the potential for youth substance abuse. Even if statistics indicate improvements in some areas, others remain problematic and there is always the threat of another epidemic outbreak. Too many youths today are or will become caught in a web of addiction—that of their own or that of a loved one.

All drugs of abuse—including nicotine, marijuana, cocaine, and others—primarily affect the brain's limbic system, what scientists call the "reward" system. Normally, the limbic system responds to pleasurable experiences by releasing the neurotransmitter dopamine, which creates feelings of pleasure. Some drugs have a similar size and shape as natural neurotransmitters and act as "counterfeit" neurotransmitters. Some drugs create pleasurable feelings by locking onto receptor sites and start an unnatural chain reaction of electrical charges, causing neurons to release large amounts of their own neurotransmitter. Other drugs work by blocking reabsorption or reuptake (brakes) of neurotransmitters, thereby causing unnatural floods of these substances.[14] The pleasurable feelings that come at first from counterfeit highs become less high with repeated use and can block individuals from feeling good naturally.

Federal and state laws have been enacted to combat abuse and the distribution of controlled substances. Federal drug convictions are typically obtained for trafficking, whereas the majority of local and state arrests involve charges of possession. Federal drug charges generally carry harsher punishments and longer sentences. State arrests for simple possession without the intent to distribute the drug tend to misdemeanors and usually result in probation, a short term in a local jail, or a fine, depending on the criminal history and age of the person being charged.

Oxycodone

Oxycodone is a very strong narcotic pain reliever that is similar to morphine. It is an effective pain reliever for mild to moderate pain, for chronic pain, and for pain associated with terminal cancer. The prescription medication is designed so that the oxycodone is released slowly over time, allowing it to be used twice daily. Oxycodone (also known by the brand name OxyContin) is abused for its narcotic effects. Rather than ingesting the pill as indicated, abusers use other methods of taking the drug. They crush oxycodone tablets to release all the narcotic in the drug at once and produce an intense, heroin-like high. Once the tablets are crushed, abusers either snort them or dissolve them in liquid for injection.

As mentioned earlier, the nonmedical use of oxycodone and other pain relievers is a growing problem. Prescription pills do not look dangerous; they appear harmless like the medicines people are accustomed to taking, such as Tylenol or Advil. This is the mindset of many teens. According to the 2008 report *Prescription for Danger* from the Office of National Drug Control Policy, one-third of teens believe there is "nothing wrong" with using prescription medicines without a prescription once in a while.[15] Acting on this belief can be the fatal mistake that leads to addiction. Family members' and friends' medicine cabinets are usually the original source of prescription drugs taken illicitly by teens. Addicts try to supply themselves by scamming physicians for prescriptions, stealing from unsuspecting acquaintances, and buying the drug on the street. Pharmacies have been forced to increase their security measures because of a rash of burglaries undertaken to obtain oxycodone and other narcotic pain relief pills such as hydrocodone (Vicodin, Lortab). Addicts who take oxycodone are prone to move on to heroin because heroin is so much cheaper to buy on the street.

Inhalants

Substances inhaled to induce psychoactive effects, such as euphoria or intoxication, can be classified into three basic groups: volatile solvents, aerosols, and anesthetics. The **volatile solvents** include the chemical components (e.g., toluene, acetone, benzene) of commercial products such as plastic (model) cement, fingernail polish removers, paint thinners, gasoline, kerosene, typewriter correction fluid, and lighter fluid. **Aerosols** are products discharged by the propellant force of compressed gas. Chemicals in the aerosol products and the propellant can be toxic. Many abused aerosols contain gases of chlorinated or fluorinated hydrocarbons, nitrous oxide, and vinyl chloride. A wide variety of aerosol products are abused, including hair sprays, spray paints, cooking sprays, and Freon gas. Many aerosols and volatile solvents are extremely poisonous and can damage body organs and systems.

Anesthetics include ether, chloroform, nitrous oxide, halothane, and related gases. Nitrous oxide (laughing gas) is the most widely used of these drugs of abuse; it is available as an anesthetic and commercially as a tracer gas to detect pipe leaks, as a whipped-cream propellant, and as a pressurized product to reduce preignition in racing cars.

Children are the most common abusers of volatile solvents and aerosols. Two major types of young inhalant abusers have been identified: (1) experimenters or transitional users, who either quit using inhalants or move on to other drugs, respectively, and (2) chronic abusers. Chronic abuse is usually limited to those persons who have limited access to more popular mind-altering substances, such as the young and the very poor. Inhalant experimentation is widespread among the young. Chronic inhalant abuse is often related to parental alcoholism and neglect or abuse.

Frequently, the abused substance is emptied or sprayed into a plastic or paper bag, which is held tightly over the nose and mouth, and the fumes are inhaled. A cloth may be dipped in a liquid solvent, or the active solvent may be applied to the cloth, which is then held against the nose and/or mouth.

Many hazards are associated with inhalant abuse, and each inhaled substance carries different hazards. Because these substances are often poisonous, long-term (e.g., brain damage, hepatitis) or short-term damage to body tissues and organs is possible. Fatal overdoses occur when the central nervous system is depressed to the point that breathing stops. The risk of accidents is high because these substances often affect reasoning, orientation, and muscle coordination. Suffocation and asphyxiation can also occur.

Anabolic Steroids

Anabolic steroids are synthetic derivatives of the male hormone testosterone. Their full name is *androgenic* (promoting masculine characteristics) *anabolic* (building) *steroids* (the class of drugs). These derivatives of testosterone promote the growth of skeletal muscle and increase lean body mass.

Anabolic steroids were first abused by athletes seeking to improve performance. Because these drugs produce increases in lean muscle mass, strength, and ability to train longer and harder, athletes in a variety of sports are attracted to these substances in hopes of enhancing athletic performance and improving physique. Young people are attracted to anabolic steroids in efforts to accelerate their physical development. Anabolic steroids are now seldom prescribed by physicians, as their current legitimate medical uses are limited to certain kinds of anemia, severe burns, and some types of breast cancer.

Athletes and other abusers typically take anabolic steroids in cycles of weeks or months, rather than continuously, in patterns called cycling. **Cycling** involves taking multiple doses of steroids over a specific period of time, stopping for a period, and starting again. In addition, users frequently combine several different types of steroids to maximize their effectiveness while minimizing negative effects, a process known as **stacking**.

Steroids are produced in tablet or capsule form for oral ingestion or as a liquid for intramuscular injection. Abusers who inject anabolic steroids run the risk of contracting or transmitting hepatitis or the HIV virus that leads to AIDS.

Steroid users risk developing serious side effects and hazards, many of which yet remain unknown, particularly when high doses are used over long periods of time. Some side effects appear quickly, such as trembling, acne, jaundice (yellowish pigmentation of skin, tissues, and body fluids), fluid retention, and high blood pressure. Others, such as heart attack and strokes, may not show up for years.

A major concern of anabolic steroid use is the impact upon physical growth and development. Among adolescents, anabolic steroids can prematurely halt growth through premature skeletal maturation and accelerated pubertal changes.

In males, use of steroids can cause shrinking of the testicles, reduced sperm count, infertility, baldness, and development of breasts. In females, irreversible masculine traits can develop along with breast reduction and sterility. Females using anabolic steroids may also experience growth of facial hair, changes in or cessation of the menstrual cycle, enlargement of the clitoris, and deepened voice.

Aggression and other psychiatric side effects may result from anabolic steroid abuse. Many users report feeling good about themselves while on anabolic steroids, but researchers report that such abuse can cause wild mood swings, including manic-like symptoms, which lead to violent, even homicidal, episodes. Depression is often seen when the drugs are stopped and may contribute to steroid dependence. Users may suffer from paranoid jealousy, extreme irritability, delusions, and impaired judgment stemming from feelings of invincibility.

Signs of steroid use include quick weight and muscle gains (if steroids are used in conjunction with weight training); behavioral changes, particularly increased aggressiveness and combativeness; jaundice; purple or red spots on the body; swelling of feet or lower legs; trembling; unexplained darkening of the skin; acne; and persistent breath odor.

Cocaine

Cocaine is a strong stimulant derived from the leaves of the coca bush, a plant that grows in the Andean Mountain region of South America (Colombia, Peru, Bolivia). Coca leaves are processed into cocaine hydrochloride, a white crystalline powder that is inhaled through the nose ("snorted") or injected. When inhaled, cocaine's effects peak in 15 to 20 minutes and disappear in 60 to 90 minutes. When injected intravenously, the result is an intense high that crests in 3 to 5 minutes and wanes over 30 to 40 minutes. Another form of cocaine is "crack" cocaine. **Crack cocaine** is made by processing cocaine hydrochloride to a base state with baking soda and water. The resulting product looks like slivers of soap but has the general texture of porcelain. It is smoked in a pipe and produces an intense cocaine high.

Cocaine directly stimulates the reward centers of the brain, producing intense feelings of euphoria. When the euphoria and excitement of the initial cocaine high taper off, the user slides into a physiological depression, a "let-down" feeling characterized by dullness, tenseness, and edginess. A user wants to take cocaine again in an effort to counteract these let-down feelings. This causes a cycle of using cocaine to achieve euphoria and to ward off the negative feelings associated with coming down from its effects.

Daily or binge users undergo profound personality changes. They become confused, anxious, and depressed. They are short-tempered and grow suspicious of friends, loved ones, and other associates. Their thinking is impaired; they have difficulty concentrating and remembering things. They experience weakness and lassitude. They neglect work and other responsibilities. They lose interest in food and sex. Some become aggressive, and some experience panic attacks. The more of the drug they use, the more profound their symptoms.

In some cases, when consumption of cocaine is frequent or the dose is high, or both, users suffer a partial or total break with reality, a condition known as cocaine psychosis. The cocaine psychotic has delusions and may become paranoid, sometimes reacting violently against those he or she imagines are persecuting him or her. Many of these users experience visual, auditory, or tactile hallucinations (one of the most common is "coke bugs," or **formication**, the sensation of insects crawling under the skin). Cocaine psychosis can continue for days, weeks, or months. Severe cases require hospitalization and antipsychotic medications.

Cocaine use can cause chest pain and irregular heartbeat, and it can worsen preexisting coronary heart disease and bring on a heart attack. Because cocaine increases acute blood pressure, it can cause blood vessels in the brain to rupture, thereby causing a stroke. Cocaine may also damage the walls of arteries. Individuals who inject cocaine—or any other drug, for that matter—are at high risk of infection from contaminated needles. HIV, hepatitis B, and hepatitis C are some of the infections that can be spread from contaminated needles.

Another serious risk associated with cocaine use is seizures. Cocaine has been known to induce epilepsy even in persons with no previous signs of this disease.

Methamphetamine

Methamphetamine is a powerful central nervous system stimulant. This drug is made easily in clandestine laboratories with over-the-counter ingredients (e.g., ephedrine, pseudoephedrine). Methamphetamine is commonly known as "speed," "meth," "chalk," "crystal," "crank," "fire," and "glass." It comes in many forms and can be smoked, snorted, orally ingested, or injected. Immediately after smoking the drug or injecting it intravenously, the user experiences an intense rush, or "flash," that lasts only a few minutes and is described as extremely pleasurable. Snorting or oral ingestion produces euphoria, but not the intense rush obtained by smoking or injections. Snorting produces effects within 3 to 5 minutes, and oral ingestion produces effects within 15 to 20 minutes.

Methamphetamine produces pronounced effects on the central nervous system: increased activity and wakefulness, increased physical activity, decreased appetite, and a general sense of well-being. The effects of methamphetamine can last 6 to 8 hours or longer. After the initial rush, there is typically a state of high agitation that in some individuals can lead to violent or irrational behavior.

Like similar stimulants (e.g., cocaine), methamphetamine most often is used in a binge-and-crash pattern. In an effort to obtain the desired effects, users may take higher doses of the drug, take it more frequently, or change their method of drug intake. In some cases, users forgo food and sleep while binging on the drug or being on a "run." After the binge or run, a user "crashes." During the crash, the user may sleep for more than 24 hours and become depressed and hungry and feel intense craving for the drug.

Methamphetamine has toxic effects. It has been shown to damage nerve terminals in the dopamine-containing regions of the brain. High doses can elevate body temperature to dangerous, sometimes lethal, levels, and can cause convulsions. Abuse can lead to inflammation of the heart lining, increased blood pressure, rapid and irregular heartbeat, and strokes in the brain. If methamphetamine is injected, the user has an increased risk of HIV, hepatitis B, and hepatitis C transmission. This is particularly true for individuals who inject the drug and share injection equipment.

Long-time users exhibit symptoms that can include violent behavior, anxiety, confusion, and insomnia. They also can display a number of psychotic features, including paranoia, auditory hallucinations, mood disturbances, and delusions including formication. The paranoia can result in homicidal as well as suicidal thoughts.

In the 1980s, "**ice**"—a smokable form of methamphetamine—was introduced. Ice is a large, usually clear crystal of high purity that is smoked in a glass pipe like crack cocaine. The smoke is odorless, leaves a residue that can be resmoked, and produces effects that may continue for 12 hours or more.

In addition to the dangers of methamphetamine abuse, the manufacturing process presents its own set of risks. The production of methamphetamine requires the use of hazardous chemicals, many of which are corrosive or flammable. The vapors that are created in the chemical reaction attack mucous membranes, skin, eyes, and the respiratory tract. Some chemicals react dangerously with water, and some can cause fire or explosion. Methamphetamine manufacturing also results in a great deal of hazardous waste; for example, the manufacture of 1 pound of methamphetamine yields 6 pounds of waste. This waste includes corrosive liquids, acid vapors, heavy metals, solvents, and other harmful materials that can cause disfigurement or death when contact is made with skin or breathed into the lungs. Lab operators almost always dump this waste illegally in ways that severely damage the environment. National parks and other preserved sites, for instance, have been adversely affected by such contamination.

Heroin

Heroin is a narcotic drug that is processed from morphine, a naturally occurring substance extracted from the seed pod of the opium poppy. It is typically sold as a white or brownish powder or as the black, sticky substance known on the streets as "**black tar heroin**." Most street heroin is cut with other drugs or with substances such as sugar, starch, powdered milk, or quinine. Street heroin can also be cut with strychnine or other poisons. Because heroin abusers do not know the actual strength of the drug or its true contents, they are at risk of overdose or death. Heroin also poses special problems because of the transmission of HIV and other diseases that can occur from sharing needles or other injection equipment.

Heroin is usually injected, sniffed/snorted, or smoked. Typically, a heroin abuser may inject up to four times per day. This drug is particularly addictive because it enters the brain so rapidly. With heroin, the rush is usually accompanied by a warm flushing of the skin, dry mouth, and a heavy feeling in the extremities, which may be accompanied by nausea, vomiting, and severe itching. After the initial effects, abusers will be drowsy for several hours. Mental function is clouded by heroin's effect on the central nervous system. Heart rate and blood pressure slow. Breathing is also severely slowed, sometimes to the point of death. As mentioned, heroin overdose is a particular risk on the street, where the amount and purity of the drug cannot be accurately determined.

Heroin use can rapidly progress to addiction. Like abusers of any addictive drug, heroin abusers generally devote more and more time and energy to obtaining and using the drug. Once addicted, the heroin abuser's primary purpose in life becomes seeking and using drugs. The drugs literally change the brain. Physical dependence develops with higher doses of the drugs. With **physical dependence**, the body adapts to the presence of the drug, and **withdrawal symptoms** occur if use is reduced abruptly. Withdrawal may occur within a few hours after the last time the drug is taken. Symptoms of heroin withdrawal include restlessness, muscle and bone pain, insomnia, diarrhea, vomiting, cold flashes with goose bumps ("**cold turkey**"), and leg muscle spasms. Taking methadone can prevent withdrawal, which explains why methadone is used in treating heroin addiction.

Club Drugs

Club drugs is a general term for a number of illicit drugs, primarily synthetic, that are most commonly encountered at nightclubs and "raves." The drugs include MDMA, ketamine, GHB, Rohypnol, LSD, PCP, methamphetamine, and, to a lesser extent, psilocybin mushrooms. This section on club drugs discusses MDMA, LSD, PCP, and psilocybin mushrooms. Ketamine, GHB, and Rohypnol, which are popular on the club and rave scene, are discussed in the following section ("Date-Rape Drugs") because they are also used as date-rape agents. Methamphetamine was discussed earlier in this chapter.

One reason why these drugs have grown in popularity is the false perception that they are not as harmful or as addictive as mainstream drugs such as cocaine and heroin. A serious danger surrounding many of these club drugs is that users are often unaware of what is contained in the pills that they acquire. Look-alike substances, such as paramethoxyamphetamine (PMA) and dextromethorphan (DXM), are sometimes sold as MDMA. These substances can cause a dangerous rise in body temperature and have resulted in the deaths of some individuals who unknowingly took them in pills they believed to contain Ecstasy (MDMA). MDMA tablets may also contain other substances, such as ketamine, PCP, caffeine, ephedrine, or methamphetamine.

MDMA

MDMA is the most popular of the club drugs and is widely abused in many areas of the United States. **MDMA**, which is also known as **Ecstasy** or "e," is a synthetic, psychoactive substance possessing stimulant and mild hallucinogenic properties. Known as the "hug drug" or "feel good" drug, it reduces inhibitions, eliminates anxiety, and produces feelings of empathy for others. In addition to providing chemical stimulation, the drug reportedly suppresses the need to eat, drink, or sleep. This enables club-scene users to endure all-night and sometimes 2- to 3-day parties. Although it can be snorted, injected, or rectally inserted, MDMA is usually taken orally in tablet form, and its effects last approximately 4 to 6 hours.

An MDMA overdose is characterized by a rapid heartbeat, high blood pressure, faintness, muscle cramping, panic attacks, and, in more severe cases, loss of consciousness or seizures. One of the drug's well-known side effects is jaw muscle tension and teeth grinding. To help relieve this tension, MDMA users will often suck on pacifiers. The most critical, life-threatening response to MDMA is hyperthermia, or excessive body heat. Recent reports of MDMA-related deaths were associated with core body temperatures ranging from 107°F to 109°F. Many rave clubs now provide cooling centers or cold showers so that participants who are using MDMA can lower their body temperatures.

Some evidence indicates that Ecstasy damages the neurons (nerve cells) that utilize serotonin to communicate with other neurons in the brain and that recreational MDMA users risk permanent brain damage that may manifest itself as depression, anxiety, memory loss, learning difficulties, sleep disorders, sexual dysfunction, and other neuropsychiatric disorders.

In addition to the dangers posed by MDMA, incidents involving look-alike tablets containing substances such as PMA, methamphetamine, and methamphetamine/ketamine are increasing. Tablets containing MDMA in combination with other illicit drugs, such as phencyclidine (PCP), have also been encountered. Users are typically unaware of the dangers posed by these drugs and may unknowingly ingest potentially dangerous or even lethal amounts. In 2000 alone, PMA ingestion was associated with three deaths in Chicago and six deaths in central Florida.

LSD

LSD (lysergic acid diethylamide) is a potent hallucinogenic drug. One liquid ounce of this colorless, odorless, and tasteless compound contains approximately 300,000 human doses. The liquid is dropped onto blotter paper ("blotter acid") or made into tiny colored pills ("microdots"). LSD is taken orally, and its effects generally last 8 to 12 hours.

In most cases, the user feels the first effects of the drug 30 to 90 minutes after taking it. LSD's physiological effects include sweating, an increase in blood pressure and heart rate, and an enlargement (dilation) of the pupils of the eye. Other effects that a user may experience include increased body temperature, loss of appetite, sleeplessness, dry mouth, and tremors.

Users refer to their experience with LSD as a "trip." The effects of LSD are unpredictable. They depend on the amount taken; the user's personality, mood, and expectations; and the surroundings in which the drug is used.

LSD is perhaps best known for its effects in altering perceptions. Psychologically, a user may experience delusional thinking and hallucinations. **Hallucinations** are alterations of vision and other senses. Some users experience **synesthesia**, which is a crossing of the senses—seeing sounds or hearing colors, for example. An LSD user may have opposite feelings at the same time, such as elation and depression or relaxation and tension. For many users, their sense of time is distorted, and hours may be perceived as much longer increments of time—perhaps days, weeks, or even years. The drug can alter perceptions to such an extent that the user engages in bizarre behavior. There have been instances in which users have jumped off a tall building or into a body of water. Another bizarre effect is the sensation that one's body is distorted or even coming apart. An LSD trip can be pleasant or terrifying; there is no way of predicting its outcome. A **"bad trip"** refers to an LSD experience that is accompanied by severe, terrifying thoughts and feelings. Fatal and serious accidents have occurred during bad trips.

Many LSD users experience flashbacks. A **flashback** is a recurrence of certain aspects of a person's LSD experience without the user having taken the drug again. Flashbacks occur suddenly, often without warning, and may arise within a few days or more than a year after LSD use.

PCP

On the street, **PCP** (phencyclidine) has many names, including "angel dust," "PeaCe Pill," "cadillac," "crystal joints," "superpot," "superweed," "monkey weed," and "horse tranquilizer." PCP is often substituted for, and sold as, LSD and mescaline to unknowing users.

PCP was first used in pill form, but now is most often snorted like cocaine or mixed with tobacco, marijuana, or parsley and then smoked. Some users inject PCP into their veins, and others swallow it in a liquid form.

PCP has depressant, stimulant, hallucinogenic, and analgesic properties—quite a combination! The effects of the drug on the central nervous system vary greatly. At low doses, the most prominent effect is similar to that of alcohol intoxication, with generalized numbness and reduced sensitivity to pain. As the amount of PCP taken increases, the person becomes more insensitive and may become fully anesthetized. Large doses cause coma, convulsions, and death.

Commonly seen physical effects of PCP use include flushing, excessive sweating, and a blank stare. The size of the pupils is not affected by PCP. At higher doses, side-to-side eye movements (**nystagmus**), double vision, muscular incoordination, dizziness, nausea, and vomiting may occur. Also, tremors, jerky movements, and grand mal and prolonged seizures may follow high doses.

PCP's psychological effects are unpredictable. Any combination of the following may occur with use: mood fluctuations, distortions in thinking, exaggerated sense of well-being, exhilaration, sedation, drunkenness, delusions, auditory and visual hallucinations, and violent behavior.

In some users, PCP causes psychotic reactions that last for weeks or months. According to some researchers, use of this drug can lead to permanent brain damage. The withdrawal effects associated with chronic PCP use include anxiety, depression, and short-term memory difficulties.

Psilocybin Mushrooms

Although they are not as popular as the synthetic drugs, **psilocybin mushrooms** are encountered at raves and clubs and may be used by high school and college students. Mushrooms can be ingested alone or in combination with alcohol or illegal drugs. They can be soaked or boiled in water to make tea, and they are often cooked and added to other foods to mask their bitter taste. The physical effects of the mushrooms appear within 20 minutes of ingestion and last approximately 6 hours. These effects include nausea, vomiting, muscle weakness, yawning, drowsiness, tearing, facial flushing, enlarged pupils, sweating, and lack of coordination. Other physical effects include dizziness, diarrhea, dry mouth, and restlessness.

The psychological and physical effects of the drug include changes to the audio, visual, and tactile senses. Colors reportedly appear brighter, and users report a crossing of the senses, such as seeing a sound and hearing a color. Some experience a sense of detachment from their body and a greater feeling of unity with their surroundings. Furthermore, the high is described as a more natural sensation than that supplied by synthetic hallucinogens. A large dose of the drug produces hallucinations and an inability to discern fantasy from reality, which in turn may lead to panic reactions and psychosis. No evidence of physical dependence exists, although tolerance does develop when mushrooms are ingested continuously over a short period of time. Individuals tolerant to LSD also show tolerance to mushrooms.

Date-Rape Drugs

Certain drugs are being used to incapacitate individuals and thereby facilitate sexual assault. The drugs that are used most frequently for this purpose are Rohypnol, GHB, and ketamine. These substances are typically slipped into a victim's beverage at a party or bar while a drink is left unattended or the person is distracted. After ingestion, the victim feels disoriented and may appear drunk. This state leaves the victim very vulnerable, and the perpetrator often volunteers to drive the victim home. Hours later, a victim may wake up in unfamiliar surroundings with little or no memory of what has happened.

Rohypnol

Rohypnol (flunitrazepam) is a powerful sedative-hypnotic that belongs to the same class of drugs as Valium (diazepam), but is 10 times stronger than Valium. Rohypnol has never been approved for medical use in the United States. It is illegal to possess in the United States but is available as a prescription drug in several countries, including Mexico. Much of the Rohypnol that comes into the United States comes from Mexico. Rohypnol has been linked to several sexual assaults. Its street names include "roofies," "roachies," "rib," "forget pill," and "mind-erasers."

GHB

GHB (gamma hydroxybutyric acid) also has high potential for abuse as a date-rape drug. GHB acts powerfully as a central nervous system depressant, taking effect within 15 minutes. Its effects are similar to those seen with Rohypnol, with the drug causing dizziness, confusion, overwhelming drowsiness, and unconsciousness. Victims often cannot remember events that occur after the drug is ingested. GHB is easily obtained and can be manufactured by amateur "basement" chemists. It comes in liquid form and can be easily slipped into drinks because it is colorless and odorless, though sometimes it may be detected because it has a slightly salty taste. Several deaths have been attributed to GHB abuse. GHB is also known by the following names: "Georgia Home Boy," "Grievous Bodily Harm" (GBH), "Liquid X," "Easy Lay," "G," and "Bedtime Scoop."

Ketamine

Ketamine is a legal drug in the United States that is approved for use as a veterinary anesthetic. It produces a dissociative effect similar to that seen with PCP. Ingestion of ketamine causes hallucinations and feelings of being separated from one's body. Amnesia and dreamlike memories make it difficult for a date-rape victim to remember whether a sexual assault was real or imagined. An unsuspecting victim of date rape could easily be given a dangerous overdose of this drug. Taking too high a dose of ketamine can cause the heart to stop. The main source of ketamine for illegal use is theft of the drug from veterinary clinics. "Special K," "K," "Vitamin K," and "Bump" are street names for ketamine.

Alcohol

Perpetrators of sexual assault now have new drugs to add to their arsenal of date-rape drugs. Alcohol, however, has a long history of use as a date-rape agent. The majority of victims of date rape are drunk or have been drinking when the assault occurs. Alcohol is a central nervous system depressant. Drinking alcohol can impair judgment and cause disorientation; drinking large amounts can cause a person to pass out. These effects place a young person at high risk of being taken advantage of sexually.

Protection against Date-Rape Drugs

A date-rape drug can be slipped into any type of beverage. For this reason, young people should be taught not to drink any beverage that they did not open for themselves. This restraint may require a person to refrain from drinking from a container that is passed around or from a punch bowl. Young people should also be instructed never to leave a drink unattended. Drinks that were left unattended are best discarded rather than drunk. When offered a drink at a party or social event, the person should go to where the drink is opened, carefully watch it being poured, and then carry the drink himself or herself. Warn young people to avoid drinking a beverage that has an unusual taste or appearance (e.g., salty taste, excessive foam, unexplained residue). Also, warn young people not to accept rides home from strangers.

Drug Injection and Disease Transmission

Increased HIV and hepatitis B and C transmission is a likely consequence of drug abuse, particularly in individuals who inject a drug and share injection equipment. HIV and other infectious diseases are spread among injection drug users primarily through the reuse of contaminated syringes, needles, or other paraphernalia by more than one person. Drug abusers may then pass on these infections to sexual partners and children. In nearly one-third of Americans who become infected with HIV, injection drug use was a risk factor, making drug abuse the fastest-growing vector for the spread of HIV in the nation.

ACTIVITIES FOR TOBACCO, ALCOHOL, AND DRUGS

7-4 Activities for Social Skills

Teaching activities in these chapters (and pages) build social skills needed for living a drug-free lifestyle.

Topic	Chapter	Pages
Problem solving and decision making	Life Skills	65–69
Self-control and goal setting	Life Skills	58–64
Coping and relaxation	Dealing with Stress	91–101
Communication and relationship building	Life Skills	49–58

7-5 Tobacco-Free Activities

The Truth

Divide students into groups and instruct the groups to make a list of all the truths about tobacco they find on the Truth Campaign and American Lung Association fact sheets available on the Internet. Have the groups then develop short PowerPoint presentations depicting the truths about tobacco. (I, J, H)

Academy Awards

Review the many Truth Campaign clips that have been aired over the years; they are readily available on the Internet. Have an "Academy Awards" ceremony where students nominate and then vote for their favorite clips. The voting process makes students pay closer attention and become more vested in the clips' messages. (P, I, J, H)

Antitobacco Posters

Have students design and make posters that make smoking or other tobacco use look stupid, unattractive, or harmful. Encourage parental involvement. Hang the posters in school hallways and have the entire student body vote on their favorites. Award the creators of the top three posters. (P, I, J, H)

Tobacco Ad Deconstruction

Have students deconstruct magazine tobacco ads. Have students identify the following elements:
1. Who the target audience is
2. What the "hooks" are (techniques used to get attention and create appeal)
3. Which emotional associations are made (e.g., happiness, power, independence, attractiveness)
4. The lies included (e.g., smoking doesn't make you attractive)
5. Why the people in the ad were chosen for inclusion by the advertiser
6. The behaviors the ad tries to create or shape
7. Important facts that were omitted (I, J, H)

(continues)

(continued)

Where Have All the Cowboys Gone?

Using Paula Cole's song "Where Have All the Cowboys Gone?" as background music, create a PowerPoint presentation that shows what happens to the "Marlboro Man" in real life. (I, J, H)

Human Beans

This demonstration helps bring numbers alive and never fails to amaze students. Count out 1,200 beans and place them in a glass jar. Give each student a handful of beans. Explain that these are "human beans." Ask students how many human beans they think die each day in the United States because of tobacco. With an empty jar in hand, walk from one student to another and have them put into the jar the "beans" they think have died that day. Keep a count tally going until the class thinks the jar has the right number in it. This will happen too soon. Say, "No, not yet," whenever they think they have the right number—this will happen several times before you collect all of their beans. After they have all placed their beans in the jar, pour all the remaining beans into it from the first jar you didn't distribute to them. Discuss the devastating effects of tobacco on human life and all the suffering it creates. (P, I, J, H)

Cancer Spots

Divide students into small groups. Pass out to each group a large outlined silhouette of a man or woman. Have groups research—using the Internet or other resources—all of the cancers, diseases, and other health problems that tobacco causes. Have them neatly indicate on their silhouette where and how tobacco hurts the body. (I, J, H)

Award Badges

Design awards, badges, or plaques and give them to tobacco users who have reduced or quit their tobacco habits. (P, I, J, H)

Letters

Have students write a letter to a family member or hypothetical friend to persuade him or her to stop smoking. (I, J, H)

Cost of Smoking: Math

This activity is very eye opening. Get the cost of a pack of popular cigarettes sold at a convenience store in your community. Have your students calculate the cost of smoking one pack of cigarettes every day for 1 or more years. Discuss how expensive smoking is, and then let students have fun "spending" the money they "saved" by not smoking. Have them create collages of things they could buy and have a competition to see who can "spend" to the closest dime what they saved (math skill practice). Bring in store catalogs or newspaper ads for their shopping spree. Suggest they do their Christmas shopping. Display students' collages and discuss how tobacco costs can affect the socioeconomic status of a family. (I, J, H)

Smoking Machine

Make a simple smoking machine as shown in the diagram. Place cotton balls in the jar to collect the tar. Have students take turns squeezing the ball to simulate taking a "drag" from a cigarette. Discuss the accumulation of tars in the body. Take care not to let tobacco smoke accumulate in the classroom or school; open windows or use fans when possible. YouTube and other Internet sources also provide clips on smoking machines. (P, I, J, H)

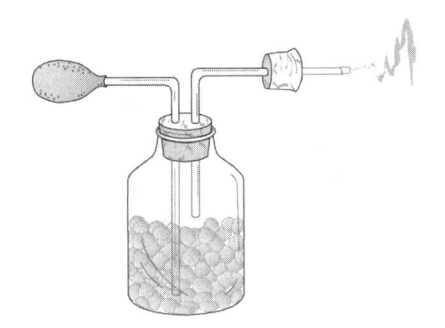

Tobacco Law: Social Studies

- Have students research and report on U.S. legislation and aid to support the tobacco industry.
- Have students check on passive smoking laws. Assign them to interview employees in public buildings and other work environments affected by the legislation.
- Have students research and report on the results of state lawsuits against tobacco companies and the ways that different states are using money gained from those lawsuits.
- Discuss the costs of smoking to all Americans in terms of medical care, lost work productivity, and loss of lives. (J, H)

7-6 *Alcohol-Free Activities*

TV Observation

Assign students to count the number of alcoholic beverages consumed by television characters during a program or over a certain time period. Have them also indicate why characters drank and consequences of drinking that were or were not depicted. (P, I, J, H)

Everyone's Not ...

Have students guess what percentage of students in your city they think drink alcohol. Access your state or city's data, available at the CDC's YRBS site. Compare and discuss the data you find on your state with use rates in other states and national averages. Discuss why students might have overestimated use and how one-third of adults do not drink alcohol. (J, H)

Picture That

Have students draw pictures or play charades that depict the reasons why people drink. Discuss alternatives for reducing stress, gaining confidence, having fun, fitting in, becoming relaxed, and so on. (I, J, H)

Alcohol Ad Deconstruction

Collect several examples of televised beer commercials you can show your students. They can be found on YouTube and other Internet sites. Study them and then help your students dissect them, looking for typical alcoholic behaviors (e.g., lying, hiding, stealing, and valuing alcohol over relationships) that

(continues)

(*continued*)

are made to look funny, or normal and acceptable. Bud has historically aired ads like this followed by the slogan, "Bud Light. Always worth it!" Uncover how ads promise the opposite of what alcohol use produces (e.g., independence, power, sexual strength, happiness.) Look for hooks, slogans, emotional transfer, and what the ads teach us about how we are to perceive and treat one another. (I, J, H)

Body Parts Skits

Break students into groups of five. Give them 5 minutes to create a skit in which each student plays different body parts affected by alcohol. Have students perform their skits. Vote on the best skit and reward the winners with a carton of milk. (I, J, H)

Bulletin Boards or PowerPoint Slides

Have students develop three bulletin boards illustrating the following: (1) alcohol's cost to society in terms of fatalities, medical costs, job absenteeism, job loss, decreased productivity, and family life; (2) the short- and long-term effects of alcohol on the body; and (3) how alcohol and drug abuse affects family life, social life, schoolwork, and the economy. Alternatively, instead of creating three bulletin boards for this activity, you can have students create PowerPoint slides. (P, I, J, H)

Walk the Line

Tape a long straight line across the front of the classroom. Ask one or two students to quickly walk the line. Have these students then twirl before again trying to walk the line. The twirling can be done in a chair, or by having students stand, bend over, and spin around a baseball bat with their foreheads held to the end of the handle. Discuss as a class the dangers of riding with a driver who cannot easily walk the line. (P, I, J, H)

Impaired

Ask for two volunteers. Have one student become "impaired" by wearing gloves and sunglasses smeared with petroleum jelly. Discuss how alcohol impairs a person's ability to do simple tasks. Have the students compete in doing the following simple tasks: tie their shoes, put on and button an oversized shirt, and pick up a penny. Discuss how alcohol affects everyone in a family. Discuss the dangers that drinking alcohol presents to both drinker and those persons around the drinker. (P, I, J, H)

Sad Story: Language Arts

In your school or community library, find books that deal with alcohol or drug abuse. Read these stories in class or have students read them as an assignment. Have student write stories about families dealing with substance abuse.

Dear Abby

Have students write and answer letters to a "Dear Abby" about substance abuse problems. (I, J, H)

Delicious Drink Recipes

Have students collect recipes for nonalcoholic beverages. Prepare and sample some of the recipes in class. Discuss how one-third of adults do not drink alcohol and how everyone can have a great deal of fun without drinking alcohol. (I, J, H)

Alcohol-Free Fun

Discuss how it is possible to have a great deal of fun at a party without any alcohol. Share your personal experiences of doing so. Challenge students to come up with some new and creative ideas of things they can do at such a party. Help them get started by giving some examples, such as to create a sound scavenger hunt or a video production competition based on a theme. Present you students with certificates for the most creative, most fun, most likely to be done activities they come up with. (I, J, H)

Service: A Better Buzz

Discuss how doing community service creates a drug-like high. Have students brainstorm creative service ideas. Here are a few to get them started:

- Bake cookies for a crabby neighbor, a shut-in, or someone feeling low.
- Cook dinner for your family.
- Read to a child or elderly person.

Challenge students to do one idea they came up and give them some incentives to do it. (I, J, H)

Alcohol Safetymercial

Review the hooks and strategies used in alcohol commercials. Have students use these same hooks and strategies to create a 20-second TV spot that argues against alcohol use. Have students act out their ads as skits in class, or have them produce their ads as video clips. (P, I, J, H)

Warning Labels

Have students design warning labels about fetal alcohol syndrome to place on all alcoholic beverages. (I, J, H)

PSA

Have students work in groups to write and record a 15-second radio public service announcement about drinking and driving. Play everyone's announcement in class and vote to determine the three most effective spots. Help winners submit their announcements to local radio stations (and potentially be aired!). (I, J, H)

Attend a Meeting

Help students identify where and when local Alcoholics Anonymous (AA), Al-Anon, and Alateen meetings take place. This can be done with Internet searches. Give students extra credit for attending and reporting on a meeting. (H)

MADD

Show a video clip from YouTube of a representative from Mothers Against Drunk Driving (MADD). Discuss as a class how drinking and driving affects a wide radius of people. (J, H)

SADD

Interview faculty, administration, and counselors to discover who in the school's "family" has been impacted by drunken driving. Gain permission to share any stories you uncover. Share these stories with your students. Help students organize a chapter of Students Against Drunk Driving (SADD) in your school. (H)

7-7 Drug-Free Activities

Circle Up

Have everyone stand in a circle facing each other around the perimeter of the classroom. Instruct students to step forward if something you say refers to them. Begin with easy things such as "Step forward if you are the oldest in your family" or "Step forward if you have read all seven Harry Potter books." The first things should be fun and help them get to know one another better.

After warming up, explain that you are now going to ask them to step forward if what you say applies to anyone they know and care about, and that they don't have to name names or talk about them. The point of the activity is to help students see how substance abuse impacts everyone and recognize that they are not alone. Ask them to step forward if anyone they know and care about is addicted to prescription medications, is a binge drinker or alcoholic, has made them cry or lose sleep because of drinking or taking drugs, uses steroids, uses inhalants, has driven drunk, or has attempted suicide. (I, J, H)

Legalizing Marijuana?

Have students search the Internet for pro and con marijuana legalization messages. As a class, analyze who created the Internet sites where they found information and discuss possible motivations for the information being placed there. (H)

Prescribe That

Challenge students to write a rap song that helps those who hear it differentiate between proper use and abuse of prescription medicines. (I, J, H)

Uncap It

Place various instructions for taking medicines inside otherwise empty medicine containers. A variety of medicine instructions can be found on the Internet and copied as images. Have volunteers come forward and take a container out of a grab bag. Have them read the instructions in the containers to the class and then try and explain in their own words how that medicine is to be taken. Discuss heart, diabetes, and other medications that their family members might be taking and the importance of taking medications properly. (J, H)

Medicine Disposal

Explain and demonstrate how to properly dispose of medicines. Do not flush prescription drugs down the toilet unless label instructs you to do so. Use city/county drug take-back programs if available. Throw drugs in the trash by taking them out of their original containers, mixing them with something yucky like coffee grounds or kitty litter, and then putting them in sealable bags to prevent them from leaking out of a garbage bag.

That Stinks!

Before class, find or create something that smells completely foul, such as dog feces. Put the foul-smelling substance in a plastic bag and zip-lock it or tie it closed. Place the plastic bag in a paper bag. Ask, "Who wants to get a whiff of something exciting?" Without letting students see what's in the bag, let some volunteers smell it. A lively interchange will follow. Ask, "Why did you volunteer to smell it?" Discuss why kids try inhalants and how inhalants hurt their bodies much more than the awful thing they just smelled. (P, I, J)

Don't Taste That

Display three white mixtures (e.g., laundry detergents, salt, sugars, rat poisons, baking powder, soda) and ask students which one they would like to taste by a show of hands for each substance. Reveal what each mixture is. Explain how drugs are cut with substances and how a person buying drugs on the street doesn't know what he or she is getting. Discuss the dangers of taking drugs available on the street without a prescription. (P, I, J, H)

Bumper Stickers

Have a competition to see who can come up with the cleverest bumper stickers against marijuana, steroid, or other drug use. Help the winners get someone in the community to print the stickers with assistance from the PTA. (I, J, H)

Lance Armstrong

Show a picture of Lance Armstrong or another athlete who has been caught cheating in his or her sport by doping. Discuss the repercussions of the athlete's doping on that person, his or her teammates, the athlete's family, and kids who looked up to the athlete as a role model.

Outdoor Activities

In groups, have students compete to see who can come up with the most ideas for outdoor drug-free fun. After giving them time, have groups take turns writing their ideas on the board. Here are some ideas you might want to contribute:

- Create a treasure hunt.
- Make and fly kites.
- Create sidewalk chalk drawings.
- Slide down a grassy slope on a block of ice.
- Slide down a mowed hay hill on cardboard.
- Do gravestone rubbing by placing a blank piece of paper on an illegible headstone and rub chalk over the paper until you can read it.
- Create a Frisbee golf course.
- Climb trees in the park.
- Play water-balloon volleyball. (P, I, J, H)

Get a Little Crazy

Emphasize how much fun kids can have without marijuana, alcohol, or other drugs. Challenge students to do one of the following activities (or others) and report on how much fun they had:

- Christmas party not in December
- Marathon dinner where the participants travel from one house to another for different courses
- Three-armed dinner where partners tie one of their arms together and then cook dinner—a dessert, salad, or main course
- Hairdo party where the boys do the girls' hair—have an awards ceremony and don't forget to videotape

(continues)

(*continued*)

- Pretend to be going on a trip, competing to see who can come up with the best vacation for a predetermined time and budget by visiting travel agencies or searching Internet sites
- Pretend to be tourists in your own town and take pictures or videos
- Play hide-and-seek at the mall
- Build sand castles (get sand at a cement company and put it into wading pools)
- Take lawn chairs to the side of the road and hold up cards with numbers 1–10 to rate the cars going by (I, J, H)

South of the Border: Geography, Social Studies

Have students research and identify where illegal drugs are grown or created in labs around the world. Depict how and where drugs are trafficked into the United States. Discuss federal laws and agencies that try to curtail illegal drug and drug war lords have on crime, politics, and daily life for people living in Mexico and other countries in Central and South America.

Instruction Plan Worksheet Tobacco, Alcohol, and Drugs

Use this worksheet to plan tobacco, alcohol and drug instruction at the grade level you will be teaching. Refer to Chapter 2 for more information on how to complete each section in this worksheet.

■ Assess Needs

Identify topics and skills state or local curricula identify to be taught at ___ grade level.

Identify additional topics or skills the T and AOD HECAT Modules indicate for this grade.

Identify tobacco, alcohol and drug needs your particular students and their families have:

- How prevalent is tobacco use among students and in the community?
- Who drinks alcohol, where, and why?
- How prevalent is drug use? What drugs are abused?
- What are the normative perceptions of students regarding tobacco, alcohol, and drug use?

■ Set Major Learning Goal(s)

Identify your major learning goal(s)—what do you want to have happen?

■ **Develop Instruction Map**

Create a map (calendar or list of days) indicating the time frame you have/need to teach the curriculum, meet student needs and reach goal(s). For each day indicate the content/skills to be taught. Work to create a good flow.

■ Write SMART Unit Objectives

Write 1 or 2 major objectives for each day you will teach. Your objectives should be in alignment with your state/local curricula, your student's needs, and your major learning goal(s).

■ Identify Assessment Tools

Preassessment	Formative-Assessment	Postassessment
How will you determine what students already know or do?	How will you know if they are "getting it"?	How will you know if students master objectives?

■ **Develop Unit Plan**

Divide the chart into the number of days you will teach. Record each day's topic and objective key words. Identify activity names (in the book) that can help you meet each day's objective. Identify tech tools you can use and possible lesson adaptations you can make for special need learners.

Lesson Topic Objectives	Instruction Activities	Tech Tools	Adaptations for Learners

■ **Develop Lesson Plans**

Use the Lesson Plan Template found in Chapter 2 and this worksheet to create detailed lesson plans for your Tobacco, Alcohol, and Drug Free Unit.

KEY TERMS

Monitoring the Future (MTF) 198
National Survey on Drug Use and Health (NSDUH) 198
Youth Risk Behavior Survey (YRBS) 198
normative education 203
peer tutors 204
peer counselors 204
wellness 206
high-risk students 210
support groups 210
nicotine 212
chewing tobacco 215
snuff 215
oral leukoplakias 215
hookahs 215
bidis 215
kreteks 215
alcohol 217
alcoholism 217
fetal alcohol syndrome (FAS) 217
fetal alcohol effects (FAE) 217
family hero 219
scapegoat 221
lost child 221
mascot 222
Al-Anon 222
Alateen 222
marijuana 223
blunts 223
THC 223
hashish 223
hashish oil 223

drug abuse 224
oxycodone 225
volatile solvents 225
aerosols 225
anesthetics 225
anabolic steroids 226
cycling 226
stacking 226
cocaine 227
crack cocaine 227
formication 227
methamphetamine 227
ice 228
heroin 228
black tar heroin 228
physical dependence 229
withdrawal symptoms 229
cold turkey 229
club drugs 229
MDMA 229
Ecstasy 229
LSD 230
hallucinations 230
synesthesia 230
bad trip 230
flashback 230
PCP 230
nystagmus 231
psilocybin mushrooms 231
Rohypnol 231
GHB 232
ketamine 232

KNOWLEDGE CHECK!

1. Define and explain the relative importance of each of the key terms in the context of this chapter.
2. Discuss substance abuse impacts on unintentional injuries, death, disease, development, schools, and students.
3. Identify trends in teenage use of alcohol, cigarettes, smokeless tobacco, marijuana, psychotherapeutic drugs, inhalants, and illicit drugs. Identify use trends in relation to race/ethnicity and location.
4. Discuss evidence that the media promote alcohol and tobacco use to youth. Discuss the Truth campaign.
5. Identify principles of effective substance abuse prevention programs. Discuss DARE's effectiveness.
6. Identify key components of information-based strategies and normative education.
7. Explain resistance strategies and personal and social skills training.
8. Identify key components of alternatives-to-drugs, student assistance, and parent approach programs.
9. Identify the topics and focus for substance abuse prevention education at various developmental levels.

10. Discuss substance abuse prevention curricular and support needs for high-risk students.
11. Describe how substance abuse prevention can be infused into the curriculum of subjects other than health.
12. Summarize the facts about tobacco use and consequences, particularly for women. Identify health consequences of using different tobacco products.
13. Identify key elements for tobacco use prevention and cessation programs in schools.
14. Discuss the effects, dangers, and problems associated with alcohol use.
15. Identify characteristics, signs, and symptoms of problem drinking and alcoholism. Discuss adolescent susceptibility to alcohol abuse.
16. Discuss the prevalence of addiction in homes, and identify the rules characteristic of an alcoholic family.
17. Discuss the four roles children of alcoholics take on and what teachers can do to help children acting in each role.
18. Discuss marijuana medical use laws and rates of teenage marijuana use.
19. Identify the effects, hazards, and additional names for oxycodone, inhalants, anabolic steroids, cocaine, methamphetamine, heroin, club drugs, and date-rape drugs.
20. Name diseases associated with drug abuse and explain how they are transmitted.

REFERENCES

1. National Institute on Drug Abuse. *Monitoring the future*. 2012. Available at http://monitoringthefuture.org. Accessed February 5, 2013.
2. Centers for Disease Control and Prevention. YRBSS: Youth Risk Behavior Surveillance System. 2012. Available at http://www.cdc.gov/HealthyYouth/yrbs/index.htm. Accessed February 5, 2013.
3. McAfee T, Tynan M. Smoking in movies: A new Centers for Disease Control and Prevention core surveillance indicator. *Prev Chron Dis*. 2012:9:120261. Available at http://www.cdc.gov/pcd/issues/2012/12_0261.htm. Accessed February 5, 2013.
4. Anderson PA, de Bruijn K, Angus K, et al. Impact of alcohol advertising and media exposure on adolescent alcohol use: a systematic review of longitudinal studies. *Alcohol Alcoholism*. 2009;44(3):229–243.
5. Legacy for Longer Healthier Life. Truth. Available at http://www.legacyforhealth.org. Accessed February 5, 2013.
6. National Institute on Drug Abuse. *Preventing drug use among children and adolescents: a research-based guide for parents, educators, and community leaders*. 2nd ed.Bethesda, MD: U.S. Department of Health and Human Services; 2009. Available at http://www.drugabuse.gov/sites/default/files/preventingdruguse.pdf. Accessed February 5, 2013.
7. Prevention First. Ineffectiveness of fear appeals in youth alcohol, tobacco and other drug (ATOD) prevention. Springfield, IL: Prevention First; 2008. Available at https://www.prevention.org/Resources/SAPP/documents/IneffectivenessofFearAppealsinYouthATODPrevention-FINAL.pdf. Accessed February 5, 2013.
8. Dusenbury L, Falco M, Lake M, Lake A. A review of the evaluation of 47 drug abuse prevention curricula available nationally. *J School Health*. 1997;67(4):127–132.
9. Botvin LifeSkills Training. Home page. Available at http://www.lifeskillstraining.com. Accessed February 5, 2013.
10. Health Education Curriculum Analysis Tool (HECAT). Available at http://www.cdc.gov/HealthyYouth/HECAT/index.htm. Accessed February 5, 2013.
11. Centers for Disease Control and Prevention. Tobacco use: school health guidelines. Available at http://www.cdc.gov/HealthyYouth/tobacco/guidelines/summary.htm. Accessed February 5, 2013.
12. Wall MM, Pho E, Cerda M, et al. Adolescent marijuana use from 2002 to 2008: higher in states with medical marijuana laws, cause still unclear. *Ann Epidemiol*. 2011;21:714–716.
13. National Institute on Drug Abuse. Drug facts: drugged driving. Available at http://www.drugabuse.gov/publications/drugfacts/drugged-driving. Accessed February 5, 2013.
14. National Institute on Drug Abuse. Drugs, brains, and behavior: the science of addiction. Available at http://www.drugabuse.gov/publications/science-addiction/drugs-brain. Accessed February 5, 2013.
15. Office of National Drug Control Policy, Executive Office of the President. *Prescription for danger*. January 2008. Available at http://www.promoteprevent.org/resources/prescription-danger-report-prescription-and-over-counter-drug-abuse-among-nations-teens. Accessed February 5, 2013.

Chapter 8
Promoting Sexual Health

Courtesy of Lindsay Hansen.

In Your Opinion

On April 5, 2013, federal judge Edward Korman ordered that all age restrictions be removed for purchasing the morning-after birth control pill, stating that it should available to anyone of any age and sold over the counter like aspirin. Korman gave the Food and Drug Administration (FDA) one month to lift all age limits on Plan B and its generic counterparts. Even as the Justice Department appealed the judge's order (saying the judge had exceeded his authority), the FDA lowered the age restriction for buying the pills from 17 years to 15 years. These events highlight the powerful roles that government and the judiciary system often play in sexual matters.

Those opposed to Korman's ruling argue that cigarettes and alcohol cannot be purchased without age ID, nor can someone vote, enlist in the military, cash a check, or open a charge account without ID. Further, schools cannot give out aspirin without parents' consent, and kids cannot drive unsupervised until they reach a certain age. Many also fear that unrestricted access to morning-after pills gives kids the message that it's acceptable to have unprotected sex—to just pop a pill and there will be no consequences. What do you think?

During adolescence, youths undergo the process of puberty and attain physiological sexual maturation. Most adolescents are extremely sensitive about their physical appearance, and many are confused about issues of sexual activity. Adolescents feel newly developed biological sexual urges and impulses. There is much in society to arouse these feelings. Sex is pervasive in advertising, television, movies, videos, music, and other media. Parents and schools encourage abstinence from sexual activity, while at the same time the mass media glamorize sex. Peer pressure related to sexual activity can be either negative or positive. For example, it is common for youths to report feeling pressure from peers to experiment and engage in early sexual activity. Even so, some youths say that they feel support for sexual abstinence from peers. Religious and cultural beliefs also exert strong influence on decisions about sexual activity. Young people observe that the issues surrounding youth sexual activity are emotionally charged and evoke a wide range of opinions and reactions from teens, parents, and educators.

In the midst of such confusion, young people must make decisions about their involvement in sexual activity. They face developmental challenges in making these decisions. Teens and preteens often lack the maturity, experience, and range of options that adults have when making decisions about sexual activity. Teens have a tendency to engage in short-range thinking, focusing more on present desires than on long-term consequences of decisions. Also, it is common for young people to feel a strong sense of personal invulnerability. As a result, they do not perceive the need to avoid risks. These factors help explain why a high percentage of young people engage in sexual behaviors that place them at great risk for unintended pregnancy, infection, disease, and emotional trauma.

SEXUAL TRENDS

Today, adolescents are maturing physically at an earlier age than did previous generations. Nearly one in two black girls and one in seven white girls begin to develop breast or pubic hair by age 8. Scientists believe this trend toward early maturation is due in part to the increase in obesity. Overweight girls tend to mature earlier. Some scientists also believe that seeing sexualized messages in the media might trigger brain chemicals to "jumpstart" sexual development,[1] and others voice concerns about the beef and chicken we eat today, which has often been bulked up using growth hormones.

Early sexual maturation creates pressures that young girls are not prepared to handle, including pressure to act much older than they are, and pressure from boys who are interested in them sexually. Early development increases the likelihood that they will not have had sex education before they experience maturation changes, and their emotional and social development may not keep pace with their physical maturity. Moreover, youths 10 to 12 years of age may be physically mature, but their still-limited cognitive reasoning abilities make providing information about or discussing sexuality issues all the more challenging. Early maturation also extends the time period of risky sexual exploration between puberty and marriage.

For the past 20 years, a consistent proportion—approximately 50%—of high school students have reported having sexual intercourse one or more times. The current rate is 47%. Improvements have been made among black and Hispanic teen sexual rates, but these groups continue to be at higher risk for engaging in sexual intercourse at a young age (**Table 8-1**).[2]

Teen pregnancy delivery rates have declined gradually since the 1990s. This decline is in part due to decreased sexual activity and the increased use of condoms.[2] The majority of babies born to teenage mothers continues to be delivered to black and Hispanic youth.[3]

Sexually transmitted diseases (STDs) among teenagers remain a persistent concern. Nearly half of all STDs diagnosed each year are among young people 15–24 years of age.[4] The average age at which young people first have sex is 17 years, and on average they wait to marry until their late 20s.

Sending and receiving sexually explicit texts or photos (**sexting**) is another problematic trend. The National Campaign to Prevent Teen and Unplanned Pregnancy reports that one in five teens has sent or posted nude or semi-nude images of himself or herself and that 50% of teens have sent and or received a sexually suggestive message via text, e-mail, or instant messaging.[5]

The ruling that the "morning-after pill," known as Plan B One-Step, can now be sold over the counter without age restrictions may influence future trends. Anyone—including 10-year-old girls—can purchase the pill at local drug stores. The pill prevents or delays ovulation and interferes with fertilization of an egg. It is more effective the sooner it is taken; in any event, it should be taken within 72 hours of unprotected intercourse. The pill is quite expensive, costing

TABLE 8-1 High School Students' Sexual Intercourse Rate

	Black (%)	Hispanic (%)	White (%)
Ever had sexual intercourse	60	49	44
Had intercourse before age 13 years	14	7	4
Had intercourse with four or more persons	25	15	13
Had intercourse in last 3 months	41	34	32
Did not use birth control before last intercourse	13	19	10

The vast majority of kids have television sets in their bedrooms.

approximately $40 to $50. There are concerns that news coverage and advertising about the drug will cause teens to think they do not have to worry about their sexual protection and, as a result, will become more sexually active and more vulnerable to STDs.

MEDIA AND SEXUAL CONTENT

Youth today are marinated in media sexual messages, many of which were taboo not too many years ago. In particular, television programs created for adult audiences are often viewed by children. For instance, when *Desperate Housewives* was first aired, the Nielsen Ratings found it to be the most popular TV show among 9-year-olds. The amount of sexual material, including sexually violent material, has dramatically increased in the media. Programs aimed for teenaged audiences are the most frequent offenders, and very few scenes contain any information about the risks and responsibilities of sexual activity. Programs also glamorize unhealthy relationships or make them seem funny and benign. Sexual intimacy is most likely portrayed in the context of hook-ups rather than in loving, healthy married relationships.

Advertisers have also increasingly used sexual titillation to attract the attention of potential customers. Sexual images to sell products are visible everywhere in our environment, from the corner store's magazine covers, to billboards, to posters plastered on public bus stops. Add to this our TV, computer, and cell phone screens, and you begin to appreciate the pervasiveness of such messages. Research has been conducted to see how sexualized media affect young people. Four longitudinal studies have linked exposure to sexy media to an earlier onset of sexual intercourse, and another study has linked early exposure of sexy media to teenage pregnancy.[6] One study followed teens over time and found that those who were exposed to high levels of television sexual content (90th percentile) were twice as likely to become pregnant in the three following years as those with lower levels of exposure (10th percentile).[7]

Given the heavy dose of sexual messages that young people receive through media sources, the entertainment industry is the United States' primary source of sex education. This is a scary fact. While school-based sex education programs may promote abstinence to avert problems such as unintended pregnancy and sexually transmitted infections (STIs), the media mock abstinence as a choice. Young teens rank entertainment media as their top source of information about sexuality and sexual health.

The proliferation of cable and satellite, which bring movie channels directly into our homes, has increased the amount of seductive material available to young people—often in their own bedrooms. The vast majority of U.S. children and adolescents have television sets in their bedrooms, and many have Internet access there as well. Even when young people view programs in a more central part of the home, their parents seldom watch with them. This is unfortunate because when parents watch programs with their children, doors are opened for discussions about relationships, responsibility, consequences, and what real love looks and feels like.

"Teen mom" reality television programs were created, according to their producers, to demonstrate how hard it is to become responsible for a baby before you are really responsible for yourself. The shows and the media publicity around them have made many people feel that these programs glamorize and encourage teen pregnancy. Some teenage girls have claimed they got pregnant to try and get on the shows. Other people feel the programs are great teaching tools when teens watch and discuss the programs with adults. Thre are numerous teaching activities at the end of the chapter that you can use to help students analyze the media's influence.

CULTURE AND SEXUAL DEVELOPMENT

The family, school, community, and ethnic cultures children grow up in greatly influence their expectations regarding gender roles, relationships, and sexual activity. Teen pregnancy, STD, and sexual violence rates are related to the culture where they take place.

By the time most youths become teenagers, they have some sense of their body image and have developed a general sense of their self-worth, for better or worse. Most of that sense of self reflects how significant adults and peers have treated them. Youth are also socialized regarding their sexual development through a range of cultural images and messages from their parents, their religious advisors, the media, and their peers. This socialization is more random that than what occurs in most other areas of development.

Consider the example of teaching youth to brush their teeth—a dissimilar activity but one that is relevant in terms of the discipline necessary to maintain a healthy lifestyle. Parents teach their children about brushing their teeth at a relatively early age and then spend considerable time coaching youngsters to develop the habit of brushing at least twice a day. In the area of sexuality, almost the reverse happens. Even in close families, parents often do not display physical affection, and most do not talk with their children about relationships or intimacy. Young people, therefore, have few relationship role models and little exposure to appropriate sexual behavior. When introduced to sexuality education and concepts such as reserving sexual activity for a loving relationship later in life, young people can grasp these ideas intellectually, but often they do not have an experiential or real-life frame of reference.

Puberty Hormones

At puberty, the hypothalamus and pituitary gland begin producing growth hormones. On average, adolescents grow 10 to 11 inches in spurts. Testosterone levels increase in boys by 1,000%, initiating the development of secondary sex characteristics (e.g., deepening voice;

armpit, pubic, and facial hair). Testosterone can also make boys moody. The amygdala is the brain's anger and alarm center, the seat of the fight-or-flight reaction. It is rich in testosterone receptors. Adolescent boys have daily surges of testosterone, five to seven of them. This helps explain why teenage boys can become aggressive and are sometimes easily angered. Amplified levels of testosterone also stimulate boys' interest in the physical aspects of sex. A small section of the hypothalamus grows in boys at puberty, which plays a role in their intense sexual interest and drive.

Estrogen and progesterone are responsible for the ebb and flow of menstruation in girls. These hormones also affect levels of the neurotransmitter serotonin. Serotonin acts like a mood stabilizer. When serotonin levels dip and rise in girls, their moods can quickly change; in addition, such changes amplify a wide range of emotions. Testosterone and oxytocin power girls' sexual awakening. Testosterone creates their interest in physical dimensions of sex. Oxytocin, the "cuddle" hormone, creates a desire to be physically close.

Males and females think differently about sex. Sex is physical for boys, but is about relationships for girls. Because males and females think very differently, misunderstandings can easily take place. For instance, Brianne, motivated by oxytocin, gets physically close to Josh. Josh thinks Brianne is interested in sex and responds warmly. Brianne, in turn, thinks Josh must really like her. It is important for girls to understand how differently boys think about sex, and for boys to understand how girls think about it.

The Big Talk

Most parents know they need to talk to their children about sex, but are very reluctant to do so. Teachers can help motivate parents by letting them know that youth who say they have good open communication with their parents about sexual matters also report delaying sexual activity. In addition, children who engage in open communication with their parents are more responsible and safe in their decision making.

Parents sometimes need help with knowing what to talk about, which is much more than physiology and sex. Sexuality involves respect, responsibility, and caring. Talking to children about these things provides parents with the opportunity to pass on their values to their children. Parents can open up discussions on this difficult subject by simply saying, "Talking about this is a little awkward for me because my parents never talked to me about it, but I know it's really important." David Walsh also provides the following tips:[8]

- ◆ Don't approach it as one "Big Talk." Make it an ongoing conversation. Cover just a little at a time. Make it a dialogue: ask and listen as well as talk.
- ◆ When you talk, don't preach. Say what you want to say and then leave it alone. When you do this, kids will listen more.
- ◆ Talk about dating, including how the media misportray it with couples ending up in bed, and how dating is a time to get to know people.

■ SEX EDUCATION

A teenager recently commented, "A popular girl just asked me, 'Are you a virgin?' She said it like virginity was a terrible disease. I feel sorry for her. I guess for her sex is like an itch that needs scratching. She seems clueless about the powerful trust and bond sex can create in a marriage. My parents have that. That's what I want. That's why I'm waiting. I'm not as afraid of what I can get from sex as what I can lose from it now."

While it is vitally important to educate young people about the risks of sexual activity, it is equally vital to help them understand what true love entails. Carefully consider the differences between lust, infatuation, and love as identified in the teaching activity *True Love* that you can find at the end of the chapter. How can discussing these differences help students identify popular misperceptions about love and sex?

The most appropriate and effective place for young people to get careful guidance in making decisions about sexual activity is from loving parents. The role of parents is a difficult job that requires support and assistance from educational institutions and community agencies. Unfortunately, many young people do not have adults in their lives who can effectively provide the nurturing and guidance that they need. Some of these young people are particularly vulnerable to involvement in sexual activity that places them at risk of unintended pregnancy and sexually transmitted infections. For this reason, schools must play an active and vital role in teaching young people how to make responsible decisions about sexual activity.

Sex education programs need to be locally determined and consistent with parental and community values. Teaching sex education requires a great deal of preparation and sensitivity to issues and policies. Those who teach sex education need to be sensitive to the attitudes of students, parents, community groups, and school administrators. Every teacher must be thoroughly familiar with his or her school districts sex education policy and follow that policy, whether or not the teacher personally agrees with it. In addition, teachers must be careful of how they interact with students, taking care to not say or do anything that could be misconstrued as sexually inappropriate. Private conversations with students should take place out of earshot, but in proximity to other people, such as in a classroom corner. This protects both the teacher and the student.

Teachers need to be well versed in state laws and policies regarding sex education. Most states require that public schools teach some form of sex or STI/HIV education. The current status of individual states' policies regarding sex education can be found on the website of the **Guttmacher Institute**. This site is updated frequently to reflect changes in state policies regarding sex education and other family life issues. Most states place requirements on how abstinence or contraception should be handled when included in a school district's curriculum.[9] One aspect that governs whether students receive instruction on sex or STIs/HIV is the existence of parental consent requirements. Sometimes called "opt-out" clauses, these policies allow parents to remove students from instruction that the parents find objectionable.

Some sex education teachers encounter negative reactions from parents or community groups opposing sex education. Most parents, however, welcome support in helping their children develop healthy relationships. Opposition to sex education is usually overcome when parents are provided with the opportunity to visit the school and learn what will be addressed and how it will be taught, and when feel they have a voice in setting the curriculum.

Effective sex education entails much more than just teaching about pregnancy and sexually transmitted infections (see **Box 8-1**); it requires going beyond just providing accurate information about risks. It must also offer life skills training (e.g., refusal, negotiation, positive relationship, decision making, goal setting, and self-management skills) to emphasize actions young people can take to avoid risks and build healthy relationships. Learning activities should also address media influences on sexual behavior. Research has clearly shown that the most effective programs are comprehensive ones that include a focus on delaying sexual behavior and that provide information on how sexually active young people can protect themselves.[4]

Sex education programs take into account the cognitive, social, and emotional developmental level of students at each grade level. Sufficient time must be devoted to building student trust, because the issues addressed in sex education programs are more complex and personal than

> ### 8-1 Application Exercise
>
> **Self-Inventory**
>
> Teaching sex education can be challenging because of the breadth and range of possible topics, especially at higher grade levels. Review the following topics and reflect on (1) how comfortable you feel discussing each topic and (2) how prepared you feel you are to teach each area.
>
> - Reproductive anatomy and physiology (e.g., male and female reproductive systems, menstruation, nocturnal emissions)
> - Sexual development (e.g., physiological development [puberty], psychological development, cultural and societal influences, sex roles)
> - Human reproduction (e.g., fertilization and conception, prenatal development, pregnancy, childbirth)
> - Family life issues (e.g., parent–child relationships, parenting skills, marriage, divorce, single parenting)
> - Relationships and interpersonal skills, including decision making, assertiveness, and peer refusal skills
> - Responsibility regarding sexual activity, including addressing abstinence and how to resist pressures to become prematurely involved in sexual activity
> - Contraception and/or birth control
> - HIV infection and other sexually transmitted infections
> - Sexual abuse and assault (e.g., date rape, incest, child sexual abuse, sexual harassment)
> - Controversial issues (e.g., abortion, homosexuality, pornography)

their counterparts in any other area of the curricula. Specialized support or immediate referral to such support must be in place for youths who, as a result of such programs, disclose sexual abuse or other serious problems.

Abstinence Education

Abstinence from sex is often stressed in school-based sex education programs because it is the most effective way to prevent unintended pregnancy and sexually transmitted infections, including HIV. The Centers for Disease Control and Prevention (CDC) states that "abstinence from vaginal, anal, and oral intercourse is the only 100% effective way to prevent HIV, other STIs, and pregnancy. The correct and consistent use of a male latex condom can reduce the risk of STI transmission, including HIV infection. However, no protective method is 100% effective, and condom use cannot guarantee absolute protection against any STI or pregnancy."[4]

Engaging in early sexual activity can also delay emotional and personal development and limit opportunities for young people to build a strong future. For all of these reasons, **abstinence education** is emphasized in all school-based sex education programs. However, there is considerable debate and lack of agreement about how to carry out abstinence education. Some sex education programs are broadly classified as "abstinence-only," whereas others are categorized as "abstinence-plus." **Abstinence-only education** generally teaches abstinence from all sexual activity as the only appropriate option for unmarried people. These programs often do not teach about contraception or condom use or, if those topics are discussed, do not provide detailed information on them. **Abstinence-plus education** emphasizes the benefits of abstinence while also teaching about contraception and disease-prevention methods, including condom and contraceptive use. Abstinence-plus programs are sometimes referred to as **comprehensive sex education** or **risk-reduction curriculum**. Educators can reinforce abstinence as a healthy choice by addressing normative expectations.

HIV Prevention Education

Most states mandate HIV prevention education in schools. Health experts urge that education about HIV should start in early elementary school and at home so that children can grow up knowing how to protect themselves against HIV infection. They further emphasize that HIV prevention education should be offered in the context of a comprehensive school health education program (grades K–12). In addition to simply providing information about HIV transmission, students should be given opportunities to develop skills for decision making and resisting personal and social pressures.

School-based programs are critical for reaching youths before behaviors are established. Because risk behaviors do not exist independently, topics such as HIV, STIs, unintended pregnancy, tobacco, nutrition, and physical activity should be integrated and ongoing for all students in kindergarten through high school. The specific scope and content of these school health programs should be locally determined and consistent with parental and community values. Research has clearly shown that the most effective programs are comprehensive ones that focus on delaying sexual behavior and that provide information on how sexually active young people can protect themselves.[4]

Kindergarten Through Third Grade

Kindergarten through third grade is the time for educators to establish a foundation for a more detailed discussion of sexuality in later grades. Children should be encouraged to feel positive about their bodies. In addition, they should know about their body parts and the differences between girls and boys. The primary goal during the early elementary years should be to dispel the fear of HIV/AIDS. To do this, teachers can tell students that young children rarely get AIDS. Teachers should also communicate that there is no need to worry about playing with children who have family members with AIDS or who have AIDS themselves—they cannot get the disease from playing with these children. Because children at this age are interested in germs and how disease is spread, teachers can discuss HIV infection as one of many diseases. They can answer questions about AIDS directly and simply; responses can be limited to questions asked by students. Children should be warned not to play with hypodermic needles that they may find in neighborhoods or elsewhere. In addition, they should be taught to avoid contact with other people's blood and the importance of cleaning up bodily fluids in a safe manner. Educators can also discuss having compassion for those living with AIDS.

Education about HIV infection should start in elementary school.

Upper Elementary Grades

Children in upper elementary grades should be provided with basic information about human sexuality. They will need help in understanding puberty and the associated changes in their bodies. Part of this understanding is affirming that their bodies will have natural sexual feelings. Children should be urged to examine and affirm their own families' values about sexuality. Upper-elementary-level children need to have answers to their questions about AIDS and HIV prevention. It is appropriate at this age level to begin discussing the ways HIV is transmitted (e.g., sexual intercourse, sharing needles). Students should also recognize that alcohol and other drugs can increase the risk of infection by lowering a person's ability to act responsibly.

Secondary Level

At the secondary level, the major emphasis of HIV prevention education should focus on teaching students to protect themselves and others from infection with HIV. Information about HIV prevention should emphasize healthy behaviors rather than the medical aspects of the disease. Students should clearly understand that they have a right to abstain from sexual intercourse and to postpone becoming sexually active. Adolescents should be taught that abstaining from sexual activity is the best way to prevent HIV infection. It should be stressed to secondary students that alcohol and other drugs influence individuals to make very poor choices. HIV prevention education needs to allow students to examine and confirm their own values. Decisions can be reinforced by providing adequate opportunities to rehearse resisting peer and social pressure to engage in risky behaviors. Questions about HIV must always be answered honestly and factually.

Educators should not assume that all students will choose to abstain from sexual activity and substance use. For those students who do not abstain, proper information concerning risk reduction (e.g., using condoms, avoiding injecting drugs) should be provided. Nevertheless, these behaviors must never be condoned by school personnel. It is important to stress that young people do not have to continue their risky behavior. High-risk youths should be offered assistance in changing their risky behavior patterns.

Effective HIV prevention programs must be implemented over the course of many years and be developmentally appropriate. Teachers should strive to provide information about HIV prevention clearly and in sufficient detail for each grade level. Students should also be encouraged to ask questions and be given the opportunity to ask questions anonymously. Moreover, HIV prevention education should include discussion of critical social issues associated with this infection (e.g., civil liberties, protection of public health, healthcare costs, compassionate care of HIV-infected people) and teach skills that will enable students to continue to evaluate HIV-related issues.

HIV prevention is too important to be left to health educators alone. All teachers and school personnel who work with young people should receive HIV prevention information as part of in-service and preservice training. In this way, all school personnel can effectively and sensitively assist in HIV prevention efforts.

Contraceptives

Young people who are sexually active need to make decisions about the use of **contraceptives**. Talking about contraceptives in schools raises many concerns and points of view. Many argue that teaching about contraceptives is necessary because many unmarried adolescents are already sexually active. However, many teachers feel uncomfortable discussing sexual matters in the classroom, and many concerned parents, community groups, and religious organizations promote the idea that it is immoral or irresponsible to suggest the use of contraceptives to young people. Further, it is difficult to get sexually active adolescents to regularly and properly use contraception because all methods require planning. School programs that promote contraceptives do not, however, lead to an increase in sexual activity. It is imperative for every teacher to know and follow the school district's policies regarding sex education. These policies often govern any discussions that transpire between school staff and students.

Successful contraception for sexually active teens requires the performance and planning of a complex sequence of behaviors. Anticipating sexual activity, acquiring contraceptives, consistently practicing contraception, and persuading partners to behave in a certain way are difficult tasks for adults, let alone teens, especially considering the cognitive inability of many adolescents to consider and plan for future outcomes. Educators should consider using simulations to teach young people these skills. Simulations should allow students to make decisions about sex, social life, relationships, school, and work, and then "live with" the consequences of their choices in all areas of their life. In some areas of the United States, contraceptive services are now available through school-based clinics. The presence of school-based clinics in schools does not appear to increase the rate of sexual activity among students attending these schools.

Controversial Issues

Most states have guidelines or mandates on how controversial sex education issues are to be addressed (or not addressed) in the classroom. The importance of educators becoming familiar with their state's and school district's policies regarding the teaching of sex education cannot be overemphasized. Knowing the policies helps educators plan curricula as well as know best how to respond to questions or comments that arise in class.

Perhaps the most emotionally and politically charged health issues today center on **lesbian, gay, bisexual, and transgender (LGBT)** people. The LGBT community wants their way of life to be seen as normal and natural, while the opposing view perceives homosexuality as deviant behavior. Students often voice these opposing views at school, in or out of class, and can become combative and militant in their expression. It is important for teachers to teach and model how to respectfully disagree. **Respectfully disagreeing** with someone entails letting the other person voice his or her point of view without interruption and then voicing your own perspective without demeaning those you disagree with. Unfortunately, disagreeing respectfully is rarely modeled in the media, where emotionally charged and derogatory comments "sell" news. It is important to help students see that bashing or harassing anyone (gay or ultraconservative) is unacceptable.

A related issue is how to handle personal questions about sexual orientation. It is not uncommon for an adolescent to question his or her sexual orientation and to seek the advice of a trusted teacher. Teachers can share two helpful points with students in a situation like this. First, let the student know that it is not uncommon for girls to have "girl crushes" on a girl and for boys to have "boy crushes" on boys. Young people often feel a strong attraction to someone whom they admire or esteem, but these feelings do not necessarily mean that they are lesbian or gay. Also let the student know that it is common for adolescents to be aroused by sexuality in general, whether from a same- or other-gender source. For instance, a 14-year-old boy might become aroused while checking in the boys' locker room to see how he compares with classmates. His arousal does not necessarily mean that he has homosexual tendencies. Second, teachers can emphasize the need for teenagers to remain sexually abstinent for reasons beyond avoiding pregnancy and STIs. Teens need time to develop socially and emotionally and to come to know who they are. Premature sexual involvement can present a major roadblock in their psychosocial maturation.

Abortion is another hotly debated topic in U.S. society and a controversial sex education issue. In states and school districts where it is included in the curricula, it is important for educators to identify the arguments and facts given both for and against abortion. Some teachers have found it helpful to poll students for their perspective and then assign them to debate in favor of the opposite point of view. This exercise helps students focus on facts and arguments rather than on being argumentative. It also helps them develop critical thinking and research skills.

Pornography can be controversial in two respects. First, there are differing perspectives on what constitutes pornography, and second, there are differing views on how harmful viewing pornography is. However, there is no controversy over the wrongfulness of children and adolescents being the subject of pornographic images or being solicited to pornographic sites. Students need to know how to protect themselves from pornographic producers and distributors, including other youths who electronically share pornographic materials. The American Psychological Association reports that pornography can warp a teenager's perspective on sexuality.[10] Students need to be warned that viewing pornography can warp their attitudes and expectations about sex and mess up their relationships. For example, girls can be affected by perceiving that the female body is an object for pleasing others.

Peer-Led Prevention Programs

Peer education is a highly effective prevention strategy with youths. **Peer education** uses exemplary young people as credible prevention messengers to promote healthy lifestyles among other young people. Peer educators can present material about the risks of sexual activity in ways that are highly relevant to young people. Adolescents often find prevention messages more believable when they are delivered by their peers.

Peer-led prevention efforts are popular at many schools, but many more such efforts utilizing peer educators are needed. An example of an innovative peer-led prevention effort is the Sex Can Wait program, in which high school students are trained to work with middle school students. The older students teach self-respect and give concrete reasons for remaining abstinent. Instead of just telling the middle school students why they shouldn't have sex, the older teens explain how to say no. They perform skits emphasizing this message and assist the younger students in practicing ways of saying no to sexual activity. The Sex Can Wait program also has benefits for the peer educators—it teaches leadership and reinforces the skills that can keep them from giving into peer pressure to have sex. When teens make a public commitment not to have sex, it reinforces their decision to remain abstinent.

Teen Parenthood Programs

Teens who have been sexually active, become pregnant, and choose to bear their babies need a considerable amount of support and help with making decisions. Educators must make comprehensive efforts to assist pregnant teens in obtaining adequate prenatal, obstetric, and pediatric care to prevent adverse consequences associated with pregnancy and childbirth. Young teens with children usually need training in parenting skills and programs to help keep them in school so that they can finish their high school degree and meet other educational and career goals. These young people need to learn skills to prevent subsequent unintended pregnancies as well. Both the adolescent mother and the adolescent father share many of these needs.

Programs for Out-of-School Youths

School-based programs do not reach all youths at risk. Those adolescents not in school—because they have graduated or dropped out—need to be reached with the same kind of basic information that schools provide to all others. Many youths at very high risk for STIs, HIV infection, and unintended pregnancy, such as homeless or runaway youths, juvenile offenders, or school dropouts, can be reached only through intensive community-based programs. Integrating prevention programs with ongoing community efforts to provide shelter, medical care, or other services to out-of-school youths is essential. Schools can play an important role in supporting these programs and referring students who drop out to these programs and services.

National Sexuality Education Standards

Numerous resources are available to help districts develop and evaluate their sex health curricula. These resources provide flexibility and help school districts meet both local needs and state sex education mandates. The Health Education Curriculum Analysis Tool (HECAT) contains healthy behavior outcomes (HBOs) for a K–12 curriculum (see **Box 8-2**). HECAT also provides a Sexual

8-2 Internet Support

Instruction Planning Resources

The following are health behavior outcomes (HBOs) recommended by HECAT for a K–12 sexual health curriculum. After reviewing these recommendations, check out the HECAT module available on the Internet for Sexual Health (SH). In this module you will find recommendations for all the content and skills to be taught at various grade levels.

HBOs:

- Establish and maintain healthy relationships.
- Practice and maintain sexual abstinence.
- Seek support to be sexually abstinent.
- Avoid pressuring others to engage in sexual behaviors.
- Return to sexual abstinence if sexually active.
- Support others to avoid sexual risk behaviors.
- Seek out healthcare professionals to promote sexual health.

Additional risk-reduction outcomes for an abstinence-plus curriculum:

- Limit the number of sexual partners if sexually active.
- Use condoms consistently and correctly if sexually active.
- Use birth control consistently and correctly if sexually active.

After reviewing the HBOs and the HECAT SH module, try to ascertain the sexual health needs in your particular community. You can do so by finding local/state data on the Internet (e.g., CDC's YRBS data) and by interviewing school staff or students. Find out if your state has guidelines for sex education and if a scope and sequence or curricula exist for your school district. Continue your instruction planning by using the guidelines provided in the Teaching Today's Students chapter and the worksheets at the end of this chapter.

These organizations provide related materials and lesson plans on their internet sites:

- Discovery Education
- Teacher Planet
- Utah Education Network
- Nebraska Department of Education
- Alberta Government

Teaching Materials:

- National Campaign to Prevent Teen and Unplanned Pregnancy: Examples of teen pregnancy in the media, audio and video clips, PowerPoint presentations
- StayTeen.org: "What would you do?" quiz
- National Campaign to Prevent Teen and Unplanned Pregnancy: "Too Young" educational video
- Kaiser Family Foundation: Fact sheet

Health (SH) module that contains lists of content and skills to be taught at various grade levels. Another resource available is a special publication of the *Journal of School Health* entitled "National Sexuality Education Standards: Core Content and Skills, K–12." This document can also be found on the Internet.[11] We will now take a closer look at using national standards to teach sexual health.

Standard 1: Key Concepts

Sex education curricula should focus on the emotional, intellectual, physical, and social dimensions of sexual health. The seven topics mentioned here represent the minimum, essential content that needs to be included in a K–12 curriculum. The appropriateness of material for students in specific grade spans needs to be considered, and the content needs to progress from concrete to higher-order thinking skills.

- Anatomy and physiology
- Puberty and adolescent development
- Identity
- Pregnancy and reproduction
- Sexually transmitted diseases and HIV
- Healthy relationships
- Personal safety

Standard 2: Analyzing Influences

Analysis is a higher-order thinking skill, but even elementary-age children can describe how culture, media, and people influence how one thinks about attractiveness and relationships. Students can describe how external influences affect sexual decision making and sexual behavior. Students in higher grades can analyze internal influences on sexual decision making. The activities in Box 8-1 and the *Media Literacy Skills* chapter can help your students analyze sexual influences.

Standard 3: Accessing Valid Information Skills

Students are often reluctant to ask parents or other adults sex-related questions. They turn to peers instead and, as a consequence, often get misinformation. Students need to be able to identify adults and community resources they can turn to for accurate information. They also need to be able to evaluate the accuracy of the sources of information they find on the Internet.

Standard 4: Communication Skills

Teenagers report that the pressures to engage in sexual activity are strong. **Refusal skill** activities can help young people to resist this pressure. Resisting the pressure to engage in sexual activity with someone a young person cares for is much more difficult than refusing sex from a "creep." Resisting pressure from someone whom they find attractive requires stronger commitment and adherence to personal values.

Parent–child communication is an important factor in deterring sexual activity among teenagers. Teens can learn skills that facilitate more open communication with their parents, and schools can help parents learn skills that will enable them to talk to their children about sensitive subjects. Many school, community, and religious groups offer parent–child sexuality classes. Such programs provide activities that increase parent–child communication about sexuality and give opportunities for parents to share their expectations and values with their children.

Standard 5: Decision-Making Skills

Providing opportunities for youths to grapple with decision making often leads to the firm decision that delaying sexual activity is best for their futures. As part of the decision-making process, students need to be able to predict short- and long-term consequences of sexual behavior and to analyze the emotional, social, and physical benefits of abstinence.

Goal-Setting Skills

Choosing to abstain from sexual activity gives youths the time and freedom to discover who they are and to make long-range goals for their future. Focusing on a bright future and avoiding adverse consequences of engaging in sexual activity is central to effective prevention education.

Self-Management Skills

Youths need to understand that they are responsible for their own behavior and that it brings consequences, both favorable and unfavorable. Abstinence gives youths time to learn how to develop high-quality relationships rather than superficial ones based primarily on physical drives. Abstinence also helps youths gain time to focus on developmental tasks and develop character as they learn self-control, delayed gratification, respect for self and others, and responsibility for their own actions.

Advocacy Skills

Demonstrating ways to encourage friends or siblings to remain sexually abstinent or return to abstinence helps both the student and the person the student talks to. Expressing compassion and support for people living with disease, such as cancer and AIDS, is another helpful advocacy skill.

At the end of the chapter you will find many activities that help students learn the skills of analyzing, accessing, communication, decision-making, goal-setting, self-management, and advocacy. You can also find helpful Internet sex education resource materials in Box 8-2.

■ PROBLEMS ASSOCIATED WITH YOUTH SEXUAL ACTIVITY

Many problems are associated with youth sexual activity, including rape, harassment, pregnancy, disease, and infection. Each state has laws, regulations, and mandated services associated with reproduction. Current in-depth information on each state's laws regarding sex education, abortion, adolescents, contraception, unintended pregnancy, services, and financing can be found on the Guttmacher Institute's website. Rape and sexual harassment are addressed in the *Promoting Safety and Violence Prevention* chapter. We will now look at other problems that arise from youth sexual activity.

Emotional Consequences

Even if promiscuous youths escape the harsh consequences of sexual activity—pregnancy, HIV infection, or an STI—they can experience negative emotional consequences. This is evidenced by the numerous young adults who state they wish they would have waited longer before becoming sexually active. It can take years for individuals to overcome the emotional baggage of early-age sexual activity. Indeed, some never completely overcome the lingering emotional effects. Following are 10 possible emotional dangers of premature sexual involvement:[12]

1. *Worry about pregnancy and STIs.* Sexually active young people can experience a great deal of stress over the possibility of being pregnant or having contracted an STI. Receiving a negative pregnancy or STI screening test can relieve their fears, but the stress reemerges at their next sexual encounter. Many youths do not seek out screening but remain sexually active, turning this stress into a chronic condition.
2. *Regret and self-recrimination.* Young women often report feeling used, stupid, and cheap after sexual encounters. Girls are especially vulnerable to this condition because they are more likely to think of sex as a way of "showing they care." They may become physically intimate in an effort to try to "keep the guy," but become ignored or "dumped." Giving oneself for nothing

can be emotionally devastating. Youths can also regret losing their virginity as they realize sex isn't exactly what it is hyped to be.

3. *Guilt.* Many people report having a guilty conscience about having sex. This can come from not living up to religious expectations or from seeing the pain they have caused in others. Guilt can also arise from knowing that their parents would be upset if they knew the teen was having sex. Parents can be crippled by guilt regarding their own early sexual activity. Their reluctance to be hypocritical can keep them from advising their children about the dangers of premature sexual involvement.

4. *Loss of self-respect and self-esteem.* Discovering that one is pregnant or has contracted an STI can have a monumental impact on a person's sense of confidence and worth. Casual sex also can lower self-esteem. An oppressive cycle can develop of casual sex leading to lowered self-esteem leading to more casual sex. When people treat other people as objects, they not only hurt them but also lose respect for themselves. Getting drunk and having sex with someone not remembered later or having sex to make a sexual conquest results in a loss of self-respect on the part of both individuals.

5. *Corruption of character and the debasement of sex.* People corrupt their character and debase their sexuality when they treat others as sexual objects and exploit them for their own pleasure. The breakdown of the character traits of self-control and delayed gratification are major factors in many of the sex-related problems plaguing society: pornography, sexual harassment, sexual abuse, infidelity in marriage, and rape. Character is also corrupted when people tell lies to get sex—anything from "I love you" to "I've never had a sexually transmitted infection."

   The debasement of sex is too often seen on school campuses. In school hallways, students can be heard using profane language. Teenage boys clubs have been reported to exist in which members compete to see how many girls they can have sex with. Elementary schoolchildren have been found playing sexual contact games in which points are earned by touching another's private parts. Sadly, many young people have stated that forced sex is permissible if a man and woman have been dating for 6 months or longer.

6. *Shaken trust and fear of commitment.* Individuals who feel betrayed or used after breaking up from a sexual relationship can experience difficulty in future relationships. Girls can see guys as interested in just one thing and wonder if anyone will ever love and accept them without demanding sex to earn that love. Boys can also feel a loss of trust and a fear of commitment. Some young men report engaging in one-night stands because they are afraid of falling in love.

7. *Rage over betrayal.* Sex can create an emotional bond that hurts terribly when broken. Rage and violence can result when an individual feels betrayed. News networks often report on the violent acts of former lovers.

8. *Depression and suicide.* The emotional pain caused by a terminated sexual relationship can be enormous, especially if one of the partners thought it was "the real thing." Sometimes the emotional turmoil of a broken relationship can lead to deep depression. Depression, in turn, can lead to suicide. Rage turned inward has also resulted in suicide.

9. *Ruined relationships.* Sex can turn a good relationship bad. It can quickly become the focal point, block other means of communicating love, and stunt the balanced growth of a relationship.

10. *Stunted personal development.* Some young people have used sex, like alcohol and drugs, ineffectively to try to cope with life's pressures. Teens caught up in intense sexual relationships stymie their individual growth and fail to develop a sense of identity. They are focusing on one thing when they need to be forming friendships with others, developing skills and interests, and taking on larger social responsibilities. Promiscuous youths can have trouble expressing and meeting their own needs and the needs of others. They can also have trouble setting long-range goals and creating a plan for their lives.

Unintended Teen Pregnancy

Birth rates among teenage mothers have declined in the past 20 years, but the United States still has the highest teen birth rate among comparable countries. Three in 10 girls in the United States get pregnant at least once by age 20.[12] The highest rates of teen pregnancy and childbirth occur among black, Hispanic, and American Indian/Alaska Native youth, and among socially economically disadvantaged youth of any race or ethnicity. Black and Hispanic youth account for more than 50% of all U.S. teen births.[3]

The vast majority of teen pregnancies are unplanned, meaning they occurred sooner than desired or were not wanted at any time. The majority of teens say they used contraceptives (most commonly condoms) the first time they had sex—but this doesn't mean they continue to routinely use them. A sexually active teen who does not use contraceptives has a 90% chance of becoming pregnant within a year.[9] Sexually active adolescents might not use contraceptives for the following reasons:

- They do not believe they could conceive.
- They do not expect to have intercourse.
- They are embarrassed to discuss sexual matters with others (e.g., partners, friends, parents, counselors, physicians, healthcare providers).
- They believe myths such as the following:
    - You cannot get pregnant the first time you have intercourse.
    - You cannot get pregnant if a girl is still having her period.
    - You cannot get pregnant if a boy withdraws in time.
    - You cannot get pregnant if you douche afterward.
    - You cannot get pregnant if you use foam or take a birth control pill afterward.

Teen pregnancy continues to be a problem, particularly in Hispanic and African American populations.

There are other reasons that teens become pregnant besides failure to use contraception. Some desire to have a baby as a sign of maturity or even as a type of status symbol. Some teens view motherhood as a way of achieving love or feeling needed by someone else. Others use pregnancy as a means of escaping an unhappy or abusive family situation. Teen mothers can obtain federal and state aid to support their babies through such programs as Medicaid, Aid to Families with Dependent Children (AFDC), and food stamps.

Teen girls who have babies are likely to become pregnant again in the short-term future. Nearly one fourth of teen mothers have a second child within 24 months of the first.[12] Children of teen mothers are also at increased risk for becoming teen parents themselves.

Teen pregnancy and childbearing bring substantial social and economic costs to the teen mother, teen father, and society:

◆ Teen pregnancy and childbirth accounted for approximately $10 billion per year in costs to U.S. taxpayers in the form of increased health care and foster care, increased incarceration rates among children of teen parents, and lost tax revenue because of lower educational attainment and income among teen mothers. Pregnancy and birth are significant contributors to high school dropout rates among girls. Only 50% of teen mothers receive a high school diploma by age 22, compared with approximately 90% of women who did not give birth during adolescence.[13]
◆ The children of teenage mothers are more likely to have lower school achievement and drop out of high school, have more health problems, be incarcerated at some time during adolescence, give birth as a teenager, and face unemployment as a young adult.[14]
◆ Teen fathers are less likely to live with their first child. By their early 20s, they are likely to have an additional child or children by a woman other than their first child's mother. When teen or young adult men have children, their opportunities decrease to finish an education and become financially stable.[15]

Laws and Teen Pregnancy

States have laws that govern many sensitive teen pregnancy issues. In most states, healthcare providers do not have to notify the parents if a teenaged girl requests birth control pills or if the teen tells the provider that he or she is sexually active. Abortion laws in most states require that

Teen mothering is associated with a plethora of problems.

Problems Associated with Youth Sexual Activity

pregnant teens younger than age 18 get parental consent for an abortion or notify their parents before an abortion takes place. Minors living in parental consent states can avoid involving their parents in an abortion by traveling to a nonconsent state or by getting a "judicial bypass" from a judge. Adoption laws also vary by state regarding the rights of grandparents and fathers, but today very few pregnant teens opt to place their babies for adoption.

DISEASES ASSOCIATED WITH YOUTH SEXUAL ACTIVITY

HIV Infection

Young people in the United States are at persistent risk for **human immunodeficiency virus (HIV)** infection. A disproportionate number of new HIV infections occur among youths, especially among black and Hispanic males who have sex with males. Infection with HIV is the most frightening potential consequence of youth sexual activity. HIV is the cause of acquired immunodeficiency syndrome (AIDS). This virus attacks the cells of the immune system, causing the body to lose its ability to fight infection and certain cancers. As a result, people with AIDS are susceptible to life-threatening diseases, called **opportunistic diseases**, that are caused by pathogens that do not cause illness in healthy people.

The most common means of transmitting HIV from person to person is through sexual contact with an infected partner. During sexual contact, HIV can enter the body through the lining of the vagina, vulva, penis, rectum, or mouth. Another common means of transmitting HIV is the sharing of needles or syringes used to inject drugs. Transmission may occur when needles or syringes are contaminated with even minute quantities of blood from someone infected with HIV.

Young people are at greatest risk of HIV infection if they have unprotected sex outside of a mutually monogamous relationship between two HIV-negative individuals, use injection drugs, or use alcohol or other drugs that impair their decision-making abilities. Those who have many different sex partners and who inject illicit drugs into their bloodstream are at even greater risk. Individuals with other sexually transmitted infections (e.g., chlamydia, herpes) are at increased susceptibility of acquiring HIV infection during sex with an infected partner.

HIV-infected females can pass the virus to their fetuses during pregnancy or birth. Approximately one fourth of HIV-infected females who do not receive treatment pass the infection to their babies. The virus can also be passed to the baby through breast milk after delivery. The chances of passing HIV to a baby are greatly reduced if the mother is given the drug AZT during her pregnancy.

Concerns that HIV can be transmitted through casual contact are unfounded. The virus is not spread through the sharing of food utensils, towels and bedding, swimming pools, telephones, or toilet seats. Closed-mouth kissing does not carry risk of HIV transmission. However, health authorities advise against open-mouthed kissing ("French" kissing) with an infected person because of the possibility of contact with blood. HIV also is not spread by biting insects such as mosquitoes or bedbugs.

Sexually Transmitted Infections

Sexually transmitted infections (STIs) continue to be a problem for American youth. According to the CDC, one fourth of the reported STI cases each year occur among teenagers. One in two sexually active persons will contact an STI by age 25.[4] Many of these young people will suffer long-term health consequences as a result. The high rate of sexual activity among young people increases the likelihood of being exposed to, being infected with , or transmitting a host of infectious diseases. **Box 8-3** identifies various STIs and their disease-causing agents.

More than 25 STIs have been identified to date. Many of these diseases are passed from one person to another unknowingly because the carrier may not feel ill or may come to feel ill only

8-3

Disease-Causing Microbes

Microbes are organisms too tiny to be seen without a microscope. They are found in vast numbers everywhere—in air, soil, water, plants, animals, and the human body. Many microbes are essential for healthy life and we could not exist without them, but some cause disease. Most microbes belong to one of four major groups: bacteria, viruses, fungi, or protozoa.

Viruses are among the smallest microbes. Viruses are not cells, but instead consist of one or more molecules of DNA or RNA, which contain the virus's genes surrounded by a protein coat. Viruses can be rod shaped, sphere shaped, or multisided. They have no way to reproduce on their own, so they must infect cells and take over their reproductive machinery to replicate. Viral diseases can be very difficult to treat because viruses live inside the body's cells, where they are protected from medicines in the bloodstream. Only a few antiviral medicines are available to prevent and treat viral infections and diseases. Antibiotics are not effective against viruses.

Thousands of types of **bacteria** have been identified. Bacteria are single-celled organisms that are much larger than viruses, yet still too small to be seen without a microscope. Under a microscope, bacteria look like balls, rods, or spirals. They are capable of reproducing on their own and often have threadlike structures, called *flagella*, that help them to move around. Bacteria may produce disease by releasing toxins into the body. Bacterial diseases are sometimes effectively treated by antibiotic drugs, but concerns about antimicrobial resistance to these drugs are increasing. Some bacteria are becoming resistant to the killing effects of these drugs. This has become a very serious problem, especially in hospital settings.

Millions of types of **fungi** can be found in our environment. Those most familiar to us are mushrooms, yeast, mold, and mildew. Fungi also live in or on the human body. Many do not cause disease, but some do. Diseases caused by fungi are called *mycoses*. Antifungal medicines are available to treat fungal infections of the skin as well as those within the body.

Protozoa are microscopic one-celled animals that come in many shapes and sizes. Protozoal infections are difficult to treat because drugs that destroy the protozoa may also destroy human cells.

The following table identifies selected STIs by type of microbe.

Viral STIs	**Bacterial STIs**	**Fungal STI**	**Protozoal STI**
HIV/AIDS	Syphilis	Candidiasis	Trichomoniasis
Genital warts	Gonorrhea		
Genital herpes	Chlamydia		
Hepatitis B			

---

after he or she has already passed the disease to unknowing victims. Some diseases regarded as STIs can be transmitted through other means (e.g., from a mother to an unborn or newborn child, through blood transfusions, by sharing contaminated needles). The primary means of transmission of these diseases, however, is through sexual contact. Therefore, the most effective means of prevention is to avoid sexual contact.

Young people who are sexually active put themselves at high risk of acquiring a sexually transmitted infection. The larger the number of partners with whom an individual has sexual contact, the greater the risk of developing an STI. *Safe sex* refers to sexual practices that are important in preventing the spread of STIs. One safe-sex practice is the use of a condom during sexual activity. Proper use of condoms reduces but does not eliminate the risk of STI transmission from one partner to another. Use of nonoxynol-9, a common ingredient in spermicidal jellies and foams, in combination with a condom further reduces the risk of spreading an STI from one person to another during sexual intercourse. Avoiding other practices, such as oral–genital and anal–genital contact, also reduces the risk of contracting an STI.

Young people who are sexually active should seriously consider the risks of developing an STI and consider postponing sexual contact. They should also know the potential signs and symptoms of STIs. If any of the following are present, early medical advice and treatment should be sought:

- Any unusual discharges from the genitals
- Pain in the genital area
- Burning sensation in or around the genitals (especially during urination)
- Sores on or near the genitals
- Frequent urination
- Lower abdominal pain
- Itching around the genital or anal area
- Growths or warts in the genital area

Common STIs Among Teens

Teens are at high risk for acquiring most STIs. Teenagers and young adults are more likely than any other age groups to have multiple sex partners and to engage in unprotected sex—both risk factors for STIs. Also, young females are likely to choose sexual partners older than themselves. Here is a closer look at common STIs in the United States.

Trichomoniasis (also called *trich*) is the most common, curable STI in young sexually active women. It is caused by parasitic protozoa. This organism can also be spread by towels, sheets, and other objects because the protozoa can remain alive on external objects for as long as 1.5 hours. Trichomoniasis may cause a green, yellow, or gray discharge; bad smell; itching in or around the vagina; pain during sex; and pain when urinating. Most males who have this infection do not exhibit symptoms.

Infection with **human papillomavirus (HPV)** often causes **genital warts**. The warts, in turn, cause considerable discomfort and embarrassment for an infected person. They are highly contagious and can easily spread to a sexual partner or to a baby during delivery. Females with HPV and genital warts are at higher risk for having cervical cancer in their lifetimes than those who have not been infected. **Gardasil** and **Cervarix** are two licensed HPV vaccines that prevent infection with the types of HPV that cause most cases of cervical cancer and genital warts. Note that this vaccine does not provide any protection for other STIs, including chlamydia and gonorrhea.

Chlamydia is the most frequently reported bacterial STI in the United States and is most common such disease among young people. It is estimated that 1 in 15 sexually active females aged 14–19 years has chlamydia. This STI is considered a "silent" disease because approximately 75% of infected women and 50% of infected men have no symptoms. It can be treated with antibiotics if detected early; if it is not detected early, the infection can progress and create serious reproductive and other health problems including pelvic inflammatory disease (PID). PID occurs in as many as 40% of women with chlamydia.[16] This major infection of the entire female reproductive tract can lead to permanent sterility, chronic pelvic pain, or even death. Yearly screening for chlamydia is recommended for sexually active women age 25 years and younger. Complications for men with chlamydia are rare but include pain, fever, and sterility. Women are frequently reinfected if their male partners are not treated. Chlamydia can also be passed from an infected mother to her baby during childbirth. Babies born to females with chlamydial infections can acquire serious eye infections that lead to blindness.

Gonorrhea is a very widespread bacterial infection that resembles chlamydia in many ways. Both of these STIs produce similar symptoms, but most females are unaware they are infected with either disease. If gonorrhea is detected early enough, it can easily be treated with antibiotics; if untreated, it can result in severe health consequences, including PID. Babies born to females with gonorrheal infections can acquire serious eye infections that lead to blindness.

Herpes simplex virus is a viral infection that cannot be cured. It is very contagious and results in recurrent and unpredictable outbreaks. Herpes infection leads to painful, blister-like sores that may appear on the sex organs, the mouth, or the face. Although the sores go away, the herpes virus remains in the body, so the sores reappear periodically throughout the person's lifetime. The herpes virus can be spread from a mother to her baby during vaginal delivery and can be fatal to the baby.

Other STIs include candidiasis, pubic lice, hepatitis B, and syphilis. **Candidiasis** is caused by a yeast-like fungus that creates intense vaginal itching and burning sensations. **Pubic lice**, also known as "crabs," are parasites that are spread by sexual contact. These lice attach themselves to the pubic hair and feed on the blood of a host. The incidence of **hepatitis B** is declining among teens and other age groups. Infection with hepatitis B virus can cause serious viral infection of the liver, but can be prevented through vaccination. **Syphilis** is a bacterial infection that, when detected early, can be treated effectively with antibiotic drugs. Untreated syphilis can cause destructive effects in the body and even birth defects in a developing baby if a pregnant female carries the infection.

8-4 Activities for Analyzing Media's Sexual Messages

You can adapt the following activities for use in many different grade levels (as indicated in previous chapters.) Also review the *Media Literacy Skills* chapter for more activity ideas.

Reality TV

Show a short clip of a reality TV program like *The Bachelor*. Discuss how "reality" programs are really staged. Identify real-life short-term and long-term consequences that might not be depicted on such a program. Identify unhealthy attitudes and values that the program promotes. (I, J, H, C)

Teen Mom

Display an image of one or more of the teenage mothers who have appeared on a "teen mom" program. Discuss how programs can glamorize teen pregnancy. Discuss the truths about teen pregnancy depicted in the programs, and the truths that are not included. (P, I, J, H, C)

Bedroom TV

Show a clip about teens' need for sleep found at www.pbs.org/wgbh/pages/frontline/shows/teenbrain/. Discuss "junk sleep" and the dangers and problems of students watching television or accessing the Web in their bedrooms. (P, I, J, H, C)

Sex Sales

Gather some TV ads from YouTube that can appropriately be shown in your classroom that use sex to sell products. As you show an ad, frequently pause and discuss details in frames. Identify the hooks used and explain how producers are trying to create emotional transversal (see the *Media Literacy Skills* chapter). Discuss how ads shape expectations about beauty and gender behavior. (P, I, J, H, C)

(continues)

(continued)

Marriage and Sex

Identify the top 20 prime-time TV programs and the top 20 movies for the past 3 years. Create a graph and have students identify the number of TV programs and movies where unmarried people were shown in some way to be sexually involved. Have them identify the number of married people shown in some way to be sexually involved in TV programs and the same movies. Discuss how media shape young people's normative expectations about sexual behaviors and the inaccuracies of their expectations (everyone is not doing it). (I, J, H, C)

TV Analysis

Assign various students to watch different TV channels for specific blocks of time during one week. (Use wisdom and care in making these assignments.) Have the students record the number and types of sexual material presented on the programming and commercials. Combine all the students' reports into a graph format for an analysis of one week. Discuss the amount and appropriateness of the sexual material presented. Have students write letters of concern to the producers of programs they found troubling or to the companies whose advertising they found distasteful. (J, H, C)

True Love

Discuss the differences between lust, infatuation, and love with your students using the chart presented here. Talk about how movies, TV programs, and books often portray lust and infatuation as love. Ask students to identify celebrities who seem to be hooked on infatuation because these individuals' relationships do not last. Discuss the many problems that can result from mistaking lust or infatuation for love. Identify the emotional dangers for being sexually intimate within lust and within infatuation. Show pictures of several married couples (young, middle age, old) whom you know and share why each couple is an example of real love. (I, J, H, C)

Lust	Infatuation	Love
Visceral.	Cupid's arrow—fall into and out of it. No control over it.	Takes time, develops, not discovered. Is something you do, not something that happens to you.
Self-centered, predatory. Uses other person as an object.	Self-gratifying—someone you want to be seen with, or fear of being left behind or missing out (everyone else is paired up).	Deep concern for the welfare of the loved one. True love gives.
Can consume thoughts, comments, and activities. Focuses on "stimuli," not person.	Feelings based on illusions and idealizations; exaggerations of the other's good points.	Feelings based on reality—mature love sees more, not less, but because it sees more, it is willing to see less.
Varying states of physical arousal.	Loss of appetite; hard to concentrate. Can be short-tempered and irritable.	Eat, study, excel because you want to be your best for the other.

No desire for relationship other than for physical gratification.	Insecure; in love with being loved; jealous.	Happy because you are sure and secure.
Tells lies to get sex.	Disagree easily. Focused on love feeling rather than on coming to deeply know and understand the other.	Readiness to listen to and understand the other's perspective.
Lacks self-control or restraint.	Feel like must have sex or must marry to cement relationship.	Recognize sex is a natural part of love, but have sexual restraint to prevent consequences for self and loved one and don't want sex to get in the way of developing the relationship. Marriage and sex can wait until the right time.

8-5 *Activities for Sex Education*

Communication and Healthy Relationships

Family Dinner

Assign students a project that has to be completed during family dinner and takes more than one night to complete. It could be a questionnaire that reveals previously unknown information. (e.g., where did you have your first kiss?). The objective is to encourage family meal time, discussion, and stronger family ties.

Warning Signs

Print out a variety of road warning signs or create PowerPoint slides with different signs on each slide. On these signs, write characteristics of unhealthy relationships: does or says things that make you feel stupid, embarrassed, or worthless; put-downs; keeps you from family and friends; keeps you from doing things you like; jealous or possessive; lies or hides things from you; always expects to get his/her way; shoves, shakes, or hits you; threatens to hurt you or himself/herself. Discuss examples of these things that students have witnessed (in real life or in the media) and examine why they are warning signs. Discuss how to get out of an unhealthy relationship. (I, J, H, C)

Iceberg

Display a picture of an iceberg. Make the analogy that unhealthy relationships are like icebergs. The small negative attitudes and behaviors that are easily seen might be just the tip of the iceberg. Write on the top

(continues)

(*continued*)

of the iceberg behaviors like name calling, slap, and push. Below the water line, write things like isolation, stalking, threats, belittling, beating, rape, pressure to have sex, and emotional abuse. Discuss why people get involved in abusive relationships and how to avoid them. (J, H, C)

Human Development

Timing

Set three or more alarm clocks to go off during class at random times. Turn each off as it sounds, but don't say anything until the final alarm sounds. Students will be eager to know what it's all about. Explain how puberty is "set to go off" at different times (ages) in different people. Have everyone line up from shortest to tallest. Tell the students to rearrange themselves to the height they think they will be at age 20. (I, J)

Body Image

Talk about how the media influence body image. Streaming videos such as the Dove ad deconstruction and "Killing Me Softly" can be found in the Media Literacy Clearinghouse link bank at http://www.frankwbaker.com/streaming_ml.htm. Be sure to get administrative clearance before using any video in class. (I, J, H)

Birth Video

Show the miracle of birth. *Nova* offers an hour-long program divided into eight chapters at http://www.pbs.org/wgbh/nova/miracle/program.html. (J, H)

"Waste" Days

On and around holidays, it is often difficult to keep students academically focused. Try out these activities on the following holidays: (P, I, J, H)

- *Halloween.* Memorize bones and then have a tag test using a decoration skeleton that is either intact or taken apart. Assemble various X-rays in a class window. Build a model of the spinal cord and nerves using empty spools of thread and string. Discover what muscle groups do by stretching large rubber bands across the body where the muscles are located.
- *Thanksgiving.* Trace where Thanksgiving dinner goes (digestive system).
- *Valentine's Day.* Discover the similarities between a valentine heart and a real heart (divide it in two and then across the top—the two upper atria and the two lower ventricles). Make a huge diagram of a heart using an old sheet or plastic table cloth and an overhead projector. Have students draw for a chance to be a red blood cell traveling through the heart.

Analyzing Consequences

Wheel of Misfortune

Divide the class into groups. Have each group design a "Wheel of Misfortune" game based on the TV program *Wheel of Fortune*. Instruct students to design their wheels so that they contain physical and emotional problems associated with premature sexual involvement. (I, J, H)

Burnt Cake

Bake two cakes, one as directed and one at much higher heat. Use the cakes as an object lesson to initiate a discussion of what happens when young people try to grow up too fast (they or others "turn up the heat"). You could also leave out one or more of the key ingredients in one cake and then liken the various ingredients to skills needed for growing up and having healthy relationships. (I, J, H)

Pass the Cookie

Hold up two cookies. Ask one or more students to wait in the hall. While they are gone, have every student take turns holding one of the cookies and doing anything they want to it except change its appearance. Invite those in the hall to come back in. Explain what happened in their absence. Ask them to identify which of the two cookies they would like to eat. Discuss how this object lesson is like HIV or STI transmission. (I, J, H)

Flour Tote

Have students carry around a 10-pound bag of flour (baby) everywhere they go for one or more days. Explore other ways of making this time resemble being responsible for a real baby. Discuss what was learned. (J, H)

Decision Making, Goal Setting, and Self-Management

Great Comebacks

Ask the class to identify and list on the board 10 or more examples of sexual pressure (e.g., "Don't worry, I'll take care of everything," "Nobody will know but us," "If you love me..."). Divide the class into pairs. Have each pair come up with a great comeback for each of the listed pressures (e.g., "If you love me..."—"If you loved me, you wouldn't pressure me!"). Have class members share their comebacks. Write the best comebacks next to their corresponding pressures on the board. (I, J, H)

Everybody's Not "Doing It"

(Read about normative education in the *Promoting a Tobacco-Free and Drug-Free Lifestyle* chapter.) Poll students to determine what percentage of the kids in their high school they believe are sexually active. Discuss how and why youths often overestimate the number of adolescents who are sexually active. Discuss the true figures. (You can find national and state YRBS data on the CDC's website.) Discuss why many youths choose to be or become sexually inactive. (J, H)

Life Line

Give each student seven small pieces of paper (3- by 5-inch). Have students write at the top of each of their papers their name, a future age (e.g., 18, 23, 28, 35, 45, 55, 65), and what they want to be doing or have accomplished by the indicated age. Have the students clip their "age papers" to a life line made by stringing a clothesline or similar cord from one end of the classroom to the other. Encourage students to read one another's papers as they are clipping theirs up. Discuss how decisions made in their adolescence can affect the rest of their lives. (I, J, H)

(continues)

(continued)

Drawing the Line

Create a sexual continuum on the board ranging from holding hands to intercourse. Ask students to mentally draw a line on the continuum that they do not want to cross at this point in their lives. Tell the following two stories to impress upon students the importance of "drawing the line" early, long before the point they don't want to cross. After telling the stories, discuss safety rules for "flying well above the trees" and staying far away from "dangerous cliffs." Such rules might include "date in groups" and "avoid being alone with the other person." (J, H)

- *Story 1.* In World War II, some pilots participated in "tree topping" to impress others with their flying skills. They would fly close enough to break off the very tips of trees. This practice became prohibited because of the number of planes that ended up in the trees. A new safety rule was set in place so that the minimum altitude at which a pilot could fly was well above the trees.
- *Story 2.* A company was interviewing truck drivers for a job hauling precious cargo across a mountain pass. When asked about a particularly hazardous curve on a steep cliff, one applicant said, "I could take that corner going 60 miles per hour while driving on the outside shoulder." A second applicant said, "I would gear down, and drive slowly and as close as possible to the hill side of the road." Which of the two applicants would you hire to drive your precious cargo?

Virginity Pledges

As part of a larger sex education program, give students the opportunity to pledge "I won't" until swearing "I do." These can be written documents that students sign on the dotted line. Those who have been sexually active can pledge to become sexually inactive. (I, J, H)

Good Clean Fun

Youths need alternative activities if they are to avoid sexual pressures and situations. Help them brainstorm group activities that would be fun, such as having a marathon dinner where they travel from one house to another for different courses. Have a three-armed dinner where partners tie one of their arms together and then cook dinner—a dessert, salad, or main course. Hold a hairdo party where the boys do the girls' hair; have an awards ceremony and don't forget to videotape the event. Pretend to be going on a trip and see who can come up with the best vacation for a predetermined time and budget by visiting travel agencies or searching Internet sites. Pretend to be tourists in your own town and take pictures or videos. Play hide-and-seek at the mall. Build sand castles (get sand at a cement company and put it into wading pools). Take lawn chairs to the side of the road and hold up cards with numbers 1–10 to rate the cars going by. (I, J, H)

Advocacy and Integration

Walk in Her Heels

Sponsor a school-wide day where every "caring" male wears a pair of girls' shoes to school. In classes, discuss what new perspectives on women's issues this activity gives.

Baby Costs: Math

Have students compute the costs of having a baby (e.g., medical, food, diapers, clothes). Cost-related information can be found at http://www.teenageparent.org/english/costofbaby2B.html.

STI Brochure: Language Arts

Have students work in groups to develop brochures on STIs that contain information on causes, facts, statistics, and treatments for these diseases. Students can get the needed information at http://www.cdc.gov/std.

The Role of Marriage: Social Studies

Have students identify and discuss the role that marriage has played in societies through time. Help students identify why cultures and governments have cared so much about marriage. Discuss economic and social problems associated with single women raising children. Analyze probable problems the United States will experience from current birth rates occurring outside of marriage.

Additional Notes

Instruction Plan Worksheet Human Development/Sex Education

Use this worksheet to plan sex education/human development instruction at the grade level you will be teaching. Refer to Chapter 2 for more information on how to complete each section in this worksheet.

■ Assess Needs

Identify topics and skills state or local curricula identify to be taught at ___ grade level.

Identify additional topics or skills the SH HECAT Module indicates for this grade.

Identify sex education needs your particular students and their families have:
- What are your student's developmental needs?
- How sexually active are the teens in your community?
- What sex related cultural values, behaviors, and attitudes do your students have?
- How is the media influencing their sexual beliefs and attitudes?

■ Set Major Learning Goal(s)

Identify your major learning goal(s)–what do you want to have happen?

■ **Develop Instruction Map**

Create a map (calendar or list of days) indicating the time frame you have/need to teach the curriculum, meet student needs and reach goal(s). For each day indicate the content/skills to be taught. Work to create a good flow.

■ Write SMART Unit Objectives

Write 1 or 2 major objectives for each day you will teach. Your objectives should be in alignment with your state/local curricula, your student's needs, and your major learning goal(s).

■ Identify Assessment Tools

Preassessment	Formative-Assessment	Postassessment
How will you determine what students already know or do?	How will you know if they are "getting it"?	How will you know if students master objectives?

Instruction Plan Worksheet Human Development/Sex Education

■ Develop Unit Plan

Divide the chart into the number of days you will teach. Record each day's topic and objective key words. Identify activity names (in the book) that can help you meet each day's objective. Identify tech tools you can use and possible lesson adaptations you can make for special need learners.

Lesson Topic Objectives	Instruction Activities	Tech Tools	Adaptations for Learners

■ Develop Lesson Plans

Use the Lesson Plan Template found in Chapter 2 and this worksheet to create detailed lesson plans for your Sex Education or Human Development Unit.

KEY TERMS

sexting 248
sex education 252
Guttmacher Institute 252
abstinence education 253
abstinence-only education 253
abstinence-plus education 253
comprehensive sex education 253
risk-reduction curriculum 253
contraceptives 255
lesbian, gay, bisexual, and transgender (LGBT) 256
respectfully disagreeing 256
peer education 257
refusal skill 259
human immunodeficiency virus (HIV) 264
opportunistic diseases 264
sexually transmitted infections (STIs) 264

viruses 265
bacteria 265
fungi 265
protozoa 265
trichomoniasis 266
human papillomavirus (HPV) 266
genital warts 266
Gardasil 266
Cervarix 266
chlamydia 266
gonorrhea 266
herpes simplex virus 267
candidiasis 267
pubic lice 267
hepatitis B 267
syphilis 267

KNOWLEDGE CHECK!

1. Define and explain the relative importance of each of the key terms in the context of this chapter.
2. Summarize teenage sexual activity trends and rates, including racial/ethnic differences.
3. Discuss how youth are exposed to high levels of sexualized images, possible consequences of such exposure, and concerns about the media being youth's primary sex educator.
4. Describe how the culture in which young people grow up affects their sexual development. Explain how hormones affect sexual development, including how boys and girls think differently about sex.
5. Identify what teachers can do to help initiate parent–child open communication about sex.
6. Explain types of sex education and laws/regulations governing sex education in various states and school districts.
7. Identify what should be taught regarding HIV in kindergarten through third grade, upper elementary grades, and secondary grades.
8. Enumerate the arguments for and against teaching about contraceptives in school. Explain when contraceptives can and cannot be discussed in school.
9. Explain how a teacher can appropriately handle classroom discussions regarding LGBT, abortion, and pornography.
10. Explain how a teacher can appropriately handle private student–teacher discussions regarding sexual orientation.
11. Describe the components and benefits of peer-led prevention programs, teen parenthood programs, and programs for out-of-school youth.
12. Identify key topics and skills included in sexual health curricula.
13. Discuss the negative emotional consequences associated with premature sexual involvement.
14. Identify trends in teen pregnancy, including those related to socioeconomic and ethnic/racial factors.
15. Discuss reasons why contraceptives are not used and myths teens often believe about pregnancy prevention.
16. Identify the consequences of teen pregnancy for the mother, the baby, and the father. Discuss laws associated with teen pregnancy.
17. Discuss HIV infection risks, rates, and complications.
18. Discuss teen risk for STIs.

19. Discuss various STI microbes and symptoms.
20. Discuss each common STI, including how prevalent it is, what causes it, how it is spread, which complications it can create, and how it can be treated.

■ REFERENCES

1. Lemonick M. Teens before their time. *Time.* 2000;156(18):66–74.
2. Centers for Disease Control and Prevention. YRBSS: Youth Risk Behavior Surveillance System. Available at www.cdc.gov/HealthyYouth/yrbs/index.htm. Accessed February 8, 2013.
3. Centers for Disease Control and Prevention. About teen pregnancy. Available at www.cdc.gov/TeenPregnacy/AboutTeenPreg.htm. Accessed February 8, 2013.
4. Centers for Disease Control and Prevention. Sexual risk behavior: HIV, STD, & teen pregnancy prevention. Available at www.cdc.gov/HealthyYouth/sexualbehaviors/index.htm. Accessed February 8, 2013.
5. National Campaign to Prevent Teen and Unplanned Pregnancy. Sex and tech: what's really going on. 2009. Available at http://www.thenationalcampaign.org/sextech. Accessed February 8, 2013.
6. Brown JD, Engle KL, Pardun CJ, et al. Sexy media matter: exposure to sexual content in music, movies, television, and magazines predicts black and white adolescents' sexual behavior. *Pediatrics.* 2006;117(4):1018–1027.
7. Chandra A, Martino SC, Collins RL, et al. Does watching sex on television predict teen pregnancy? Findings from a national longitudinal survey of youth. *Pediatrics.* 2008;122(5):1047–1054.
8. Walsh, D. *Smart parenting, smarter kids.* New York, NY: Free Press; 2011.
9. Guttmacher Institute. State policies in brief: sex and HIV education. February 1, 2013. Available at www.guttmacher.org/statecenter/spibs/spib_SE.pdf. Accessed February 8, 2013.
10. DeAngelis T. American Psychological Association: Web pornography's effect on children. Available at http://www.apa.org/monitor/nov07/webporn.aspx. Accessed May 7, 2013.
11. American Alliance for Health, Physical Education Recreation and Dance. National sexuality education standards: core content and skills, K–12. January 2012. Available at http://www.ashaweb.org/files/public/sexuality%20education/josh-fose-standards.pdf. Accessed February 11, 2013.
12. National Campaign to Prevent Teen and Unplanned Pregnancy. National data. Available at http://www.thenationalcampaign.org/national-data/. Accessed February 11, 2013.
13. Perper K, Peterson K, Manlove J. *Diploma attainment among teen mothers.* Fact Sheet Publication #2010-01. Washington, DC: Child Trends; 2010.
14. Hoffman SD. *Kids Having kids: economic costs and social consequences of teen pregnancy.* Washington, DC: Urban Institute Press; 2008.
15. Scott ME, Steward-Streng NR, Manlove J, Moore KA. The characteristics and circumstances of teen fathers: at the birth of their first child and beyond. *Trends Child Res Brief.* June 2012. Available at http://www.childtrends.org/wp-content/uploads/2013/03/Child_Trends-2012_06_01_RB_TeenFathers.pdf. Accessed February 9, 2013.
16. Centers for Disease Control and Prevention. Chlamydia: CDC fact sheet. Available at http://www.cdc.gov/std/Chlamydia/STDFact-Chlamydia.htm. Accessed February 11, 2013.

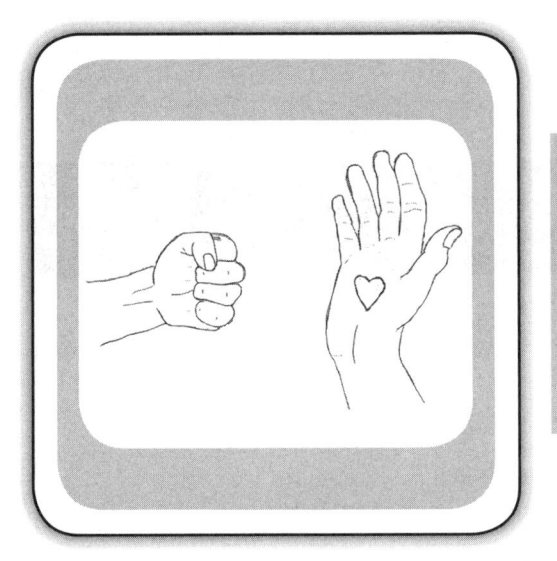

Chapter 9
Violence Prevention and Safety

Tragedy Strikes

Tragedies like those that took place in Sandy Hook Elementary School in Newtown, Connecticut (in 2013); Minnesota's Bemidigi High School (in 2005); and Colorado's Columbine High School (1999) have made us think twice about how safe our society is and what we can do to prevent such events from ever happening again. Each tragedy rekindles efforts to enact state or federal laws on gun-dealer licensing, gun registration, background checks, gun-purchase waiting periods, assault-weapons bans, and concealed carrying of guns. Proponents of these measures argue that new laws are needed to protect our children; opponents argue that none of the newly proposed laws would have saved lives in these tragedies. Mass shootings also promote national conversations about whether violence in entertainment has a significant role in inciting real-life acts of violence.

A Time/CNN poll conducted in January 2013 showed an even divide between survey respondents on issues related to gun ownership. Half of the national respondents said someone in their household owned a gun, and half said no one did. When asked who was to blame for gun violence ("What is the primary cause of gun violence in America?"), 37% said it was the way in which parents raised their children, 37% pointed to the influence of pop culture, and 23% identified the availability of guns as the key issue.

While the tragic and heroic stories from mass shootings can give the impression that our children are at great risk, it is encouraging to note that the odds of a student being killed at school are 1 in 3 million; children are three times more likely to be hit by lightning.

Source: *The next gun fight.* Time. February 28, 2013.

This chapter addresses the leading causes of death and disability for school-age youth. Injuries can be classified as either intentional (resulting from violence) or unintentional. Unintentional injuries are often called "accidents," even though many of the situations that cause injuries can be prevented. Motor vehicle crashes, drowning, poisoning, fires and burns, falls, sports- and recreation-related injuries, firearm-related injuries, choking, and suffocation are major causes of unintentional injuries. Types of violence include assault, sexual violence, rape, child maltreatment, dating and domestic violence, homicide, suicide, and self-inflicted injuries.

Injury-related causes account for approximately two thirds of all deaths among children and adolescents. The leading causes of injury deaths in school-age youth are motor vehicle crashes, homicide, and suicide. In fact, motor vehicle crashes are the leading cause of death throughout childhood and adolescence. Homicide, however, is the second leading cause of death among adolescents aged 15 to 19 years and the fourth leading cause of death among children aged 5 to 14 years. Suicide is rare among children ages 5 to 9 years, but is the third leading cause of death among adolescents aged 10 to 19 years. In addition to deaths, injuries—both intentional and unintentional—lead to enormous suffering in the lives and families of young people, such as pain, emergency room visits, hospitalizations, disability, fear, and other negative emotional consequences. Injuries also cause billions of dollars in medical costs.

> **9-1 Application Exercise**
>
> ## What Would You Do?
>
> The following are scenarios you will likely find yourself in. Consider what you would do in each situation. Read the chapter and check out Internet support resources for insights into how you can best handle each situation.
>
> 1. You overhear students talking about voting online for the school's ugliest girl.
> 2. A student confides that vicious rumors have been spread about him/her or another student.
> 3. You come upon some students intimidating another student.
> 4. One of your students comes to class with a black eye or other visible bruises and simply says, "I tripped."
> 5. You observe that students rarely if ever wear helmets while riding their bikes.

In this chapter, we look first at bullying and violence and then at injury-related issues. Violence and safety issues often require teachers to respond instantaneously. Quickly think of how you would respond to each of the scenarios in **Box 9-1**. As you continue reading the chapter, mentally rehearse how you could best handle each issue and possible related problems.

■ BULLYING*

Bullying is a widespread form of youth violence. For aggressive behavior to be termed bullying, it must entail (1) unwanted, aggressive behavior that involves (2) a real or perceived power imbalance and (3) is repeated, or has the potential to be repeated, over time. Children who bully use their power (e.g., physical strength, access to embarrassing information, or popularity) to control or harm others.

There are three types of bullying: verbal, social, and physical. Verbal bullying includes teasing, name-calling, inappropriate sexual comments, taunting, and threatening to cause harm. Social bullying involves hurting someone's reputation or relationships and includes leaving someone out on purpose or telling others not to be friends with someone, spreading rumors about someone, and embarrassing someone in public. Physical bullying includes hitting/kicking/pinching, spitting, tripping/pushing, taking or breaking someone's things, and making mean or rude hand gestures.

Bullying can occur during or after school hours. While most reported bullying happens in the school building, a significant percentage also happens in places like on the playground or the bus. It can also happen when students are traveling to or from school, in the youth's neighborhood, or on the Internet. National data indicate that 1 in 5 students experiences bullying.

There are many roles that children can play in a bullying situation, and it is important to understand these roles to effectively prevent and respond to bullying. When referring to a bullying situation, it is easy to call the children who bully others "bullies" and those who are targeted "victims," but such labeling may have unintended consequences. When children are labeled as "bullies" or "victims," it may send the message that the child's behavior cannot change, or fail to recognize the multiple roles children might play in different bullying situations. Labeling also

---

*Unless otherwise indicated, this section has been condensed and adapted from the stopbully.gov website provided by the U.S. Department of Education; Department of Health and Human Services, Centers for Disease Control and Prevention, Health Resources and Services Administration, Substance Abuse and Mental Health Services Administration, and Department of Justice. It is available at http://www.stopbullying.gov/what-is-bullying/roles-kids-play/index.html. Accessed February 14, 2013.

tends to disregard other factors contributing to the behavior, such as peer influence or school climate. Instead of labeling the children involved, focus on the behavior. For instance, you can refer to the parties involved as "the child who bullied" or "the child who was bullied."

Some researchers talk about the "circle of bullying" to define both those directly involved in bullying and those who actively or passively assist the behavior or defend against it. This "circle" may include children who assist or encourage the bullying behavior, children who reinforce the bullying by laughing or encouraging it, outsiders who watch without taking a side, and children who defend the child being bullied. Most children play more than one role in bullying over time.

Cyberbullying

Cyberbullying is bullying that takes place using electronic technology. Such technology includes devices and equipment such as cell phones, computers, and tablets as well as communication tools including social media sites, text messages, chat, and websites.

Examples of cyberbullying include mean text messages or e-mails, rumors sent by e-mail or posted on social networking sites, and embarrassing pictures, videos, websites, or fake profiles.

Children who are being cyberbullied are often bullied in person as well. Additionally, those who are cyberbullied have a harder time getting away from the behavior. Cyberbullying can happen 24 hours a day, 7 days a week, and reach a kid even when he or she is alone. Cyberbullying messages and images can be posted anonymously and distributed quickly. It can be difficult or sometimes impossible to trace the source. Deleting inappropriate or harassing messages, texts, and pictures is extremely difficult after they have been posted or sent.

Whether done in person or through technology, the effects of bullying are similar. Children who are cyberbullied are more likely to use alcohol and drugs, skip school, experience in-person bullying, be unwilling to attend school, receive poor grades, have lower self-esteem, and have more health problems.

Risk Factors

Depending on the environment, some groups—such as lesbian, gay, bisexual, or transgendered (LGBT) youth, youth with disabilities, and socially isolated youth—may be at increased risk of being bullied. Although there are no clear data indicating race, ethnicity, or national origin factors confer a higher risk, we do know that black and Hispanic youth who are bullied are more likely to suffer academically than their white peers. Generally, children who are bullied have one or more of the following risk factors:

◆ Are perceived as different from their peers
◆ Are perceived as weak or unable to defend themselves
◆ Are depressed, are anxious, or have low self-esteem
◆ Are less popular than others and have few friends
◆ Do not get along well with others or are seen as annoying

Nevertheless, even if a child has these risk factors, it does not automatically mean that the individual will be bullied.

Children who bully tend to fall into two categories. Some are well connected to their peers and like to dominate or be in charge of others. Others are more isolated and not able to identify with the emotions or feelings of others. Children with these characteristics are more likely to bully: aggressive/easily frustrated; home issues; think badly of others; difficulty with rules; view violence in positive way; have friends who bully others. Remember, those who bully do not need to be stronger or bigger than those they bully. The power imbalance can come from a number of sources—popularity, strength, cognitive ability—and children who bully may have more than one of these characteristics.

Effects and Warning Signs

Bullying is linked to many negative outcomes, including impacts on mental health, substance use, and suicide. Media reports often link bullying with suicide. However, most youth who are bullied do not have thoughts of suicide or engage in suicidal behaviors. Although children who are bullied are at risk of suicide, bullying alone is not the cause of such self-inflicted violence. Many issues contribute to suicide risk, including depression, problems at home, and trauma history. Additionally, certain groups have an increased risk of suicide, including American Indian and Alaskan Native, Asian American, lesbian, gay, bisexual, and transgender youth. This risk can be increased further when these children are not supported by parents, peers, and schools. Bullying can make an unsupportive situation worse.

Not all children who are bullied ask for help. Children may want to handle matters on their own to feel in control again. They may fear being seen as weak or a tattletale. Some may not want adults to know what is being said about them, whether true or false. They may also fear that adults will judge them or punish them for being weak. Children who are bullied may already feel socially isolated—as if no one cares or could understand. Signs that may point to a bullying problem include unexplained injuries, lost or destroyed items (e.g., clothing, books, electronics), suddenly skipping meals, difficulty sleeping or frequent nightmares, and avoidance of social situations. Signs that indicate a child may be bullying others include getting into fights, unexplained extra money or new belongings, blaming others for problems, not accepting responsibility for the child's own actions, and being overly competitive and worrying about the child's own reputation or popularity.

Responding to Bullying

When adults respond quickly and consistently to bullying behavior, they send the message that it is not acceptable. Research shows this action can stop bullying behavior over time. There are simple steps adults can take to stop bullying on the spot and keep children safe.

Do:

- Intervene immediately. It is okay to get another adult to help. Model respectful behavior.
- Separate the children involved. Make sure everyone is safe.
- Stay calm. Meet any immediate medical or mental health needs.
- Reassure the children involved, including bystanders.

Avoid these common mistakes:

- Don't ignore it. Don't think children can work it out without adult help.
- Don't immediately try to sort out the facts or make children apologize on the spot.
- Don't force other children to say publicly what they saw.
- Don't question the children involved in front of other students.
- Don't talk to the children involved together, only separately.

Get police help or medical attention immediately in the following circumstances:

- A weapon is involved.
- There are threats of serious physical injury.
- There are threats of hate-motivated violence, such as racism or homophobia.
- There is serious bodily harm.
- There is sexual abuse.
- Anyone is accused of an illegal act, such as robbery or extortion—using force to get money, property, or services.

Preventing Bullying

One highly effective bullying prevention program achieved reductions in bullying among elementary, middle, and junior high school students by instituting the following measures:[1]

- Determination of the nature and prevalence of the school's bullying problem by surveying students anonymously
- Increased supervision of students during breaks
- School-wide assemblies to discuss bullying
- Regular classroom meetings with students to discuss bullying
- Establishment and enforcement of classroom rules against bullying
- Staff intervention with students who bully, students who are bullied and their parents to ensure that the bullying stops

School staff and parents can help children know what bullying is and create open communication about it. They can tell children bullying is unacceptable and make sure they know how to get help. Most important, staff and teachers can model how to treat others with kindness and respect. When parents and teachers openly discuss bullying, students are more likely to turn to them if they have been bullied. Teachers and parents can:

- Encourage children to speak to a trusted adult if they are bullied or see others being bullied. The adult can give comfort, support, and advice, even if he or she cannot solve the problem directly. Encourage the child to report bullying if it happens.
- Talk about how to stand up to children who bully. Give tips, such as using humor and saying "stop" directly and confidently. Talk about what to do if those actions don't work, such as walking away.
- Talk about strategies for staying safe, such as staying near adults or groups of other children.
- Urge children to help other children who are bullied by showing kindness or getting help.
- Watch the short webisodes on bullying and discuss them with children.

The stopbullying.gov website contains many resources for educators to use to prevent bullying, including Recent Blogs, News Releases, a Video Gallery, Live Webcasts, and Policies and Laws.

VIOLENCE

Media reports often contain sobering details of school shootings, hazing, gang activities, suicide, and other examples of youth violence. Such violence leaves young people and their families struggling to cope with injury, disability, and death, and it leaves lasting scars on victims, perpetrators, and their families and friends. Youth violence is an ongoing, troubling problem afflicting every community, albeit some communities more than others. YRBS data reveal that black and Hispanic students, compared to whites, report higher rates of being threatened or injured with a weapon on school property, of getting into physical fights, and of not going to school because they didn't feel safe.[1]

Youth violence includes aggressive behaviors such as verbal abuse, bullying, hitting, slapping, and fist fighting. These behaviors have significant consequences and can leave emotional scars, but do not generally result in serious physical injury or death. Youth violence also includes serious violent and delinquent acts committed by and against youth, such as aggravated assault, robbery, rape, and homicide.

Several factors must be considered to understand why children and adolescents exhibit violent behavior. Awareness of these factors enables educators and parents to develop and implement strategies to reduce and prevent violent behavior. This section reviews the following contributing factors: family, media, substance use, access to weapons, personal and peer characteristics, and gang involvement.

Family Factors

Violence is often a learned response to conflict and frustration, which explains why violent children often come from violent families. Within these families, violence is modeled by parents and other family members as a problem-solving strategy. As a consequence, children have ample opportunities to observe parents attempt to resolve conflict by violent means. Through this modeling of violent behavior, children learn to solve their personal conflicts and stress by violent means.

Lack of appropriate parenting is also often an important factor in the development of violent behavior. A lack of parental monitoring and discipline, poor supervision, inconsistent rule application, and aversive interactions are likely to be present within parent–child interactions of families of children exhibiting violent behavior. Family rejection also increases the likelihood of long-term violent behavior. Conversely, good parental and family relationships are associated with reduced risk of adolescent violent behavior.

Exposure to Media Violence

A large proportion of the media to which children and adolescents are exposed includes acts of violence. It is estimated that by the age of 18, the average young person will have viewed 200,000 acts of violence on television alone. Many television programs contain interpersonal violence—and much of this violence is portrayed in an entertaining or glamorized manner with little to no depiction of realistic pain or harm. The suffering, loss, and sadness of victims and perpetrators are rarely shown.

American films are the most violent in the world. It is not uncommon for a young person viewing a major motion film to see numerous people shot, stabbed, crushed, punched, slapped, raped, maimed, or blown up during the course of the movie. Even children's shows often depict violence. In fact, the level of violence during Saturday-morning cartoons is higher than the level of violence during the prime-time viewing hours. Much of the music that young people listen to contains lyrics with violent messages on themes such as suicide, sexual violence, murder, Satanism, and substance abuse. Music videos often contain violence, sexism, suicide, and substance abuse.

Violent video games may pose greater risks than passively watching violence on television or in a move. Game players are more likely to identify with violent characters that respond to their directions. This identification increases a player's ability to learn and retain the aggressive thoughts and behaviors portrayed in the game. Research suggests that exposure to violent video games increases angry and hostile feelings in players and decreases compassionate feelings for others with whom they interact.[2] Unfortunately, restrictive age and violent-content labels seem to increase the attractiveness of video games for both boys and girls.[3]

Influence of Media Violence

What is portrayed on television appears to be shaping behavioral patterns with respect to violence. Television often teaches children that violence is an acceptable response to anger or frustration. Few researchers now bother to debate the contention that bloodshed on TV and in the movies has an effect on children who witness it.[4] According to the American Academy of Pediatrics (AAP), more than 3,500 research studies have examined the relationship between

Bullying is a widespread form of youth violence.

media violence and violent behavior; all but 18 have shown a positive relationship.[5] The strongest single correlate with violent behavior is previous exposure to violence. As a result, healthcare professionals are increasingly recognizing that exposure to media violence can cause violent behavior to occur.

The AAP alerts parents and those who work with children that media violence affects children in the following ways:[6]

- Increasing their aggressiveness and antisocial behavior
- Increasing their fear of becoming victims
- Making them less sensitive to violence and to victims of violence
- Increasing their appetite for more violence in entertainment and in real life

According to the AAP, media violence is associated with a variety of physical and mental health problems for children and adolescents, including aggressive behavior, desensitization to violence, fear, depression, nightmares, and sleep disturbances. Children and adolescents may mirror conflict resolution techniques they see on television and in movies. Viewing aggressive acts on television tends to increase aggressive behavior among children, particularly among those children most inclined to aggression initially. In particular, a strong relationship exists between heavy television viewing and aggression during the preschool years. Children whose parents use physical punishment are more likely to be aggressive themselves or to become more aggressive after exposure to television violence. Children younger than 8 years cannot discriminate between fantasy and reality. As such, they are particularly vulnerable to adopting as reality the values and attitudes that are portrayed in the media they watch.

Substance Use and Abuse

Alcohol and drug use increase the potential for violent behavior and victimization by reducing behavioral inhibitions and facilitating aggressive responses. Alcohol and other drugs can make people feel more aggressive and powerful, yet less able to control themselves and less aware of the consequences of their actions. Abuse of alcohol and other drugs is strongly associated with suicide, assault, child abuse, rapes, manslaughter, and murder (see the *Promoting a Tobacco-Free and Drug-Free Lifestyle* chapter).

Immediate Access to Weapons

The immediate accessibility of a weapon is another critical factor that increases the potential for violent behavior affecting both the weapon carrier and others. The proliferation of guns and the relative ease with which young people can acquire them appear to be some of the most potent factors accounting for episodes of lethal youth violence.

Weapon-carrying behavior for some youths may be a defensive strategy in response to the profound fear of being a victim of a violent act. However, research has shown that weapon carrying among youths appears to be more closely associated with criminal activity, delinquency, and aggressiveness than with purely defensive behavior. Handgun ownership by high school youth is associated with gang membership, sale and use of drugs, interpersonal violence, being convicted of crimes, school truancy, and either suspension or expulsion from school. Gun carrying among junior high students is also strongly linked with indicators of serious delinquency, such as having been arrested.[7,8] Having access to weapons is linked to suicide as well, and suicide attempts made with guns are much more lethal than attempts made with other methods. The *Dealing with Crises and Critical Issues* chapter addresses suicide and self-harm in depth.

Personal and Peer Characteristics

Young people who behave violently and aggressively often engage in other high-risk behaviors (e.g., alcohol abuse, illicit drug use, sexual promiscuity). Thus youths who display violent behavior also share the following characteristics with youths engaging in other high-risk behaviors, early initiation of delinquent behavior, lack of parental support and guidance, school failure, and inability to resist peer influences.

Violent children and adolescents often seem not to fit in with their "mainstream" peers. They may feel rejected or isolated as a result of their displays of aggressive behavior, or they may have become aggressive in response to feeling left out or different. These feelings may be compounded by difficulties in learning. Early academic skill deficits and difficulty cause school failure and frustration. As a consequence, those experiencing this frustration do not "bond" to the school culture. Instead, they are more apt to bond with peers who are likewise experiencing school failure and who do not fit in with their mainstream peers. Attachment to these peers often reinforces participation in violent behaviors and increases the likelihood of alienation from prosocial peers and institutions (e.g., school, church, youth groups). These factors also heighten the likelihood of gang involvement.

Gang Involvement

The term "gang" can refer to any group of young people who engage in activities ranging from troublesome to criminal. Consider which groups may be present in the school where you teach.[9]

- ◆ *Troublesome youth groups*: young people who hang out together at places such as malls and may be involved in minor forms of delinquency.
- ◆ *Delinquent groups*: a small number of friends who commit delinquent acts such as vandalism or burglaries.
- ◆ *Subculture youth groups*: groups such as "goths," "straight edgers," and "anarchists," which are not gangs but rather share special interests.

- *Taggers*: graffiti vandals. They are often called gang members but typically engage only in graffiti contests.
- *School-based gangs*: groups of young people who may function as a gang only at school.
- *Street-based gangs*: semistructured groups of adolescents and young adults who engage in delinquent and criminal behavior.
- *Drug gangs*: groups loosely organized for drug-trafficking operations. They are generally led by young and older adults but sometimes include adolescents.
- *Adult criminal organizations*: small groups of adults who engage in lucrative criminal activity primarily for economic reasons.

Young people are attracted to gangs for many reasons, but primarily because the gangs fill needs that are not otherwise being met. Gangs become an extended family of sorts or even a surrogate family, where the banding together provides a sense of security. The gang also provides some youths with a sense of identity, belonging, power, and protection. Thus young people lacking a sense of security are vulnerable to gang involvement. Among those feeling powerless and lacking control, gang activities become an outlet for their anger.

Large cities have historically had problems with juvenile gangs, but now their appearance in smaller cities and communities is a growing concern. The emergence of gangs in smaller populations is the result of several factors, including the injection of newly arrived racial or ethnic groups into the community. Immigrant youth often experience difficulty merging with the dominant youth group. They may feel different or ostracized, may have language barriers, and may feel alienation toward their parents' "old ways." In the face of these pressures, they may band together in groups to create a social group where they are understood and where they can maintain a strong ethnic identity. This does not mean, however, that all immigrant youth groups or other bands of youths are gangs.

It is reassuring to note that in smaller communities, in most cases, a gang problem is short-lived, dissipating as quickly as it develops. Small towns and rural areas simply do not have a large enough population base to sustain a gang as members are arrested or drop out. In cities with typically longer-standing gang problems, approximately half of the youth who join a gang leave it within a year.[10] The following community conditions often precede the transition of typical youth groups into established gangs:

- Families or schools, or both, being ineffective and alienating
- Adolescents having a great deal of free time not consumed by other healthy activities
- Limited access to appealing career lines
- Having a place to congregate, such as a well-defined neighborhood

Violence and Learning Potential

Violence can adversely interfere with a child's development and learning potential. When children constantly confront the threat of violence, they must learn to protect themselves by setting up defenses against their fears. These defenses take considerable emotional energy to maintain, robbing from the energy needed for other developmental tasks, including learning in school.

The presence of violence in the home is often associated with feelings of guilt and responsibility by children and consequent feelings of being bad or worthless. These feelings are not compatible with a child's potential for learning and commonly result in the feeling that one is incapable of learning. This, in turn, contributes to a lack of motivation to achieve in school.

Children who face the threat of violence, or who have suffered trauma from violence, have difficulty seeing themselves in meaningful future roles. Children who cannot perceive a positive and secure future for themselves are unable to give serious attention and energy to the tasks of learning and socialization. The unpredictability of violence contributes to a sense of little or no control over one's life. Such a sense of helplessness interferes with the development of autonomy, which is essential for healthy growth and maturation.

■ VIOLENCE-FREE SCHOOL ENVIRONMENT

Safety and violence prevention begins by making sure the school campus is a safe and caring place. Compared to home and other settings, school is one of the safest places where young people spend their time. Unfortunately, the tragic episodes of violence that have occurred on school campuses across the nation highlight the point that no school and community can afford to be complacent about making and keeping schools safe.

School Security Measures

Schools must ensure that weapons are not carried onto school premises and that students remain safe at school. In recent years, far too many violent episodes involving weapons on school campuses have led to tragedy. Providing a safe and violence-free school requires school districts to consider such provisions and controls as locker searches, security guards or police who patrol school premises, and possibly metal detectors through which students must pass before entry into the school. Some schools have eliminated lockers altogether. Some schools employ uniformed security guards or install hallway cameras to monitor students. Some school systems have created separate alternative schools for young people with a history of violent and abusive behavior.

School Gun Laws

In nearly every state, possession of a firearm on school property is a felony. Schools have the right to file criminal charges in such a case, and every school district must automatically expel any student caught with any type of weapon on school property under the Gun-Free Schools Act of 1994. The automatic expulsion can be appealed on a case-by case basis, and special education students have some protection from the automatic expulsion rule. Some states—for example, Kansas and Florida—also have laws that allow for students' driver's licenses to be revoked if they are found guilty of possessing a gun or drugs on school property.

A Safe Physical Environment

The physical condition of the school building has an impact on student attitude, behavior, and motivation to achieve. Typically, there tend to be more incidents of fighting and violence in school buildings that are dirty, too cold or too hot, filled with graffiti, in need of repair, or unsanitary. To ensure a safe physical environment, regular safety and hazard assessments need to be made. Structures, equipment, and grounds need to be maintained. All student activities need to be actively supervised.

A Safe Social Environment

The social climate of a school can promote safety and prevent unintentional injury, violence, and suicide. To ensure a safe social climate, school personnel need to establish a supportive environment that does not tolerate any type of harassment or bullying. They can create a culture of empathy and harmony by helping students understand how ineffective teeter-tottering is and by facilitating hydraulic-lift activities. High academic standards need to be maintained and students' connectedness to school needs be encouraged. School personnel must develop, implement, and enforce written policies including disciplinary policies. School programs and policies need to be assessed at regular intervals.

Discipline and Dress Codes

School officials may consider discipline and dress codes as strategies to curb violence. For instance, some schools have banned students from wearing gang-claimed colors or clothing typically worn by gangs. Administrators, teachers, parents, and students must craft these codes collaboratively, and the district's legal staff must review them so that they are in accordance with state law. An effective discipline and dress code clearly explains to students which behavior is acceptable and what will happen to students who break the rules. Discipline and dress codes must be firmly, fairly, and consistently implemented and enforced. Every student, parent, and teacher must be given a copy of a discipline or dress code.

Warning Signs of Violence

Schools should take special care in training all school personnel to understand and identify **early warning signs** of violence that may indicate a child needs help or the child is prone to violence toward self or others. When early warning signs are observed, teachers should be concerned, but should not overreact and jump to conclusions. In no way should early warning signs be used to exclude, isolate, or punish a child, nor should children be inappropriately labeled or stigmatized because they exhibit a set of early warning indicators.

When educators observe early warning signs, their first and foremost responsibility should be to get timely help for a child. They should immediately speak to available professionals such as school psychologists, social workers, counselors, and nurses. Referrals to outside agencies or professionals may be necessary. School administrators can help facilitate this process. Educators must keep in mind that all referrals to outside agencies based on early warning signs must be kept confidential and made with parental consent (except for referrals for suspected child abuse or neglect).

Educators can increase their ability to recognize early warning signs by establishing close, caring, and supportive relationships with students. This requires getting to know students well enough to be aware of their needs, feelings, attitudes, and behavior patterns.

In contrast to early warning signs, **imminent warning signs** indicate that a student is very close to behaving in a way that is potentially dangerous to self and/or others. Imminent warning signs require an immediate response. No single warning sign can predict that a dangerous act will occur; rather, imminent warning signs usually comprise a sequence of overt, serious, hostile behaviors or threats directed at peers, staff, or other individuals. Usually imminent warning signs are evident to more than one staff member, as well as to the child's family. Imminent warning signs may include the following:

- Serious physical fighting with peers or family members
- Severe destruction of property
- Severe rage for seemingly minor reasons
- Detailed threats of lethal violence
- Possession or use of firearms and other weapons
- Other self-injurious behaviors or threats of suicide

When warning signs indicate that danger is imminent, safety must always be the first and foremost consideration. Action must be taken immediately. Immediate intervention by school authorities and possibly law enforcement officers is needed whenever a child exhibits the following behaviors:

◆ Presents a detailed plan (time, place, method) to harm or kill others, particularly if the child has a history of aggression or has attempted to carry out threats in the past
◆ Carries a weapon, particularly a firearm, and threatens to use it

In situations where students present other threatening behaviors, parents should be informed of the concerns immediately. Schools also have the responsibility to seek assistance from appropriate agencies such as child and family services and community mental health. These responses should reflect school board policies.

Effective Violence Prevention Programs

The most highly effective violence prevention programs combine components that address both individual risks and environmental conditions, particularly building individual skills and competencies, parent effectiveness training, improvements in the social climate of the school, and changes in type and level of involvement with peer groups. In schools, interventions that target change in the social context appear to be more effective on average than those that attempt to change individual attitudes, skills, and risk behaviors. Involvement with delinquent peers and gang membership are two of the most powerful predictors of violence.

Another factor relating to effectiveness is the quality of program implementation. Many programs are ineffective not because their strategy is misguided, but because the quality of implementation is poor.

Violence Prevention Curriculum

In addition to health classes, schools can infuse violence prevention content into various disciplines, including family and consumer education, social studies, and English. Schools can work with communities to increase the availability of early childhood education for those at increased risk. Early childhood education for children at risk has been demonstrated to decrease unintentional injury, violence and delinquency, and educational difficulties.

Educational programs should be appropriate to the culture of the community in which they are located. Educators can consider issues of social class, race, ethnicity, language, sexual orientation, and physical ability when choosing and implementing prevention strategies. In addition, educational efforts might need to be tailored for students with special needs. Activities that promote tolerance and respect for differences are critical. Involving students in developing and implementing programs can help ensure their relevance. Obtaining input from student members of various cultural groups is essential. Educational activities can help students understand social influences on health- and safety-related behaviors and how to resist cultural, media, and peer pressure to make unsafe choices.

Violence prevention curricula need to focus on building skills identified in the National Health Education Standards. The Health Education Curriculum Analysis Tool (HECAT) health behavior outcomes (HBOs) for K–12 violence prevention curricula are identified in **Box 9-2**. These behaviors are best taught through approaches that incorporate modeling, role-playing, performance feedback, and adequate time for practicing the skills. The HECAT Module V (violence prevention) can be accessed online. Within this module, you will find grade-level lists of core concepts that need to be taught as well as multiple examples of how to teach the national standard skills. After reviewing the HBOs and Module V, you will be prepared to proceed with planning to teach a violence prevention unit. Follow the outline presented in Box 9-2. Teaching activities for violence prevention skills are found in **Box 9-3**.

9-2 Internet Support

Violence Prevention Resources

The following are health behavior outcomes (HBOs) recommended by HECAT for K–12 violence prevention curriculum. After reviewing these recommendations, check out the HECAT Module V (violence prevention) available online. In this module, you will find recommendations for all the content and skills to be taught at various grade levels.

HBOs:

- Engage in positive, helpful behaviors.
- Manage interpersonal conflict in nonviolent ways.
- Manage emotional distress in nonviolent ways.
- Avoid bullying, being a bystander to bullying, or being a victim of bullying.
- Avoid engaging in violence, including coercion, exploitation, physical fighting, and rape.
- Avoid situations where violence is likely to occur.
- Avoid associating with others who are involved in or who encourage violence or criminal activity.
- Get help to prevent or stop violence including harassment, abuse, bullying, hazing, fighting, and hate crimes.
- Get help to address inappropriate touching.
- Get help to stop being subjected to violence or physical abuse.
- Get help for self or others who are in danger of hurting themselves.

After reviewing the HBOs and HECAT Module V, try to ascertain the specific violence prevention needs in your community. You can do so by finding local/state data on the Internet (e.g., CDC's YRBS data) and by interviewing school staff or students. Find out if your state has guidelines for violence prevention education and if a scope and sequence or curricula exist for your school district. Continue your instruction planning by using the guidelines provided in the Teaching Today's Students chapter and the worksheets at the end of this chapter.

These Internet sites contain teaching resources and lesson plans for violence prevention:

- Stop Bullying Now
- Youth Violence Prevention Resource Center
- National Youth Gang Center

CHILD ABUSE

Child abuse affects children of all ages, races, and income levels. Most state laws recognize four major types of child abuse: physical abuse, neglect, emotional abuse, and sexual abuse. Although any form of child abuse may be found separately, they often occur in combination. The following discussion provides definitions and descriptions of the major types of child abuse.

Physical abuse is the infliction of a nonaccidental physical injury upon a child. This may include burning, hitting, punching, shaking, kicking, beating, or otherwise harming a child. It may also be the result of overdiscipline or physical punishment that is inappropriate to the child's age.

Neglect is the failure to provide for a child's basic needs. Neglect can be physical, educational, or emotional. *Physical neglect* can include not providing adequate food or clothing, appropriate medical care, supervision, or proper weather protection (e.g., hat or coat). *Educational neglect* is failure to provide appropriate schooling or special educational needs or allowing excessive truancies. *Psychological neglect* includes not providing emotional support and love, chronic inattention to the child, exposure to spouse abuse, or drug and alcohol abuse.

Emotional abuse, also referred to as *emotional maltreatment*, is a pattern of behavior that impairs a child's emotional development or sense of self-worth. It may include constant criticism, threats, or rejection, as well as withholding love, support, or guidance. Emotional abuse is often difficult to prove without evidence of harm to the child. Such abuse is almost always present when other forms of child abuse are identified.

Sexual abuse is inappropriate adolescent or adult sexual behavior with a child. It includes fondling a child's genitals, making the child fondle the adult's genitals, intercourse, incest, rape, sodomy, exhibitionism, sexual exploitation, or exposure to pornography. To be considered child abuse, these acts must be committed by a person responsible for the care of a child (e.g., baby-sitter, parent, day-care provider) or related to the child. If a stranger commits these acts, the matter would be considered **sexual assault** and handled solely by the police and criminal courts.

Reported cases of child sexual abuse represent only the tip of the sexual abuse iceberg. Because sexual abuse is largely a secretive act, most occurrences go unreported. Also, offenders are likely to force, bribe, coerce, threaten, or deceive child victims to prevent them from telling. As a result, it is difficult to determine with certainty the number of children who are sexually abused, and estimates of its incidence vary widely.

Although some child sexual abuse involves sexual intercourse, most cases of child sexual abuse do not. Child sexual abuse can take the form of genital handling, oral–genital contact, sexual abuse of the breasts or anus, or requiring a child to undress and/or look at the genitals of adults. Sexual abuse typically involves less force than adult rape. Children often comply with the wishes of their abusers because of their smallness of physical stature, their innocence, and the persuasive powers of abusers. Sexual contact between relatives is **incest**, often a part of sexual abuse.

In many cases, child sexual abuse is not limited to a single episode. Many children are repeatedly abused and victimized over periods of months or even years. Sexual offenders against children often have abused many children before they are discovered. Those who abuse children are most frequently individuals with whom the child is familiar or acquainted. Often the abuser is a parent or other family relative, neighbor, family friend, baby-sitter, or day-care worker. Child sexual abuse is more likely to occur in the home of the child victim than in any other place. Although only a small percentage of sexual abuse cases involve strangers to the child, most child sexual abuse prevention programs focus on "stranger dangers." Consequently, few children learn about the possibility of abuse by a relative or friend.

Individuals who abuse children very often had been abused themselves as children. Thus there is a vicious cycle in which the abused grow up to be abusers. Interestingly, boys who are abused are far more likely to turn into eventual offenders, and girls are more likely to produce children who are abused by others (possibly because they tend to associate with males who are abusive). More prevention efforts should be directed toward helping abused children not become abusers.

Recognizing Abuse

Children and adolescents may not tell supportive adults that they have been or currently are a victim of abuse for many reasons. Some common reasons include that they are afraid of the offender, they are worried that they will not be believed, they are afraid of what people will think of them, and they are concerned what will happen (or will not happen) if they tell.

Teachers need to be sensitive to possible signs of abuse. Physical indicators of abuse include evidence of physical trauma, complaints of pain or itching in the groin, and torn or stained clothing. Some family indicators for abuse include extreme paternal dominance, family isolation, role reversal between child and parent, parental or sibling substance abuse, and history of domestic violence. Behavioral indicators of abuse include wearing many layers of clothing, regardless of the weather; reluctance to go home and/or constant early arrival at school; use of alcohol and/or other drugs; lack of affect; extreme absence of expressiveness; and continual avoidance of physical education activities or the bathroom. A student who engages in any one of these behaviors should signal to a teacher that something is amiss, that the student needs help, whether or not abuse is involved. Teachers also need to know that children with the following characteristics are more vulnerable to victimization: are poorly supervised, are cared for by someone with a substance abuse problem, have a low sense of self-worth, and are hungry for attention.

Handling Disclosure

Responding to a student's disclosure of abuse presents a difficult and delicate situation for a teacher or school professional. The following guidelines can assist teachers in properly handling the disclosure.

Do:

- Believe the student.
- Find a private place to talk.
- Reassure the student that he or she has done the right thing by reporting.
- Listen to the student.
- Tell the student help is available.
- Let the student know you must report to someone who can help him or her.
- Report the incident immediately to appropriate persons or agencies.
- Seek out your own support system.

Don't:

- Promise confidentiality.
- Panic or express shock.
- Ask leading or suggestive questions.
- Make negative comments about the perpetrator.
- Disclose information indiscriminately.

In addition, educators must reassure the student that he or she is not at fault and should not take the blame for the abuse. They must determine the student's immediate need for safety and ensure that the student will be protected and supported. It is also important for teachers to discuss with the student what will happen when the report is made.

Reporting Abuse

Teachers and school administrators are required by law to report suspected abuse to the appropriate child protective agencies. Teachers who report their suspicions of child abuse only to a school administrator or counselor are not meeting the full requirements of the law. Because mandatory reporting statutes vary from state to state, it is imperative that you become familiar with the specifics of the law within the state where you teach. Information about state child abuse laws is available from the school district superintendent's offices or from the state attorney general's offices. Teachers reporting suspected child abuse without malice are generally immune from prosecution for any civil or criminal damages that may result from the report.

Preventing Child Abuse

Recognizing and reporting child maltreatment is important to prevent abuse and neglect from continuing or recurring.* Schools also must be involved in working to prevent maltreatment from ever occurring at all. A school's involvement in prevention can be divided into school-based programs, school–community programs, and individual action on the part of educators.

---

* This section has been condensed and adapted from Crosson-Tower C. Preventing child abuse and neglect. In: *The role of educators in preventing and responding to child abuse and neglect.* Fairfax, VA: Caliber Associates; 2003: Chapter 6. Available at www.childwelfare.gov/pubs/usermanuals/educator/educatorg.cfm. Accessed February 13, 2013.

School-Based Programs

Some child abuse prevention efforts consist of specifically designed programs, whereas existing school curricula integrate other efforts. Some of the more common areas that prevention activities address or strengthen are the following:

- *Life skills training.* These skills include conflict management, peer mediation, communication, problem-solving skills, and parenting.
- *Socialization skills.* Children and adolescents need to learn at least four socialization skills to grow into happy, successful adults:
    - How to get their needs met appropriately. Often, maltreated children are not able to express their needs and ask for help.
    - How to express feelings, which enables children to separate these feelings from actions. For example, children must learn that it is acceptable to feel anger toward someone, but it is not appropriate to hit another person.
    - How to take responsibility for their actions.
    - How to make decisions and solve problems.
- *Problem-solving and coping skills.* The *Life Skills* and *Dealing with Stress* chapters address these skills and give suggestions for how to teach them to students.
- *Preparation for parenthood.* To help stop the intergenerational cycle of violence and prevent new cycles of child abuse, many schools have curricula on learning how to parent adequately. To do so, students must be armed with knowledge in three areas: reproductive processes, child development, and parenting skills. Students who are trained to understand what children do at specific ages may be better able to cope as parents. Numerous lessons and exercises exist that teach what is expected of new parents, as well as the social, financial, physical, and psychological implications of sexual activity and potential parenthood.
- *Self-protection training.* This usually includes educating children about what sexual abuse is (e.g., distinguishing among "good," "bad," and "confusing" touches), making children aware of potential abusers, and teaching children what to do when they are abused or feel that they are vulnerable to abuse. Some programs bring in experts to educate the children, whereas others train teachers to conduct the training seminar or to integrate the information into their curriculum. Opinions on such programs vary, with some sources maintaining that they make children feel responsible for their own protection and cause them to feel guilty if they are molested. Programs with a minimum of four sessions have been shown to be the most effective, and active, long-term programs have the greatest impact on children.
- *School-based programs for families.* These programs can offer support for at-risk families and support for adolescent parents and their children. After-school care for children and after-school recreation programs for adolescents are a great help for working parents or parents who need relief from child-care responsibilities. At-risk adolescents often have more problems with their parents, and schools can make efforts to alleviate some stress that mounts between parents and teens.
- *Support for adolescent parents and their children.* Some schools have programs designed for adolescent parents that focus on specific activities and skills to help them stay in school and strengthen their family life. Some schools provide special programs such as child care for the children of adolescent students, whereas others assign special teachers and counselors to monitor and support the students. Some schools also offer these teens training in parenting, birth control, budgeting, child development, and time management.

School–Community Programs

Cooperative efforts between schools and the community can be an effective means of preventing child maltreatment. Training and staff development programs for those who work with children should stress identifying, reporting, treating, and preventing child maltreatment; furnish information on professional roles and responsibilities; and offer opportunities for free and frank discussion of mutual interests and problems among professionals in various disciplines. Schools can participate in public awareness programs through parent–teacher groups and other school–community organizations. They can offer their facilities, such as auditoriums or conference rooms, for use by self-help groups, such as Parents Anonymous or Circle of Parents, or for school-sponsored public forums and workshops on child abuse and neglect prevention. Schools can also offer joint school–community adult education programs on such topics as alternative disciplinary methods and early childhood growth and development. School buildings can be made available for day-care, crisis-care, and after-school programs operated by social service agencies. School staff can serve as consultants, leaders, and facilitators of these programs, and school newsletters can be used to announce them. In addition, school-owned films and books can be lent to other agencies and organizations for training programs and meetings.

Individual Action

Although the school as a whole is important in preventing child maltreatment, it is the individual who is often in a position to carry out these efforts. As mentioned previously, reporting suspected child maltreatment is necessary to prevent it from continuing. The attitude of the reporter can affect the progress the family is able to make once the report is filed. The educator who recognizes the strengths of both children and their parents and is supportive and available to the family throughout the investigation, treatment, and rehabilitation process helps the family maintain its dignity and protects the child.

Educators must consider how their actions will affect family functioning. For example, if behavior management is a point of contention between the parents and their child, a terse note from the school about the child misbehaving in class may increase the child's risk of maltreatment. In such a case, it may be better to meet with the parents to decide together which techniques of behavior management should be used.

If grades are an issue, a parent–teacher conference to discuss academic performance may be a better choice than sending home a report card with a failing grade. Whenever possible, the educator should stress the child's positive performance while suggesting ways to improve any negative aspects. Reiterating the child's faults may reinforce the child's negative self-image and further the parent's view of the child as a disappointment. In contrast, emphasizing the child's assets will increase the child's self-confidence and indicate to the parent that the child is worthwhile, capable, and someone of whom to be proud.

The positive influence of an educator on the life of a child can be significant. As one survivor of an abusive home commented:

> I don't think my fourth-grade teacher, Mr. Evans, had any idea what an impact he had on my life. He was my father's opposite and taught me much about how men could be. He was consistent and concerned while my father was drunk or ignored me. He praised me while my father criticized. He prized my mind and my accomplishments; my father cared only about abusing my body. I learned a great deal from that teacher about who I was and that I was an important person. I think I became a teacher myself to be like him, so that I could make a difference for some other child.

Many survivors of child abuse name an educator who made a real difference in their lives by showing that he or she cared.

The actions of these vital educators helped prevent survivors of abusive homes from repeating the negative behaviors from their childhoods. Every educator has the opportunity to make a difference for an abused or neglected child. It is a challenge worth meeting.

SEXUAL VIOLENCE

Sexual violence is any sexual act that is perpetrated against someone's will. It includes rape, abusive touching, harassment, voyeurism, exhibitionism, and unwanted exposure to pornography. **Rape** is the act of forcing or coercing someone to have sexual relations against her or his will. Rapes that occur to victims younger than the age of consent are considered **statutory rape**, whether or not force is involved. **Acquaintance rape** involves individuals who know each other casually prior to the rape, including coworkers, neighbors, and friends. **Date rape** occurs between two people who are spending time together with the possibility of building a closer relationship. **Marital rape** occurs between spouses. **Stranger rape** occurs between a victim and an offender who had no prior relationship.

Many myths and erroneous perceptions associated with rape persist. These include the following:

- Victims "ask for" rape by their clothing, behavior, or actions.
- Males cannot be raped.
- Old or unattractive women do not get raped.
- Any victim can resist a rapist if she or he really tries.
- Rapists are mentally ill or sexually perverted.
- Victims secretly want to be raped.
- Rapes almost always occur in dark alleys or deserted places.

No one is immune to rape. Rape can happen to anyone regardless of age, social class, educational level, occupation, or race. The most common age range of rape victims is 13 to 19 years, with 14 and 15 years being the most frequent ages at which this crime occurs. This finding underscores the importance of rape prevention activities within the secondary schools.

Date Rape

Unfortunately, it is not uncommon for females in our society to have an experience in which a male dating partner forces sex against their will. The aftermath of date rape can be devastating. Victims may experience any or all of the following:

- Anxiety
- Sleeplessness/nightmares and flashbacks
- Guilt and feelings of responsibility
- Lowered sense of self-worth and power
- Questioning of personal judgment
- Feelings of shame/sense of humiliation
- Altered attitude toward sex
- Other physical or verbal battering

To help prevent date rape, secondary curricula should teach students to be cautious of the inappropriate dating behaviors or characteristics of dating partners, such as demonstrating a lack of respect or jealousy, insensitivity for the partner's feelings or wishes, attempts to manipulate the partner to engage in sex, physical roughness, or abuse while drinking.

Intimate-Partner Violence

Intimate-partner violence is a serious, preventable public health problem that affects millions of Americans. **Intimate-partner violence** comprises physical, sexual, or psychological harm by a current or former partner or spouse; it also includes threats of physical or sexual violence and stalking. This type of violence can occur among heterosexual or same-sex couples and does not require sexual intimacy. **Teen dating violence** is a form of intimate-partner violence. It can occur in person or electronically, and may occur between current or former dating partners.

Recently, efforts to prevent teen dating violence have expanded, such that many states and communities are now working to stop this type of violence. To help these efforts, the CDC has developed *Dating Matters*, a comprehensive teen dating violence prevention initiative based on the current evidence about what works in prevention.[11] The CDC was prompted to create this prevention initiative because of data showing almost 10% of high school students said they had been hit, slapped, or physically hurt on purpose by their boyfriend or girlfriend.[12]

■ SAFETY

Young people face many safety concerns. Unintentional injuries come from what are often called "accidents," even though many situations that cause injuries can be prevented. Motor vehicle crashes, poisoning, drowning, fires, and falls are major causes of death and unintentional injuries. This section reviews data that help put in perspective the various risks.* As you consider these facts, think about what you can do as a teacher to limit your students' risks for unintentional injury.

Traffic-Related Injuries

Motor vehicle injuries are the United States' top safety concern. In fact, vehicle injuries are the greatest public health problem facing children today. Among children and adolescents, 70% of unintentional injuries and deaths are the result of motor vehicle crashes. That rate translates into, on average, 4 children dying and 500 others being injured each day. Alcohol plays a large role in this devastation. Approximately 25% of motor vehicle crashes involve drinking drivers, and more than half of these incidents occur while a child is riding with a drinking driver. In any month, 30% of high school students will ride with a driver who has been drinking.[12] Cell phone use (particularly texting while driving) and driving while drowsy are other major traffic safety concerns.

Wearing seat belts and using booster seats saves lives. Restraint use among young children often depends on the driver's seat belt use, however: children are much less likely to wear a seat belt or be properly restrained in car seats when they ride with drivers who are themselves unbelted.

Traffic-related injuries also include those injuries sustained while walking and while riding a bicycle. Each year, more than 700 children die from injuries sustained while walking, most often while walking in traffic.[13] The most serious bicycle-related injuries are head injuries. Wearing a bicycle helmet is as important as wearing a seat belt, yet high school–age youths rarely or never wear bike helmets. Younger children tend to be more compliant. Approximately 30% of motor vehicle–related deaths involve bicyclists.

Home-Based Injuries

Poisoning is the second leading cause of unintentional injury–related death in the home. Each year, approximately 2.4 million people—more than half younger than age 6—swallow or have contact with a poisonous substance. Children are involved in 75% of all poison control center

---

*Statistics in this section come from the Centers for Disease Control and Prevention/YRBS and Injury, Violence, and Safety websites unless otherwise indicated.

cases. The American Association of Poison Control Centers (AAPCC) estimates that 70% of accidental poisonings are preventable. Generally, poisonings in the home break down as follows: kitchen (41%), bathroom (21%), bedroom (12%), and all other places (26%).

Fire is another leading cause of unintentional injury deaths among children and adolescents. Fire kills more Americans than all natural disasters combined, and more than three fourths of all civilian fire deaths occur in homes.

Outdoor Injuries

Drowning is the third leading cause of injury death for children aged 5 to 14. On average, 15 people drown each day from swimming or boating-related incidents. More than one in four fatal drowning victims are children 14 years or younger. For every child who dies from drowning, another four receive emergency department care and survive but might suffer brain damage. Fatal drownings are more prevalent in some racial/ethnic populations. The fatal drowning rate of African American children is three times that of white children, and it is two times higher in American Indian/Alaskan Native children than in white children.

Outdoor sports are also involved in injury and death. More than 1 million serious sports-related injuries occur each year to adolescents aged 10 to 17 years.

Playgrounds are often the site of injuries. Approximately 4 million children and adolescents are injured at school each year, with many of these injuries occurring on school playgrounds. Approximately 45% of playground-related injuries involve severe fractures, internal injuries, concussions, and dislocations. More injuries occur from falls among climbers than on any other school playground equipment. Swings are responsible for most playground-type injuries that take place at the home.

Safety and Hazard Assessments

The CDC recommends that schools consider doing a comprehensive safety assessment at least annually. More frequent assessments (e.g., monthly) are needed for some areas of the school, particularly playgrounds and sports fields. One person can be given the responsibility for identifying hazards and ensuring maintenance of the school environment. Procedures for reporting hazards to the responsible person should be developed and publicized. Sufficient funding is necessary to support inspection, repair, and upgrades as needed.

Safety Curricula

A variety of educational approaches are used in schools to promote safety. When selecting these educational strategies, educators must take into account which are developmentally appropriate. Young children might not fully understand abstract concepts or different perspectives; for example, young children might think a driver can see them and will stop just because the child can see the car approaching. Consequently, efforts directed toward young children need to focus on concrete experiences (e.g., practice in safely crossing a street or resolving conflicts). More abstract associations become appropriate as students approach middle school. By the time children enter middle school, they can understand and act on the connection between their behaviors and injury.

Several resources are available to help develop and evaluate safety curriculum. The HECAT HBOs for a K–12 curriculum are identified in **Box 9-4**. HECAT also provides a Safety Module (S) that contains lists of content and skills to be taught at various grade levels. Activities that can help you teach safety skills are found in **Box 9-5**.

9-3 Internet Support

Safety Resources

The following are HBOs recommended by HECAT for K–12 safety curriculum. After reviewing these recommendations, check out the HECAT Module S (safety curriculum) available on the Internet. In this module you will find recommendations for all the content and skills to be taught at various grade levels.

HBOs:

- Use appropriate seat restraints when riding in a motor vehicle.
- Sit in the back seat of the vehicle when age appropriate.
- Avoid using alcohol and other drugs when driving a motor vehicle.
- Avoid riding in a car with a driver who is under the influence of alcohol or other drugs.
- Use appropriate safety equipment.
- Refuse to engage in or encourage others to engage in risky behaviors.
- Practice safety rules and procedures to avoid injury.
- Plan ahead to avoid dangerous situations and injuries.
- Seek help for poisoning, sudden illness, and injuries.
- Provide immediate help to others with a sudden illness or injury.

After reviewing the HBOs and Module S online, try to ascertain your community's specific safety needs. You can do this by finding local/state data on the Internet (e.g., CDC's YRBS data), interviewing school staff or students, and making personal observations. Find out if scope and sequence or safety curricula exist for your school district. Once you have done this, set safety learning goals for your students. Map out your instruction time and then continue your instruction planning using the guidelines provided in the *Teaching Today's Students* chapter. Box 9-5 contains activities you can use. The following organizations/websites also provide activities, videos, games, materials, lesson plans, and information you might like to use.

- Lesson Plan Central
- CDC's Home and Recreational Safety
- Kidd Safety
- CodeRedRover
- AARP Driver Safety Online Course
- Tips for Teachers: Road Safety Lesson Plans
- CDC's "Walk to School Day"
- National Bike Safety Network
- U.S. Environmental Protection Agency Sun Wise Program
- Environmental Protection Agency
- U.S. Fire Administration for Kids
- A to Z Teacher Stuff
- Natural Disaster Preparation
- FEMA for Kids

9-4 Activities for Violence Prevention

Life Skills

Life skills are key components of safety and violence prevention curricula. More than 50 activities previously given in this book can be modified for use in violence prevention curricula. The following list identifies where specific skill activities can be found.

Analyzing influences	(*Media Literacy Skills* chapter)
Accessing valid information	(*Media Literacy Skills* chapter)
Interpersonal communication	(*Life Skills* chapter)
Empathy	(*Life Skills* chapter)
Resistance skills	(*Life Skills, Dealing with Stress, Promoting a Tobacco-Free and Drug-Free Lifestyle*, and *Promoting Sexual Health* chapters)
Decision making and problem solving	(*Life Skills* chapter)
Goal setting and impulse control	(*Life Skills* chapter)
Anger management	(*Life Skills* chapter)
Conflict management	(*Life Skills* chapter)
Stress management	(*Dealing with Stress* chapter)

Here are a few additional activity ideas.

Family Feud

Play a game similar to the TV version of *Family Feud* where students guess violence-related statistics from the YRBS ("Survey says . . ."). Take time to discuss the relevance and implications of each statistic, including differences in various areas of the United States. (I, J, H)

What's My Line?

This is another game based on an old TV show where contestants try to guess the identity of the mystery guest. Have the "mystery student" take the role of a victim of abuse. Use the activity to dispel myths and identify how to get help. (I, J, H)

Out of the Hat

Have students take turns drawing a bully-related scenario out of a hat. Discuss how each could/should be handled. Emphasize the need for empathy. (I, J, H)

Calloused Analogy

Locate one or more students with calluses on their hands. (Playing on playground equipment, manual labor, and lifting weights are some activities that might create calluses.) Discuss as a class how and why the body develops calluses (protection). Tickle the calloused hands with a feather. Ask the students what they felt. Discuss how calluses can desensitize us. Explain how we can become emotionally calloused (e.g., through exposure to media violence) and how this makes us lose sensitivity to others' feelings.

Advocacy

Have students develop and air safety promotion or violence prevention announcements over the school's public address system.

Integration into Other Subjects

- *Math.* Create graphs on violence statistics and discuss how to avoid risky situations.
- *Language Arts.* Write captions for photographs. Create short stories on violence related topics. Contribute to a bully-free blog.
- *Social Studies.* Research safety or violence risks in various cultures or at various times in history.

9-5 *Activities for Safety*

Road Safety

Buckle Up, Egg Head

Roll a large plastic car into a wall with an egg sitting in the driver's seat. The first time, have the egg taped in, simulating wearing a safety belt. The second time, do it with no tape. You might want to cover the floor with plastic to contain the mess. (P, I, J, H)

Bike Rodeo

Create a bike "obstacle course" with simulated hazards on the playground. (P, I)

Safety Check

Have students conduct a seat belt and other safety behavior observational survey before and after school. (P, I, J, H)

Melon Drop

Draw a face on a cantaloupe and then put it in an old bike helmet. Drop the helmet onto the ground so that the helmet takes the impact. The cantaloupe usually survives the fall, but the helmet will lose its strength integrity and should not be worn for protection in the future. Now drop the cantaloupe without the helmet—use a plastic tarp to contain the mess. (P, I, J, H)

Home Safety

Safety Fair

As a class or school, design a safety fair with booths and activities for various safety topics. Here are a few possibilities: fire extinguisher use; stop, drop, and roll relay; spot the hazards; first aid station, and blindfold smoky room demonstration. Invite other classes to participate and learn from your expert students. (I, J, H)

(continues)

(continued)

Song Writers' Competition

Have students write safety-related lyrics to familiar tunes on assigned safety issues. Have groups perform and vote on the best song for teaching safety concepts. (I, J, H)

Safetymercial

Have students create and record a 30-second spot that could be aired as a public safety commercial. Skits could be performed instead of videotaping. (I, J, H)

Poison Collage

Have students create a collage of pictures of poisonous household materials with a Mr. Yuck sticker prominently displayed, along with the local poison control phone number. (P, I)

Fire Fighters

Arrange for a field trip to a local fire station or have a fire truck visit your school.

Outdoor Safety

Face Paint

Compete to see who can apply sunblock on the face, arms, and legs in the most creative way. (I, J, H)

Safety Signs

Have students design and display original safety signs. (I, J, H)

ABCs of Summer Safety

Have students come up with a summer safety concept for every letter of the alphabet. (P, I)

Mock Disaster

Have students participate in mock disaster training held by the local fire department. Alternatively, have students create their own mock disaster scenarios and rehearse appropriate first responder actions. (J, H)

PSA

In conjunction with a local TV or radio station, have students develop and air a safety promotion public service announcement.

Integration into Other Subjects

- *Math.* Contact insurance agencies to obtain information so students can compare rates for various age groups and high-risk drivers. Identify home insurance rates based on risks.
- *Language Arts.* Tweet, blog, or place on Facebook safety-related information.
- *Social Studies.* Research traffic safety risks and identify population and urbanization contributing factors.

Instruction Plan Worksheet Violence Prevention and Safety

Use this worksheet to plan violence prevention and safety instruction at the grade level you will be teaching. Refer to Chapter 2 for more information on how to complete each section in this worksheet.

■ Assess Needs

Identify topics and skills state or local curricula identify to be taught at ___ grade level.

Identify additional topics or skills the V and S HECAT Modules indicate for this grade.

Identify violence and safety needs your particular students and their families have:
- Where and how is bullying taking place among students?
- What violence concerns/fears do your students have?
- What are your student's major injury risks?
- What particular safety risks exist within your community?

■ Set Major Learning Goal(s)

Identify your major learning goal(s)—what do you want to have happen?

■ **Develop Instruction Map**

Create a map (calendar or list of days) indicating the time frame you have/need to teach the curriculum, meet student needs and reach goal(s). For each day indicate the content/skills to be taught. Work to create a good flow.

■ Write SMART Unit Objectives

Write 1 or 2 major objectives for each day you will teach. Your objectives should be in alignment with your state/local curricula, your student's needs, and your major learning goal(s).

■ Identify Assessment Tools

Preassessment	Formative-Assessment	Postassessment
How will you determine what students already know or do?	How will you know if they are "getting it"?	How will you know if students master objectives?

Instruction Plan Worksheet Violence Prevention and Safety

■ **Develop Unit Plan**

Divide the chart into the number of days you will teach. Record each day's topic and objective key words. Identify activity names (in the book) that can help you meet each day's objective. Identify tech tools you can use and possible lesson adaptations you can make for special need learners.

Lesson Topic Objectives	Instruction Activities	Tech Tools	Adaptations for Learners

■ **Develop Lesson Plans**

Use the Lesson Plan Template found in Chapter 2 and this worksheet to create detailed lesson plans for your Violence and Safety Unit.

KEY TERMS

bullying 282
cyberbullying 283
early warning signs 291
imminent warning signs 291
physical abuse 293
neglect 293
emotional abuse 294
sexual abuse 294
sexual assault 294
incest 294

sexual violence 298
rape 298
statutory rape 298
acquaintance rape 298
date rape 298
marital rape 298
stranger rape 298
intimate-partner violence 298
teen dating violence 299

KNOWLEDGE CHECK!

1. Define and explain the relative importance of each of the key terms in the context of this chapter.
2. Provide examples of verbal, social, and physical bullying and cyberbullying. Describe the roles children play in the circle of bullying.
3. Identify risk factors for children who are bullied. Explain the two types of children who bully.
4. Discuss warning signs of bullying, responding to bullying, and preventing bullying from the teacher's perspective.
5. Identify what constitutes youth violence, characteristics of youth who engage in violence, and family factors that contribute to youth violence.
6. Discuss the various forms of media violence and their impact on young people.
7. Discuss the role that alcohol and drugs play in violent acts. Discuss how immediate access to weapons affects violence, criminal acts, and suicide.
8. Discuss various types of "gang" groups, including youths' reasons for getting involved in such groups, aspects of a community that promote gangs, and small town/rural gang exposure.
9. Describe how violence interferes with learning potential.
10. Describe the measures school can take to ensure a physical and social violence-free environment. Discuss how dress and discipline codes can help.
11. Describe how schools should conduct safety and hazard assessments.
12. Identify the early warning signs of violence, and describe what a teacher can/should do to see them and respond to them. Identify imminent warning signs of violence, and discuss what teachers must do when they are present.
13. Identify the components of effective violence prevention programs. Identify actions that must take place when a student has a gun on school grounds and why.
14. Identify some of the physical, family, and behavioral indicators of child abuse and child sexual abuse. Explain how teachers should report child sexual abuse, including the *dos* and *don'ts* in handling the child's disclosure.
15. Describe the various programs and actions educators can provide to prevent child abuse and neglect.
16. Identify rape myths, the most common age range for rape, and possible effects of date rape.
17. Identify resources for addressing teen dating violence.
18. Discuss the prevalence of traffic-related injuries and measures that can be taken to prevent or reduce such injuries and deaths.
19. Discuss the prevalence of poisoning and fires and measures that can be taken to prevent or reduce such injuries and deaths.
20. Discuss the prevalence of drowning, sports, and playground injuries and death. Identify racial/ethnic rate disparities in these types of incidents.

REFERENCES

1. Ericson N. *Addressing the problem of juvenile bullying.* Washington, DC: U.S. Department of Justice, Office of Juvenile Justice and Delinquency Prevention. Available at http://www.ncjrs.gov/pdffiles1/ojjdp/fs200127.pdf. Accessed February 15, 2013.
2. Anderson CA, Carnagey N, Flanagan M, et al. Violent video games: specific effects of violent content on aggressive thoughts and behavior. *Adv Exp Soc Psychol.* 2004;36:199–249.
3. Pediatrics News Briefs. Violent video game content more attractive to youth. March 2009. Available at http://www.aap.org/en-us/about-the-aap/aap-press-room/pages/Violent-Video-Game-Content-More-Attractive-to-Youth.aspx. Accessed February 15, 2013.
4. Strasburger VC. Why do adolescent health researchers ignore the impact of the media? *J Adolesc Health.* 2009;44: 203–205.
5. American Academy of Pediatrics. Media violence: policy statement. *Pediatrics.* 2001;108(5):1222–1226.
6. American Academy of Pediatrics. Role of the pediatrician in youth violence prevention. *Pediatrics.* 2009;124(1): 393–402.
7. Page RM, Hammermeister J. Weapon-carrying and youth violence. *Adolescence.* 1997;32(127):505–513.
8. Simon RR, Richardson JL, Dean CW, et al. Prospective psychological, interpersonal, and behavioral predictors of handgun carrying among adolescents. *JAMA.* 1998;88(6):960–963.
9. Howell JC. *Preventing and reducing juvenile delinquency: a comprehensive framework.* Thousand Oaks CA: Sage; 2003.
10. Lumsden L. Preventing violence. *ERIC Digest.* March 2002:155. ERIC Clearinghouse on Educational Management. Available at http://www.ericdigests.org/2001-3/violence.html. Accessed February 13, 2013.
11. Centers for Disease Control and Prevention. Dating matters initiative. Available at http://www.cdc.gov/ViolencePrevention/DatingMatters/index.html. Accessed February 15, 2013.
12. Centers for Disease Control and Prevention. YRBSS: Youth Risk Behavior Surveillance System. Available at http://www.cdc.gov/HealthyYouth/yrbs/data/index.htm. Accessed February 15, 2013.
13. Centers for Disease Control and Prevention. Injury prevention: reducing childhood pedestrian injuries: summary of a multidisciplinary conference. June 2002. Available at www.cdc.gov/ncipc/pub-res/childhood_pedestrian/child_pedestrian.htm. Accessed February 15, 2013.

Chapter 10
Dealing with Crises and Critical Issues

Courtesy of Sabrina Squires.

David Disappeared

When I was in fourth grade the kid that sat in the desk next to mine was killed in an automobile accident. On the school bus Monday morning, all the kids were talking about it. When we got to school, we found that his desk had mysteriously disappeared and the rows had been rearranged. No adult at school said anything about his death—it was as if David had never existed to them. At recess, the kids whispered all kinds of stories about David's death for weeks. Looking back, I can see we needed to talk about it and these stories were generated by fears, imagination, and sometimes by wanting to be the center of attention. Because our teacher never spoke of David, we didn't dare ask her about him or the rumors that we were hearing. I never said anything about it to my parents, even though it really affected me. I was scared I might die, too, and then everyone would forget me.

This chapter addresses some of the more difficult situations educators are called upon to deal with. Every semester, students express appreciation for the opportunity to discuss the issues covered in this chapter. They readily see the importance of becoming prepared now for something they may have to deal with in the future, as individuals and as teachers. This chapter can help educators gain insights into how to prepare for crises and offers classroom tools for dealing with suicide, self-injury, terminal illness, and death.

■ CRISIS RESPONSE PLANS*

Schools need to be responsive to crises and disasters that could affect the school community, including environmental disasters (e.g., fires, floods, tornadoes, blizzards, earthquakes) and other situations that threaten safety (e.g., chemical spills, explosions, terrorist acts). School teachers and administrators also have to be prepared to deal with the serious injury or death of one of their students, a member of a student's family, or a fellow teacher. A school plan for dealing with crises can be comprehensive, addressing response needs for multiple types of disasters and emergencies. Such plans should outline responses for both short- and long-term services.

Many states require districts and schools to have crisis response plans. School administrators should review their district and state crisis intervention manuals and adapt them to address local needs. The school plan could include the formation of a crisis response team with a designated contact person to coordinate the school's response. The plan and team could be developed with input from key members of the local community, including school administrators; law enforcement; fire and rescue departments; emergency medical services (EMS); mental health agencies;

---

*This section is adapted and condensed from Centers for Disease Control and Prevention. School health guidelines to prevent unintentional injury and violence. *MMWR.* 2001;50(RR-22):350.

parent–teacher organizations; hospitals; domestic violence shelters; health, social services, and emergency management agencies; rape crisis shelters; the faith community; teachers' unions; and organizations such as the Red Cross. Crisis plans can do the following:

- Assign roles and responsibilities in the event of an emergency to all members of the team and to the broader school community
- Consider the potential need for backup assistance from the district, other schools, or outside groups
- Consider that the crisis might be based in the community and that the school might need to serve as a shelter
- Include plans for dismissing school early, canceling classes, and evacuating students to a safer location
- Include strategies for informing school staff members, families, and the community regarding the school's plans and assignment of responsibilities
- Include procedures for handling suspicious packages or envelopes, including actions to minimize possible exposure to biological or chemical agents and mechanisms for informing law enforcement

A communication system could provide for communicating internally as well as for contacting community resources (e.g., law enforcement) and families in the event of an emergency. As part of preparation activities, schools can communicate basic emergency procedures to families so that they will know where to report or call for information in the event of a crisis. A communication system can also include methods for families, community members and agencies, students, and others to communicate potential crises to the school. Floor plans might be shared with local law enforcement, fire and rescue, and EMS agencies. Crisis plans can be produced in writing and copies given to all school staff members and all relevant community organizations, even if they do not participate in developing the plan. Such plans can also be updated annually.

Schools can train faculty, staff members, students, community organization and agency staff members, and the crisis response team regarding the crisis response plan and their individual roles and responsibilities in a crisis. Plans should be practiced regularly and whenever updates are made.

Preparations for a Crisis

Responsiveness during a crisis depends on preparation. In addition to the crisis response plan, schools could have a current list of personnel who are trained and certified to administer first aid and cardiopulmonary resuscitation (CPR); a phone tree for expediting communication with school staff members and families; clothing or badges to signify members of the crisis response team; fact sheets and letters for distributing information regarding the school to the media; an emergency contact list; and a "go box." The go box contains tools and information to be taken to the crisis response post—for example, the phone numbers, current lists, and items described previously, as well as a bullhorn, a complete list of students, and maps and floor plans that include locations of power and utility connections. A laptop computer and a cell phone or walkie-talkie system could also be made available. The contents of the go box might be reviewed and updated at least annually. Several persons should have access to the go box and know how to use it.

Schools should establish evacuation procedures for moving students to safety, making appropriate provisions for persons with special needs. Adequate transportation should be available to move students to the preestablished safe location, taking into account transportation requirements for students with special needs. Reunion areas should be established for students and families to meet each other. Assigned staff members can manage a standardized procedure for

Schools often become emergency shelters at times of crises. The school building and school staff can offer both physical and emotional refuge.

releasing students to family members. This procedure could include keeping records of when each student left the school grounds and with whom the student left.

Schools can anticipate demands from the media and be proactive in delivering the information that the school wants released to the media. For example, schools can decide in advance which types of information will be released during a crisis and have templates of press releases already assembled. When a crisis occurs, schools can then control the message that will be released to the media. A school official trained in providing information through the media could be designated to speak to the media. A specific location for media contacts can be assigned. This location and the name of the media contact can be communicated to local media outlets when releasing the school crisis response plan.

Short-Term Responses and Services

Schools should consider reopening as quickly as possible after a crisis has ended. In the aftermath of such an event, school personnel can be a substantial source of assistance to students. Developmentally appropriate and culturally competent mechanisms are essential for dealing with the psychological consequences of traumatic events in counseling centers, classrooms, and assemblies. Depending on the situation, these mechanisms might involve teachers, administrators, counselors, families, and local safety professionals (e.g., fire fighters after a fire).

After a crisis, grief counselors could be made available to students and staff members on both group and individual levels. The school can communicate with students, families, and staff members regarding recognizing and treating post-traumatic stress disorder.

Depending on the scope of the crisis, all or some of the students and staff members might not be able to return immediately to their regular class schedules. Community resources might need to be sought for counseling and psychological services.

In the event of a death, students, families, and staff members should be allowed to grieve. Gatherings or other tributes might be appropriate, except in the case of suicide, where public tributes might increase the risk for copycat suicide attempts. Schools can be proactive in identifying and assisting students who want or need to discuss their feelings. In addition, schools can continue to work with the media so that students and staff members can return to school without disruption while ensuring that the media and the public receive the information they need.

Long-Term Responses and Services

Crises have lingering consequences and should be treated over the long term. Some students might require ongoing counseling and psychological services. Schools can anticipate anniversary dates and other occasions that might be painful for members of the school community and can provide any necessary additional services at these times. Schools should continue to communicate with students, families, and staff members to recognize and treat post-traumatic stress disorder and depression. They can also teach students coping and grieving strategies that students can use throughout their lifetimes.

Schools as a whole can learn from crises. After a crisis affects the school or community, the school crisis response team might meet to analyze the school's response, consider revisions to the crisis response plan, assess how to prevent future recurrences, and make necessary changes based on lessons learned.

■ YOUTH SUICIDE*

Youth suicide is a serious public health problem. For youths between the ages of 10 and 24 years, suicide is the third leading cause of death. In addition, suicides among children younger than the age of 10 have been reported. Approximately 4,600 young people's lives are lost each year through suicide. The top three methods used in suicides of young people are firearms (45%), suffocation (40%), and poisoning (8%).

Deaths from youth suicide are only part of the problem. More young people survive suicide attempts than actually die. A nationwide survey of youths in grades 9 through 12 in public and private schools in the United States found that 16% of students reported seriously considering suicide, 13% reported creating a plan, and 8% reporting trying to take their own life in the 12 months preceding the survey. Each year, approximately 157,000 youths between the ages of 10 and 24 receive medical care for self-inflicted injuries at emergency departments across the United States.

Suicide affects all youths, but some groups are at higher risk than are others. Boys are more likely than girls to die from suicide. Of the completed suicides in the 10- to 24-year-old group, 81% of the deaths are males and 19% are females. Girls, however, are more likely to report attempting suicide than are boys. Cultural variations in suicide rates also exist, with Native American/Alaskan Native and Hispanic youth having the highest rates of suicide-related fatalities. A nationwide survey of youths in grades 9 through 12 in public and private schools in the United States found Hispanic youth were more likely to report attempting suicide than their black and white, non-Hispanic peers were.

Several factors can put a young person at risk for suicide. Nevertheless, having the following risk factors does not always mean that suicide will occur:

◆ History of previous suicide attempts
◆ Family history of suicide
◆ History of depression or other mental illness
◆ Alcohol or drug abuse
◆ Stressful life event or loss
◆ Easy access to lethal methods
◆ Exposure to the suicidal behavior of others
◆ Incarceration

*The statistics found in this section on suicide are taken from the Centers for Disease Control and Prevention. Suicide Prevention. Available at http://www.cdc.gov/ViolencePrevention/suicide/index.html.

Most people are uncomfortable with the topic of suicide. Too often, victims are blamed, and their families and friends are left stigmatized. As a result, people do not communicate openly about suicide. Thus an important public health problem is left shrouded in secrecy, which limits the amount of information available to those working to prevent suicide.

Warning Signs of Suicide

An attempted suicide must be taken very seriously. In addition to being a potentially lethal event, it is a risk factor for completed suicide and often an indicator of other problems such as substance abuse, depression, or adjustment and stress reactions. Unfortunately, many youths who try to commit suicide do not receive medical or psychological treatment following their attempt. Suicide researchers estimate that 25 attempted suicides occur for every completed suicide.[1]

Many signs can indicate suicidal thoughts or behavior in young people. These signs can be grouped in four categories: verbal, behavioral, situational, and depressive symptoms. Educators should be alert for these signs in the children and adolescents they work with.

Most suicides are planned rather than committed on impulse. Educators should be alert for verbal, behavioral, situational, and depressive symptoms.

Verbal Signs

Quite often educators dismiss or overlook direct or indirect statements about suicidal intentions or wishes as not being serious statements. In fact, these statements do indicate suicidal intentions and should be treated seriously. One of the most dangerous misconceptions about suicide is that people who talk about killing themselves rarely do it. Actually, more than three fourths of all suicide victims mention it beforehand. Most suicides are planned rather than committed on impulse. Statements like the following may indicate suicidal intentions:

- I wish I were dead.
- I'm going to kill myself.
- People (or my family) would be better off without me.
- Nobody needs me.
- If (such and such) happens, I am going to kill myself.
- I just can't go on living anymore.
- You won't have to worry about me anymore.
- How do you donate your body to science?
- Why is there such unhappiness in life?

Behavioral Signs

The most serious and predictive sign of suicide is a previous unsuccessful suicide attempt. Any suicide attempt should be considered serious. It is common for some youths to make weak attempts to gain attention. If these attempts are ignored or not taken seriously, the individuals may turn to more lethal methods.

"Setting one's affairs in order" is another behavioral sign that needs serious attention and is strongly suggestive of suicidal thoughts. This includes activities such as making arrangements to be a donor of vital body organs and giving away prized possessions. Educators should question any changes in behavior, whether positive or negative. Behavioral signs include the following:

- Poor adjustment to a recent loss
- A suicide note that is left in advance
- A sudden, unexplained recovery from a severe depressive episode
- Alcohol and other drug abuse
- Extreme changes in mood or behavior
- Excessive irritability
- Feelings of guilt
- Unexplained crying (particularly if male)
- Truancy or running away from home
- Academic difficulty or poor schoolwork
- Aggressive behavior
- Promiscuity
- Self-mutilation
- Resignation from clubs or other groups
- Repeated episodes of accidental injury
- Social isolation or withdrawing from friends

Situational Signs

The most important situational signal is family strife. Family disruption by death of a parent or sibling, separation, or divorce is associated with suicidal behavior. Disruption or disorder in the family is frequently associated with alcohol or other drug abuse among parents. Suicidal behavior by an immediate family member is more prevalent among youth suicide attempters than among those who have not attempted suicide. In such case, the suicidal behavior by other family members may serve as a model for coping with stress. Young people growing up with these family models may, in turn, be more likely to resort to suicide in response to stress. Other situational signs include the following:

- Loss of a job
- Loss of a boyfriend or girlfriend
- A fight with a peer
- A fight or serious disagreement with a parent
- Chronic illness
- Survival of an illness with a disability
- A move to a new city
- Academic failure
- Being caught for a crime, such as shoplifting or vandalism

Depressive Symptoms

Depression is strongly associated with youth suicide. Educators should be alert for the signs associated with depression discussed in the *Dealing with Stress* chapter. Feelings of hopelessness are particularly highly correlated with suicidal ideation and behavior, so any signs of depression and hopelessness require serious attention (see **Box 10-1**).

Prevention and Intervention

Often, suicidal behavior is a cry for help with problems that seem—at least to the student—impossible to solve. Showing that you care and listening are the most critical preventive measures that you can employ. Take warning signs and threats seriously and establish a sense of trust. A student's trust in a teacher often requires confidentiality, which places a great deal of responsibility on the teacher to determine whether the situation warrants informing parents or others. When intervention is necessary, the teacher can advise the student on how to get professional help. It is beneficial when teachers serve as a liaison between the school and the professional help.

Daily contact with and knowledge of their students put teachers in an excellent position to detect the warning signs of suicide. Any suspicions about suicide cannot be ignored. It is best to

10-1 Internet Support

Suicide Prevention Resources

Numerous organizations focus on suicide prevention and offer resources and immediate help. Here are some resources you or your students can check out on the Internet:

- National Suicide Hotlines USA (1-800-SUICIDE, 1-800-TALK); state- and city-specific numbers can be located online
- American Foundation for Suicide Prevention
- CrisisLink
- Survivors of Suicide
- National Suicide Prevention Lifeline (1-800-273-8255)
- SAVE (Suicide Awareness/Voices of Education)
- SPRC (Suicide Prevention Resource Center)
- YSPP (Youth Suicide Prevention Program)

ask a student calmly, "Are you thinking about suicide?" This direct approach helps lower a student's anxiety and lets him or her know that someone cares enough to simply listen.

Teachers should not back away from talking to young persons who disclose that they are considering suicide. By discussing suicide, you are not putting the idea into the student's head or increasing the likelihood of suicidal behavior. An open discussion can help decrease some of the anxiety that students in crisis feel and open up the door for seeking help. It also conveys the message that someone cares about them and wants to help them. A discussion can help them see other options.

By being a concerned listener, you help a young person know that he or she is being taken seriously. Listening to the young person indicates to him or her that you care and that the student is not alone. Failure to listen may be perceived as a sign of an individual's sense of worthlessness.

Teachers must not act shocked if a student discloses that he or she is thinking about suicide. You can help the individual to realize that he or she is not so different because of thinking of suicide in response to problems or stresses. Thoughts of suicide are normal; suicidal actions are not. Teachers must take disclosure of suicidal thoughts seriously and not dismiss them lightly. *They must take appropriate action.*

Educators must not attempt to deal with a suicidal person alone. Enlist the support and help of parents, school counselors, and other mental health professionals, clergy, and friends. Most states have laws mandating school personnel to report student suicide ideation. It is very difficult for students to obtain professional assistance on their own, so teachers can serve a critical role in the referral process. Trust your suspicions that a student may be contemplating suicide and take the appropriate action.

Teachers must not allow themselves to be sworn to secrecy by a suicidal student. You may be confronted by a student who says, "I have something important to tell you, but first you must promise not to tell anyone else." Your response should be, "If someone is hurting you or you are considering hurting yourself, I cannot promise that I will not tell anyone else. If it is a personal matter, I will not tell anyone and I will help and support you. However, if it is a problem for which you need assistance from others, I will help you get the help you need."

Young people are often relieved that teachers are willing to help with their problem and that they are comfortable talking about it. In discussing their problems and situation, take a positive approach and help them see the alternatives to suicide. It is important that they realize other choices are available. Share some strategies that work for you in dealing with stressful situations, failure, loss, and disappointment. Ask them to share with you some strategies that have worked for them in the past. Convey the message that suicidal thoughts are normal but that students do not need to act upon those thoughts. Suicide is a normal thought, not a normal behavior.

It is important that depressed and unhappy youths understand that most problems resolve themselves over time. Help them break out of the thought pattern that things always get worse and worse. Emphasize the temporary nature of most problems. Explain that the immediate crisis will pass in time and that time will help in the healing. Tell them that suicide is a permanent solution to a problem that is usually temporary.

Help the young person develop a network of support. Identify people whom he or she can be with and talk with. Sometimes signing a **contract for life** helps. A contract for life is a formal, written agreement in which suicidal people state that they will ask for help before they hurt themselves. A contract for life should be dated and signed. Educators must never let a contract for life expire without formal acknowledgment of its termination. *Young people who pose an immediate suicide risk should never be left alone.*

More schools and school personnel need to be involved in suicide prevention and intervention programs (see **Box 10-2**). Educators must become adept at identifying and helping potential suicide victims. Effective suicide prevention programs are developed when teachers, school administrators, school staff members, parents, and community agencies become actively involved. Box 10-3 provides suggested classroom activities for dealing with the topic of suicide.

10-2

Suicide Prevention Strategies

Suicide prevention methods are best used in conjunction with other strategies rather than in isolation. Schools and communities can implement several suicide prevention strategies to counter suicide among students:

- **School-based suicide awareness curricula.** These curricula generally focus on the following areas: dispelling myths and increasing correct knowledge about youth suicide, increasing the ability of students to recognize another student potentially at risk for suicidal behaviors, encouraging troubled students to seek help, and providing students with knowledge concerning school and community resources that are available should they need help or should they encounter a peer who needs help. Lessons about suicide can be incorporated into existing classes such as health, social studies, physical education, and others.

- **Life skills training for youth.** Some schools offer skills training for students as a way to protect young people against depression, hopelessness, and drug abuse—all risk factors for suicidal behaviors or thoughts. Problem-solving skills, social skills, coping skills, and help-seeking strategies may be included in such programs.

- **Screening.** This prevention strategy involves efforts to identify students who are potentially at risk for suicide through interviews and self-report questionnaires. Screening can focus on such indicators as depression, hopelessness, psychiatric disorders, substance abuse problems, suicidal ideation, and past suicide attempts. Referrals of students with indications for suicide risk should then be made to the proper professionals and agencies.

- **Gatekeeper training.** Gatekeeper training refers to education and training for teachers and other school staff (e.g., counselors, coaches) about youth suicide. Because these adults are often in a position to be among the first to detect signs of suicidality and offer assistance to youths in need, they are sometimes known as "natural community helpers." Gatekeepers are trained in school policies that relate to dealing with students deemed to be at high risk for suicide and making appropriate referrals for professional help for these students. They are also trained to recognize that their role is not to go beyond the gatekeeping role. Mental health counseling needs to be left to trained professionals.

- **Educating parents.** Schools can provide information to parents about youth suicide warning signs, risk factors, protective factors, community resources, and actions to take following a suicidal crisis. These efforts can be combined with education on other youth-risk topics such as alcohol and other drug use. Parents should be alerted to the heightened risk that easy access to firearms in the home poses for youth who are suicidal. Firearms are the most common method of suicidal death in the United States.

- **Crisis centers and hotlines.** Schools can inform students about crisis centers and hotlines, which provide immediate, accessible, and confidential support for individuals in need. These services are often available during times when other services are not open or accessible, such as late at night and on weekends.

- **Peer support groups.** Another strategy for students potentially at risk for suicidal behaviors is the use of peer support groups. These students are more likely to confide in and feel comfortable with peers rather than adults. Support groups that allow vulnerable students to meet with other students in a comfortable group climate might foster peer relationships and coping skills. Such groups may also help alleviate feelings of isolation, loneliness, and hopelessness. Despite the potential benefits of peer support groups, they should not be used as a substitute for professional counseling or therapy.

- **Positive and safe school climate.** Interventions that target the improvement of school climate might have an impact in terms of reducing youth suicide. All students, including those at high risk of suicide, benefit from a positive and safe school climate. It is important for students to feel connected to their school.

Sources: Doan J, Roggenbaum S, Lazear K. *Youth suicide prevention school-based guide—Issue Brief 5: suicide prevention guidelines.* Tampa, FL: Department of Child and Family Studies, Division of State and Local Support; 2005. Gould MS, Kramer RA. Youth suicide prevention. *Suicide Life-Threatening Bhvr.* 2001;31(suppl):6–31.

SELF-INJURY

Some young people engage in acts of self-injury. **Self-injury**, also known as *self-harm* or *self-mutilation*, includes deliberate attempts to cause harm to one's own body; the injury is usually enough to cause tissue damage. Any method used to harm oneself might be used in self-injury, such as cutting, hair pulling, skin picking, burning, biting, bone breaking, head banging, self-poisoning, self-strangulation, or limb amputation. Self-injury is not generally an attempt at suicide, but it has resulted in deaths when sustained injuries were serious enough to cause fatality, and it can be a marker for possible future suicide attempts. Self-injury appears to be more common in girls than in boys. Some studies suggest that self-injury may be practiced by as many as 5% to 9% of people in Western societies.[2]

Why would a young person intentionally harm himself or herself? Self-injury might be used to help someone relieve intense feelings such as anger, sadness, loneliness, shame, guilt, and emotional pain. It is believed that those who cut themselves do so in an attempt to release intense emotional feelings. Some young people troubled by a sense of emotional numbness report that seeing their own blood when they cut themselves helps them to feel alive because they usually feel dead inside. Others report that they injure themselves because dealing with the physical pain is easier than dealing with emotional pain. Self-injury is also used by some as a way to punish themselves for the guilt, shame, and blame that they carry for an abuse that they have suffered. Some people harm themselves out of a sense of self-hatred for themselves and their body. Sometimes, self-injury is an attempt to get attention or a cry for help; in other cases, self-injurers go to great extremes to keep their behavior a secret. Whatever means is used for self-injury and whatever the reasons behind it, the practice usually provides a release from built-up feelings and emotions. This emotional release is only temporary, however.

Many young people who engage in acts of self-injury have a troubled past. Some have a history of sexual or physical abuse, have emotionally absent parents, come from broken homes, or have substance-abusing parents. These factors could potentially contribute to a young person's use of self-injury as a way to cope with or block out the emotional pain resulting from these situations.

The act of cutting and other forms of self-injury are signs of disturbance or emotional difficulty that need to be recognized. For some individuals, self-injury is a last resort or a coping mechanism keeping them from committing suicide. In essence, they are choosing self-injury instead of death. Self-injury often becomes a habit, and some mental health experts describe it as an addiction. One woman who struggled with cutting said that "there was nothing like seeing your own blood dripping off your arm or leg and knowing you control it." Some participants say they are addicted to the blood, some to the scars, and some to the pain, and some cite a mixture of all three. The compulsion to self-injure becomes increasingly more dangerous. When a young person self-injures and feels emotional release, the next time he or she is feeling depressed or angry, the individual's thoughts are likely to turn to self-injury. If the person succumbs to the urge, he or she is perpetuating a cycle of addiction.

Young people suffering from this dangerous behavior need to understand that accepting help is not a sign of weakness, but a sign of strength. Many adults do not understand how to react to someone who is injuring himself or herself. Educators and adults need to react not with shock, but with understanding. They should understand that self-injury is a coping mechanism. They need to support a young person suffering from self-injury and to help him or her obtain help from mental health professionals who are trained to deal with this problem. The road to recovery may be long; through the recovery process, however, the self-injurer may find understanding from informed adults.

HELPING CHILDREN AND ADOLESCENTS DEAL WITH DEATH

Bereaved children face the arduous tasks of coming to terms with a terminal illness, death, grieving, and resumption of the appropriate progression toward development of personality. Sensitive and skilled school personnel can help children accomplish these tasks. However, many teachers are either uncomfortable or inadequately trained to offer appropriate support to bereaved children. These teachers cannot help children resolve their grief in a healthy manner, and some may even complicate the grieving process. Teachers who are comfortable with their own grief and prepared to help students as they grieve play a vital role dealing with death in the classroom. Completing the application exercise in **Box 10-3** will help you become more comfortable with talking about death.

The process of acceptance of a death or loss is often referred to as **grief work**. The death of a loved one, such as a parent or sibling, often requires 2 or more years before grieving is completed. A child's reactions to death depend on his or her age and cognitive developmental level, but resemble the adult patterns of mourning. Typically, the initial responses are denial, anger, and anxiety. Later, these feelings are replaced by periods of sadness, despair, and depression. When the child has worked through these feelings, acceptance of the death emerges.

These same grief patterns take place when a child loses a parent to something other than death. Children grieve when parents walk out on them or simply relocate to another city. This grief work is amplified for a child whose parent deploys for military action. In this case, the child has to deal with not only the parent's physical absence, but also the fear of the parent possibly becoming injured or dying. **Box 10-4** provides a list of normal emotional, physical, and behavioral reactions to death and loss.

Culture and Death Practices

An understanding of cultural practices regarding death can help school personnel more effective in helping children and adolescents deal with death. The evolving nature of cultures and the vast variety of religious affiliations people can have within an ethnic group make it impossible to

10-3 Application Exercise

Am I Ready?

Take out a blank piece of paper and without much thought draw whatever comes to mind when you think of the word "death." When you are finished, step back and look at your drawing. Ask yourself the following questions:

1. What experience do I have with death?
2. How comfortable am I talking about death and grieving with others?
3. What do I need to do to become more prepared for dealing with a death that affects my students?

Complete one or both of the following challenges.

1. Talk to a parent or other loved one about death. Approaching the subject while they are healthy is much easier than when their death is eminent. Use this assignment as an excuse to initiate the conversation. Discuss their feelings about death, living wills, resuscitation orders, and preferred funeral arrangements.
2. Visit a funeral home. Check out caskets and urns. Ask about funeral options and costs. Doing this long before you must deal with the emotional loss of a loved one is extremely helpful. It will assist you in making wise choices, fulfilling the deceased person's requests, and navigating major decisions in a time of grief.

10-4 Internet Support

Bereavement

The following are normal reactions to death. Knowing that these emotions and behaviors are normal can help you and your students work through your grief.

Emotions

- *Shock and numbness.* It seems like a dream.
- *Sadness.* Sadness might come and go over a long period of time, depending on how well you knew the person and how much you depended on him or her.
- *Anger.* You might feel anger possibly at those perceived to be responsible, yourself, the world in general, or the person who died.
- *Depression.* You might feel like you are on a rollercoaster of laughing one minute while remembering funny incidents and then immediately feeling depressed again.
- *Guilt.* You might have regrets about what you did or said to the deceased or what you didn't do or say, or guilt that you are still alive. In time, you might experience guilt that you cannot always remember what the person looked like.
- *Fears.* You might experience fear for the future and possibly about getting close to others.
- *Special emotional days.* You might feel highly emotional on special days, such as holidays, death date, anniversaries, birthdays, or other special days.

Physical Sensations

- Fatigue or weakness, like your body is weighted down
- Trouble breathing, like the wind has been knocked out of you
- Dry mouth
- Hallucinations—seeing or hearing the deceased

Behaviors

- Crying at random and at unexpected times
- Withdrawing from others
- Loss of appetite
- Insomnia
- Dreams or nightmares
- Treasuring or avoiding mementos of the deceased
- Absentmindedness or preoccupation
- Reverting to acting like a younger age
- Hostility and aggression, especially in children who do not have other means of expressing their anger and frustration

Read more about coping with grief and loss on the HELPGUIDE Internet site.

---

declare with certainty what an ethnic family might believe or do regarding death. The following paragraphs highlight general cultural practices.[3]

The Hispanic culture is tightly knit and offers strong emotional support. It views the world through a fatalistic lens, which helps members prepare for death and eases the grieving process. Women may wail and openly mourn, but males do not grieve openly because of "machismo." Funerals are marked by open caskets, Catholic mass, and funeral processionals.

Death beliefs and practices among African Americans vary widely because of the vast diversity in religious affiliations, geographic regions, education, and economics. Some grieving African Americans wail openly, while others are more stoic. Their sense of family includes extended relatives, neighbors, and church members. Members of this culture resist advance planning, including the making of a living will or plans for the survivors after a person's death. Funeral directors have high status in the community. Funeral services include dynamic storytelling and exhortations to be strong in hardship. The number of funeral attendees is reflective of the character of the deceased.

People in Asian and Pacific Islander cultures may wear white clothing or headbands for a period of time after a death. They believe talking about bad things can make them happen. Death is a taboo subject among Chinese Americans, and they are likely to not tell a dying individual that he or she is dying. Care for the dying, funeral services, and mood for mourning are all established by the patriarch of the family. Funerals are very important in establishing and maintaining relationships between the living and the dead. Mourning tends to be very conservative and may include a processional in which mourners line up in hierarchical order and proceed to the graveside, where food offerings are burned. During transit, money may be thrown to ward off evil spirits. Continued graveside visits and upkeep are important.

Native Americans view death not as a linear path, but as a circular progression—a perspective depicted in their art and oral histories. They tend to believe that talking about death may cause it to happen and, therefore, do not make advance directives such as do not resuscitate (DNR) orders or living wills. They also tend to keep personal issues to themselves. Funeral rituals are elaborate and tribe specific. Grief is expressed by punctuated immediate shared emotional releases and then a physical outward return to calm. Survivors have 4 days to clean and prepare the body, bury, grieve, and dispose of the deceased's belongings.

Age-Related Concepts and Needs

It is important to identify young people's perceptions and needs regarding death (see **Figures 10-1 through 10-4**). For most children, the understanding of death follows an orderly sequence. This sequence begins with total unawareness in very early childhood and progresses

FIGURE 10-1 When children are asked to draw pictures about death, many different perceptions and experiences emerge. This child's grandfather had recently died. Notice the detail of the tears and coffin, and also the missing feet on the people who cannot walk away from the pain.

FIGURE 10-2 This child drew about her pet being put to sleep. The child had mixed feelings about this procedure. Notice the smile on the person and the intensity of the water coming out of the faucet.

through stages to the point where death is conceptualized as final and universal and where abstract thinking about death occurs. Mature concepts about death develop in a progressive, developmental sequence that generally follows Piaget's model of conceptual development. Many children, however, attain mature death concepts at younger ages than suggested by

FIGURE 10-3 This child's depiction of death possibly reveals a fear of drowning.

324   Chapter 10   Dealing with Crises and Critical Issues

FIGURE 10-4 This child had had no real experience with death and depicted it with cartoons and Halloween images.

Piaget. The comprehension of death concepts such as irreversibility, universality, and cessation of function has been found to vary widely among the chronological ages of children.

Here are 10 needs children have concerning death:[4]

1. *To learn how to mourn.* Children need to learn how to go through the process of giving up some of the feelings they have invested in the deceased and go on with the living, to remember, to be touched by the feelings generated by their memories, to struggle with guilt over what they could have done, and to deal with their anger over the loss.
2. *To mourn small losses.* Mourning small losses, such as animals, helps children to deal better with larger, closer losses.
3. *To be informed about a death.* When they are not told about a death but see parents upset, children may invent their own explanations or blame themselves.
4. *To understand the finality of death.* Because abstract thinking is difficult for young children, they may misunderstand adults who say a deceased person "went away" or is "asleep."
5. *To say good-bye to the deceased.* Children can participate in funerals or viewings, even if only for a few minutes, to say good-bye.
6. *To work out their feelings and perceptions.* Opportunities to work out their feelings and deal with their perceptions of death come through talking, dramatic playing, reading books, or expressing themselves through the arts.
7. *Reassurance that their parents will take care of themselves and probably won't die until after their children are grown.* It is important that children know that sometimes children die, but only if they are very sick or if there is a bad accident. It is equally important that they understand that almost all children grow up and live to be very old.

8. *To know that everyone will die someday.* It may be hard for adults to be honest about this fact, but if it is denied, children will not be prepared for dealing with death during their lives.
9. *To be allowed to show their feelings.* Children need to be able to cry, become angry, or laugh uncontrollably. The best approach is for adults to empathize with their feelings.
10. *To feel confident that their questions will be answered honestly and not avoided and that adults will give them answers they can understand.*

Preschool-Age Children

Children 3 to 5 years of age tend to see death as gradual and happening only to the very old, and as a departure that is reversible—as they have seen portrayed in cartoons. Many children believe that a magical power can bring a deceased person back to life. They are very curious about death, which is likely to lead to questions that parents and teachers may find unsettling.

When a deceased person continues to stay away, a child may become angry or hurt. A child may feel that he or she is responsible for the person's absence, believing that a thought or behavior may have caused the death. This evolves as a result of the child's egocentric thinking. Fears of abandonment and anxiety also occur.

Concern about the dead person's physical well-being after death is common. A child is typically concerned with how the dead person will stay warm and get food after burial.

In the mind of a young child, death is associated with a cessation of body functions. A person or animal is considered to be dead when there is no longer any breathing or voluntary movement.

Middle Childhood

Early in the middle childhood period (from about first to third grade), death is often personified as a monster, ghost, skeleton, or other predatory form. Because of this conception, children think death can be fought and overcome by magic. As a result, children consider themselves to be immortal and believe that only those who are weak or old are susceptible to death.

At about 9 or 10 years of age, children are able to conceptualize that death is final and not reversible. Although death remains an abstract thought, they come to realize that they, too, will die. Such realizations can create fears and concerns about dying. Such realizations also heighten their interest in the details of dying and the state of the body after death and stimulate questions.

It is common for children to believe that a deceased person can see and hear them. As a result, children may feel pressure to "be perfect" for the deceased. Misunderstandings about death can also accelerate fears about dying. The religious beliefs of the family concerning death gain new importance to children as they come to understand the finality of death.

Adolescence

Adolescents are capable of comprehending that death is final, irreversible, and universal. This understanding brings concern about personal mortality. Adolescents often defend themselves against the resulting anxiety by denying the possibility of their own death—except as an abstract event in a remote future. Denial serves as a buffer against this anxiety and contributes to an illusion of invulnerability and immortality. These illusions may contribute to risk-taking behaviors such as speeding and reckless driving and drug use.

Adolescents can also formulate abstract ideas about the nature of death. Piaget refers to this developmental period as "the period of formal operations." As such, young people can make generalizations about death beyond what they experience. They formulate their own theologies about life after death as they examine the religious views of their parents and others.

Death of a Parent

Parental deaths can be sudden, as from a car crash, or prolonged, as from a lingering terminal illness. When death comes suddenly, children and surviving family members have little opportunity for preparation—a surviving parent is likely to be in a state of shock that makes it difficult for children to obtain parental assistance and support with their grief.[5] When a parent is terminally ill, the family can "live with death" for a long time.

Responses to the death of a parent and to a fatal diagnosis may include a host of emotions and behaviors. The death or news of the illness may frighten, stun, shock, bewilder, or overwhelm a child. Also, feelings of guilt, anger, loneliness, helplessness, and abandonment or rejection may occur. Behavioral responses that typically result are aggression, hostility, and noncooperation. Withdrawal and regressive behaviors also occur. Sometimes children experience disturbances in school performance.

Losing a parent in the teen years can be particularly problematic. Well-meaning adults sometimes say things like, "You need to be strong and take care of your family." Such comments deny the teen the opportunity to mourn. Often children experience a sense of guilt or unfinished business if a parent dies while an adolescent, in the normal course of development to gain autonomy, is emotionally and physically pushing the parent away. Adolescents might lack the emotional support they need because the adults in their lives assume that they will find comfort in their friends. In fact, this rarely happens unless the teenager's peers have had some experience with grief themselves.[5]

Although such an event is a major source of distress, most children survive the terminal illness and death or sudden death of a parent without long-lasting effects on their mental health. The support and care that a child receives from adults during the illness and after a parent's death are crucial factors in the healthy acceptance of the death.

When a parental death is sudden, school personnel need to provide support to the child immediately upon return to school. When a child is isolated or feels rejected because of the death, class discussions may help. Class discussions can also help other children overcome their fears that such a loss will happen to them. When a child did not have an opportunity to say good-bye to a deceased person, the need to do so remains (this often happens when a child was shielded from the death and not allowed to attend the funeral). Counselors can assist by helping a child write a letter or draw a picture to say good-bye to a loved one. Further, children should be allowed to express their feelings about the death freely. Later psychiatric problems often result from incomplete grief work. School personnel can play a key role in initiating and assisting children in their grief work.

Students dealing with the terminal illness of a family member or a friend go through a long, protracted series of stages. Helping students understand and successfully navigate these stages can be very helpful.

The first stage takes place at the time of diagnosis and is characterized as a time of crisis and anxiety. At this point it is important for teachers, coaches, and other school staff to know about the family situation.

The next stage is unity, where unified efforts are made to "fight" the illness. During this stage, students need to be kept up to date with what is happening and appreciate any efforts to help "fight" such as fundraising or expressions of encouragement. During the ongoing illness process, students need to be encouraged to keep their life at home as normal as possible and to stay involved in school and other activities. They need to know that it is okay to spend time with friends having fun and that the sick person would want them to do so. Teachers should also be aware of and sympathetic toward students who take on burdensome responsibilities at home.

The third stage is characterized by upheaval, as the wear and tear of the prolonged illness continues. In this stage, the student needs to be able to honestly communicate with a trusted adult about things like changes in family dynamics, previously suppressed thoughts and feelings, and lowered life quality for the ill loved one.

The fourth stage of grief deals with resolution, as memories and emotions about roles emerge and rivalries and resentments are handled. Teachers can help students resolve any troubling relationship dynamics.

The final stage of grief occurs at the funeral. It features mixed emotions of sadness and relief and can be a time of celebration of a life as much as it is a marking of a loss. Teachers need to be present and mourn and celebrate with grieving surviving students.[6]

School personnel should be alert for the following behaviors in a bereaved child. According to Brenner, a combination of two or more of these behaviors may indicate the need for additional support, counseling, or therapy:[7]

◆ Deep and persisting fears that other loved ones will die or that the child himself or herself will die
◆ Repeated expressions of wanting to die to be with the dead parent
◆ Angry and violent outbursts combined with feelings of guilt for the parent's death
◆ Attempted role reversal, from depending on the surviving adult to taking care of him or her
◆ Continual movement; inability to be quiet or to express sad feelings
◆ Marked reduction in activity by a formerly very active child

Death of a Sibling

The loss of a sibling during childhood is a very traumatic experience. A sibling's death may be more difficult to accept and understand than a parent's death is. Because the deceased sibling is close in age, the death represents the reality of a child's or adolescent's mortality. Further, the surviving sibling's need for support may be ignored by others in light of the needs of parents or the dying child.

Parents' reactions to the sibling's death/terminal illness profoundly influence a child's own quest for acceptance of the death. Some parents react by overprotecting surviving children, taking excessive precautions to make sure they are free from any risks. In such cases, a child may have difficulty developing independence as a result of these efforts to restrict the child's

The death of a sibling may be more difficult to accept and understand than a parent's death is.

vulnerability to perceived danger. Such overprotectiveness can seriously thwart a child's normal development process.

Some parents may come to idealize the dead child, such that surviving siblings may feel inadequate by comparison to the deceased sibling. Other parents try to recover from the loss by unconsciously pressuring a remaining child to take on the personality or behavior of the dead one.

The siblings of a terminally ill child must deal with the stress of witnessing the pain and discomfort of their dying brother or sister. Because the parents must focus on the overwhelming needs of the dying sibling, other children in the family may suffer the loss of attention and companionship of their parents. An additional stressor faced by surviving siblings is that parents expect them to be well behaved and to take care of their own needs. Feelings of guilt are common among survivors, because they are allowed to go on living while the sibling must die.

When a sister or brother is actively involved in circumstances that lead to a sibling's death, extreme feelings of guilt are likely. Professional help is necessary for such children to gain an understanding of the death and to come to the point that they can forgive themselves. Another concern focuses on the reactions of the other family members to this sibling. Some have difficulty trusting and forgiving the child. Some direct anger toward the child as other family members deal with the death.

In response to the death of a sibling, it is common for children to experience feelings of shock, confusion, numbness, depression, anger, and loneliness. Thoughts about the dead sister or brother linger. The surviving siblings may have thoughts about suicide, experience sleeping and eating disturbances, or report hallucinations in which a deceased sibling either speaks to them or reappears to them.

Death of a Pet

The death of a pet is often a child's first experience with death and grief. When a pet dies, children are likely to feel significant sorrow, pain, and grief. It is important for educators not to underestimate the depth of a child's grief. Children love their pets and often consider the pet to be a member of their family. Pets provide young people with companionship, acceptance, emotional support, and unconditional love. Youths often feel responsible for their pets because they feed them, groom them, and clean up after them. When a pet dies, children may blame themselves, their parents, or the veterinarian for not saving the pet. They may feel depressed and frightened that others they love may also leave them.

Children need extra support in dealing with the loss of a pet. Teachers can encourage a child to talk freely about the pet. It is important to be patient because the child may repeatedly return to the topic. During this process, teachers can give the child lots of reassurance and discuss death, dying, and grief honestly. They can use correct terms and avoid euphemisms such as "put to sleep." Children often develop misunderstandings about death and hearing "put to sleep" could make a child become afraid of going to sleep. Educators can also encourage grief work by having the child draw a picture, write a story, or engage in imaginary play about the deceased pet. Sharing personal experiences with grief can reassure the child that sadness is okay and help the child work through his or her feelings.[8]

■ PROVIDING A SUPPORTIVE ENVIRONMENT FOR THE TERMINALLY ILL CHILD

The presence of a terminally ill school-age child or adolescent in school involves and affects many people. In addition to the terminally ill child and his or her family, school personnel and students need support as they cope with the situation. (Working with children with chronic illnesses is discussed in the *Teaching to Make a Difference* chapter.)

If feasible, dying children are encouraged to continue to attend school for as long as possible. School offers frequent opportunities for creative expression and art activities, which provide natural outlets for working through the dying process. Schoolwork is often something that terminally ill youngsters can do, so it provides a means through which they can perform successfully. This sort of activity can be extremely important as a source of maintaining feelings of self-worth. School also allows a terminally ill young person to fulfill social needs.

Of course, the physical limitations of a terminal illness make full-time school attendance difficult, if not impossible. Absences are necessary for treatments and on days when a child feels too ill to attend school. Therefore, arrangements for partial days and homebound teaching support are usually necessary.

When the illness progresses to the point that school attendance is no longer possible, it helps if small groups of classmates visit the child. This maintains contact between the child and his or her class, which can be very supportive to a terminally ill child.

Understanding the Dying Child

Children with terminal conditions come to understand death at younger ages than their same-age healthy peers. Dying children often demonstrate remarkable knowledge about the seriousness of their condition despite attempts by physicians and parents to conceal the child's impending death. Therefore, children do need to be informed that their condition is fatal.

Terminally ill children feel a great deal of anxiety regarding their illness and their future. However, open communication about the illness by medical personnel and family members is associated with lower stress and anxiety levels, increased relief about their concerns, and improved ability to cope among dying children.

Dying children experience many losses in their lives. They are often separated from their family and school environment for long periods of time as they receive medical care. In the dying process, they may lose hair or undergo disfiguring surgery. Particularly to an adolescent, these changes in physical appearance result in severe blows to self-esteem.

Although school-age children lack the cognitive ability to grieve the loss of their future, adolescents do not. Preparatory grief can be overwhelming and debilitating for adolescents with terminal illness and for their families. **Preparatory grief** typically includes five stages. A person can experience these stages in any order, revisit some stages, go through more than one stage at a time, and skip stages.

- **Denial** ("No, not me. It can't be true") is often the first stage and works as a buffer to reduce the initial shock of news of a terminal illness.
- **Anger** and resentment can follow, as the realities of the illness can no longer be ignored ("Why did God let this happen?" "Those stupid doctors . . .").
- The ill person often attempts **bargaining** with a supreme being for full recovery or more time to delay or prevent the inevitable ("God, I'll do . . . if you . . .).
- When the person realizes that death is inevitable, he or she feels a sense of deep **depression**. This sense of depression and loss is a normal part of preparatory grief, not a mental disorder.
- With adequate support and time, the dying individual works through the previous stages and comes to **acceptance**. Acceptance is neither a happy nor sad time, but a period of accepting her or his fate. The depression and pain are mostly gone, and it is a time for rest and reflection.

Recognizing these stages helps people work through the emotions that come with grief. The preparatory grief of the terminally ill child is best facilitated when supportive adults understand why a dying young person feels and behaves in a particular manner, and then responds to his or her needs.

The Teacher's Role

The classroom teacher can play a special role in the life of a terminally ill child. Bryant describes this role as follows:

Remember that as a teacher you have a special place. You represent the child's normal world; you are an oasis for him. The doctors and nurses bring shots and machines; the parents hover with tears and anguish. You, however, know the child's work-a-day world. You are part of his business and social community. You, more than many, can maintain a semblance of his former world by your visits, news of the classroom, and occasional work assignments. Your interaction with a dying child can keep him among the living a little longer.[9(p.65)]

The Classmates' Role

Throughout the terminal illness, the child needs to continue to feel included as a member of the class. When possible, classmates should be informed about the terminal illness and guided to deal with the situation in a constructive manner. Bertoia and Allan explain why this is important:

> By including the child as part of the class throughout the treatment phase and during the course of an illness, the class as a whole can deal with the situation in a positive manner. Generally, class members will become very supportive of the child in class and protective on the playground. When the teacher or child explains something about the disease to class members, their fear of getting the same thing is diminished and the sick child is not isolated. Because family members are frightened by names such as "cancer" or "AIDS," general terms such as "blood disease" can be used. The counselor should get permission from the child's family if the proper name is to be used. Classmates will understand when standards do change and seem unfair because the sick child cannot complete as much work in the assigned time. Class discussions about feelings and behaviors help clarify what is happening in the classroom.[10(p.34)]

Teachers should never ignore questions that classmates have about the illness or the eventual death of their terminally ill classmate. It is important that children have the opportunity to ask questions and to have them answered. Further, the parents of classmates should be informed that their child was exposed to a death so that they can recognize behaviors or other characteristics that indicate their child's grief and mourning. The parents can then help their children in their grief work.

■ RESPONDING APPROPRIATELY TO DEATH

During your teaching career, it is likely that you will have to deal with death in the classroom. Whether a student, fellow teacher, member of the community, or family member of a student dies, it can affect your entire school. This section provides additional insights into how educators can respond appropriately to death. **Box 10-5** identifies some resources available on the Internet.

Death of a Student

It is apparent that children's reactions to the death of a schoolmate can be hindered by the behavior of school personnel. The most powerful hindrance is the teacher's denial of children's capacity to deal with death. Studies reveal that teachers who are open to the painful feelings aroused by death are the best facilitators because they help their classes deal with death as a unit to explore together.[11] Some children need counselors or outside agencies, but the most effective method of handling children's reactions to the death of a schoolmate is within the classroom. The classroom was found to provide the best environment for children to deal with the trauma of a fellow student's death.

Immediately upon the news of a student's (or teacher's) death, the involved teacher(s), principal, school counselor, and school nurse should meet to make a plan of action for talking to classmates about the death, removing the dead student's belongings, working with the family, and engaging in some form of memorial activity.

> ### 10-5 Internet Support
>
> ### Resources on Death and Dying
>
> There are many resources for helping children and adolescents deal with death and dying.
>
> - Cincinnati Children's Hospital Medical Center's StarShine Hospice provides a list of suggested books about death and grief for preschoolers through adolescents. It also has a list of books that help children prepare for hospital and doctor visits.
> - Parenting Book Reviews has a page devoted to reviews of books about children and death.
> - Hospice Net has a children's section and information on helping younger people cope with death and funerals.
> - "Discussing Death with Children" provides insights into dealing with death in the classroom as a planned or unexpected event. Included are listening guidelines, classroom considerations, and classroom projects.
> - Compassion Books is a commercial website with an annotated listing of more than 400 resources to help children and adults through serious illness, death, loss, grief, and bereavement. The books have been reviewed and selected by knowledgeable professionals.

School personnel should be designated to inform schoolmates of the death, to discuss the death with them, and to answer questions. It is preferable if the classroom teacher, who has an ongoing relationship with the students, is involved in these discussions. When the teacher is too uncomfortable to lead the discussion, it helps if she or he is present while someone else, such as a counselor, leads the discussion. Children should be encouraged to ask questions, and teachers should remain open for questions and comments beyond this initial discussion. Many questions and concerns will surface in the days and weeks that follow, and teachers should be prepared to deal with them as they arise. Teachers have to acknowledge their own feelings about loss so that they can be emotionally available to help their students. By displaying their own emotions, teachers validate the emotions of their students and provide a model for grieving.

The grief work of schoolmates is facilitated by planning and participating in memorial activities for the deceased child and communicating condolences to family survivors. Children need to express their sorrow and to participate in activities such as attending memorial activities, writing notes or drawing pictures for the bereaved family, and creating a memorial book, bulletin board, or memorial garden.

Suicide

Many children and adolescents die from accidents, suicides, or homicides. When death is the result of suicide, young people need a lot of help in understanding why the suicide occurred. It is common for surviving friends, siblings, and children to feel considerable guilt about something they said or did to the deceased individual, and to feel responsible for the suicide. When this occurs, the young person needs adult support and professional counseling to come to terms with the death and to find relief from this sense of responsibility.

Family survivors of a suicide victim are inclined to feel shame about the death. Many may hold religious and personal views in which a person who commits suicide is condemned. These are difficult feelings for family members and friends to work through and require extra support.

In the school setting, teachers can allow students to express their emotions surrounding the suicide, especially through classroom discussions of the death and memorial activities. Depressed students, who might view the suicide as a path to follow, need special help.

Survivors of suicide victims need to talk and vent their feelings. Willingness of friends and school personnel to listen is one of the most important types of support. Survivors must be allowed to relate their feelings over and over if they desire; this action enables them to begin the healing process. While listening, friends and school personnel should be careful not to place blame or rationalize reasons for the suicide. Educators must affirm survivors' right to feel the way that they do.

Adults should avoid making comments such as these:

- It was God's will.
- You must forget her or him.
- He or she must have been insane.
- Don't cry.
- You have other friends.
- You have other children.
- I know how you feel.
- Time will make it easier.

Adults must realize that there is no appropriate timetable for the grief process. Students must be allowed time for recovery, even if it takes months or years.

When Tragedy Comes to School

This section provides an actual account of how a school coped with the tragic death of a student.* Its experience provides an example of all the different needs and issues schools must address in these types of situations.

Coping with the Trauma of a Violent Death

A member of the junior class was murdered one weekend, following a party with friends. She was killed by her boyfriend, a classmate. Both students were well known and well liked in the school. As can be imagined, there was considerable anguish and confusion on the part of all who knew them. The student body was stunned, the small New England community shocked.

The loss of their classmate prompted a variety of emotions among the students. After initial shock and grief, our students experienced anger and varying levels of fear and depression. It was not unusual that at times these emotions commingled indiscriminately. The students needed to be guided through this difficult time so they could deal with their grief and the grieving period would be brought to some sort of acceptable closure.

I hope you never have to deal with such a condition. However, if it does occur, perhaps by knowing our experience you may be better able to manage the situation. The following was our reaction and process.

A Meeting with Classes

Each grade level was addressed on the next school day following the tragedy. The first class to meet was the class of the victim. The students were talked to softly and gently, told that their grief was natural and had a purpose. They were told that the grieving period and subsequent time would help to heal the hurt while preserving the memory of their classmate.

---

*This section on coping with the trauma of a violent death is taken from Franson JP. When tragedy comes to school: coping with student death. *NASSP Bull.* October 1998:88–91. It is reprinted here with permission.

Many students were afraid after the tragic event. They envisioned themselves as experiencing the same tragedy. Many said that they were afraid to be alone, or that they were afraid of the dark. They were comforted and urged not to live their lives in fear. The mere statement gave considerable reassurance. Repeated with confidence and conviction, it had a calming effect.

Finally, students were warned to give no credence to rumor. Rumor, whether true or false, has a destabilizing impact on the entire school. One cannot stress this point often enough. Students must be given as much information as possible from credible sources. They should be urged to reject all statements that begin with, "I heard that . . .". In the absence of personal knowledge, they must assume nothing.

The main office, guidance office, and library were set up as in-school information centers. Students were urged to seek factual information there.

A Place to Be Apart

Grieving students were allowed a place in the school where they could express their grief. They were often too upset to go to their classes, and needed a place where they could talk, cry, or simply sit and reflect. The library was closed for general use and made available to anyone who needed to be apart from classes or classmates.

A Memorial Service

A memorial service conducted in the school gym had a considerable healing effect. Probably its most significant accomplishment was to bring closure to the period of public grieving, while accelerating the end of personal grieving.

The service was primarily for the students; however, since the parents of the victim did not have a memorial service open to the public, we were able to provide a medium by which friends of the family could participate and express their sentiments. The parents also attended the service, and they, too, were consoled.

The service was held after school and was primarily directed to the students. They had "reserved" seating by the podium. Other guests were given the remaining available seats and bleacher seats. More than 1,000 persons attended.

Journalists from all media were invited to the service, although cameras of all types were prohibited. Advance notice of this restriction was given the media where possible; others were informed of the restrictions at the entrance to the gym. This decision lent much to the dignity and solemnity of the service.

A clergyman known to many of the students delivered the eulogies and the prayers. As principal, I spoke, and at various times during the service, the choir sang.

At the conclusion of the service, there was no rush to leave. People stood around talking quietly. Students hugged each other, cried softly, or otherwise consoled one another. Townspeople came by to talk. They were pleased with the sensitive way in which the school managed events. It was an important part of the healing process. Great care should be taken not to miss this opportunity.

Student Support Services In-House and Out-of-House

When students left the memorial service, they were given a paper that told them how they could find support during the next five days in school, and indefinitely out of school. This information was also posted in the halls and office area.

In school, a hotline and drop-in center were established by the guidance directors. The school was open 24 hours a day for the next five days (which included a long weekend).

The telephone numbers of area emergency services and mental health centers were made available. An area outpatient clinic was also available to provide immediate therapeutic services to those in need.

The hotline was active during the first couple of days of its availability. By the fourth and fifth days, there were only one or two calls. Seemingly, the students who used the outreach opportunities felt satisfied. Others may have found comfort simply in knowing that the help was available.

Bereavement Counseling for Staff

It was important not to overlook the emotional needs of staff members during this time. Teachers often have deep personal ties to their students. We contacted a mental health clinic in a neighboring town and requested the services of their bereavement counselors. (The counselors donated their services.) The counselors came to school and talked to the staff members, explaining the stages of the grieving process and the symptoms that the staff members could expect to see in themselves and in the students. They gave suggestions on how to cope with the different situations. Further, they explained how just their coming together had a therapeutic effect that contributed to the healing process.

The knowledge and comfort that staff members gained in this session contributed greatly to their ability to calm themselves and their students.

Staff and Administrative Presence

The first school day after the tragedy was the most difficult day of all. There was much congregating in the halls, cafeteria, gymnasium, and other places with general access. The professional staff members were visible and accessible to students at every opportunity. Questions were answered. Opinions and solace were given with love, caring, and sensitivity. Nothing would have been more devastating than a "business as usual" approach.

Class time was given up freely for the discussion of events. School rules regarding punctuality were relaxed. A caring and sheltering atmosphere pervaded the school building. The students responded with relief and affection. As mentioned earlier, the staff counseling contributed much toward the effectiveness of staff–student counseling.

Civil Officials

The local police chief and an officer came to school to meet with interested students to explain the sequence of legal events that were to follow. They shared as much information as possible, and further explained the potential consequences for their other classmate.

At the courthouse where the trial was to be held, the district attorney met with a delegation of students to discuss the legal process in homicides. Both meetings provided authoritative information with which students could make personal judgments.

The Media

The media provided one of the thorniest problems during the entire process. While some journalists behaved with sensitivity and in a professional manner, others could best be described as carnivores. The latter sought to sensationalize events and intruded on the grief of students with impunity and without apology.

Journalists have a vested interest in all news, but particularly in the spectacular. A middle ground must be found whereby the school can help them meet their professional responsibilities and yet protect individual privacy.

To this end, on school grounds, all interviews with journalists were done exclusively by school administrators and guidance counselors. Journalists and students were kept apart. Any student interviews initiated by journalists were conducted off school grounds. We did not do this until the second school day after the tragedy. In that short time, considerable student animosity developed toward the media.

One young-looking female reporter hid herself in the girls' room, eavesdropped on conversations, and printed them in the evening paper out of context. In another incident, our students were photographed in their grief and ended up on the 6:00 news. It was not surprising, then, that the students requested that their privacy be protected. We supported their request wholeheartedly. From that point on, the members of the media behaved much more responsibly.

During the entire process, no student file information was released. There are statutes that prohibit release of private information; however, in the absence of such statutes, it is still a good idea to maintain confidentiality.

Memorial Tributes

Different kinds of memorials were established on behalf of the deceased student. Members of the school and community sent contributions for a memorial scholarship. The company for whom the victim's father worked matched all contributions on a two-for-one basis. It has turned into our largest scholarship award with an endowment of approximately $20,000.

During the week following the girl's death, the school flag was flown at half-mast.

Students planted a cherry tree and provided a memorial stone. A dedication ceremony was held for the junior class and all others who wished to participate. The school choir also participated.

A page in the class yearbook was dedicated to the student in memoriam. When the class graduated, the parents, in a private meeting with me, were presented a diploma granted in memoriam.

Strength is supposed to come from adversity. I would have to say that such was the case here. In addition, there was a certain coming together of the school and community as a result of heightened sensitivity by those who sought to comfort and those who sought to be comforted.

We are all changed by the past events and yet we are still the same. We shall never forget that year. But there is comfort in knowing that in this very difficult time, we helped.

■ DEATH EDUCATION

Education about life and death assists students and teachers in confronting one's own mortality and that of others. This awareness allows the development of the mature perspectives necessary for decision making about matters of life and death. Death education aims to help students find more depth and meaning in family relationships and friendships, to set goals and priorities, and to better understand the feelings of those who experience dying and bereavement. In addition to gaining an understanding of bereavement and grief processes, students practice and acquire listening and communication skills so that they can assist others through grief work. These skills also help in coping with personal losses.

The following are possible areas of study in a death education unit or course:

- The life cycle
- Definitions, causes, and stages of death
- The meaning of death in American society
- Cross-cultural views and practices related to death
- Funeral ceremonies and alternatives
- Bereavement, grief, and mourning
- Cremation
- Cryogenics
- Organ donations and transplants
- Extending condolences to a relative or friend
- Legal and economic aspects of death
- Understanding the dying relative or friend
- Euthanasia

Before a teacher initiates a death education unit, she or he must confront personal feelings about death and come to terms with these feelings. The teacher, of course, must also be knowledgeable about the subject matter. Components of death education are often included in mental and emotional health units. The activities in **Box 10-7** can help you teach the content and skills often included in units addressing death.

10-6 Activities for Dealing with Suicide

The following are examples of teaching activities that deal with suicide—a subject usually addressed at the high school level. These activities help students review the warning signs of suicide, the proper steps to take in prevention and intervention, and the importance of life. Be sure to invite your school counselor to participate. One or more of the students in your class may have experienced the loss of someone close as a result of suicide, and you need to be prepared to handle appropriately any emotional needs that may surface.

Lesson Plans

You can find lesson plans on suicide prevention at the SOS Signs of Suicide: Suicide Prevention Program for High Schools website at http://www.mentalhealthscreening.org/highschool. This school-based program produced a reduction in suicide attempts (by 40%) in a randomized controlled study (*American Journal of Public Health*, March 2004). The main teaching tool of the SOS program is a video that teaches students how to identify symptoms of depression and suicidality in themselves or their friends and encourages help seeking. The program's primary objectives are to educate teens that depression is a treatable illness and to equip them to respond to a potential suicide in a friend or family member using the SOS technique. SOS is an action-oriented approach instructing students how to ACT (acknowledge, care, and tell) in the face of this mental health emergency.

Chalk Line

Draw a horizontal line across a chalkboard. Tell the class that this line represents the timeline of a person's life. Have the students identify the gender of the person and name the person. Divide the class into three groups. Have one group come up with important events that take place in the "chalk person's" school years. Have the second group identify events in the person's young adult years, and have the third group identify events for midlife and beyond. Give the groups a few minutes to work independently to determine their life events. Then, have the first group come up to the chalk line and mark in the important events, followed by the second group, and finally the third group. Don't be surprised if students mark in both good and bad events. Let them have fun with it. When they are finished, say, "I'm sorry, this was to have been Jane Doe's life, but on (give a specific date and time indicating she died as a teenager) she committed suicide." Draw a very heavy line showing time of death. At this point, the students will most likely become very quiet as they think about all that this fictitious person would have missed out on. This activity can be useful in introducing the topics of suicide and how life should be celebrated.

Letters

Assign students to write a letter to an imaginary friend who is contemplating suicide.

Speaker

Invite a suicide hotline crisis worker or other mental health specialist to talk with your class about suicide prevention and intervention.

(continues)

(continued)

Brainstorm

Have students brainstorm the warning signs of suicide. Discuss how and why each sign makes suicide a likely possibility.

Dos and Don'ts

In small groups, have students compile lists of *dos* and *don'ts* in helping suicidal students. Have each group share its lists with the rest of the class.

Role-Play

Have students role-play situations in which they practice suicide intervention and prevention. Examples of role-play situations include pretending to be a worker at a suicide hotline or responding to a friend who is contemplating suicide. Be sure to guide students in active listening skills and enlisting the help of adults.

10-7 Activities for Teaching Loss as a Part of Life

The teaching activities described here deal with loss and seeing death as a part of life. The appropriate grade level for each activity is indicated. As you prepare to teach this topic, tell your school counselor about your plans and invite him or her to attend and participate. Be aware that one or more of your students may have recently had someone close to them die. Be prepared to respond appropriately to any unexpected emotions.

Confronting Mortality and Dealing with Bereavement

Falling Leaves

Collect leaves and make a display in the classroom of a variety of shapes, sizes, and colors. Liken them to the uniqueness of individual lives. Discuss the finite nature of life and the reassurance that our world goes on. (P, K, I, J, H)

Pets

Allow children to talk about the death of pets or of relatives. This gives you an opportunity to teach the acceptance of death as part of life. (P, K, I, J)

Literature

Comment on death and loss as it occurs in the literature that you read in the classroom. Discuss how grieving characters act and help your students understand the need for grief work. Reinforce the fact that loss is universal, that it hurts, and that life goes on. (I, J, H)

In the News

Discuss violent deaths that are prominent in local or national news. Help students empathize with grieving families. Teach students safe ways to express verbally or nonverbally any anger they feel. (I, J, H)

Draw

Have students draw a picture entitled "Death." This is a good groundbreaking activity for the subject. It will also give you a quick preview of who has experience with death, who sees it as an abstract cartoon, and who may have fears concerning death. These pictures can then serve as a starting point for discussions on death. (I, J, H)

Panel Discussion

Invite representatives from different religions to discuss their beliefs about death and life after death. Have students prepare questions for panel members in advance. (H)

Finding Deeper Meaning in Life and Relationships
Obituary

Have students write their own obituaries. The purpose of this activity is to help them identify all the things they want to fill their lives with. It demonstrates the fact that each of their "stories" has a beginning and an end. Provide your students with examples of actual obituaries from newspapers. Instruct students to select the age and cause of death and to enumerate on their accomplishments and activities. (I, J, H)

Two Years

Have students close their eyes, take a deep breath, and relax. Tell them: "Imagine yourself in your favorite place to be alone, someplace you like to go when you want to think something through. It is very comfortable, warm, and quiet there. You feel very calm and relaxed, and at peace. Your feelings are a little surprising, because you have been told you have only 2 years to live. You have already gone through denial, anger, and bargaining, and have come to accept your circumstances. You have come to this special place to think about what it is you want to do with the time you have left. Take a few moments now and visualize what it is you want to do with the 2 years you have left." Give students about 5 minutes to think this through. You may need to speak occasionally, helping them through this visualization. At the end of the visualization, instruct students to take a deep breath, let it out slowly, and to slowly come back to the present and open their eyes. Discuss their visualizations and what they wanted to do with their limited time. This activity helps students identify their priorities in life. It can also help illustrate the point that everyone dies, but not everyone lives. (J, H)

Role-Play

Have students role-play the following situations: talking to a very ill grandparent, talking to a terminally ill friend, asking their healthy parent about their living will or funeral desires, talking to a grieving person, and talking to a person with suicidal thoughts. (I, J, H)

Roots

Have students fill out a family tree with their parents or guardians. In addition to becoming familiar with ancestors' names and dates and places of birth and death, suggest that students inquire about their ancestors' personalities and characteristics. (I, J, H)

(continues)

(continued)

Decision Making

Funeral
Have students plan and enact a funeral for an imaginary person or animal. (I, J, H)

Other Customs
Have students research other cultures' perspectives on death and funeral customs. In addition, have them look for changes that have taken place in their own culture related to death and funerals over the past 200 years. (I, J, H)

Mortuary
Have students visit a mortuary and report on itemized costs of funerals and other services. (H)

Living Will
After discussing the importance of organ donations and transplants, create a living will as a class. (I, J, H)

Do Not Resuscitate
Discuss what a DNR order is. Have students do Internet searches for details on what DNR orders do and don't do and when and how they are created.

Organ Donation
Have students do Internet research on organ donation.

Hospice
Ask a representative from a local hospice to speak to your class about the needs of those with terminal illnesses and about hospice services. (I, J, H)

Instruction Plan Worksheet Suicide and Death Education

Use this worksheet to plan suicide prevention and possible death education topics at the grade level you will be teaching. Refer to Chapter 2 for more information on how to complete each section in this worksheet.

■ Assess Needs

Identify topics and skills state or local curricula identify to be taught at ___ grade level.

Identify additional topics or skills the ME HECAT Module indicates for this grade.

Identify suicide and death needs your particular students and their families have:
- Have deaths occurred in recent years to students, staff, or family members?
- What perceptions do students have about suicide and death?
- What cultural practices regarding death exist within your community?
- How comfortable are you with talking about death/mourning with others?

■ Set Major Learning Goal(s)

Identify your major learning goal(s)–what do you want to have happen?

■ **Develop Instruction Map**

Create a map (calendar or list of days) indicating the time frame you have/need to teach the curriculum, meet student needs and reach goal(s). For each day indicate the content/skills to be taught. Work to create a good flow.

■ Write SMART Unit Objectives

Write 1 or 2 major objectives for each day you will teach. Your objectives should be in alignment with your state/local curricula, your student's needs, and your major learning goal(s).

■ Identify Assessment Tools

Preassessment	Formative-Assessment	Postassessment
How will you determine what students already know or do?	How will you know if they are "getting it"?	How will you know if students mastered objectives?

Instruction Plan Worksheet Suicide and Death Education

■ **Develop Unit Plan**

Divide the chart into the number of days you will teach. Record each day's topic and objective key words. Identify activity names (in the book) that can help you meet each day's objective. Identify tech tools you can use and possible lesson adaptations you can make for special need learners.

Lesson Objectives	Instruction Activities	Tech Tools	Adaptations for Learners

■ **Develop Lesson Plans**

Use the Lesson Plan Template found in Chapter 2 and this worksheet to create detailed lesson plans regarding suicide and death education.

KEY TERMS

contract for life   318
self-injury   320
grief work   321
preparatory grief   330
denial   330

anger   330
bargaining   330
depression   330
acceptance   330

KNOWLEDGE CHECK!

1. Define and explain the relative importance of each of the key terms in the context of this chapter.
2. Summarize the key elements of crises plans, preparations, short-term responses and services, and long-term responses and services.
3. Discuss the prevalence and risk factors for suicide, including age, gender, ethnicity, and means.
4. Identify various verbal, behavioral, and situation warning signs of suicide.
5. Explain in detail what to do when someone confides he or she is thinking about committing suicide.
6. Identify resources for suicide prevention and suicide prevention strategies.
7. Explain why young people engage in acts of self-injury and how educators should respond.
8. Discuss various culture-related practices regarding death and explain how knowing these practices can be helpful for a teacher.
9. Identify age-related concepts that preschoolers, children, and adolescents have regarding death. Identify the needs that children have concerning death.
10. Identify the stages a family passes through when a family member has a terminal illness, and explain what teachers and school personnel can do to help in each of the stages.
11. Describe the possible responses a child and an adolescent may have to the death of a parent. Identify normal emotional, physical, and behavioral reactions experienced in bereavement.
12. Identify when additional support, counseling, or therapy may be needed by a student.
13. Enumerate some of the unique emotions, stresses, and needs a student can experience with the death of a sibling and of a pet. Identify how teachers can be helpful in each situation.
14. Describe how schools can provide a supportive environment for a terminally ill child.
15. Identify the needs of a dying child and explain the stages of preparatory grief.
16. Describe the roles a teacher and classmates can fulfill for a terminally ill student. Describe how classmates can be guided to deal with the situation.
17. Describe the best environment for students to deal with the trauma of a fellow student's death. Discuss all that needs to happen upon the news of a student's or teacher's death.
18. Discuss the particular needs young people have when dealing with a suicide and what teachers need to do following a suicide.
19. Outline how to deal with the needs and issues a school must address after a violent death.
20. Identify why death education is included in curricula, what it can contain, and which kinds of special preparation teachers need to successfully deal with the subject in the classroom.

REFERENCES

1. Centers for Disease Control and Prevention, Suicide and National Center for Injury Prevention and Control, Division of Violence Prevention. Facts at a glance 2012. Available at http://www.cdc.gov/violenceprevention/pdf/suicide-datasheet-a.PDF. Accessed February 25, 2013.
2. Skegg K. Self-harm. *Lancet.* 2005;366(9495):1471–1483.

3. Lobar SL, Youngblut JM, Brooten D. Cross-cultural beliefs, ceremonies, and rituals surrounding death of a loved one. *Pediatric Nurse.* 2006;32(1):44–50.
4. Butler AR. Scratchy is dead. In: Thomas JL, ed. *Death and dying in the classroom: readings for reference.* Phoenix, AZ: Oryx Press; 1984.
5. Wolfelt AD. Helping teenagers cope with grief. 2005. Available at http://www.hospicenet.org/html/teenager.html. Accessed August 24, 2009.
6. HELPGUIDE. Stages of grief: saying goodbye when a family member is dying. Available at http://www.helpguide.org/harvard/saying_goodbye.htm. Accessed February 25, 2013.
7. Brenner A. *Helping children cope with stress.* Lexington, MA: Lexington Books; 1984.
8. Kaufman KR, Kaufman N. And then the dog died. *Death Studies.* 2006;30(1):61–76.
9. Bryant EH. Teacher in crisis: a classmate is dying. In: Thomas JL, ed. *Death and dying in the classroom: readings for reference.* Phoenix, AZ: Oryx Press; 1984.
10. Bertoia J, Allan J. School management of the bereaved child. *Elementary School Guidance Counseling.* 1988;23:30–39.
11. Keith CR, Ellis D. Reaction of pupils and teachers to death in the classroom. In: Thomas JL, ed. *Death and dying in the classroom: readings for reference.* Phoenix, AZ: Oryx Press; 1984.

INDEX

Note: Page numbers followed by *b, f* and *t* indicate material in boxes, figures and tables respectively.

A

AAHE. *See* American Association for Health Education
AAP. *See* American Academy of Pediatrics
AAPCC. *See* American Association of Poison Control Centers
abortion, 256
abstinence education, 253
abstinence-only education, 253
abstinence-plus education, 253
abstract learning style, 30
absurdity, 116
abuse, 320. *See also* alcohol use and abuse; drug use and abuse
   child abuse. *See* child abuse
   emotional, 294
   physical, 293
   sexual, 294
   youth violence, 285–286
acceptance, preparatory grief stage, 330
accessing valid information skills, 259
acquaintance rape, 298. *See also* rape
acquaintance stage, relationships, 62
acquired heart disease, 19
acquired immunodeficiency syndrome (AIDS), 16, 226, 264
active learning, 27
active listening, 60
activities. *See* application exercise
acute stress, 98. *See also* stress
ad creep, 139–140
Adderall, 16
addiction, 219–222. *See also* alcohol use and abuse; drug use and abuse
ADHD. *See* attention-deficit/hyperactivity disorder
adolescents, 8
   dealing with deaths, 321–329, 332*b*
   early age maturation, 248
   peer-led prevention programs, 257
   to prevent HIV infection, 255
   unintended teen pregnancy, 262
adult-onset diabetes, 172
advertising
   alcohol and tobacco use, 200–201
   overweight and obesity, 165–166
   placement of, 139
   power of, 138–141
   sexual content, 249
advocacy
   communication skills, 60–61
   sexual health, 260
   substance abuse prevention, 206

aerosols, 225
affective skill, 42
aggressive expression, feelings, 60
AIDS. *See* acquired immunodeficiency syndrome
Al-Anon, 222
Alateen, 222
Alcohol and Other Drug-Free (AOD) HBOs, 207*b*
alcohol use and abuse, 217. *See also* substance abuse
   activities, 235*b*–237*b*
   addiction in families, 219–222
   alcoholism, 14, 217–218
   date-rape, 232
   driving, 217, 223
   media promotion, 200–201
   overview, 217–222
   problems associated with, 218*f*
   trends, 198
   violent behavior, 287–288
alcoholism, 217–218
alertness, relaxed, 26
all-or-nothing thinking, 100
American Academy of Pediatrics (AAP), 137–138, 148, 286
American Association for Health Education (AAHE), 37
American Association of Poison Control Centers (AAPCC), 300
American Legacy Foundation, 201
amygdala, 28
anabolic steroids, 226
anemia, 168
anesthetics, 225
angel dust, 230
anger, 330
   management, 68–69
angina, 174
anorexia nervosa, 170–171
antibiotics, 18
anxiety disorders, 110–112. *See also* stress
application exercise
   death, 321*b*
   diet and activity, 165*b*
   favorite activities, 52*b*
   marks on you, 12*b*
   personal stress management, 100*b*
   self-inventory, 253*b*
   substance use, 199*b*
   TV review, 136*b*
   Web tools, health education, 34*b*

arthritis, 175
arts, 118–120
assertiveness, 60–61
asset development, 71–72
asthma, 19
atherosclerosis, 173
attention-deficit/hyperactivity disorder (ADHD), 15–16
attitude, 39–40
attractiveness, influence of, 8
auditory learning style, 30
autogenic training, 117–118

B

B cells, 99
bacteria, 265*b*
bad trip, 230
bargaining, 330
behavior
   bereavement, 322*b*
   put-down behavior, 10–11
   student, expectations for, 9
   suicide, signs of, 316
   teachers' 10 commandments, 9
Bennett, William, 7
bereavement, 322*b*
   counseling for staff, 335
Bergsma, Lynda, 133
bidis, 215
binge eating, 171
bipolar disorder, 109–110
birth rates, teenage, 262
bisexual people, 256, 283
black humor, 116
black tar heroin, 228
blaming, distorted thinking, 101
Bloom's Taxonomy, 42
blunts, 223
BMI. *See* body mass index
bodily-kinesthetic intelligence, 30
body image, media's influence on, 167–168
body language, 13, 58
body mass index (BMI), 162
boredom, student, 105
brain, 23–25
   levels of, 25*f*
   teaching and, 25–29
brain plasticity, 25
brain stem, 24–25
branded environments, 141
breakfast, importance of, 168
bulimia, 171

347

bullying, 105, 137, 282. *See also* violence
  behavior, 284
  cyberbullying, 283
  effects and warning signs, 284
  prevention, 285
  risk factors, 283
burnout, teacher, 107
buzz marketing, 139

C

calcium, 174
calories, 164
cancer, 19, 174
candidiasis, 267
cannabis, marijuana and, 223–224
casual sex, 261
CDC. *See* Centers for Disease Control and Prevention
celebrities, self-image and, 55
cell phones, 60
Centers for Disease Control and Prevention (CDC), 17, 31, 134
  abstinence education, 253
  categories of risk behavior, 32–33, 33*f*
cerebral palsy, 19
Cervarix, 266
cessation programs in schools, 216
chalk, 227–228
Channel One, 140
character, corruption of, 261
character education, 55–56
characteristics of effective health education curricula, 34–35
chewing tobacco, 215
child abuse, 13
  handling disclosure, 295
  physical indicators, 294–295
  prevention
    individual action, 297
    school-based programs, 296
    school–community programs, 296–297
  reporting statutes, 295
children
  dealing with deaths, 321–329, 332*b*
  HIV prevention education, 254–255
  marketing and advertising to, 140
  of teenage mothers, 263
  terminal illness, supportive environment for, 329–331
  vulnerable to advertising, 140
chlamydia, 266
cholesterol, 173
chronic abuse, 225
chronic health conditions, 18–19, 105
chronic stress, 98. *See also* stress
cigarettes, 198, 211–212
  advertisements, 201
  daily deaths from, 213*f*
Cipher in the Snow, 1–2
circle of concern, 3–4
circle of influence, 3–5
circulatory system, 118
civil officials, 335
classmates' role, in terminal ill child, 330–331
classroom policies, 8, 10*b*
clove cigarettes, 215
clown, family roles, 222
club drugs, 229–231
cocaine, 227
cognitive distortion, 100–101
cognitive restructuring, 117
cognitive skill, 42
cold turkey, 229
collaboration, school personnel, 176
communication
  crisis response, 312
  nonverbal, 8
  skills
    activities for, 76*b*–80*b*
    assertiveness and advocacy, 60–61
    electronic, 60
    empathy, 61–62
    relationship building, 62–65, 63*f*
    sending and interpreting messages, 58–60
    sexual health, 259
    styles, 61*f*
community involvement, 37, 177
competition, stress and, 105
comprehensive sex education, 253
compulsions, 111
concern, circle of, 3–4
Concerta, 16
concrete learning style, 30
conditional worth, 53
conflicts, 63
  management, 70
  parental, 104
congenital heart disease, 19
connectedness, 7
Consumer Product Safety Commission (CPSC), 145
contact, relationships, 62
contemplation, 40
contraceptives, 255–256
contract for life, 318
conversation skills, 60
coordinated school health program (CSHP), 35–37, 36*f*
coordination, learning disabilities, 15
coping skills, stress, 115–117
  activities, 123*b*–124*b*
coronary heart disease, 173–174
cortisol, 98
counseling services, 36
counselors, 13–15
crabs. *See* pubic lice
crack cocaine, 227
crank, 227–228
crisis centers and hotlines, 319*b*
crisis response plans, 333–336
  long-term responses and services, 314
  preparations for, 312–313
  short-term responses and services, 313–314
cross-cultural understanding, 13
crystal, 227–228
CSHP. *See* coordinated school health program
culture, 13
  and death practices, 321–323
  and sexual development, 250–251
  suicide and, 314
curriculum
  health education, 34–35
  HECAT, 34, 206
  sex education, 259
  substance abuse prevention, 206–211
  suicide awareness, 319*b*
cutting, self-injury, 320
cyberbullying, 137, 283
cycling (anabolic steroids), 226

D

DARE. *See* Drug Abuse Resistance Education
date rape, 298
  drugs, 229, 231, 232
death, 323*f*–325*f*
  activities about, 338*b*–340*b*
  age-related concepts and needs, 323–326
  bereavement, 322*b*
  from cigarettes, 213*f*
  cultural practices, 321–323
  dealing with, 321–329
  education about, 336
  parental, 327–328
  per year from substance abuse, 212*f*
  of pets, 329
  responses to, 331–336
  of sibling, 328–329
  stress of, 105
  from youth suicide, 314
decision-making skills, 69–72
  activities for, 85*b*–89*b*
  sexual health, 259
delayed gratification, 67–68
delta-9-tetrahydrocannabinol, 223–224
denial, 330
dental decay, 175

depression, 226, 261, 330
   student support teams, 14
   suicide and, 109, 315, 317
   types, 109–110
depressive disorder, 108
deterioration stage, relationships, 63
determinism, 66
Dexedrine (dextroamphetamine), 16
diabetes, 19, 172–173
diaphragmatic breathing, 117
diazepam (Valium), 231
Dietary Guidelines for Americans, 177
digital advertising, 139
discipline, 8–10
disease transmission, drug injection and, 232
dissolves, relationships, 63
distorted thinking patterns, 100
distress, 98
diversity, 12–13
divorce, 14, 104–105
dopamine, 28
downshift, 26
Drug Abuse Resistance Education (DARE), 202
drug-free activities, 204, 238*b*–240*b*
drug injection and disease transmission, 232
drug-resistant microorganisms, 18
drug use and abuse, 224. *See also* substance abuse
   addiction in families, 219–222
   anabolic steroids, 226
   club drugs, 229–231
   cocaine, 227
   date-rape drugs, 231–232
   eating disorders, 14
   heroin, 228–229
   inhalants, 225–226
   methamphetamine, 227–228
   oxycodone, 225
   student support teams, 14
   trends, 198–199
dysfunctional families, 105
dysthymia. *See* dysthymic disorder
dysthymic disorder, 109

E

e-mail, 60
early sexual maturation, 248
early warning signs of violence, 291
eating disorders, 169
economic stressors, 102
Ecstasy, 229
effective teachers, characteristics of, 5
electronic communication, 60
emotional abuse, 294
emotional climate, 10

emotional concerns, 14
emotional maltreatment, 294
emotions, 61–62
   death and, 322*b*
emotive reasoning, 101
empathy, 61–62
endocrine system, 98
energy drinks, 166
English language skills, 29
environment, 11
   supportive school, 176
environmental determinism, 66
epilepsy, 19
estrogen, 251
ethnicity, 12, 199
ethnocentricity, 13
eustress, 98
evacuation procedures, 312
Evans, Cliff, 1–2, 7
exercise
   resistance, 174–175
   weight-bearing, 174
expectations, 7–8
experience, learning through, 25
exploration, learning through, 29
extension activities, 46
external assets, 71
external rewards, behavior, 39

F

factual questions, 46
families
   addiction and, 219–222
   food choices and, 164–165
   involvement of, 37
   stress in, 14
family clown, 222
family hero, 219–221
fashion models, body image and, 167–168
fat burning analogy, 170*b*
FDA. *See* Food and Drug Administration
fear, 101, 110
Federal Trade Commission (FTC), 145
fetal alcohol effects (FAE), 217*b*
fetal alcohol syndrome (FAS), 217*b*
fight-or-flight response, 97
filtering, 100
financial skills, 113
fire (methamphetamine), 227–228
flagella, 265*b*
flashback, 230
flunitrazepam (Rohypnol), 231
food allergy, 166–167
Food and Drug Administration (FDA), 145
food, choices about, 164–165, 167–168
formative assessment, 42

formication, 227
Frankl, Victor, 66
FTC. *See* Federal Trade Commission
fungi, 265*b*

G

GAD. *See* generalized anxiety disorder
gamma-aminobutyric acid (GABA), 110
gamma hydroxybutyric acid (GHB), 232
Gardasil, 266
GAS. *See* general adaptation syndrome
gatekeeper training, 319*b*
gender differences
   self-injury, 320
   smoking and, 214–215
   stress, 99–100
   suicide, 314
general adaptation syndrome (GAS), 97
generalized anxiety disorder (GAD), 111
Generation M, 134, 135
genetic determinism, 66
genital warts, 266
GHB. *See* gamma hydroxybutyric acid
Girls Intelligence Agency (GIA), 140
glass (methamphetamine), 227–228
Glasser, William, 7
global learning style, 30
globesity, 162
"go box," 312
goal-setting, 32
   activities for, 81*b*–85*b*
   anger management, 68–69
   being proactive, 66–68
   overview, 65–66
   sexual health, 260
gonorrhea, 266
government, 29
grading
   assessments, 42
   substance abuse prevention, 206–210
Grady, Melissa, 13
gray matter, brain, 23
grief, 313, 321–336
grief work, 321, 332
guilty conscience, 261
Guttmacher Institute, 252

H

Hall, Bill, 4, 5
hallucinations, 230
hallucinogenic drug, 230
hand washing, 17
hashish, 223. *See also* drug use and abuse
hashish oil, 223
health behavior outcomes (HBOs), 51, 178*b*, 207*b*, 292
Health Belief Model, 38

health conditions, 17–19
health consequences of smoking, 212–214
health education
    behavior change
        Health Belief Model, 38
        SCT, 38–39
        stages of change model, 40
        theory of planned behavior, 39–40
    CDC's categories of risk behavior, 32–33
    CSHP, 35–37
    curriculum, effective, 34–35
    HECAT, 34
    NCATE preparation standards, 37
    NHES, 31–32
    state and district guidelines, 33
Health Education Curriculum Analysis Tool (HECAT), 34, 292
    healthy eating and physical activity, 178b
    mental and emotional health, 50, 51b
    safety, 300, 301b
    sexual health, 258b
    substance abuse prevention, 207b
    violence prevention, 292, 293b
health information
    reliable, 144
        sources of, 145
    unreliable, 144
health literacy, 29–31
health organizations, 145
health services, 36
healthy behavior outcomes (HBOs), 207b, 257, 258b
healthy eating. *See also* obesity; overweight
    breakfast, 168
    dietary guidelines, 177–179
    MyPlate, 179–180, 179f
    national standards, 180–181
    overview, 161
    and physical activity
        activities for, 183b–188b
        community involvement, 177
        parental involvement, 176
        School Health Guidelines, 175–176
        school personnel collaboration, 176
        supportive school environment, 176
Healthy People 2010, 163
heart attack, 174
heart disease, 19
HECAT. *See* Health Education Curriculum Analysis Tool
helper's high, 114
hepatitis B, 267
hero identification, 54–55
heroin, 228–229
herpes simplex virus, 267
high blood pressure, 173

high-risk students, 210
high school, substance abuse prevention, 209–210
higher-order thinking skills, 42
HIV. *See* human immunodeficiency virus
H1N1 virus, 18
home alone, stress and, 104
home-based stress, 103–105
homeostasis, 97
homicide, 32
hookahs, 215
hormones, 98
human immunodeficiency virus (HIV), 226
    infection, 264
    prevention education
        kindergarten through third grade, 254
        secondary level, 255
        upper elementary grades, 255
human papillomavirus (HPV), 266
humor, 115–116
hydraulic lift, 11
hyperactivity, 15

I

"I" messages, 59
ice (methamphetamine), 228
ideal-self, 53
    character and values education, 55–56
    hero identification, 54–55
illicit drugs, 199
illness, 17–19
imagery, 118
immigration, 102
imminent warning signs of violence, 291
immune system, 99
immunization schedule, 18
impulse control, 67–68
impulsivity, 15
inattention, 15
incest, 294
influence, circle of, 3–5
influenza, 19
information-based strategies, substance abuse, 202–203
information literacy, 144–146
inhalants, 199, 225–226
injuries. *See also* violence
    alcohol and, 217
    self-injury, 320
    substance abuse and, 197
inner monologues, 115
innovative teachers, 29
instruction design template, 43, 43f
instruction mapping, 41
instructional planning
    assessing needs, 40–41

instruction mapping, 41
lesson plan, 44–46
for MEH, 51
setting learning goals, 41
unit design, 42–43
unit planning, 41–42
insulin resistance, 173
internal assets, 72
internal rewards, behavior, 39
Internet. *See also* Web resources
    evaluating information on, 145–146
    marketing, 141
    use concerns, 136–137
interpersonal intelligence, 30
interpersonal skills
    assertiveness and advocacy, 60–61
    empathy, 61–62
    relationship building, 62–65, 63f
    sending and interpreting messages, 58–60
interpreting art, 119t
intimacy stage, relationships, 62
intimate-partner violence, 298
intrapersonal intelligence, 30
iron-deficiency anemia, 168
irony, 116

J

Jillian, Ann, 54
journals, 116
jumping to conclusions, stress and, 100
junior high school, substance abuse prevention, 209
junk sleep, 114

K

ketamine, 232
Kilbourne, Jean, 138
kinesthetic learning style, 30
kreteks, 215

L

labels, 101
language, 14–15
learning disability (LD), 14, 15
learning goals, setting, 41
learning styles, 29–31
lesbian, gay, bisexual, and transgender (LGBT), 256
lesson plan, 44–46, 44f, 45f
LGBT. *See* lesbian, gay, bisexual, and transgender
Lickona, Tomas, 55
life skills, 49–50
    communication and interpersonal
        assertiveness and advocacy, 60–61

empathy, 61–62
relationship building, 62–65, 63f
sending and interpreting messages, 58–60
decision-making and problem-solving, 69–72
goal-setting and self-management
anger management, 68–69
being proactive, 66–68
overview, 65–66
self-awareness and evaluation, 51–58
standards for, 31–32
suicide and, 319b
teaching, 50–51
Life Skills Training program, 203–204
life-threatening diseases, 264
limbic system, 24, 142
linguistic intelligence, 30
listening skills, 59–60, 59f
logical-mathematical intelligence, 30
long-term crisis responses and services, 314
lost child, 221–222
lower-order thinking skills, 42
LSD. *See* lysergic acid diethylamide
lymph, 99
lymphocytes, 99
lysergic acid diethylamide (LSD), 230

M

magnification, distorted thinking, 101
maintenance, behavior change, 40
major depression. *See* major depressive disorder
major depressive disorder, 109
Make It Happen—School Nutrition Success Stories, 167
manic-depressive illness, 109
mapping instruction, 41
marijuana, 198–199, 223–224
marital rape, 298
marketing. *See* advertising
mascot, 222
mastery experiences, 39
MDMA. *See* Ecstasy
media, 146, 335. *See also* media literacy
activities for analyzing and monitoring, 152b–154b
activities for sexual messages, 267b–269b
alcohol and tobacco use, 200–201
analyzing and technology influences, 146–148
exposure, concerns about, 137–138
influence on body image, 167–168
instruction resources, 146b
management, 148
creative alternatives, 150–151

limitations, 149
online safety tips, 149
positive media choices, 150
producers, consolidation of, 135
reinforces stereotypes, 135
and sexual content, 249–250
stress and, 104
use and concerns, 134–138
violence, influence of, 286–287
youth, use by, 165–166
media literacy, 133–134. *See also* media
accessing valid information activities, 151b
advertising, power of, 138–141
exposure concerns, 137–138
information literacy, 144–146
medications, 16, 110. *See also* drug use and abuse
meditation, 68
MEH. *See* mental and emotional health
memorial service, 334, 336
mental and emotional health (MEH), 51
activities for, 72b–75b
mental disorders
anxiety disorders, 110–112
depressive disorders, 108–110
mental imagery, 118
methamphetamine, 227–228
methylphenidate (Ritalin), 16
microbes, disease-causing, 265b
middle childhood, dealing with deaths, 326
middle/junior high school, substance abuse prevention, 209
military deployment, stress and, 104
minor depression, 109
mixed messages, 59
mobile marketing, 140
modeling, 3, 5, 38
money management, 113–114
Monitoring the Future (MTF), 198
morals, 54–56. *See also* sexual behavior and health
motor skills, 15
motor vehicle crashes, 32, 217
muscular system, 117
mushrooms, psilocybin, 231
music, 118
musical intelligence, 30
mycoses, 265b
MyPlate, 179–180, 179f

N

naming rights, 139
National Campaign to Prevent Teen and Unplanned Pregnancy, 248
National Council for Accreditation of Teacher Education (NCATE), 37

National Health Education Standards (NHES), 31–32, 50
National Health Information Center (NHIC), 145
National Institute on Drug Abuse, 198
National Sexuality Education Standards, 257–260
National Standards, for healthy eating, 180–181
National Survey on Drug Use and Health (NSDUH), 198
natural calamities, 102–103
naturalist intelligence, 30
NCATE. *See* National Council for Accreditation of Teacher Education
NCATE Health Education Teacher Preparation Standards, 37
negative thinking patterns, 101
neglect, child, 293
neural branching, 25
neural pruning, 25
neustress, 98
NHES. *See* National Health Education Standards
NHIC. *See* National Health Information Center
nicotine, 212, 214, 215
nitrous oxide, 225
nonoxynol-9, 265
nonverbal communication, 8
nonverbal learning disorders, 15
normative beliefs, 40
normative education, 203
November, Alan, 144
nutrition services, 36
nystagmus, 231

O

obesity, 162
rate of, 149
trends and influencing factors, 162–168
energy drinks, 166
excessive intake of calories, 164
family and social factors, 164–165
food in schools, 166–167
media and marketing, 165–166
media's influence on body image, 167–168
physical inactivity, 162–164
obsessions, 111
obsessive–compulsive disorder (OCD), 111
O'Malley, Frank, 6, 7
omnipresent media, 134
online safety, 149
open-ended questions, 46
opportunistic diseases, 264

INDEX 351

oral leukoplakias, 215
orchestrated immersion, 27
organization skills, 113
osteoporosis, 174–175
out-of-school youths, programs for, 257
overgeneralizing, 100
overscheduling, 103
overweight, 162, 163f
   rate of, 149
   trends and influencing factors, 162–168
      energy drinks, 166
      excessive intake of calories, 164
      family and social factors, 164–165
      food in schools, 166–167
      media and marketing, 165–166
      media's influence on body image, 167–168
      physical inactivity, 162–164
oxycodone, 225
oxytocin, 251

P

panic attacks, 112
panic disorder, 112
parasympathetic nervous system, 98, 118
parental conflict, 104
parents
   communication with child, 259
   death of, 327–328
   educating youth suicide, 319b
   healthy eating and physical activity promotion, 176
   substance abuse prevention, 205–206
parody, 116
Partnership for 21st Century Skills, 29
passive expression, feelings, 60
passive listening, 60
PCP (phencyclidine), 230–231
PECAT. See Physical Education Curriculum Analysis Tool
peer approaches, substance abuse prevention, 204
peer counselors, 204
peer-led prevention programs, 257
peer pressure, 105
peer support groups, suicide and, 319b
peer-to-peer marketing, 139
peer tutors, 204
perceived behavioral control, 40
personal development, stunted, 261
personal skills, substance abuse prevention, 203–204
persuasion, 39
pets, deaths of, 329
phencyclidine, 230–231
physical abuse, 13, 293, 320
physical activity
   brain function and, 29
   curriculum, 181–183
   healthy eating and
      activities for, 183b–188b
      community involvement, 177
      parental involvement, 176
      School Health Guidelines, 175
      school personnel collaboration, 176
      supportive school environment, 176
   lack of, 162–164
      diseases related to, 171–175
      problems related to, 168–171
   stress and, 117
Physical Activity Guidelines for Americans, 182
physical attractiveness, 8
physical dependence, 229
physical education, 36, 182
Physical Education Curriculum Analysis Tool (PECAT), 183
physical fitness, 182
physical ideal, 54
physical sensations, death and, 322b
planned behavior, theory of, 39–40
planning skills, 24
play, 116. See also physical activity
policies, classroom, 8, 10b
pornography, 137, 256–257
portion distortion, 164
positive emotional state, 39
positive interpersonal relationships, 62
post-traumatic stress disorder (PTSD), 112
postassessments, 42
poverty, 102
PowerPoint technology, 142–143
preassessment, 42
precontemplation, 40
prefrontal cortex, brain, 24
pregnancy. See also sexual behavior and health
   alcohol use, 217
   and STIs, 260
   teen
      delivery rates, 248
      laws and, 263–264
      unintended, 250
prejudice, 13
preparation, behavior change, 40
preparatory grief, 330
preschool-age children, dealing with deaths, 326
prescription drug, 199
primitive brain, 24–25
proactive people, 4, 66–67
probing questions, 46
problem-solving skills, 69–72
   activities for, 85b–89b
procedures, classroom, 8
product placement, 139
progesterone, 251
progressive muscular relaxation, 118
protective factors, resilience, 71
protozoa, 265b
psilocybin mushrooms, 231
psychic determinism, 66
psychological services, 36
psychologists, 13, 14
psychomotor skill, 42
psychotherapeutic drugs, 199
PTSD. See post-traumatic stress disorder
puberty
   hormones, 250–251
   premature, 168
pubic lice, 267
puns, 116
purging, weight control, 171
put-down behavior, 10–11
Pygmalion effect, 56–57
Pygmalion-self, 53, 56–57
pyramid of influence, 2, 4

R

racism, 12, 13, 199
RAD teaching, 27–28
rape, 298
RAS. See reticular activating system
raves, 229–231
reactive people, 4, 66–67
reading, 15
reasoning skills, 24
reducing stress, activities for, 121b–122b
Reeve, Christopher, 66, 67
reflective listening, 60
refusal skills, 203, 259
reinforcements, behavior, 38–39
relationship bank account, 64–65
relationships, 62–65, 63f
   activities for, 76b–80b
   ruined, 261
relaxation skills, 117–120
   activities for, 125b–126b
relaxed alertness, 26
remediation activities, 46
resilience, 71
resistance exercises, 174–175
resistance strategies, substance abuse, 203
respect, 55
respectfully disagreeing, 256
respiratory system, 117
responsibility, 55
restaurant eating, 165
reticular activating system (RAS), 27
reverse teeter-tottering, 11
rewards, behavior, 39
risk behaviors, 198–199
   activities for, 72b–75b

CDC categories of, 32–33, 33*f*
risk-reduction curriculum, 253
Ritalin, 16
Rohypnol, 231
role-playing, 70
rubrics, 42

S

SAD. *See* seasonal affective disorder
safe sex, 265
safe weight-loss programs, 169*b*
safety
   activities for, 303*b*–304*b*
   and hazard assessments, 300
   home-based injuries, 299–300
   outdoor injuries, 300
   resources, 300, 301*b*
   traffic-related injuries, 299
sarcasm, 116
satire, 116
scapegoat, 221
schedule, stress and, 103
school
   district guidelines, 33
   environment, 37, 176
   personnel collaboration, 176
   psychologists, 14
school-based marketing, 140–141
school-based programs
   sex education, 250, 253
   substance abuse prevention, 202
school-based stress, 105–107
school-based suicide awareness curricula, 319*b*
school gun laws, 290
School Health Advisory Council (SHAC), 37
School Health Guidelines, 175–177
screening
   learning disabilities, 15
   suicide and, 319*b*
SCT. *See* social cognitive theory
Search Institute, 71–72
seasonal affective disorder (SAD), 109
self-awareness skills
   ideal-self
      character and values education, 55–56
      hero identification, 54–55
   overview, 52–53
   Pygmalion-self, 56–57
   self-esteem, 53
   self-evaluation, 57–58
   self-worth, 53–54
self-blame, 101
self-control, 8–9, 53, 68, 69
self-discipline, 68
self-efficacy, 39, 57
self-esteem, 53, 261
self-evaluation, 57–58

self-fulfilling prophecies, 7
self-harm. *See* self-injury
self-image, 53
self-injury, 14, 320
self-management
   activities for, 81*b*–85*b*
   anger management, 68–69
   being proactive, 66–68
   overview, 65–66
   sexual health, 260
self-mutilation. *See* self-injury
self-recrimination, regret and, 260–261
self-respect, loss of, 261
self-worth, 53–54
Selye, Hans, 97
separation, parents, 104–105
sequential learning style, 30
service to others, 114–115
sex
   debasement of, 261
   education, 251–253
      abstinence, 253
      activities for, 269*b*–273*b*
      contraceptives, 255–256
      controversial issues, 256–257
      HIV prevention, 254–255
      National Sexuality Education Standards, 257–260
      peer-led prevention programs, 257
      programs for out-of-school youths, 257
      teen parenthood programs, 257
Sex Can Wait program, 257
sexting, 248
sexual abuse, 13, 294, 320
sexual assault, 294
sexual behavior and health, date-rape drugs, 231–232
sexual health
   culture and sexual development, 250–251
   diseases associated with youth sexual activity
      HIV infection, 264
      STIs, 264–267
   media and sexual content, 249–250
   overview, 247
   problems associated with youth sexual activity
      emotional consequences, 260–261
      unintended teen pregnancy, 262–264
   trends, 248–249
sexual intercourse rate, 248*t*
sexual predators, 137
sexual violence, 298
   date rape, 298
   intimate-partner violence, 298–299
sexually transmitted diseases (STDs), 248
sexually transmitted infections (STIs), 250, 264–267

SHAC. *See* School Health Advisory Council
short-term crisis responses and services, 313–314
sibling, death of, 328–329
skill-based health education, 50
slapstick, 116
sleep deprivation, 103
SMART objects, 41–42
smokeless tobacco, 198, 215
smoking
   and body weight, 169
   early onset of, 211*f*
   and girls, 214–215
   health consequences of, 212–214
   marijuana, 224
   media promotion, 200
   overview, 210–211
snuff, 215
social cognitive theory (SCT), 38–39
social factors, food choices and, 165
social intelligence, 30
social media, 137, 143
   in classroom, 143–144
social networking, 136, 137
social phobia, 112
social services, 36
social skills
   activities for, 233*b*
   substance abuse prevention, 203–204
social workers, 13, 14
solvents, volatile, 225
special education students, substance abuse prevention, 210
speed, 227
spina bifida, 19
split-second decisions, 70
stacking (anabolic steroids), 226
stages of change model, 40
state guidelines, 33
statutory rape, 298
Steinberg, Laurence, 24
stereotypes, 13
steroids, anabolic, 226
STIs. *See* sexually transmitted infections
stranger rape, 298
stress, 97
   anxiety disorders, 110–112
   coping skills, 115–117
   depressive disorders, 108–110
   disease and, 98–99
   eating disorders, 169
   families and, 14
   overview, 97–98
   relaxation skills, 117–120
   of students, 101–107
   suicide and, 315
   of teachers, 105, 107
stress reduction skills, 112–114

stressor, 97
student assistance programs, substance abuse prevention, 204–205
student-support team, 14
students
　behavior, expectations for, 9
　death of, 331–332
　diversity, sensitivity to, 12–13
　expectations, 7–8
　high-risk, 210
　interacting with, 6–13
　stress of, 101–107
　support services, 334
study skills, 114
subjective norm, behavior, 40
substance abuse, 14, 197. *See also* alcohol use and abuse; drug use and abuse
　deaths per year from, 212*f*
　monitoring trends, 198–199
　prevention, 201–206
　　curricula, 206–211
　　drug-free activities, 204
　　information-based strategies, 202–203
　　normative education, 203
　　parent approaches, 205–206
　　peer approaches, 204
　　personal and social skills training, 203–204
　　resistance strategies, 203
　　school-based programs, 202
　　student assistance programs, 204–205
　suicide and, 315
Substance Abuse and Mental Health Services Administration (SAMHSA), 198
sudden infant death syndrome (SIDS), 215
suicide, 261
　activities for dealing with, 337*b*–338*b*
　behavioral signs, 316
　depression and, 109, 315, 317
　overview, 314–315
　prevention and intervention, 317–319, 319*b*
　responding to, 332–333
　situational signs, 316–317
　student support teams, 14
　verbal signs, 316
SuperTracker, 180, 180*f*
supervision, at home, 104
support groups, 210
sympathetic nervous system, 98, 117
synesthesia, 230
syphilis, 267

T

T cells, 99
teachers
　emotional concerns, 14
　interacting with students, 6–13
　making difference, 2–5
　personal and professional characteristics, 5
　role in terminally ill children, 330–331
　stress, 105, 107
　ten commandments, 9
team approach, 13
technology in classroom, 141–144
teen parenthood programs, 257
teen pregnancy. *See* pregnancy
teeter-totter syndrome, 11
teeter-tottering, 11
television, 135, 137, 138, 165, 201. *See also* media; media literacy
terminal illness, 14, 329–331
test-taking skills, 114
testosterone, 250–251
texting, 60
THC. *See* delta-9-tetrahydrocannabinol
theory of planned behavior, 39–40
thoughts
　cognitive distortions, 100–101
　coping skills, 115
　organization of, 24
time management skills, 113
tobacco use
　activities, 207*b*, 233*b*–235*b*
　advertisements, 147
　media promotion, 200–201
　overview, 210–215
　prevention and cessation programs, 216
　trends, 198
Tremor, 139
trichomoniasis, 266
Twenge, Jean M., 53
type 1 diabetes, 172
type 2 diabetes, 172

U

unconditional self-worth, 54
undercover marketing, 139
undernutrition, 168
unhealthy eating and inactivity, 162–164
　diseases related to, 171
　　arthritis, 175
　　cancer, 174
　　coronary heart disease, 173–174
　　dental decay, 175
　　diabetes, 172–173
　　osteoporosis, 174–175
　problems related to, 168
　　anorexia nervosa, 170–171
　　bulimia, 171
　　unsafe weight-loss methods, 169
unintended teen pregnancy, 250, 262–264
unit design, 42–43
unit planning, 41–42
unsafe weight-loss methods, 169
U.S. Department of Agriculture (USDA), 177
U.S. food industry, 166

V

Valium, 231
values clarification, 55
values education, 55–56
verbal persuasion, 39
vicarious experiences, 39
video sharing services, 140
violence
　bullying
　　behavior, 284
　　cyberbullying, 283
　　effects and warning signs, 284
　　prevention, 285
　　risk factors, 283
　child abuse
　　handling disclosure, 295
　　physical indicators, 294–295
　　prevention, 295–297
　　reporting statutes, 295
　death, coping with trauma of, 333
　family factors, 286
　gang involvement, 288–289
　and learning potential, 289–290
　media, 286–287
　personal and peer characteristics, 288
　safety
　　activities for, 303*b*–304*b*
　　and hazard assessments, 300
　　home-based injuries, 299–300
　　outdoor injuries, 300
　　safety resources, 300, 301*b*
　　traffic-related injuries, 299
　sexual. *See* sexual violence
　stress and, 105
　substance use and abuse, 287–288
　violence-free school environment
　　discipline and dress codes, 291
　　prevention resources, 292, 293*b*
　　safe physical environment, 290
　　safe social environment, 290–291
　　school gun laws, 290
　　school security measures, 290
　　warning signs of, 291–292
　　weapon-carrying behavior, 288
viral marketing, 139
virtual advertising, 139
viruses, 17, 18, 265*b*
visual learning style, 30
visual-spatial intelligence, 30
visualization, 118
volatile solvents, 225

W

water pipes, 215
Web resources
   ADHD, 17*b*
   death and dying, 332*b*
   healthy eating, 178*b*
   mental and emotional health, 51*b*
   mental disorders, 111*b*
   safety, 301*b*
   sexual health, 258*b*
   substance abuse, 207*b*
   suicide prevention, 317*b*
   violence prevention, 293*b*
weight-bearing exercise, 174
weight-loss programs, 169*b*
wellness, 206
white matter, brain, 23, 24*f*
Willis, Judy, 27
willpower, 68
win–win solution, 70
withdrawal symptoms, 229
women, smoking and, 214–215
World Health Organization (WHO), 31, 50
writing, 15, 116

Y

youth
   sexual activity
      diseases associated with, 264–267
      emotional consequences, 260–261
      unintended teen pregnancy, 262–264
   suicide
      overview, 314–315
      prevention and intervention, 317–319, 319*b*
      warning signs of, 315–317
   violence
      aggressive behaviors, 285
      gang involvement, 288–289
      media, 286
      Weapon-carrying behavior, 288
Youth Physical Activity Guidelines Toolkit, 182
Youth Risk Behavior Survey (YRBS), 34, 198
YouTube, 140